Ferdinand [Mount] [is a] political journalist. He [...] [...]ement for over a decade a[nd, be...] [...] [...]t [Po]licy Unit. His political columns in *The Spectator*, the *Daily Telegraph* and the *Sunday Times* were required reading in the '80s and '90s. Since then he has published the dazzling memoir *Cold Cream*, the controversial polemic *The New Few* and a bestselling history of the British in India, *The Tears of the Rajas*. He was born in 1939 and lives in north London.

Further praise for *Prime Movers*

'Like many of his books, this one works because he writes so beautifully and with such an appealing personality ... In our polarized times there is something to be said for his temperate open-mindedness, and certainly for his sense of humour.'
Jeffrey Collins, *Times Literary Supplement*

'Mount's idea is to map the stars in the firmament of political thought ... Thought is the point here, rather than biography, but *Prime Movers* shines best when the dense intellectual filleting takes a back seat to quirky life story ... a beautifully efficient writer.'
Hugo Rifkind, *The Times*

'One of the finest essayists in the English language. Mount assesses 12 great political thinkers from Pericles and Jesus to Marx and Gandhi. His book encourages us to go back and read the originals again.'
Chris Patten, *The Tablet*

'An engaging collection of extended essays on a disparate bunch of thinkers. Ferdinand Mount is an accomplished writer, he has the knack of summarising complex ideas without giving the reader indigestion, and he contrives to be opinionated without being overly obtrusive.'
The Oldie

'The book surveys in extraordinary detail, and with exceptional insight, the ideas of 12 "Prime Movers" ... readers should expect the

PRIME MOVERS

*The Real Stories of Twelve Great Thinkers
from Pericles to Gandhi*

FERDINAND MOUNT

**SIMON &
SCHUSTER**

London · New York · Sydney · Toronto · New Delhi

A CBS COMPANY

First published in Great Britain by Simon & Schuster UK Ltd, 2018
This paperback edition published by Simon & Schuster UK Ltd, 2019
A CBS COMPANY

1 3 5 7 9 10 8 6 4 2

Simon & Schuster UK Ltd
1st Floor,
222 Gray's Inn Road,
London WC1X 8HB

www.simonandschuster.co.uk
www.simonandschuster.com.au
www.simonandschuster.co.in

Simon & Schuster Australia, Sydney
Simon & Schuster India, New Delhi

A CIP catalogue record for this book
is available from the British Library

Paperback ISBN: 978-1-4711-5601-4
eBook ISBN: 978-1-4711-5602-1

Typeset in the UK by M Rules
Printed and bound by CPI Group (UK) Ltd, Croydon, CR0 4YY

In memory of David Miller

'The science of political right is yet to be born, and it is to be presumed that it never will be born.'

JEAN-JACQUES ROUSSEAU,
Emile, Book V

'The science of politics is in its infancy.'

MARY WOLLSTONECRAFT,
A Vindication of the Rights of Woman

'All faiths constitute a revelation of Truth, but all are imperfect and liable to error. Reverence for other faiths need not blind us to their faults.'

M. K. GANDHI,
From Yeravda Mandir, Chapter X

CONTENTS

THE FATAL BLANDISHING

There is a chamber cut into the rock face at Mount Rushmore. Inside it you can see the texts of the American Declaration of Independence and the Constitution of the United States reproduced on porcelain enamel panels. On the cliff above, Thomas Jefferson, the author of that Declaration, stares out over the Dakota plains in lofty serenity. Of the four presidents carved on Mount Rushmore, only Jefferson can lay claim to be a great political thinker. How his opening lines still sing out to us: 'We hold these truths to be self-evident, that all men are created equal, that they are endowed by their Creator with certain inalienable Rights, that among these are Life, Liberty and the pursuit of Happiness.'

Yet at the time, Jefferson's Declaration didn't make much of a splash. The acidulous John Adams, later to become president with Jefferson as his Veep, called it 'a commonplace compilation, its sentiments hacknied in Congress for two years before'. Three hundred miles away in Richmond, some weeks earlier, the Commonwealth of Virginia had already drafted its own Declaration of Rights, in wording almost identical to Jefferson's, down to Life, Liberty and the pursuing of Happiness. The Virginia Declaration was mostly written by George Mason, of whom nobody much outside Virginia has heard (he's not even the original of the Mason–Dixon Line). As for the Constitution of the United States, Jefferson was in Paris the whole time it was being drafted, and he didn't think much of the text when they sent it to him. Yet it is Jefferson who still hogs the imperishable glory of inventing American democracy.

In the same way, it is to Jeremy Bentham that posterity has awarded the credit for the coining of that indelible mantra of the Utilitarians: 'the greatest happiness of the greatest number'. Years later, Bentham wrote an excited account of his discovery of the phrase, talking of himself in the third person, as great men sometimes do. Browsing in the library of Harper's coffee house near his Oxford college, Queen's (he was a child prodigy and the youngest undergraduate the university had ever had), he had chanced upon the phrase in a pamphlet by the great scientist-philosopher Dr Joseph Priestley: 'At the sight of it he cried out, as it were in an inward ecstasy like Archimedes on the discovery of the fundamental principles of hydrostatics, *Eureka*.' As it happens, the actual phrase occurs nowhere in Priestley's works, although something like it can be found there and in the writings of earlier philosophers all over Europe, including the Italian Beccaria, the French Helvétius and the Irish Francis Hutcheson. Not quite such a eureka moment then.

Sometimes it is not the authorship but the circumstances of the resonant phrase that are not quite what they seem. There's no doubt about who composed that unforgettable opening line of *The Communist Manifesto*: 'A spectre is haunting Europe – the spectre of communism.' Karl Marx dashed the whole thing off in six weeks, with a little sub-editing from Friedrich Engels. But what a huge claim it makes. In reality, the Communist League was only a few months old, having just changed its name from the League of the Just, itself a fairly insignificant group of revolutionary émigrés, many of whom weren't sure they wanted a manifesto at all. It was only after a bad-tempered wrangle at the League's Congress in Soho at the beginning of December 1847 that Marx and Engels secured the commission to write one. Neither the League nor the manifesto played much part in the revolutions that swept across Europe in 1848, except in Germany. After further internal wrangles, the League disbanded in 1852, and the manifesto disappeared from view until the 1880s. Far from haunting the minds of a continent, communism was mostly haunting the minds of Marx and Engels. They were not reporting the existence of a spectre, they were setting out to create one.

There is a larger audacity, a more boundless presumption about the manifesto. At the time when Marx issued his final trumpet call – 'Workers of the world, unite! You have nothing to lose but your chains!' – he had scarcely met any flesh-and-blood workers. A lawyer's son from the prosperous Jewish bourgeoisie of the Rhineland, he had mixed almost exclusively with philosophers and journalists. At the age of nearly thirty, he knew nothing of industrial life. How could he be sure that the workers of the world would ever wish to unite across national boundaries (as 1914 was to prove so calamitously, they didn't)? How could he claim to have any legitimate clue about what sort of society they might wish to live in?

Giuseppe Mazzini was equally ignorant of his huge target audience when he sent out a stream of clarion calls for a united Italy from his hideout in an attic above a Chelsea post office. Before he had been exiled to England, he had scarcely seen anything of Italy outside his native Genoa. When he became briefly ruler of the Roman Republic in 1849, it was his first-ever visit to the Eternal City. He had no idea whether the inhabitants of Naples and Italy thought of themselves as Italians at all, still less of the views of the German-speaking peasants of the Alto Adige (it is doubtful whether he even knew that so many of them spoke German). In fact, he soon became uncomfortably aware that peasants all over Italy were conspicuous by their lack of aspiration to nationhood, confining their loyalties to their local patch. Scarcely a single *contadino* was to join Garibaldi's Redshirts.

There is a no less daring innocence about the two greatest pioneers of sexual liberation in England, Jeremy Bentham and Mary Wollstonecraft. When the latter wrote *A Vindication of the Rights of Woman* in her early thirties, she had never had a serious boyfriend. Bentham was a lifelong celibate. Their combined experience of relations between the sexes was then close to zero, although Mary was to have a bucketful in the last few years of her life, most of which confirmed her views. Yet they shared a heroic disrespect for the old taboos and conjured up a universe of free sexual relations, unconstrained either by convention or the law, and kicked over centuries of moral teaching without a backward glance.

Such pioneers are not deterred by practical hitches. Gandhi's insistence that India should return to village life, the tradition of the spinning wheel and wearing homespun cloth, the *khadi*, entranced his contemporaries and has since attracted simple-lifers the world over. Yet Mohandas Gandhi was himself essentially a city-dweller, and had never spent more than a few nights in any village. When the campaign got under way, his followers discovered to their chagrin that there were few spinning wheels in working order to be found, and even fewer teachers of the craft available. By this time, the cotton mills of India had finally managed to overcome the competition from Lancashire, and the country was self-sufficient in cotton.

If these are failings, they are noble, or at any rate excusable. But the later disciples often discovered that their heroes had other, less palatable flaws – Gandhi's cruelty to his own children being one painful example. The editors of the abundant correspondence between Marx and Engels all too often came across repellent wise-cracks about Jews and blacks that they felt compelled to excise. The standard biographers of Thomas Jefferson, notably Dumas Malone in his six volumes, played down or omitted altogether Jefferson's obsession with the inferiority of African Americans and his urgent determination to arrange for as many of them as possible to be shipped back to Africa, not to mention his harsh treatment of his own slaves and his reluctance to free them, even on his death, as other slaveholders such as George Washington often did. Bentham's editors had a different problem: their hero's vicious mockery of all organized religion. This stuff had to be kept out of Sir John Bowring's massive edition of Bentham's works, for fear that it might discredit his ingenious political schemes.

Yet these men and women are the Prime Movers of our minds. Their passion and eloquence, above all their unshakeable certainty, have shaped our politics. Our political habits and institutions mutate – sometimes gradually, sometimes violently – in response to what we have learned from them. These standout individuals are themselves formed by their intellectual inheritance and by the hubbub of their own times, but it is they who express, with unique and memorable intensity, a new way of looking at the world – and of changing it. The debate is never quite the same thereafter.

Some people don't like the thought of this. Both academics and practising politicians often prefer to abstract from the individual discourse to the general theory, to turn personal preachings into 'isms'. The 'great man theory' of history is supposed to be hopelessly out of date. Yet at the level of serious study, we are driven back to examine the thought of named individuals. Half a century ago, my Oxford university course on philosophy ordered me to study Plato, Descartes and Kant; my course in political theory directed me to Hobbes, Locke and Rousseau. The reason for this was and is simple. Only by listening closely to these individual voices can we absorb and test their arguments with any hope of accuracy. To grapple with a depersonalized theory is to wrestle in mud.

Let's say you wish to make a critique of socialism (or liberalism or communism or conservatism or anarchism – the same problem applies to them all). You can write down how Karl Marx or Saint-Simon or Harold Laski defined socialism, and you can identify what seem to you the virtues and defects of that definition. But it is impossible to say, without fear of contradiction, what 'socialism' really is, where its limits fall, what is and is not to count as genuine socialism. You can at best sketch the political ethos of a certain historical period. But if you want to engage in hard and exact analysis, you have to focus on the individual perspective of Marx or Saint-Simon or Laski. That's the only way to catch the living doctrine as its first supporters and opponents encountered it.

So, whether you like it or not, if you aspire to be a serious student of political ideas, you are compelled to examine, and in some detail, what Rousseau, or Marx, or Gandhi actually said and wrote – and did. You can attach ironic capitals or scare quotes to the idea of 'Great Thinkers', but their collected works are inescapably your raw material. Often these are horrendously profuse; the *Marx-Engels-Gesamtausgabe* will run to over a hundred volumes when it is complete. Thomas Jefferson's works are getting on for fifty, Gandhi (by means of a certain patriotic stretching) manages to clock up the ton. Within these forbidding shelf-fuls, you will find all sorts of stuff, much of it dross: self-serving whines and excuses, petty feuds conducted with fanatical vituperation, vaporous cant, along with brilliant insights, acute analysis of social conditions, searing criticism of the conventional wisdom of the times. From all this you have to extract a coherent and sustained theory or set of theories. At least that is how devoted historians of ideas tend to see their task.

But what if no such coherent and consistent theory is really there? What if there are glaring gaps and contradictions, some no doubt minor and superficial, but others intrinsic and disabling? What if, over his lifetime, your subject shifts, either consciously or unconsciously, from one theory set to another set that cuts across and undermines the first?

All too often the devoted disciple, and even the supposedly impartial historian of ideas, then succumbs to what I call 'the fatal blandishing'. He or she smoothes out the wrinkles, ignores or underplays the contradictions, homogenizes the message. I call this a 'blandishing' not merely in the usual sense of smooth flattery, but to describe a process of making bland.

Often, too, there is a double blandishing at work. Internally, the theory is smoothed out and homogenized. Externally, it is linked up into a flawless chain with the thinker's predecessors and successors. Political theory develops its grand narrative; ideas are fitted into a logical progress (including the idea of progress itself). We have the comforting sensation of forward movement. Michael Oakeshott in his entrancing treatise *On Human Conduct* speaks of clambering from one platform of understanding to the next. That may be an apt metaphor to describe progress in the natural sciences, but does political theory really work like that?

This book, by contrast, will describe a scatter of eruptions, in which the lava flows in unpredictable quantities and directions, and often at terrible human cost. Some of these volcanoes may lie dormant for centuries before erupting or re-erupting in a different place; others bubble on in a continuous but variable flow.

Nor are these eruptions necessarily related to one another. They may explode out of the same geopolitical terrain, but their authors often have quite different starting points and reach conclusions that are totally unconnected and sometimes quite opposite. Their critiques of one another tend to be fierce and unrelenting. See, for example, how mercilessly Mary Wollstonecraft disposes of Edmund Burke, Jean-Jacques Rousseau and, in a couple of sentences, Adam

Smith too. Wollstonecraft pales in comparison, though, with the bucketloads of abuse Karl Marx poured over Burke, Bentham and Mazzini.

Prime Movers also have entirely different, and highly personal, methods of appealing to their audiences and stirring them into action – from the sweet lyricism of Jean-Jacques Rousseau at his best, to the harsh contempt of Karl Marx at *his* best. In studying the content, we cannot overlook the rhetoric that colours it and seduces the audience. As well as the content of their doctrines, we have to be alert to the tricks and quirks of their argument, their recurring stresses and omissions. For that reason, I make no apology for quoting sizeable chunks of what they have said and written. Paraphrasing – the besetting sin of many biographers – too often blurs the awkward gaps and contradictions that spring out from their original words. Only by hearing what they actually said can you gain a full sense of how and why they made such a mark. And only by fully quoting them can you understand properly what Rousseau and Iqbal thought about the place of women in society, or know in detail what Jefferson felt about African Americans and what Gandhi thought about Africans in Africa, or how Burke and Smith viewed the poor, or gauge Marx's relish for violence.

We have to pay close attention, too, to the circumstances of their life and background that shaped their thought. In political theory, it really matters to gain some idea of where the speaker is, literally, coming from, of what deprivations and stimulations have driven him or her on. So I make no apology either for the strong dose of biography in these essays. It is crucial to get a sharp idea of who the thinker was as well as of what he wrote and how his contemporaries and posterity have viewed him. In fact, if I have a single prime motive in writing this book, it is to reunite the person and the dogma, to get as vivid an idea as possible of how one gave birth to the other.

A great political theory will jump national boundaries and spread out from the culture in which it was born into an entirely different type of society. My twelve apostles not only preach very diverse creeds; they are diverse in their origins too. They comprise a Greek, a Palestinian Jew, a Frenchman, a Scot, an Irishman, an American, an Englishman and an Englishwoman, an Italian, a German, a Hindu who invented India and a Muslim who invented Pakistan. In every case, their ideas have spread far beyond their countries of origin.

This is not, I think, a consequence of the particular selection I have made. For me, these Prime Movers are the most resonant voices, the voices in human conversation that have left the loudest echoes behind them. But I could have chosen a dozen others, from among, for example: Plato, Machiavelli, Hobbes, Locke, Grotius, Voltaire, Montesquieu, Herder, Proudhon, Mill, Bakunin, Nietzsche and Lenin, not to mention Napoleon Bonaparte, Adolf Hitler and Chairman Mao – all of them remarkable writers or orators with a claim to have changed the ways we think and act. I can only say that the Prime Movers I have chosen seem to me to have said things of abiding interest and value. Though the defects in their doctrines may live after them too, the good is certainly not interred with their bones. We cannot un-know what they have taught us.

But even if I had chosen this other team, two things would be true of them too: the violent antagonism between reason and passion that runs through them, and the fact which their respective fan clubs try to dodge for as long as humanly possible and often never confront at all: that just as each of them offers unique and lasting insights, so there is also something defective, partial and sometimes even dishonest about every one of them. Ever since I started reading political theory more than fifty years ago, I have been struck simultaneously by two things: the remarkable charm of all the Prime Movers I have encountered, and the gaping hole in some crucial part of their doctrine.

Every theory has its unwelcome side effects. There is always blowback. I am not talking about mere collateral damage. These unwelcome outcomes are usually due, not to a misunderstanding of the Mover's intentions, or to some defect in the implementing of them, as the theory's defenders will claim, but to inherent faults in the design. A theory may be brilliant, seductive and even profound, but still it will offer only a partial glimpse of the truth about human political arrangements. The more the theory's defenders call for a pure and thorough implementation of the theory, the more corrosive the effect of its flaws – and the more terrible the possible consequences.

This is not a collection of hatchet jobs. It is not my intention here to debunk utterly any or all of these Movers. On the contrary, I hope to evoke something of their zest and charm and also to show their genuine and lasting contributions to the ways we think about the world. But what I want to do as well is to show how, in moving us, they also remove us from reality; in persuading, they select and distort; in enchanting, they also seduce. I hope that this selection will encourage rather than discourage readers to go back to the original texts. But I also hope that it will encourage them to read those texts, not only with an open mind, but with a wary eye.

I

PERICLES

and the invention of democracy

OLD SQUILL-HEAD – THE LEGEND AND THE REALITY

Was there ever such a man, so inspiring a leader in war and peace, so bold a thinker, such an irresistible orator, such a paragon of public – and private – virtues? Posterity has swooned at the feet of Pericles of Athens, ever since George Grote entranced readers all over Europe with his twelve-volume *History of Greece* in the 1850s:

> Taking him altogether, with his powers of thought, speech and action – his competence civil and military, in the council as well as in the field – his vigorous and cultivated intellect, and his comprehensive ideas of a community in pacific and many-sided development – his incorruptible public morality, caution and firmness, in a country where all those qualities were rare, and the union of them in the same individual of course much rarer – we shall find him without parallel throughout the whole course of Grecian history. (Vol. V, p. 443)

More than a century later, Donald Kagan, the *numero uno* of American classicists, writes in *Pericles of Athens and the Birth of Democracy* (note the jamming together of the man and the system): 'The story of the Athenians in the time of Pericles suggests that the creation and survival of democracy requires leadership of a high order. When tested, the Athenians behaved with the required devotion, wisdom and moderation in large part because they had been inspired by the democratic vision and example that Pericles had so effectively communicated to them.' (Kagan, p. 292)

When Boris Johnson as Mayor of London sought a model, it was Pericles of Athens that he fastened on in a mixture of hero worship and self-worship. He claimed to see in his London the same 'spirit of freedom that Pericles exalted, a spirit of democracy and tolerance, and cultural effervescence and mass political participation'. (*Spectator*, 13 September 2014)

Thus, Pericles was famous both as a political leader and as an orator. He led the greatest democracy that we know of in ancient times, perhaps in any times; he formed that democracy and brought it to its peak – Periclean democracy. In his famous speech at the funeral of those who had died in the Peloponnesian War, as reported by Thucydides, he paid the dead an imperishable tribute, still often quoted today: 'famous men have the whole earth as their memorial; it is not only the inscriptions on their graves in their own country that mark them out; no, in foreign lands also, not in any visible form but in people's hearts their memory abides and grows.' (*The History of the Peloponnesian War*, Book II, Chapter 43)

In that same speech, which we know inspired both Abraham Lincoln in framing his Gettysburg Address and Winston Churchill in the Second World War, he also glorified the democracy he had shaped:

> Our constitution is called a democracy because power is in the hands not of a minority but of the whole people. When it is a question of settling private disputes, everyone is equal before the law; when it is a question of putting one person before another in positions of public responsibility, what counts is not membership of a particular class but the actual ability which the man possesses ... we are free and tolerant in our private lives: but in public affairs we keep to the law. This is because it commands our deep respect. (Ibid., II, 37)

A hero for all times, then, leading a democracy that is still an example to us all.

Yet the Founding Fathers of the United States, the world's

greatest present-day democracy, took a very different view. In *The Federalist*, that matchless repository of political wisdom, Pericles and Athens are most definitely *not* the model to follow. Nothing could exceed the contempt of Alexander Hamilton for Pericles and his role in Athens' twenty-year war with Sparta:

> The celebrated Pericles, in compliance with the resentment of a prostitute [in fact his second wife, Aspasia], at the expense of much of the blood and treasure of his countrymen, attacked, vanquished and destroyed the city of the *Samnians* [Samos]. The same man, stimulated by private pique ... was the primitive author of that famous and fatal war, distinguished in the Grecian annals by the name of the *Peloponnesian* war; which terminated in the ruin of the Athenian commonwealth. (*Federalist*, No. 6)

James Madison was no less scornful of the Athenian political system. Their assembly, the *ecclesia*, in which every adult male citizen had a vote, was disastrously large and unmanageable: 'Had every citizen been a Socrates, every Athenian assembly would still have been a mob.' (*Federalist*, No. 55) Madison agreed with Plato that 'such democracies have ever been spectacles of turbulence and contention; have ever been found incompatible with personal security or the rights of property; and have in general been as short in their lives as they have been violent in their deaths.' (*Federalist*, No. 10)

Jacob Burckhardt, the great Swiss historian of the Italian Renaissance, was equally hostile to Pericles. Like later Roman emperors, the Athenian leader had debauched the people: 'he was also forced to humour their greed with pleasures of all sorts – not to satisfy it would have been impossible.' According to Burckhardt, Pericles may even have *welcomed* the outbreak of the Peloponnesian War because it deflected the anger that the people felt against him. (Azoulay, p. 213). Vincent Azoulay offers perhaps the best modern account of Pericles' life and times. In his last three chapters, Azoulay offers a brilliant account of the ups and downs of Pericles' reputation, from heroic leader to forgotten man, then warmonger and mob orator, then, in the nineteenth century, model statesman, before finishing up in a more equivocal light in our own time). Another great nineteenth-early, twentieth-century historian, Karl Julius Beloch, in his history of Greece claimed that Pericles 'had unleashed the fratricidal Hellenic conflict for personal reasons and had thereby been guilty of the greatest crime known in the whole of Greek history'. (Beloch, pp. 319–20, tr. Azoulay, p. 213)

The extraordinary thing is that these two wildly contradictory assessments are based, almost exclusively, on the same two sources: Thucydides' *History of the Peloponnesian War* and Plutarch's *Lives of the Noble Greeks and Romans*. These two marvellous works are pretty much all we have to go on for Pericles and his times.

Thucydides, about fifty years younger than Pericles, was regarded as the greatest of all historians in his own time and is still so regarded today: clear, acute, painstakingly fair and a superb narrator. He was a general in the Athenian navy, and like many another unlucky Athenian commander was sent into exile after a reverse that was scarcely his own fault. Yet he betrays no hint of resentment or bias, either pro or anti Athens, and it takes a tortuous mind (of which there have been plenty in the world of classical scholarship over the centuries) to detect any.

Plutarch is very different, so different that austere classical scholars have often failed to grasp the depth and subtlety of his portraits of the great men of Greece and Rome. The well-known ancient historian Frank Walbank describes him as 'a mediocre talent': 'ambling pleasantly along the surface, he sacrifices literary form to a wealth of anecdote.' (*Oxford Classical Dictionary*, 'Plutarch') This utterly misses the point. Plutarch is not simply a charming gossip, he is a supreme analyst of character and the impact of individual character upon events. He is writing five centuries after Thucydides, but his portraits are carefully based on earlier biographies and annals now lost to us. His Life of Pericles is not simply a masterpiece in itself, it is the first biography we have of a dedicated professional politician, a man utterly consumed with the art and practice of power.

Pericles was born to great wealth and of a great family. His mother's clan, the Alcmaeonids, had been prominent in Athenian politics for three generations. His father, Xanthippus, had clawed his way to the top in 489 BC by leading a vicious prosecution of Miltiades the Younger, who had led the Athenians to the immortal victory at Marathon only the year before. Miltiades came from the Alcmaeonids' rivals, the Philaids, so this was clan warfare rather than a prosecution based on the misdeeds of Miltiades. Xanthippus demanded the death penalty. Instead, Miltiades was fined a huge sum that he couldn't hope to pay, and flung into jail as a debtor, where he died of his wounds. For a brief moment, Xanthippus enjoyed supreme power as the leader of the aristocratic faction, but almost immediately he was overthrown by the populist leader Themistocles, and in 484 BC, only five years after he had got rid of Miltiades, Xanthippus was ostracized, that is, exiled by popular vote for a period of ten years. Pericles was ten or eleven at the time, not too young to realize how rough Athenian politics could be.

Plutarch introduces us to Pericles as a seductive youth, fond of philosophy and music, supposedly hanging out with Damon, the great teacher of the lyre (whose virtuosity did not save him from being ostracized for some political intrigue), and Anaxagoras, the first thoroughgoing materialist philosopher we know of. Anaxagoras too was to be attacked, perhaps even prosecuted, for declaring that the sun was not a god but a lump of hot rock, and Pericles helped him to get out of town alive.

Even in adolescence, Pericles seems to have been already the coolest of customers, a rationalist who did not really believe in the gods, but who was careful all his life never to expose himself to any charge of atheism. He had plenty of natural advantages, apart from birth. He had a sweet voice and an eloquent tongue. Plutarch says he was reasonably good-looking, except for his bulb-shaped head and long neck. The comic writers called him *Schinocephalos*, or Squill-head. Plutarch hazards that the images and statues of him always show him wearing a helmet in order to make him look less peculiar. Others have pointed out that Pericles was a *strategos*, one of the elected generals, and *strategoi* always wore helmets. Well, Miltiades, Sophocles the playwright, Thucydides the historian, Aristides nicknamed the Just and (Pericles' successor) the great Nicias were generals too, and they are often shown without helmets; Pericles never. So I wouldn't rule out vanity, but I would definitely rule in Pericles' determination to be known as a military man. In fact, Plutarch tells us that Pericles deliberately adopted the military option as the safest path to power: 'Reflecting, too, that he had a considerable estate, and was descended of a noble family, and had friends of great influence, he was fearful all this might bring him to be banished as a dangerous person, and for this reason meddled not at all with state affairs, but in military service showed himself of a brave and intrepid nature.' (Plutarch, 'Pericles')

When he came back from his campaigns, having scored a decent measure of success, he 'reinvented himself'. That is not an anachronistic piece of modern jargon, it is precisely what Plutarch tells us he did: 'He immediately entered, also, on quite a new course of life and management of his time. For he was never seen to walk in any street but that which led to the market-place and council-hall, and he avoided invitations of friends to supper.'

The only time he ever went out to dinner, when his kinsman Euryptolemus was getting married, he remained present only until the toast and then went home.

Pericles then took the momentous decision that was to ensure his enduring fame. Having seen what had happened to his father, he abandoned his aristocratic connections and became a red-hot democrat. As a young man, 'his natural bent was far from democratical', Plutarch tells us. In fact, 'he stood in considerable apprehension of the people', but now he realized that populism was the future. 'Fearing he might fall under suspicion of aiming at arbitrary power, and seeing Cimon on the side of the aristocracy, and much beloved by the better and more distinguished people, he joined the party of the people, with a view at once both to secure himself and procure means against Cimon.'

So he deliberately becomes a leader of the people, a *demagogos*, as Isocrates, the great Athenian orator of the next generation, describes him. The first project of the new democratic Pericles is to bring down Cimon, the son of Miltiades, whom Pericles' father had destroyed. The family feud continues alongside the ideological struggle. The contrast between Cimon and Pericles is one of the great contrasts of history, between the cheerful, unbuttoned, boozy old campaigner and the thin-lipped, austere, political ascetic; it's rather like the contrast between Charles James Fox and William Pitt, or between Danton and Robespierre.

Cimon (better written as Kimon, as it's a hard 'C') was the most brilliant general of his day. He had fought bravely at Salamis, he had destroyed the Persian fleet at Eurymedon and he had commanded the Delian League of Greek city states around the Aegean. But he was also a man of peace, always trying to improve relations with Sparta, the other great power in Greece. He had a great admiration for Spartan society, and he called one of his sons Lacedaemonius ('the Spartan').

It was for Cimon's goodwill towards Sparta that Pericles managed to get him ostracized, if only at the second attempt. Not unnaturally, the Spartans felt warmly towards Cimon too. This is another of the surprises that await the new reader of Thucydides. Sparta, that austere, militarized society that sounds to us like one big boot camp, was most of the time peaceable in its relations with Athens, slow to take offence, even slower to mobilize its troops, usually taking the first opportunity to bring the troops home and put feelers out for a lasting peace. Only a besotted admirer of Athens (and there have been plenty) could warp the testimony of Thucydides to find Sparta the consistent aggressor of the two powers in the fifth century BC. And we must remember that Thucydides was not only an Athenian but a respectful admirer of Pericles.

Yet nobody could have been less 'Spartan' in his habits than Cimon – this big, dark, curly-headed squire, fond of a post-prandial sing-song and legendary in his generosity: in Athens, he kept open house for the poor, and in the country he pulled down the walls and hedges of his gardens and fields, so that any stranger could help himself to the fruit and vegetables. He was forgiving to tax default-ers and would have no pressed men in his fleet: 'he forced no man to go that was not willing, but of those that desired to be excused from service he took money and vessels unmanned, and let them yield to the temptation of staying at home, to attend to their private business.' (Plutarch, 'Cimon')

We shall be struck by the contrast between Cimon's relaxed view of civic obligation and the tense, demanding tone of Pericles.

You could certainly describe Cimon as a conservative. He

thought that the Athenian constitution was pretty much ideal as it stood. He believed in retaining the powers of the old institutions like the Areopagus, a sort of senate, with life membership for former *archons*, the top city executives who mostly came from the richer classes. But what he stood for was not a narrow oligarchy, but a loose, tolerant type of conservative democracy that was hedged by constraints but acknowledged the ultimate authority of the people.

It was this entrancing character, to me one of the most attractive figures in the ancient world, that Pericles set about demolishing. He carefully refrained from leading the prosecution himself, leaving the attack-dog role to his tough associate Ephialtes, but he was one of the commission appointed for the prosecution. When Cimon's sister, the equally ebullient and unbuttoned Elpinice, came to plead for her brother, Pericles brushed her off with a smile: 'O Elpinice, you are too old a woman to undertake such business as this.' Elpinice was not scared off. When Pericles was being garlanded in the funeral ceremony for those who had died in the brutal Athenian suppression of the Greek island of Samos, she came up to him again and said, 'These are brave deeds, Pericles, that you have done, and such as deserve our garlands, for you have lost us many a worthy citizen, not in a war with Phoenicians or Persians like my brother Cimon, but for the overthrow of an allied and kindred city.'

To which stinging rebuke he quietly riposted with a well-known verse: 'Old women should not seek to be perfumed.' You often cannot help noticing the sheer unpleasantness of Pericles, as, for example, when he refers to the nearby island of Aegina, which the Athenians have reduced to servitude, as 'the pus in the eye of the Piraeus'.

Athens was a society fuelled by eloquence. It was by his oratory, far more than by his military successes, that Pericles maintained his hold over the Athenian public for nearly three decades until his death. Whenever he was in trouble, accused of personal corruption or of a mistaken military strategy, he rescued himself by his sweet tongue. His contemporaries, as relayed by Plutarch, were obsessed by how he did it. Was it the untroubled serenity and calm of his manner on the platform, or the sonority of his speaking voice, or the way he seemed to speak so frankly, so directly, sometimes even roughly to his fellow citizens? Certainly the three speeches of his that Thucydides reconstructs for us at length have an electric, irresistible quality. Even at a distance of two and a half millennia, you want to keep listening until he leaves the podium as quietly and unostentatiously as he stepped up to it. Yet, if you reflect on the actual content of what he has just said, you may gain a rather different impression.

Anyone who comes fresh to Thucydides and Plutarch will, I think, be struck not so much by the high-flown praise of Athenian democracy for which Pericles has become immortal, as by the hard nationalistic tone of his words and deeds. And in this he does seem to embody the mood of Athenian democracy. How else could he have been elected *strategos* fifteen years running? As the fifth century BC wears on, we realize that Athens has become a military sort of democracy – and one with relentless imperial ambitions.

The key power in the state now seems to be not so much the *ecclesia* of all adult citizens, which still has to approve all major decisions, nor yet the *boule* or council, made up of 500 representatives chosen by lot from the ten tribes of Athens, which frames and debates the issues. What really counts is the board of generals, who each have to undergo re-election each year but, unlike most other officials, can be re-elected again and again. As Athens becomes obsessed with her growing empire, the *strategoi* take more of a leading role in non-military matters, such as taxation and public works. At times, one is almost tempted to describe the regime as a military junta tempered by democracy.

The spirit of imperial expansion had penetrated deep into Athenian culture. Every Athenian citizen had to do a two-year stint of state service, including military training, called the *ephebeia*. By the mid-fourth century at the latest, every *ephebe* had to recite a long oath of allegiance that included the pledge: 'And I shall fight in defence of things sacred and secular, and I shall not hand down to my descendants a lessened fatherland, but one that is increased in size and strength, as far as lies within me.' (Samons, *Democracy*, p. 47) This is the same boast that Pericles makes in his final speech when he is trying to persuade the Athenians to stick with the war against Sparta: 'Yet still it will be remembered that of all Hellenic powers we held the widest sway over the Hellenes.' (*History*, II, 64)

By the 450s BC, Athens is the dominant power in the Greek world. She collects tribute from her colonies, euphemistically described as 'allies', all over the Aegean; the number of talents stumped up by each colony is proudly inscribed on a pillar on the Acropolis. The noble intentions of the Delian League – formed initially as an alliance to fend off the Persians – have degenerated into an Athenian protection racket. The Treasury has been removed, allegedly for safer keeping, from the sacred island of Delos to the Acropolis, where part of the cash is being diverted to build temples and theatres to the glory of Athens, and to provide a fixed daily payment – the *misthos* – for the poorer citizens to attend first the law courts as jurymen, then later on the Assembly and the Council.

Those temples and theatres, and the statues and friezes that adorned them, still dazzle us today. We tend not to notice how flagrantly they proclaim the new imperial spirit driving the city. The old temple of Athena Polia was dedicated to the homely civic cult of Athena, goddess of fertility, agriculture and the household. The enormous new temple is dedicated to the warrior maiden Athena Parthenos, who offers protection and brings victory in war. From the sixth century onwards, it is an even more militant deity, Athena Promachos (foremost fighter), who appears on the sacred vases and on the silver coins of Athens.

The heart of the building was the 'room of the virgin', the Parthenon, which later gave its name to the whole structure, originally known simply as 'the Great Temple'. Set behind the central hall that housed the huge statue of Athena, the Parthenon was where all the city's treasure was stored, in particular the tribute collected from the Delian League. So, as Azoulay points out, 'far from being a temple, the Parthenon was a treasury and a monument that glorified imperialism and symbolized the hardening or even the petrification of Athenian domination'. (p. 66) Significantly, it was begun in 447, a year before Athens smashed the Euboean revolt, and completed in 438, a year after Samos got the same treatment. It is this Athenian self-glorification that attracted the admiration of even such a rabid anti-democrat as Adolf Hitler.

Not everyone in Athens accepted that these unscrupulous appropriations from the often poor and rocky island states were the legitimate spoils of empire. Plutarch tells us that the enemies of Pericles

> cried out in the Assembly that Athens had lost her good name and disgraced herself by transferring from Delos into her own keeping the funds that had been contributed by the rest of Greece ... The Greeks must be outraged, they must consider this an act of barefaced tyranny, when they see that with their own contributions, extorted from them by force for the war against the Persians, we are gilding and beautifying our city, as if it were some vain woman decking herself out with costly stones. (Plutarch, 'Pericles', 12.1–3)

To this indictment, Pericles replied, in effect, 'tough'. 'They do not give us a single horse, nor a soldier, nor a ship. All they supply is money, and this belongs not to the people who give it, but to those who receive it, so long as they provide the services they are paid for.' (Samons, *Pericles*, pp. 95–6)

States that tried to leave the League, like the island of Naxos in 470, were swiftly and often brutally brought to heel. Democratic governments were forcibly installed in mutinous states, often with Athenian garrisons to keep order. Some residents were expelled and their lands given to mostly poor but armed Athenian settlers, known as *cleruchs*, who remained citizens of Athens and formed a cheap sort of garrison. On the Ionian coast and on some of the islands, local fortifications were pulled down. Some locals were appointed *proxenoi*, or friends of Athens. These designated quislings were often so unpopular that the Athenians passed legislation protecting them from assassination. (Samons, *Pericles*, pp. 116–19) The subject nations could be compelled to swear humiliating oaths of loyalty to Athens. The people of Chalkis, one of the two important city states on the island of Euboea, had to declare: 'I shall not revolt from the people of Athens by any artifice or any contrivance at all, neither by word nor by deed, nor shall I be persuaded by anyone in revolt, and if anyone revolts I shall denounce him to the Athenians.' (Samons,

Pericles, p. 119) Anyone who failed to swear the oath was to lose his citizen rights and his property.

Of course, there have been more brutal empires. Except in the notorious case of Melos, the Athenians carried out relatively few massacres of rebels or prisoners. But there is no doubt that this was an empire acquired and held down by force, and squeezed dry for the benefit of the imperial power. Yet such is the aura of Athens and her civilization that quite a few scholars have sought to maintain that the empire was not unpopular with its subjects. Grote claimed that 'practically, the allies were not badly treated during the administration of Pericles' and that, even when they were, 'it was beyond the power of Pericles practically to amend' the abuses. (Grote, Vol. IV, pp. 517–31) A century later, the rumbustious Oxford Marxist Geoffrey de Ste Croix argued that 'the masses in the cities of the Athenian empire welcomed political subordination to Athens as the price of escape from the tyranny of their own oligarchs'. It was only the local oligarchs who itched to stir up rebellion. (de Ste Croix, 'The Character of the Athenian Empire', p. 38)

This seems improbable, to put it mildly, especially because Thucydides says exactly the opposite. He has Pericles warn of 'the loss of our empire and the hatred which we have incurred in administering it . . . Your empire is now like a tyranny; it may have been wrong to take it; it is certainly dangerous to let it go.' (II, 63) The bellicose Cleon, a fierce opponent of Pericles, was in no doubt about the realities: 'What you do not realize is that your empire is a tyranny exercised over subjects who do not like it and who are always plotting against you.' (III, 37) Later, Thucydides reports the Athenian admiral Phrynichus as specifically rebutting de Ste Croix's contention that it was only the upper classes who wanted to revolt against Athens: 'the cities now in revolt', Phrynichus said, 'were more interested in being free under whatever kind of government they happened to have than in being slaves, whether under an oligarchy or a democracy.' (VIII, 48) Throughout Thucydides' majestic account of the two big wars with Sparta, there is the hubbub of colonies of all sorts revolting against Athens all over the Aegean. Sir Moses Finley sums up quite simply: 'Athenian imperialism employed all the forms of material exploitation that were available and possible in that society.' (Samons, *Cambridge Companion*, p. 24)

Of course, Thucydides might have made up some of this, but de Ste Croix himself calls him 'an exceptionally truthful man and anything but a superficial observer', claiming only that he deceived himself about the unpopularity of the Athenian empire, because of his own class background. This is clearly baloney. There was never anyone less blinkered than Thucydides nor readier to speak ill of the upper classes when they deserved it.

The truth is that Pericles was a hard man leading a hard regime. The very first words that Thucydides puts in his mouth are: 'Athenians, my views are the same as ever; I am against making concessions to the Peloponnesians.' (I, 140) He was giving this flinty response to a delegation from Sparta, the message of which was simply: 'Sparta wants peace. Peace is still possible if you give the Hellenes their freedom.' In particular, war could be avoided if Athens would revoke the trade embargo she had imposed on Megara. Pericles refused to budge. He warned the Assembly: 'Let none of you think that we should be going to war for a trifle if we refuse to revoke the Megarian decree.' It would be better that the Megarians should starve than the Athenians give in on a single point, which would only lead to demands for more concessions. Two years later, in the last of the speeches that Thucydides reports, he was adamant as ever. The war had become unpopular, and so had Pericles himself, but Athens must not give up now. 'Athens has the greatest name in all the world because she had never given in to adversity, but has spent more life and labour in warfare than any other state, thus winning the greatest power that has ever existed in history.' (II, 64) His proudest boast had nothing to do with the glorious culture for which Athens would in fact be remembered. It was simply that Athens had ruled over more Greeks than any other power.

Yes, Pericles' most famous funeral oration does contain passages of eloquence and beauty. So do the other two speeches that Thucydides reconstructs for us. But we cannot forget that all three speeches have a single purpose: to persuade the Athenians to stick with the war against Sparta. All three speeches use the same

arguments that war ministers always use: we are the greatest, we
have right on our side, this war has been forced upon us, but we
are bound to win it. These propositions were all highly dubious:
the Athenians had been ruthlessly assembling their empire in order
to smash the supremacy of Sparta. Most of the time, the Spartans
wanted nothing more than to be left in peace. Pericles did succeed in
steadying the nerve of the Athenians, but at a terrible cost. The war
went on for another twenty years after his death (probably in the
same plague that killed his two elder sons); it destroyed the power of
Athens and, for a time, Athenian democracy too. Yet Pericles himself seems to have been blind to the horrors he had inflicted upon his
people. His dying words, as reported by Plutarch, are breathtaking
in their self-deception: 'No Athenian now alive has put on mourning
clothes because of me.' (Plutarch, 'Pericles')

So far we have not said a word about what Pericles contributed
to the development of Athenian democracy. He made three such
notable contributions: first, he and Ephialtes (who was murdered
soon after) neutered the Areopagus, so that the Assembly enjoyed
untrammelled power.

Second, as we have seen, he diverted the tribute from the 'allies'
to ladle out the *misthos* to everyone who attended the jury courts
(later, the *misthos* was extended to attendance at the Council and
the Assembly).

Third, and no less important, he restricted citizenship to those
who could claim two Athenian-born parents. This restriction had
a tinge of racism about it, because the Athenians, almost alone
of all the tribes swirling about the Aegean, claimed to be *autoch-
thonoi* – sprung from the earth they dwelled upon. You couldn't
become an Athenian, you had to be born one, and of unimpeachable
Athenian ancestry.

Of course, women, slaves and resident aliens (the *metoikoi*, or
metics) already had no role in Athenian public life. Now thousands
more were excluded, to great distress, not least that of Pericles himself later on. After his two sons by his first marriage had died in the
outbreak of plague, he had to appeal for special dispensation for
his remaining son, Pericles the Younger, by his second marriage, to
Aspasia, who was an immigrant from Miletus.

These three changes combined to make the democracy simpler and narrower. Power and money were heaped upon the 25,000 or so lucky people who qualified as citizens, probably no more than a quarter of the adult male population, if that. For them to continue to enjoy this happy state of affairs, they had only to keep voting in Pericles as *strategos*. He had secured a captive client base.

The opponents of Pericles, from Thucydides, son of Melesias (not to be confused with the historian), down to the Founding Fathers of the United States, have been dismissed as spokesmen for the well-to-do, running scared of the mob. But they did and do have a point. There really is merit in having political structures to restrain headstrong elected majorities: second chambers for second thoughts, independent unelected judges, and written constitutions too, all have their place in a stable and long-lasting system. Pericles is perhaps the first of the 'terrible simplifiers' whom Burckhardt in the late nineteenth century identified as the menace of the coming age. Of course, Pericles was not remotely a Hitler or a Stalin. He was a deeply cultivated man, the very opposite of a barbarian totalitarian dictator. Yet that itch to simplify the system was insidious then, and it remains insidious today.

The critics of Pericles in his own day were acutely alive to the danger. Aristotle's majestic *Politics* a century later is one long dissertation on the virtues of plurality and complexity in a political system. That was why he was so keen on the importance of a large middle class to prevent either the poor or the rich from achieving an uncontested dominance: 'they are nearer the truth who combine many forms; for the state is better which is made up of more numerous elements.' (II, 6.18) In the West today, we are deceived by our own rhetoric, which is all about democracy, but our systems are by no means purely democratic: unelected magistrates and judges deal out justice in our courts; unelected or indirectly elected second chambers review and revise new legislation; international courts impose codes of human rights; our daily lives are largely administered by bureaucracies with their own codes of practice. None of this prevents the elected representatives from having the ultimate say, but we recognize these other institutions and practices as necessary to ensure fair play for the vulnerable and the voiceless and to protect all sorts of rights. Far from aspiring to the sort of simplification that Pericles went in for, our instinct is rather to complicate, by setting up fresh commissions and quangos to improve standards of justice and equality.

Who really invented Athenian democracy?

Whatever we may think of the way Pericles simplified the democracy he inherited, one thing is clear: he did not invent it. In the desire to magnify Pericles and Periclean Athens there is sometimes concealed a worship of national power and glory. Grote, writing in the heyday of the British Empire, and Kagan, a passionate believer in American power (he and his son Robert were among the founders of the neo-conservative movement), share a reverence for Pericles as a strong leader who brought a second-rank power to greatness. But that is not the same thing as inventing or even enriching democracy.

If there is a single date to which the invention of Greek democracy can be assigned, it is 508/7 BC, about ten years before Pericles was born. And if that invention had a single author, it was the younger Cleisthenes, who happened also to be Pericles' great-uncle. For many centuries, exactly what happened in 508/7 was unclear, as were the nature and magnitude of Cleisthenes' achievement. Virtually all we had to go on were a couple of references in Aristotle's *Politics* (III, 2.3 and VI, 4.18) and the mention in Herodotus of 'the same Cleisthenes who organized the tribes in Athens and instituted democracy there'. (VI, 131) Herodotus is the first writer we know of to use the word 'democracy' (VI, 43), rather than the more frequent *isonomia* (equality of the laws). But what did this democracy amount to? How did Cleisthenes do it? Herodotus does tell us the story of how Cleisthenes seized power (V, 69–73), but he does not explain exactly what he did with it. For all the huge resources devoted to classical scholarship over two millennia, we were pretty much in the dark.

Then, on a January morning in 1890, readers of *The Times* opened their newspaper to read the equivalent of a front-page splash. Actually, this being 1890 and *The Times*, the story was on page 9 and carried no sort of headline, but you can feel the tremble of excitement in its opening words: 'We announce this morning a literary discovery almost unprecedented in the whole history of classical learning.' The British Museum had acquired a papyrus manuscript from a dealer in antiquities somewhere in Egypt. On one side of the scroll were scribbled the accounts of a farm manager on the Nile in the time of the Emperor Vespasian, about AD 79. On the other side was written the text of Aristotle's long-lost work *The Athenian Constitution*, composed some four centuries earlier. Scholars had always known of this treatise but had given up hope of ever seeing a copy. Yet here it was, acquired for the museum by a short-sighted, self-taught clerk from Cornwall, Ernest Wallis Budge, who made regular forays into the alleys of Cairo where the dealers lurked, then as now a murky milieu. He had acquired the papyrus, *The Times* said, 'from a source which, for obvious reasons, it is not expedient to specify'. No other manuscript of *The Athenian Constitution* exists anywhere, and no other work tells us in detail how the Athenian democracy came into being, what it was like at the beginning and how it developed. Mr Budge's murky find has lit up the whole history of political ideas, or should have, if we read it carefully enough.

The first shock is that democracy at Athens was not a slow-growing, organic sort of thing. It started with a bang, and with bloodshed. The American scholar Josiah Ober calls it 'democracy's revolutionary start'. Ober has been twitted by some nervous colleagues for this melodramatic dubbing, yet it does seem to fit the facts, or what we know of them. There was something uniquely abrupt and dramatic about what happened in Athens in 508/7 BC. Of course, ordinary Greeks then as now were not slow to speak up for themselves. In the sixth and seventh centuries BC, there had been popular revolts against the local tyrant in various Greek cities – Argos, Delphi, Megara. One strong man would be turfed out, but then, as often as not, another tyrant would be installed. Many of these city states also had popular assemblies and councils, and the ruler who wished to survive would be well advised to listen to their views. There was at least an element of people power in most of these city states. In some of them, the ruler could not take major decisions, like declaring war, without the assent of the popular assembly. But these places could not be described as democracies in our sense, and there was little tradition of stable government based on an established constitution.

What happened at Athens in 508/7 BC was extraordinary. Not for the first time, there was a struggle for power going on. One faction, led by Isagoras, had called in King Cleomenes I of Sparta to help them take control of the city. Cleomenes turned up with a small force and ejected several hundred Athenians, including their leader, Cleisthenes, the *capo* of the Alcmaeonid family, one of the city's leading clans. Cleomenes then tried to dissolve the city council and install as the ruler Isagoras, who was now his puppet. But the council refused to be dissolved, and the common people gathered in numbers to support the exiled Cleisthenes. Cleomenes had assumed that the whole business would be a pushover, but now he and his tiny force suddenly had to flee to the Acropolis. The Acropolis was and is a fine defensive position on its rock above the city, but only if you have food and water, which Cleomenes had not. After two days of siege, he surrendered. Half his supporters were killed, the others sent into exile. Cleisthenes and his supporters returned in triumph, having burnished the Alcmaeonids' reputation as the most determined enemies of the tyrants. This was reckoned, both at the time and increasingly by modern historians, as the true beginning of Athenian democracy. (Herodotus, V. 66, 69–73)

This was a popular revolution, and one carried out with bloodshed on both sides. Such birth pangs are anything but unique in the history of constitutional upheaval. Think of Magna Carta: civil war rampaging across the whole country – Scotland, Wales and Ireland, too, being caught up in it – King John on the verge of being toppled, and the aftermath no less violent: the civil war goes up a notch, and the rebel barons call in the French Prince Louis to replace John on the throne. Or take the Bill of Rights: again, a foreign king called in, as James II flees. Or the American Declaration of Independence, this time signalling the beginning rather than the climax of a huge rebellion. Or the Fall of the Bastille and the framing of the Declaration of the Rights of Man and of the Citizen. Only upheaval on such a scale can generate the momentum for a total rewriting of the rules.

The crucial detail of what Cleisthenes actually did is only to be found in Mr Budge's papyrus. Instead of just taking over and ruling more or less decently, as *turannoi* sometimes did, Cleisthenes set about reorganizing the whole structure of politics. We don't know what he looked like, we don't have a single direct quote from him, but we know what he did. The fact that we know so little about him is simply a question of sources and the haphazard way in which they survive or don't. Pericles became a hero of democracy to posterity only because Thucydides wrote down (or imaginatively recreated) the words of his famous funeral oration. Herodotus, by contrast, records no words of Cleisthenes, although he does recreate the speeches of many other key actors in his *Histories* – the Kings of Persia, Darius and Xerxes, for example, and the speeches in a debate on the most suitable form of government for Persia after Darius and his gang had slaughtered the Medes – a debate so sophisticated that Herodotus tells us the Greeks could not believe it ever took place, but Herodotus swears it did. (III, 80) Plutarch does not include a portrait of Cleisthenes, nor does he pair up Cleisthenes among the twenty-odd leading figures he contrasts with their Roman equivalents in his *Parallel Lives*. Lysias, the fourth-century orator, tells the Athenians that their ancestors chose Solon, Themistocles and Pericles as their lawgivers. (Azoulay, p. 135) No mention of Cleisthenes. He never quite made the Great Man podium, perhaps because he seems to have held power for only a short time, before falling from grace for dabbling with the Persians. At any rate, he disappears from history. His personality remains a mystery to us. No doubt he possessed remarkable powers of advocacy. He certainly possessed inherited prestige as the leader of the Alcmaeonid family.

The Alcmaeonids were big landowners on the south-west coast of Attica, but they had also a longstanding reputation as friends of the people. A modern scholar has called them 'the Kennedys of Athens', and like the Kennedys or the Bushes, they contributed leaders to Athenian politics for several generations; not only Pericles but Alcibiades were of Alcmaeonid descent. Like the Kennedys, too, they were loathed almost as much as they were loved, and their reputation was by no means untarnished. Herodotus tells us that the family was rumoured to be cursed and that, when they were exiled in Delphi, they not only built a splendid new temple but bribed the Delphic Oracle to advise any Spartan who visited her that he must throw the Peisistratid tyrants out of Athens. Herodotus does, however, acquit the Alcmaeonids of the worst smear against them: that, after the battle of Marathon, they had waved a shining shield off the cliff at Sounion as a prearranged signal to the Persian fleet that the coast was clear for it to sneak into the Piraeus – a sort of primitive semaphore. Herodotus indignantly denies this, declaring not only that 'the Alcmaeonids indisputably set Athens free' but that they 'were at least the equals of Callias in their loathing of tyrants' (Callias being the most indefatigable intriguer against the previous long-term strong man of Athens, Peisistratus). The Alcmaeonids had been in exile for most of Peisistratus's reign and had never stopped manoeuvring to get rid of him. They had earned their street cred.

Cleisthenes was undoubtedly the star of his generation. Though we don't know his date of birth, we do know that he had already served as *archon* in Athens in 525/4 BC, so by 508/7 he must have been well advanced into middle age as well as experienced in the intricacies of politics. The fact of his archonship – one of the nine chief officers in the city – also tells us that his family cannot have been in exile for the whole of the Peisistratus dictatorship, so he was by no means out of touch with the latest political ideas.

Yet the mud has stuck, and quite a few modern scholars have characterized Cleisthenes as 'an opportunist who would try anything for political power (like many of his family)'. (O'Neil, p. 30) Professor Paul Cartledge of Cambridge, in his introduction to Tom Holland's superb new translation of Herodotus, argues that even in Herodotus, 'the manner in which Cleisthenes is said to have achieved his reform is bathed in a sharply opportunistic light'. (p. xxvii) For Herodotus tells us that 'when Cleisthenes was having the worst of it in his power struggle with Isagoras, he set himself up as a special friend of the people'. (V, 66) Democratic ideas were all the rage in Athens, so the argument goes, and Cleisthenes simply displayed all his family's notorious agility in jumping on the bandwagon at the right moment, and finding the right language to be allowed to grasp the reins. It is obviously true that he made the most of his opportunities, but then that is the definition of a successful statesman. We would not think of denying JFK and Lyndon Johnson the credit for civil rights legislation simply because they were ambitious and unscrupulous operators.

It is hard to argue that the reforms were undertaken solely in the interests of Cleisthenes himself and his family; the sheer complexity and thoughtfulness of them suggests otherwise. Cleisthenes and the Alcmaeonids could easily have returned to power by making only token gestures in the direction of people power. The system they set up was intended to last, and it was intended to act as a bulwark against the permanent domination of any single family, even of the Alcmaeonids.

It is true, of course, that the Athenian democracy would probably not have taken off in the way it did and lasted as long as it did if Athens had not already enjoyed a long tradition of popular assemblies and a degree of popular participation in government. Athenian citizens were well aware that a successful city, what Aristotle called a '*politeia*', required a common spirit and an instinctive obedience to the law. For, as Aristotle put it, 'a state is not the growth of a day, neither is it a multitude brought together by accident'. The law's only power to command obedience was that of habit, which had to be acquired over time. Rulers and ruled were all in it together, for 'he who would learn to command must first of all learn to obey'. (*Politics*, V, 3.11, II, 8.25, III, 4.14, VII, 14.6)

But the crucial point remains that Athens did not just grow gradually into full-blown democracy. The structure of the system that became a glory to the city and an example to posterity was deliberately designed, and by an identifiable individual. Cleisthenes knew from his own experience how fragile every political regime was liable to be, and he set out to construct a system that would have its inbuilt protection both against overmighty would-be oligarchs and against the negligence or gullibility of the people.

The first thing he did was to divide the peninsula of Attica by *demes* into thirty parts – ten parts in the city of Athens, ten along the coast and ten inland. (*Athenian Constitution*, 21) *Demes* are originally local districts – villages, wards, hundreds, call them what you will. For political purposes, they are what we would call 'constituencies'. It's only by extension that the word came also to mean the people who lived in that district. *Demos oneiron* in Homer's *Odyssey*, for example, means 'land of dreams', not 'people of dreams'. So democracy at the very beginning is more about geography than population; it's about power to the constituencies.

What Cleisthenes is up to is this: he wants to break up the allegiances to the old clans and to mix the citizens up 'so that more men should have a share in the running of the state', Aristotle tells us. Every contrivance was to be adopted to mingle the citizens. The powerful private religious centres were to be split up and amalgamated with the local countryside, so that their patrons no longer exercised undivided control over the local people. And he tells us something of even deeper significance: Cleisthenes 'made the men living in each deme fellow-demesmen of one another'. The strangers whom you passed by on the street or on the country roads were henceforth to be your fellow citizens. For *deme*-ocracy is a society of strangers who recognize each other as a new sort of kin. You're related by neighbourhood and not by blood. No profounder revolution in human society can be imagined. It is a revolution that has still not fully conquered what we used to call the Third World, where blood and clan still exert much of their old power. The constituency is the building block of any genuine democracy.

Cleisthenes then takes the mixing up one stage further. He groups one *deme* from each region (coastal, inland and city) into a threesome, which he calls a 'tribe'. Each of these new tribes – there are to be ten of them – chooses fifty men for the grand council of 500 at Athens, the *boule*. So these are not tribes in the old sense – the McTavishes or the Cohens or the Patels. A Cleisthenes tribe is an amalgam of the inhabitants, let's say, of Southampton, Oxfordshire and Birmingham South. Every bloc has all sorts of men in it. The state cannot be dominated by any professional or economic faction – not the admirals or the army or the merchants or the artisans. True, the Alcmaeonids' own strongholds seem to have been left more or less intact, but even so they could not hope to exert overall control without genuine popular support.

The new politics starts with the local. The *deme* governs itself

under an elected '*demarch*', and it selects, sometimes by lot, sometimes by vote, the officials who are to exercise power at the national
level: the generals, the judges, the tax collectors and the auditors,
the officials in charge of the religious and sporting festivals. Power
comes from below. This is *deme*-ocracy through and through.

And it works. In no time, the Athenian army sees off the armies
of Chalcis and Boeotia, the Athenian navy rules the Aegean, and
a period of peace and plenty begins. Cleisthenes took control
only about thirty or forty years before Herodotus was born, so
Herodotus would have known people who had lived through this
golden age, and he was in no doubt about the reason for it:

> So Athens came to flourish – and to make manifest how impor-
> tant it is for everyone in a city to have an equal voice, not just on
> one level but on all. For although the Athenians, while subjects
> of a tyrant, had been no more proficient in battle than any of
> their neighbours, they emerged as supreme by far once liberated
> from tyranny. This is proof enough that the downtrodden will
> never willingly pull their weight, since their labours are all in
> the service of a master – whereas free men, because they have a
> stake in their own exertions, will set to them with enthusiasm.
> (Herodotus, V, 78)

You may think this tribute a little flowery, but it is a remarkable one,
coming as it does from one who was no less sceptical about democracy than his fellow intellectuals. Even Aristotle, who was inclined
to regard Athenian democracy as having gone too far and to fear
that the people might exercise their own form of despotism, thought
much the same: 'the victory of Salamis, which was gained by the
common people who served in the fleet, and won for the Athenians
the empire of the sea, strengthened the democracy.' (*Politics*, V,
4.8) Salamis was the crucial Athenian naval victory in 480 BC over
Xerxes and the invading Persians.

The Spartans won a no less decisive victory on land at Plataea the
following year. Yet Aristotle does not wax lyrical about Plataea as
he does about Salamis, because, unlike his master Plato, he dislikes
the rigid, militaristic society that Sparta had forged. He thought

that the Spartans brutalized their children by laborious exercises.
(*Politics*, VIII, 4.2) They had 'lost the better end of life' by failing to
understand that the ultimate purpose of toil was to make space for
leisure. Even for the sceptical Aristotle, however fragile Athenian
democracy might sometimes appear, it was enormously attractive,
with its citizens enjoying a rare combination of liberty and equality.

What's more, the new experiment had staying power. It lasted
for more than a century and a half, until Philip II of Macedon and
his son Alexander the Great came down from the north and took
control of most of Greece, including Athens. Even after that, in
what came to be called the Hellenistic age, democracy continued
in much the same outward forms, although the reality of it was
crippled by the Macedonian supremacy. Hellenistic democracy
continued only in so far as it suited Philip or Alexander, and it
was a strictly internal affair, all foreign business being reserved
for the overlord.

During the democracy, there were a couple of interruptions,
notoriously in 404 BC when a bunch of thugs known as The Thirty
became briefly masters of the city. But the democracy was restored
with amazing rapidity, more or less undamaged. In fact, Aristotle
tells us that, from the return of the exiled democrats, 'the constitution has continued to that in force today [about eighty years later],
continually increasing the power of the masses. The people have
made themselves masters of everything and control all things by
means of decrees and jury-courts, in which the sovereign power
rests with the people; even the jurisdiction of the council has been
transferred to the people.' (*Athenian Constitution*, 41)

The modifications introduced by Pericles had no effect on the
staying power of the Athenian democracy, and became accepted
features of it. Aristotle regarded the payment of citizens for public
service, introduced by Pericles, as one of the most characteristic
features of any democracy. When the state could not afford an obol
or two per day for all serving citizens, it would pay at least those
who sat on juries or were responsible for choosing the magistrates.
It is worth pondering the fact that it was not until the twentieth century that pay was introduced for British MPs, under the Parliament
Act of 1911. *Misthos* became a standard ingredient of Athenian

democracy in its heyday, and continued through good times and bad until it was abolished in the Hellenistic period.

This unquenchable thirst for democracy is all the more remarkable because the literati of Athens, the chattering classes, were almost to an egghead instinctively and enduringly hostile to democracy. They hankered for government by an elite of wise men – 'the Guardians', as Plato called them in *The Republic* – or, better still, by a single wise ruler. Plato, Aristotle, Thucydides, almost any notable thinker you care to name – none of them could bring himself to imagine that the masses might be capable of governing themselves. Professor Cartledge says that the exceptions to this hostility can be counted on the fingers of one hand (in fact, he comes up with only three names). The word 'democracy' itself seems to have been coined by its opponents, rather as 'Whig', the Scots word for cattle-rustler, and 'Tory', the Irish word for brigand, were first deployed in politics as terms of abuse. In the fledgling Greek democracies, the name more frequently given to the system was *isonomia* – equality of rights. (Herodotus, III, 80; but see VI, 43 for the first use of *democratia*) The tumble of pejorative words beginning with *demo-* in Liddell and Scott's great Greek lexicon show how the idea of the people terrified the intelligentsia, then as now: *demagogos*, a demagogue; *demegoria*, popular oratory, claptrap; *demizo*, to affect popularity, cheat the people; *demoeides*, vulgar, low; *demokolax*, mob flatterer; *demokopia*, love of mob popularity; *demopithikos*, charlatan; *demoteros*, common, vulgar; *democharistes*, mob courtier.

What was wrong with democracy, its critics argued, was that the poor always grabbed everything they could. And they were as gullible as they were greedy, being fatally vulnerable to the sweet talk of demagogues. Herodotus summed up the prevailing attitude of the intelligentsia: 'a crowd is more easily fooled than a single man.' (V, 97)

Time and again, to the despair of the elites, democracy reared its vulgar head in Greek city states. Aristotle in his *Politics* (V, 4–5) mentions half a dozen of them: at Cos, Rhodes, Megara, Argos and Syracuse, for example. He became fascinated by the rise and often speedy fall of these tiny democracies and by the various oligarchies and tyrannies that preceded or succeeded them.

The history of Greece is a unique history of overseas expansion from the homeland into myriad colonies all over the Mediterranean, most notably in Sicily and southern Italy (*Magna Graecia*) and on the coast of what is now Turkey, the new Ionia as it came to be called. These colonies needed constitutions, and they needed politicians to devise and run them; no other empire in history has been such a seed ground for political experiment. And Aristotle, with his restless curiosity, set his research students to carry out surveys of each polity, new or old, large or small. We are told that no less than 158 of these research papers were written – the first ever large-scale exercise in political science. Unfortunately, only one such paper survives: Mr Budge's papyrus. The other 157 have disappeared. *The Athenian Constitution* was probably not the work of the great man himself but by one of his post-grads; these days, it is usually described as 'Aristotelian' rather than actually 'by Aristotle'.

So Athens was not just the most famous, successful and long-lived of these Greek democracies; it happens to be the only one we have a detailed picture of. The Greeks not only deliberately designed their democracy; they also invented the idea of appraising political systems coolly and objectively and comparing them with other systems. Which was a staggering departure from the time-honoured practice of following tradition more or less unthinkingly, until you were forced by the pressure of events to make adjustments to the way your fathers and grandfathers did things. Aristotle is a pioneer not only in studying the intrinsic virtues and vices of each system, but also in paying close attention to the ways in which oligarchy may turn into democracy or tyranny, and vice versa. In the language of social science, his research is diachronic as well as synchronic. How remarkable it is that this sort of political science, which we congratulate ourselves as being a modern invention (the school of Politics, Philosophy and Economics at Oxford used to be known as 'Modern Greats'), should in fact have been practised at the dawn of human thought. But then it is scarcely less remarkable that democracy should be among the first political systems of which we have any detailed record.

The Athenian democracy had its notorious faults: women didn't count as citizens, nor did the slave labourers who performed the manual work both in the fields and in the towns. But we should not feel too superior about that. In the UK, it was not until 1930 that all adult women were granted the vote, and we were not the last Western democracy to do so. The franchise had been extended to all adult males only a decade earlier, at the end of the Great War. So our inclusive democracy is a fairly recent creation.

OSTRACISM AND THE NATION

Cleisthenes invented something else, with which we are less comfortable: ostracism. (*Athenian Constitution*, 22) Any citizen could be expelled for a period of ten years if he was thought to be a threat to the state or even a potential tyrant. Every year, the Athenians were asked in the Assembly: anyone you fancy ostracizing this year? If they voted yes, then a couple of months later they piled back into the *agora* and scratched whatever name they had in mind on pottery shards – *ostrakoi*. The 'winner', the man whose name appeared on the most shards, had to leave the city. There would be no specific charge against him, and he had no right of appeal. On the other hand, ostracism was not quite as harsh a fate as it sounds. The victim did not forfeit his property, and he was allowed to keep in touch with his family and friends. You could charitably describe it as a system for removing an unpopular minister in a society that had as yet no concept of a loyal opposition.

Aristotle regards this practice as a regrettable necessity: ostracism 'is a policy not only expedient for tyrants or in practice confined to them, but equally necessary in oligarchies and democracies'. In democracies, 'equality is above all things their aim, and therefore they ostracise and banish from the city for a time those who seem to predominate too much through their wealth, or the number of their friends, or through any other political influence'. (*Politics*, III, 13.18, 15) He tells the story of Thrasybulus, the ruler of Miletus, sending a herald to Periander, the ruler of Corinth, to ask his advice. Periander said nothing, but took the herald for a walk in a wheat field and cut off the tallest ears of corn till he had brought the field to a level, meaning that, in order to retain control, Thrasybulus must cut down his principal rivals. Herodotus tells the story the other

way round, with Periander asking Thrasybulus for advice. (V, 92)
The 'tall poppy syndrome' has ancient roots.

Any such system allows dangerous scope for the settling of
scores and for vindictive organized campaigns. In a well near the
Acropolis, archaeologists have found a heap of 190 *ostrakoi*, all
scrawled with the name of Themistocles in fourteen identifiable
hands. These must have been the equivalent of voting cards, to
be handed out to floating or possibly illiterate voters. And the
campaign seems to have worked, because the great Themistocles,
a populist politician/general of modest origins who had himself
engineered the ostracism of Pericles' father, was in fact ostracized
in 471 BC, on the charge, dreamed up by the Spartans, that he had
collaborated with Persia, as their own treasonous general Pausanias
had done. Quite a few distinguished Athenians were ostracized for
no better reason than that their political opponents had gained
the upper hand, including two nephews of Cleisthenes himself and
Aristides the Just, whom Herodotus called 'the best and most honourable man in Athens'. But it is the ostracism of Themistocles, who
had commanded the Athenian fleet at the crucial battle of Salamis,
the man who had saved Greece, according to Plutarch, which shows
us most shockingly how ostracism could destroy even the greatest
of Athenian citizens.

'Ostracism' has crept into the English language because it is such a
useful word to describe a recurring problem and a universal practice
in most societies. The problem is especially touchy in democracies
that pride themselves on the wide social freedoms permitted to their
citizens. Yet even the most liberal of these democracies operate on
codes and assumptions that prohibit or fiercely discourage certain
opinions and certain sorts of behaviour and hence make life difficult
or intolerable for certain sorts of people. In Ireland until recently, for
fear of the social disapproval and the secular power of the Catholic
Church, unmarried women who found themselves pregnant would
migrate to England to have their babies. In England, until the law
reforms of the 1960s, homosexuals would often feel compelled to
move away to more tolerant climates. France's strong traditions of
laïcité have excluded religion from the public sphere; the extreme
instance being the law banning Muslim women from wearing the

veil in public. Nor is it any more comforting to reflect that the grounds of ostracism may vary quite sharply from one generation to the next. Homophobia is now as unacceptable as homophilia once was. By contrast, while the rules of adult sexual behaviour have been loosened to a once unthinkable extent, paedophilia is now regarded as the vilest of crimes, almost as bad as murder. We may think that we have rid ourselves of the old taboos about the human body, but the 'Naked Rambler' is regularly arrested in every part of the United Kingdom that he trudges through.

By contrast, long-lasting empires such as the Roman, Ottoman and British required only that their inhabitants should not stir up opposition to the regime. The religious beliefs of the natives were of little interest to the authorities, except in so far as they might threaten civil order. That is what the trial of Jesus was all about. Nor were empires much concerned about the tribal origins of the myriad hordes within their territories. Residents in such empires usually had little or no share in the government. They could come from anywhere and believe more or less what they liked.

In ancient Greece, the moral codes differed from state to state. Herodotus often pauses in his narrative to describe the variations in the treatment of women as between one small city state and the next; women had a bad time everywhere, but decidedly worse in some places than in others. Most Greek states were strictly monogamous; most 'barbarian' states were not. Nakedness was de rigueur for young men exercising in the open-air gymnasium (*gymnos*, after all, only means naked), but it was a shameful thing for a woman to be seen unclothed. Today we comfortably assume that we have settled the woman question, but have we settled the question of what opinions may legitimately be voiced in our democracy, or whether a democracy has a right to set any boundaries or make any distinctions in this area? Not long before he died, Isaiah Berlin pointed out that the record of democracies is anything but flawless in this respect:

> Let me point out that democracies can be exceedingly oppressive, and diminish civil and political liberties very greatly indeed. Do you really think that Athenian democracy, in its actual functioning ... was compatible with the basic liberties, whether negative

or positive, of Socrates, Anaxagoras, Diagoras and other thinkers punished by exile or death (Aristotle only just escaped such a fate)? Do you think that American democracy, which is real, in spite of the flaws in practice which we all recognize, was not oppressive vis-à-vis all kinds of minorities, not merely in McCarthy's day but in New England in the seventeenth century – the witches of Salem? Would you say that the New England communities were not democratic, ruled by majorities? Would you say that the majority of Iranians under the Ayatollah Khomeini would not have voted to repress those who disagreed with them, or, as some did, looked forward to the rule by a majoritarian populist Islam over the world, and the elimination of the basic rights of, say 'the Great Satan' (the USA)? (Letter to Professor Frederick Rosen, 17 July 1991, reprinted *TLS*, 21–28 August 2015)

We can think of many other examples, ancient and modern, of religious minorities or resident aliens or awkward individuals being harshly treated by regimes that are undeniably democratic. But let us go back to Berlin's starting point, Athens. In his famous funeral oration on the dead of the Peloponnesian War, Pericles (as recounted by Thucydides) claims among the many glories of Athens that 'we are free and tolerant in our private lives, but in public affairs we obey the law'. But what is private and what is public? Fifth-century Athens found it no easier to answer that question than we do.

It so happens that, in that amazing blaze of the fifth century BC, the birth of democracy coincided with the first flourishing of scientific thought. And there was a spectacular clash between the two. We have already heard something of Anaxagoras (500–428 BC), who came to Athens from the Ionian coast, no doubt to escape from Persian rule, where he became a friend of Pericles. In middle age, he came under attack for impiety, and Pericles had to help him escape into exile. What had he said? That the sun was not a god, but a large rock glowing with heat. He also taught that the universe was made up of infinitely small components too tiny for us to observe. These mites were constantly moving and rearranging of their own accord. Anaxagoras was one of the founders of what we call atomism – in other words, a thoroughgoing materialist. At the time when he was forced to flee, Pericles was the most powerful man in Athens. Thucydides tells us that the people 'put all affairs into his hands' and 'regarded him as the best man they had', so much so that 'in what was nominally a democracy, power was really in the hands of the first citizen'. (II, 65) Yet even Pericles could not save Anaxagoras from inflamed public opinion, expressed through impeccably democratic channels.

Of Diagoras we know much less, except that he was notorious for his atheism. He mocked the Mysteries of Eleusis, and perhaps divulged their secrets, regarding them as mere mumbo jumbo. He is also said to have chopped up a wooden statue of Heracles to boil his turnips, declaring this to be the hero's final Labour. What may be equally to the point is that he seems to have been friendly with several Ionian states that were on hostile terms with Athens. All in all, he looks like the sort of unpatriotic intellectual who sneers at the simple beliefs of the people, the kind of figure George Orwell so much disliked. Whatever the precise mixture of reasons, Diagoras was condemned to death and had to flee Athens.

Of Socrates, we know a great deal more, via Plato, but argument still rages as to exactly why he was condemned to death. It seems so bizarre to us that he should have been killed simply for teaching the young men of Athens to question the accepted pieties. But when you consider that many of his young friends and hangers-on were well known for attacking the democratic system of the city, and might even be secretly in league with the Spartan oligarchs, the death sentence becomes more understandable, if not more forgivable. Democracy was so new, and seemed so fragile, that it needed protection from juvenile snipers and their middle-aged pied pipers.

More peculiar still to us is the fact that even sober old Aristotle should have fallen foul of an enraged majority and should have had to flee to Chalcis, where he died a year later. But here too we must consider the circumstances. Aristotle's pupil, Alexander the Great of Macedon, had just died and there was an outburst of anti-Macedonian feeling in the city. At last they were free of their overwhelming overlord, and how better to express their feelings than by turfing out his resident guru?

City states that resisted the Athenian embrace could not expect tender treatment. The inhabitants of Melos had to endure a long lecture from the Athenian delegates on why they would be fatally misguided if they refused to become part of the Athenian Empire. (the famous Melian Dialogue, Thucydides, V, 84–116) When the Melians said they would still prefer to stay neutral, the Athenians besieged the city of Melos, and after the Melians surrendered unconditionally, massacred all their men of military age, sold the women and children as slaves and seized the island. Not unique behaviour certainly by the standards of the day, but nasty enough to rid us of any illusion that democracy injected new standards of tolerance and compassion. Thucydides tells us that he himself was banished from Athens for twenty years on the grounds that he had failed to prevent the fall of Amphipolis, although the city had surrendered to the Spartans before his army got there. Generals who lost a battle in these colonial wars were often reluctant to return to Athens for fear of what might happen to them. Fifth-century Athens was not a forgiving culture. Burckhardt muses on whether 'the Greeks were not somewhat lacking in gentleness'. (pp. 133, 200) There is certainly little feminine gentleness in their founding myths that are full of rapacity and violence and delight in pitiless revenge and the spectacle of human suffering.

The Athenian democracy, alas, exhibited almost all the varieties of intolerance that have since become familiar to us: intolerance of atheism and all religious deviation, suspicion of innovations in scientific thought, hatred of foreigners and, underneath it all, the lurking fear that their beloved democracy was really a feeble thing and would fall apart at the first efforts to subvert it – and that the most likely subverters would be aliens.

The question that nagged lawmakers everywhere in the Greek world was how to define a citizen – i.e. what rights should they offer or deny immigrants and resident aliens? These problems have never ceased to vex modern democracies. Think of the years before West Germany admitted her *Gastarbeiter*, guest workers, usually from Turkey, to full citizenship. Germany and Israel have been, by a grim irony, the two Western democracies that have had a racial definition of citizenship.

To this day, like the ancient Athenians, we in Britain deny foreign residents the vote. Non-UK citizens in this country enjoy the
dubious privilege of taxation without representation, unless they
are lucky enough to be able to claim tax exemption through their
'non-dom' status. Cleisthenes, by contrast, was pretty liberal on
this question, for Aristotle tells us in his *Politics* (III, 2.3) that, after
making his revolution, Cleisthenes enrolled in his tribes a number
of strangers and slaves and resident aliens; that is, he made the
definition of who was to be counted an Athenian citizen as wide
as possible.

Aristotle is extremely dubious about this. 'Who is the citizen?'
was for him, as for all Greeks, one of the most vexing questions. He
doubted not merely whether the new citizens enrolled by Cleisthenes
ought to be citizens, but whether they could be counted as the genuine article, lacking as they did the qualification of two Athenian
parents stipulated by Pericles in his citizenship law of 451/0. And he
more or less accuses Cleisthenes of smuggling as many foreigners
as possible into the new citizenry in order to strengthen his popular
base. (*Politics*, VI, 4.16) But of course the reforms of Cleisthenes,
like all other legislation, had to be passed by the Assembly, which
was composed of men who already had votes, and the strong local
bias of the reforms was obviously appealing. In any case, Aristotle
does also tell us (*Politics*, III, 5.7) that many states do admit aliens as
citizens, especially when they are short of labour, some for instance
admitting men who had fought for the city or who had only one
local parent.

Metics – from *meta-oikos*, change of house – may have made
up as much as half the population of Athens, if you combined
foreign residents and slaves, who were, after all, only involuntary
foreign residents. The word did not catch on in English as it has, for
instance, in French, where the *métèques* of the wretched *banlieues*
surrounding Paris and other cities are alternately pitied and reviled.
One French commentator remarked that ancient Athens treated its
metics better than France does today.

In Britain, over the past fifty years, Parliament has passed a
succession of laws to control immigration and to redefine who is to
qualify for British citizenship by birth or ancestry. The complicated

rules defining 'patrials' under the 1971 Immigration Act are pretty close to those that the ancient Athenians used to include or exclude. Not merely have these laws failed to settle the problem permanently, they have been overtaken by two new waves of settlement: the first following British entry into the European Economic Community, and the consequent freedom of movement for all EEC, later EU, citizens; the second caused by the recent mass migrations out of North Africa and the Arab world. Those illegal immigrants who do manage to cut their way through the wire or hide out in the cross-Channel lorries face a shifting and uncertain future; if they succeed in reaching Britain, at what point will the British state recognize them as legal residents? And if they are to be deported, where are they to be deported to? These questions go all the way to the new British Supreme Court and have caused a bitter breach between the government and the judges. The boundaries of any democracy, including our own, remain as uncertain and open to challenge today as in the days of Cleisthenes.

DEMOCRACY IS NOT ENOUGH

How then did Cleisthenes manage to leave behind a democracy that endured when all the intellectuals said it wouldn't? First of all, he insisted that the constituencies must all be equal in size, so that no faction could gain an unfair advantage. That may sound simple, but of all the rules of democratic systems this has proved the most difficult to police effectively. When in power, politicians have always found it an irresistible temptation to rig the boundaries to their advantage. There is even a word for it – 'gerrymander' – after Governor Elbridge Gerry of Massachusetts, who in the early nineteenth century is said to have contorted the boundaries of one district in Boston into a shape resembling a salamander in order to make it a safe seat for his party. Gerrymandering continues in rude health in many American states today. In Britain, we prefer to practise it at national level. In 1969, Prime Minister Jim Callaghan instructed his MPs to vote down the report of the impartial Boundary Commission in order to preserve a useful number of Labour rotten boroughs for the next general election.

There is also what might be called 'passive gerrymandering'. By this I mean the failure to readjust city boundaries to take account of shifts in wealth and population. This has been prevalent in the United States. There the 'white flight to the suburbs' has too rarely been accompanied by the enlargement of the city boundaries to maintain the tax base. As a result, the city becomes poorer and less populous and is consequently trapped in a cycle of decline that makes it even less appetizing as a place to live and do business and bring up children. Cleisthenes would not have allowed Detroit and Baltimore to degenerate into no-go areas.

It is the meticulous vigilance of Ancient Greek democracy that provides us with enduring lessons. They had strong safeguards against jury-packing. And in the courts they had water-clocks to measure the time each speaker spouted for, so that no powerful plaintiff got an unfair advantage. When the water dripping out of one bowl had filled the receiving bowl, the speaker had to sit down, whoever he was. To prevent jurors being intimidated, each man was given two voting sticks – one hollow, one solid, but looking just the same – so that the litigant could not see which stick the juror put into the bronze jar that collected the votes and which was put into the wooden jar for the rejected sticks: in other words, a secret ballot.

Above all, Athenian democracy was face to face. Everyone came to the *agora* to vote in the Assembly. As we have seen, fifty members were chosen by lot from each tribe to make up the executive council of 500. It could be your turn tomorrow, no matter who you were. And for a tenth of the year, just over a month, you and your fellow tribesmen ran the whole show: convening the meetings, drawing up the timetable and the agenda, taking the vote on whether to hold an ostracism, organizing the games, and – not to be sneezed at – eating in the official quarters at the state's expense.

Imagine if democracy today were as direct as that. Imagine if we chose our MPs and councillors by lot, just as we still choose our juries. We have the technology now to throw any decision out to the public. We could select citizens' juries by lot to deliberate on important long-term questions. We could hold referenda online; anyone could cast his vote in the post office or the internet café. Instead of having to summon everyone to the *agora* (even more of a problem in the far-flung Roman Republic than in fifth-century Athens), our modern *archons* are in a position to consult the people overnight. But apart from the odd national referendum (usually held to get the party leaders out of a fractious situation – for example, the June 2016 referendum on membership of the European Union), we don't dare. In fact, whenever faced with the choice, we tend to shy away from democratic decision-making in favour of top-down administration. We 'contract out' decisions, away from Parliament and the council chamber, to unaccountable boards and quangos. We say to ourselves that modern society is far too complicated for simple folk to take big decisions – the Eurocrats say this every time the people of a member state vote No to the latest treaty. Leave it to the experts. Which, as it happens, is just what Plato was saying more than 2,000 years ago. Yet, operating on just such a dicey system, Athens became the most prosperous city in the Greek world, built the most beautiful buildings in history and conquered most of her immediate neighbours. And other city states across the Greek world began to copy the Athenian model of democracy, more specifically the Cleisthenes model. Whenever and wherever they were given the chance, the people voted for Cleisthenes.

There is another disquieting thought too. It is not just that by comparison with ancient Athens our representative democracy is remote and pallid and that the ordinary citizens' contact with their rulers is so distant and sporadic; it is that our form of democracy has been getting steadily more remote over the past hundred years. At the beginning of the twentieth century, 90p in the £1 of all local expenditure in Britain was raised locally, and local councillors decided how it was to be spent. By the end of the twentieth century, 90p in the £1 of that expenditure was raised centrally, and Whitehall had the deciding say in how it was to be spent.

It is not simply that administration and taxation have been centralized remorselessly and progressively over recent decades. Political parties, too, have been brought firmly under the control of the leadership. The rank and file, distrusted as too 'extreme' or 'out of touch', have been excluded from any real share in power and policy; party conferences have been turned into PR rallies; despite many promises to the contrary, the selection of candidates in both

Labour and the Conservatives has been gathered into the hands of the party leadership; so-called 'open primaries' admit only candidates who have been preselected by Central Office.

Yet Aristotle would have thought that a modern Western society like Britain offered ideal conditions for full-hearted popular participation in government. For modern Britain is predominantly middle class, to a degree almost unimaginable to the ancient world; both the aristocracy and the industrial proletariat are impotent shadows of their former selves. And this is the kind of society that Aristotle dreamed of:

> Thus it is manifest that the best political community is formed by citizens of the middle class, and that those states are likely to be well-administered, in which the middle class is large, and larger if possible than both the other classes, or at any rate than either singly; for the addition of the middle class turns the scale, and prevents either of the extremes from being dominant ... democracies are safer and more permanent than oligarchies, because they have a middle class which is more numerous and has a greater share in the government. (*Politics*, IV, 11.10, 14)

But Athens, too, had second thoughts about the full-blown democracy they had inherited from Pericles. In the fourth century, there was a shift, gradual but marked, back towards the more complex and nuanced type of democracy that Cleisthenes had devised. Although Aristotle only mentions Cleisthenes a couple of times in his great work, the *Politics* (III, 2.3, VI, 4.18), that whole treatise is saturated with the spirit of Cleisthenes, largely, I am sure, on the basis of his team's exhaustive researches. In Periclean Athens, all magistrates and major officers of state, except the generals, were chosen annually by lot. But in the fourth century we find a growing suspicion of the view that any ordinary person could carry out these jobs and a growing prejudice in favour of elected officials with a record of efficiency. The new official in charge of management was elected for a four-year term, and though he could not then be re-elected, it was possible for him to find frontmen who would allow him to go on doing the work: in this way, rather

like Vladimir Putin, Lycurgus managed to act as the city's financial
manager for twelve years. Other managerial posts, those in charge
of the navy and public architecture and religious ceremonies, for
example, also became elective and enjoyed longer terms. Aristotle
grumbles that 'nowadays, for the sake of the advantage which is
to be gained from the public revenues and from office, men want
to be always in office'. (*Politics*, III, 6.10) Just as we do today, he
feared the emergence of a class of greedy professional politicians.
'The short tenure of office prevents oligarchies and aristocracies
from falling into the hands of families; it is not easy for a person
to do any great harm when his tenure of office is short, whereas
long possession begets tyranny in oligarchies and democracies.'
(*Politics*, V, 8.7)

There was a revival, too, in the powers of the Areopagus, the
city's equivalent to the House of Lords, in which former *archons*
sat for life. The *archons* were the nine chief magistrates – three for
civil affairs, three for military and three for religious affairs. They
had originally been elected for ten-year terms from among the
wealthier citizens. Under full-blown democracy, the *archons* were
chosen by lot each year. Even then, the Areopagus was, by virtue
of its life membership, an elite organization. When it was revived,
it had a less aristocratic bias because archonship was now open to
the poorer classes, but the revival was evidence of the new emphasis
on experience and efficiency. This increased once Athens became
part of the Macedonian Empire. Notably, it was in the Hellenistic
period that *misthos*, by then amounting to three obols a day for
attendance at the Assembly, was abolished, thus restoring the bias
towards attendance by the wealthier citizens.

The argument for professionalization is seductive and familiar
to us. To make *isonomia* – equality before the law – a reality, there
must be equal standards of justice and welfare across the whole
nation. We cannot leave delivery of public services to the amateurish
bungling of local men. Nor can we abandon our fellow citizens to
the rough mercies of a postcode lottery. The Athenians might have
said 'a *deme* lottery' – they were certainly familiar with lotteries.

Yet by our modern standards, even Hellenistic Athens was
unthinkably democratic. Debates in the Assembly were still open

to all Athenians. The *demes* still sent fresh representatives to the Council every year. But even Athenian democracy was vulnerable to corrosion, not merely by open corruption but by the professionalizing and centralizing tendencies of an elite that, then as now, distrusts the rough and tumble of democracy and dislikes the hot breath of the people down its neck.

What the example of ancient Athens teaches us is how demanding genuine democracy is: demanding of our vigilance, our ingenuity and our honesty. The example of Cleisthenes teaches us something else too. At a moment of extreme fragility in the history of Athens, when the Spartan invaders had only just been forced off the Acropolis, Cleisthenes gained power and hung on to it, not by imposing the brutal simple remedies of the strong man, but by devising a complex and articulated system of popular rule that permeated every part of Athenian society, from the *demes* along the coast of Attica to the law courts and the Assembly in the heart of the city. He chose democracy. This must have taken a rare kind of courage, the courage to choose the difficult. We have drifted into thinking that democracy is the default setting of a modern state. But it remains an arduous form of government, durable if well handled, but with rules and habits that stand in perpetual need of maintenance and refreshment.

What democracy and democrats often lack is modesty. In particular, they are reluctant to consider whether democracy on its own is a sufficient quality to ensure a happy and prosperous society. It may be instructive finally to compare the Athenian democracy with the other celebrated polity of ancient times, the Roman Republic. We do not often think of the two alongside each other. Notoriously the Greeks have precedence, both in time and quality. Did not even the greatest Romans feel grossly inferior when they looked at the art and literature of the Greeks? It was as a homage to their cultural superiors that the Roman elite continued to speak and write in Greek for so many centuries, much as the nineteenth-century Russian aristocracy preferred to speak French. Disraeli famously mocked his wife: 'She is an excellent creature, but she never can remember which came first, the Greeks or the Romans.' Yet if you consider politics alone, the answer is not so clear-cut. The crucial

starting points are in fact startlingly close together: the best date for
the beginning of the Roman Republic is 509 BC, when the last king
was ejected; for the Athenian democracy, we begin with the reforms
of Cleisthenes only two years later, in 508/7 BC.

Over the following years, the Romans developed a system that
was every bit as sophisticated and complex as the one being refined
at Athens: two consuls elected each year for a single year by popular vote; a senate consisting of former elected officials, thus rich
in experience of civil and military administration as well as rich in
land and money; and two elected assemblies, the *comitia centuriata*
elected by classes (and so heavily weighted towards the rich), which
chose the magistrates and censors, and the *comitia plebis tributa*,
which elected the other officials and approved the laws of the city.
This plebeian assembly was elected by territorial constituencies
à la Cleisthenes, and every male citizen had a vote. Latin, and by
derivation English, is full of terms that came from the hustling hustings of Roman politics: *ambitio*, ambition, from the going round
his constituency that every Roman had to do to solicit votes for
the humblest office; *rostrum* or bird-beak, from the curved ship's
prows that were taken from captured galleys to adorn the speaker's
platform in the Forum; *candidatus*, from *candidus*, 'white', because
those seeking office wore glittering white togas; and, of course,
forum, 'an outdoors place', but already extended by the Romans to
mean any place for discussion. This was a society saturated in politics, and we should not undervalue its democratic vitality because it
was also a plutocracy steered and managed by the elite. The people's
consent mattered.

So, there were quite a few similarities between Athens and the
Roman Republic, but there were two major differences. The Romans
had no hang-ups about openly allowing the major landowners and
plutocrats a preponderant say in affairs; they were content to allow
the fat cats who had grown rich on the spoils of office to loll on the
benches of the Senate indefinitely. The Romans did not insist that
their democracy should be constantly refreshed by new blood. They
had no tradition of choosing their rulers by lot. Romans did cast
lots, but it seems entirely for purposes like assigning plots of land or
spheres of command for civil and military officers, much as we toss

coins or pick a card to decide who goes first in a game or chooses the end to play from. Roman sortition, to use the technical term, was more of a randomized queuing system, not a basic feature of their democracy. In selecting their officers, Romans were happy that experience, wisdom and wealth should be taken into account.

The other big difference was that the number of Roman citizens was constantly and deliberately expanded, just as it has been in the United States of America: by opening Roman citizenship to freed slaves, to men of conquered nations who had been conscripted into the Roman army, and eventually to ordinary citizens in those conquered territories. That was how the population of Rome rose to more than a million under the Republic. By contrast, the dominant tendency in Athens was always to restrict citizenship, preferably to those who could prove they had two Athenian parents. Far from slackening the criteria for citizenship, the great Pericles took considerable trouble to tighten them. This tendency weakened Athens in two ways: first, there were thousands of non-citizens in the city who had little prospect of gaining citizenship and so were likely to be, if not actively disloyal, then at least disenchanted and disengaged. Second, unlike Rome, Athens could not count on an ever-widening pool of manpower to defend her widening borders; in this sense, the Athenian Empire was bound to be self-limiting and fragile.

All in all, the Roman Republic was less restrictive, less pure and idealistic if you like, but also looser and more flexible. It had a relaxed attitude towards wealth and power. Money talked, but the people could always answer back, and frequently did – much as they can and do in the greatest modern republic, which is at the same time a plutocracy and a democracy, the United States of America. Both republics are uninhibited in their acquisition of wealth, power and population. The Athenian democracy, by contrast, remained a glittering but smallish metropolis on a rocky peninsula, its efforts to acquire an empire short-lived and troubled by guilt. As a fully independent democracy, Athens lasted just under two centuries, from Cleisthenes in 507 BC to the Macedonian takeover in 322 BC. The Roman Republic lasted seven centuries, and several of its institutions, the senate, the curia and the consulate, for example, continued to have a shadowy life even under the empire. The impurer, more worldly form of popular government proved to have the greater staying power.

This comparison between the two great societies of the ancient world is a rather chastening one. For it suggests that democracy is not the beginning and end of good government. Popular participation in politics is necessary for a people to be at ease with itself, but it may not be sufficient to secure a sustainable economy or long-term independence. It is a reality that we are reluctant to confront: democracy is a good thing, but it is not the only thing.

The usual criticism of Athenian democracy, as we have seen, is that it was too exclusive: the rights of citizenship were denied to women, to slaves and to resident aliens, the metics. Well, we in the West have belatedly enfranchized women and abolished slavery, though we are still as vexed as Pericles was about how to treat our metics. We are conscious, too, that this is not enough to make our democracy fully inclusive. Majorities can be cruel, unthinking steamrollers. We need additional rules and practices that make it impossible to squash unpopular minorities, or to maltreat individuals we find odious or to suppress opinions we disagree with. This is more or less what we mean when we put the prefix 'liberal' in front of democracy. It is a matter for argument how far we have succeeded in this secondary ambition.

But even if we manage these fine-tunings of democracy, there are still other desirable qualities in politics, and they are qualities that democracy may not naturally supply: financial prudence, for example. Democracies are as vulnerable as any other system to the perennial temptation to buy popularity by bribing voters with their own money. Many of the great economic crises of recent years were sparked by overspending or by thoughtless gestures to win popularity. The great crash of 2007–08 was essentially caused by reckless lending in Britain and the United States, often under schemes sponsored or encouraged by government, notably the grant of 'trailerpark mortgages' to people who could not conceivably afford to pay them back. It is equally tempting for political leaders under any system to launch unnecessary or disastrous wars in search of splashy headlines and a reputation for strong leadership. The Athenian democracy, Pericles very much included, was just as guilty of this as any old tyranny of the time, and in the long run Athenian warmongering destroyed the state. The Athenians were just as eager to 'export democracy' as the Americans have been in our own day, and inflicted (and suffered) appalling loss of blood and treasure as a result.

The most advanced democracy can be as cocksure and self-righteous as any other type of regime. The democracy's consciousness of its own moral superiority often entrenches it in a refusal to admit error or to shift course to reach an accommodation with its neighbours – faults in which Pericles himself abounded. Those other qualities that make for good government – prudence, continence, foresight, modesty, a clear-headed calculation of odds and practicalities – are not inherent in any political system, but derive from a political tradition and ethos that, with luck, will come up with thoughtful leaders more often than not.

No, democracy is not enough. And the belief that it is the answer to every question is one of the worst things about it.

II

JESUS

and the brotherhood of man

IT'S YOU WHO JESUS LOVES

Even now, it doesn't take much to bring back how fresh it all felt when I first heard it – how direct, how thrilling. Dozing in the pew, scratching at a loose piece of skin, watching simple Charlie mumbling into his prayer book two pews ahead, I would suddenly be arrested by the beginning of the parable of the Good Samaritan (Luke 10:30): 'A certain man went down from Jerusalem to Jericho and fell among thieves'; or the raising of Lazarus (Luke 16:19): 'There was a certain rich man, which was clothed in purple and fine linen, and fared sumptuously every day: and there was a certain beggar named Lazarus, which was laid at his gate, full of sores.'

It required the vicar's sermon to explain that the Jews loathed and despised the Samaritans. But it needed no sermon to press home the electrifying message: 'thou shalt love the Lord thy God with all thy heart, and with all thy soul, and with all thy strength; and thy neighbour as thyself.' The commandment had an unforgettable force and passion. The way it tied together the duty to love our actual neighbours, the Miss Felthams and Colonel Oliver (whom my father certainly did not love), to the love that we were to pour upon God gave the everyday world a tingle and glow that it had not possessed before. Whether by accident or design, many of these Gospel readings setting out Jesus's teachings were prescribed for the long row of sleepy Sundays after Trinity, and so sliced through the summer torpor with even greater force: the lost sheep, the poor and the maimed and the halt and the blind being winkled out of the highways and hedges and brought into the rich man's banquet, the healing of the lepers – again, the vicar's sermon was needed to point up just how untouchable lepers were in that society and that the only leper who said thank you to Jesus was another Samaritan.

What struck me then as it has struck so many others – and still strikes me today – is the vividly comprehensive nature of Jesus's embrace: publicans (tax-gatherers) and sinners, cripples and outcasts, boozers and thieves, foreigners (especially unpopular foreigners), and women and children who are treated with an attention and a warmth almost unknown to the Roman Empire of the first century.

Sometimes, the story has an element of mystery and wonder that removes it from the time and place in which Jesus is telling it. The tale of the woman taken in adultery (John 8:1–11 in the Authorized Version) seems to have been inserted into St John's Gospel at a late stage, which is why the New English Bible excludes it from the main text and runs it as a postscript instead. Wherever it is placed, the story sticks in the mind: after a night spent on the Mount of Olives, Jesus appears in the temple at daybreak, and the crowds gather. The doctors and the Pharisees bring in a woman who has been caught committing adultery, we assume on the very night that has just passed. 'Master, she was caught in the act. Moses laid down that such women are to be stoned. What do you say?' The question is an obvious trap. Either Jesus says go ahead and stone her, and he contradicts his message of mercy and forgiveness; or he absolves her and he betrays the law of Moses.

But, to start with anyway, he does neither. Instead, he bends down and writes with his finger in the dust. Nobody can see what he is writing, so they press forward, repeating the question: 'What's your answer?' It is only then that he says: 'Let he among you who is without sin cast the first stone.' Baffled, the crowd trickles away, until Jesus and the woman are left alone. It is as if he has been abstracted for a few minutes, his mind on other things, for he asks her: 'Where are they all? Has no one condemned you?' 'No one, sir.' And Jesus says: 'Well, I'm not condemning you either. Go away and don't do it again.'

So what has Jesus been writing in the dust? Perhaps he has just been doodling in the sand to give his hyped-up audience time to calm down, restoring the crucial qualities of reflection and moderation to the business of judging others. He is not pretending that adultery is a trivial matter: go away and sin no more, he says in the resonant language of the King James Bible. Why has this odd story stuck in so many minds ever since it slipped into St John's Gospel (other early versions of the New Testament had it elsewhere in John or in Luke)? Not only because of its lingering mystery of the writing in the sand, I think, but also because of its delicate pausing, its removal of the moral question from snap judgements and the shouted Q&A of the crowd to the quiet chambers of conscience and to a one-to-one conversation.

As with so many other incidents in Jesus's ministry, there is an intimate, person-to-person quality. Jesus certainly delivers grand homilies to large crowds, the greatest of them being the Sermon on the Mount, but it is the personal nature of his teaching that strikes us as peculiarly Christian. His manner is quintessentially conversational, rather than oracular. And in the conversation lies the beginning of conversion.

The actual content of the teachings of Jesus can find plenty of parallels among other religions founded both before and after Christianity, among the Hindus and their Buddhist offshoots, in the teachings of Confucius, and among the Greek Stoics who were to have such an influence on the Early Fathers of the Church. Loving your neighbour, boundless forgiving, non-violence, the brotherhood of man – all these ideas crop up again in the earliest texts of these other faiths. It is as though all religions start out from the same universal impulses, however different their founding myths and the social circumstances of their births. Perhaps because they arise at roughly similar stages of development, their prophets and teachers are naturally drawn to answer the great questions of how to live your life in roughly similar ways.

But there does seem to be something different about the teaching of Jesus, this personal insistence that He loves you, regardless of what or who you may be. One might almost, if it were not considered blasphemous, give the You an initial cap as well as the He. For this is the purpose of his incarnation as a man, not to judge and scold and put you in your place, not to come down upon you but to put himself beside you, to make his love real and vivid. Even after its endless repetition over the centuries, mumbled by Catholic priests facing the altar, bellowed by revivalist preachers in huge halls, there remains something queer and unnerving about this doctrine, something that continues to entrance millions who are hearing it for the first time, often in cultures where it is an entirely alien idea.

What imaginative force this idea gives to our duty to our neighbours. Again and again, Jesus insists that the love we show to others, or don't show, is the same as the love we show or don't show to Him. In the scorching chapter 25 of St Matthew's Gospel, He tells the righteous that when He was hungry and thirsty, they gave Him meat and drink; when He was a stranger, they took Him in; when He was sick or in prison, they came and visited Him. They ask, quite baffled, when had they seen Him in these wretched states and done these acts of kindness, and He responds: 'Inasmuch as ye have done it unto one of the least of these my brethren, ye have done it unto me.' It is even more telling when He tells the unrighteous: 'Verily I say to you, inasmuch as ye did it not to one of the least of these, ye did it not to me. And these shall go into everlasting punishment: but the righteous into life eternal.'

It is out of this basic commandment that Christianity derived its lasting social force. From its earliest days, the new faith spoke up for the outcasts and the aliens, and cared for the sick and destitute. St Paul insists on the common humanity of all Christian people: 'for ye are all the children of God by faith in Christ Jesus ... There is neither Jew nor Greek, there is neither bond nor free, there is neither male nor female: for ye are all one in Christ Jesus.' (Galatians 3:26–28) From the Middle Ages if not before, the Church's hospitals and alms houses provided refuges from the cruelties and misfortunes of life. It was a few brave priests who protested against the brutality of the conquistadors and the horrors of the slave trade. In our own times, Catholic priests stood out against the oppression in Eastern Europe, and Anglican and Methodist priests protested against the iniquities of apartheid, to be joined, ultimately and decisively, by the repentant pastors and congregations of the Dutch Reformed

Church. As Christian faith began to wane, its causes were largely taken up, if not taken over, by the new 'religion of humanity'. Some humanists have gone on to argue that it was their influence rather than that of the Church that had implanted these ideas in the bloodstream. But the historical evidence is against them. Even in the darkest days, it was the teachings of Jesus that never ceased to offer a critique of man's cruelty to man. The teachings of humanists were, and still are, an honourable dilution of those teachings.

A VERY PRIVATE CREED

How surprising it is that this nuanced, intensely personal message of compassion, this thoughtful and private creed, should have conquered the Western world, and later on, large parts of the rest of the globe. It was an extraordinary achievement, but it was also a puzzling one. And you can detect a puzzled note in most honest histories of the early Church, even those written by the Church's apologists. How did this quiet, reflective faith, at first confined to small, sober, austere communities, living simply among themselves and scattered across the Roman Empire, and according to the Acts of the Apostles sharing their goods in common, become the master force in the whole civilized world?

There is, after all, something different about the teachings of Jesus as opposed to those of many other prophets and gurus. It is something that Christians have struggled with through the ages and are still, I suspect, struggling with today. I don't mean the peculiar intensity of Jesus's commandment that we should love one another, though that is certainly hard to live up to. What I mean is that there is something missing from the teachings of Jesus. There is an absence – a crucial absence and also a deliberate one.

These other faiths – and the same was to be true of Islam when it came along a few centuries later – are deeply entrenched in the societies where they grow up. They are firmly attached to the prevailing social and economic rules and customs. They do add fresh glosses and perspectives to those rules, but they do not separate themselves and their adherents from their old familiar worlds. They are in dialogue with the existing priests and lawgivers, reinforcing, refining, sometimes contradicting the orthodox codes of ethics and social behaviour. They have practical advice to offer, backed up by theoretical argument, on the questions that never go away: on land ownership, on waging war, on slavery, on capital punishment, on forms of government ranging from tyranny to democracy. They have as much to say about social conduct as about man's relationship to God. Religion and politics belonged together, bleeding into one another, both part of the human world.

The extreme example was the religion of Rome, which was oriented entirely towards the flourishing of the city and its empire. Its priests were not a separate caste. They were secular state officials, like Cicero, who regarded this dual role as one of the great advantages that Rome possessed: the system ensured 'that the most eminent and illustrious citizens might ensure the maintenance of religion by the proper administration of the state and the maintenance of the state by the prudent interpretation of religion'. (Cicero, *On His House*, I; see also, Mary Beard et al., *Religions of Rome*, Vol. I, p. 115) Roman religion did not offer salvation outside the city. The salvation of the city and its people was the supreme law.

The Jews too, for all their differences from the Romans, regarded religion and society as one single human sphere. It was not merely that Jews felt, and still feel today, the observance of ritual to be a central part of who they were and are; Jewish faith and Jewish society flourished together, or they decayed together. Modern scholarship, led by the great Géza Vermes, has turned our attention to Jesus as a Jew preaching to other Jews in the context of the Torah. This is no doubt a desirable shift, but it should not and cannot disguise the sharpness of the eventual breach between Jesus and the Jews and the scandalous originality of his teaching.

The breach between the old law and the new law was inevitable. Separation between the sacred and the secular was at the heart of the new faith. To save their immortal souls, Christians had in some important senses to keep themselves apart. Miles Hollingworth argues in his Life of St Augustine of Hippo that 'the idea that the spiritual aspect of life is by definition separate from the secular is very much a Christian invention'. (p. 16)

You cannot help noticing how little Jesus has to say about what his teaching implies for civil society. Much of what he does say is to stress this separation between the secular and the sacred. What's more, he usually opens up on the subject only when he is being questioned by the civil authorities. Most famously, when the Pharisees ask him whether it is lawful to give tribute or not, and he asks them to bring him some tribute money. They bring him a penny, and he says: 'Whose is the image and superscription?' Caesar's, they answer. And he says: 'Render therefore unto Caesar the things which are Caesar's; and unto God the things which are God's.' (Matthew 22:18–21)

Then again when Pontius Pilate asks him whether he is the King of the Jews, and Jesus says: 'My Kingdom is not of this world.' If it had been, his servants would fight to prevent him from being delivered to the Jews; but because it isn't, they have no right to resist the jurisdiction of the civil powers, whether Jewish or Roman. (John 18:33–37)

The story of Jesus driving the moneychangers from the temple occurs in all four Gospels, though at different points in his ministry, and it became popular with artists from Giotto to El Greco. Jesus overturns the tables and scourges the merchants and bankers with cords, because they are a bunch of thieves who are rooking the thousands of pilgrims who have come for Passover. But he does so also because, even if they had been honest traders, they do not belong there: 'Is it not written, My house shall be called of all nations the house of prayer?' (Mark 11:17) His actions infuriate the scribes and chief priests, for whom this commercial activity is all a legitimate part of the Passover as well as being a source of profit to the temple.

Not surprisingly, this queer, withdrawn, violent faith unnerved both the civil authorities and the local people. In the centuries that followed, Christians found themselves under persistent pressure to prove that they were not disloyal citizens and that their separate lifestyle was not a sign that they were plotting rebellion. In their letters dispatched to followers across the Roman Empire, to Rome itself, to Corinth and Philippi and Thessalonica in Greece, to Ephesus and Galatia in present-day Turkey and to the Hebrews in Jerusalem, Paul and his fellow missionaries pour out a stream of advice that amounts to 'keep your head down and stay out of trouble'. In Romans 8, Paul hammers home this message of civil docility: everyone must submit to the authorities; their authority comes from God; obey the law and pay your taxes. The author of I Peter (probably not St Peter himself) writes to the Christian flock scattered through Asia Minor from the Ionian coast to the hills of Cappadocia and the Black Sea: you must set a good example to the pagans, so that they will stop abusing you as criminals; submit to every civil authority, honour the king; if you're a servant, you must put up with maltreatment from your master; women must submit to their husbands. (I Peter 2, 3) To this day, you will see painted on old boards in many an English parish church: fear God, honour the King.

Despite this conspicuous submission to the civil authorities, not only the Roman rulers but local non-Christian populations continued to find something creepy about the Christians. They were standoffish, they did not join in the social rituals. In particular, they did not honour their ancestors (which even the scarcely less suspect Jews did). Devotees of other 'Eastern' faiths were not so exclusive in their devotions. Christians did the minimum in fulfilling their civil obligations, and it showed. By the end of the second century AD, this complaint had become so widespread that the security of the now far-flung Christian communities was threatened. Tertullian, the most prolific of the Church Fathers, writing in AD 197, responded vigorously in his *Apologeticus*:

We are neither Brahmins nor Indian fakirs. We despise none of God's gifts, but we use them with discretion and understanding. Moreover in living in this world, we make use of your forum, your meat market, your baths, shops and workshops, your inns and weekly markets, and whatever else belongs to your economic life. We go with you by sea, we are soldiers or farmers, we exchange goods with you, and whatever we make as a work of art or for use serves your purposes. But we do not join in your festivals to the gods, we do not press wreaths upon our heads, we do not go to plays, and we buy no incense from you. It is true that your temple dues are continually becoming smaller; we prefer to give to the poor in the streets rather than to the treasuries of the gods. Other dues, however, are conscientiously met by Christians. (*Apologeticus*, 42; see also Lietzmann, II, pp. 155–7)

None the less, the Christian way of life continued to provoke suspicion and hatred. Tertullian wearily remarked that, every time there was a public disaster – flood, drought, earthquake, pestilence, famine – the mobs gathered, yelling: 'The Christians to the lions!' The Roman governors were, on the whole, perplexed rather than vindictive, much as Pilate had been when faced with the local mob's demand that Jesus be crucified. Tacitus says (*Annals*, XV, 44) that Nero had blamed the great fire that broke out in Rome in AD 64 on the Christians, although he was rumoured (in all probability falsely) to have started the fire himself. But sustained official persecutions of the Christians were rare in the first two centuries AD. In a famous exchange of letters in AD 112, Pliny the Younger consults the Emperor Trajan on how he is to deal with Christians who refuse to give up their faith. Trajan replies that he must not seek out such recusants, nor should he rely on the reports of anonymous informers, 'for they give the worst example and are foreign to our age'. If stubborn Christians are brought before him, they must be punished, but only after having been given every opportunity to recant and worship the Roman gods. (Pliny, *Letters*, X, 96, 97)

The first great official empire-wide persecution did not happen until AD 250, when the Emperor Decius issued an edict requiring everyone in the empire to perform a sacrifice to the gods in the presence of a magistrate and obtain a signed and witnessed certificate, a *libellus*. Several of these *libelli* survive, for example:

> To those in charge of the sacrifices of the village Theadelphia, from Aurelia Bellas, daughter of Peteres, and her daughter Kapinis. We have always been constant in sacrificing to the gods, and now too, in your presence, in accordance with the regulations, I have poured libations and sacrificed and tasted the offerings, and I ask you to certify this for us below. May you continue to prosper. [Second person's handwriting] We, Aurelius Serenus and Aurelius Hermas, saw you sacrificing. (see Wikipedia: 'Persecution of Christians in the Roman Empire: Decius')

A number of prominent Christians who refused to sacrifice did not survive. The edict continued in force for only eighteen months. The martyrdoms continued under the persecutions of the Emperors

Valerian, Diocletian and Galerius. But although it may not have seemed like it to the Christians of the time, the age of persecution was nearing its end, for a variety of reasons: there were now just too many Christians, quite a few of them in positions of authority up to and including the emperor's household; the empire was racked by internal squabbles and external threat. The new emperors hoped to consolidate their shaky hold on power by issuing edicts of toleration rather than by pursuing divisive and difficult campaigns of persecution. In 306, Constantine, on being proclaimed emperor in Britain, restored Christians to full legal equality and returned property that had been confiscated during the persecution.

But that was only the start of the most momentous change in the whole history of Christianity.

THE GREAT DOUBLE CONVERSION

It took Constantine another six years to make himself master of Gaul and Spain as well. His rival, Maxentius, clinging onto control of Italy, had made overtures to the Christians and appointed Eusebius as the new Bishop of Rome as a gesture of goodwill. Already the Christians were being conscripted into the deadly struggle. Constantine, himself no more a Christian than Maxentius, journeyed south for the final confrontation.

At Arles or thereabouts, he had his famous vision: of the Cross superimposed upon the sun above the words '*In hoc signo vinces*' – 'in this sign you will conquer'. He crossed the Alps to advance on Rome, ordering his troops to mark their shields with the sign of the cross. Against the odds, in the battle of Milvian Bridge, just outside Rome, Constantine triumphed. The gentle God of Jesus had been transformed into the God of Battles. In March 313, the Edict of Milan put a final end to the persecution of the Christians.

Constantine was still not himself formally a Christian. Like many others in the early Church, he was baptized only on his deathbed. But from now on, Christianity was a '*religio licita*', a permitted religion, not by any means the only religion practised in Constantine's now undisputed empire, but an officially lawful creed that basked in his favour. Long before Christianity was raised to become the state religion under the Edict of Thessalonica in 380, it had become an established faith, its new status emphasized by Constantine's great new basilicas in Constantinople, those kingly throne halls redesignated as cathedrals.

The emperor introduced one or two cosmetic reforms as a nod to the new faith: crucifixion was replaced as a punishment by hanging, and the shops were closed on Sundays. But, in essence, the Roman Empire continued on its brutal Roman way. For the Church, though, things were never the same again. It was the emperor who became the supreme arbiter of Christian orthodoxy, with all his immense power to enforce that orthodoxy. In return, bishops became great secular princes, mandarins who administered large parts of the imperial territories. Soon bishops were seen in battle. According to the *Song of Roland*, at the Battle of Roncesvalles, Charlemagne's great defeat, Archbishop Turpin of Rheims was everywhere, slashing away with abandon. If the emperor had been converted to Christianity, the Christian Church had been converted to his service and his glory.

So it was a double conversion, and the Christian prelates played their part with enthusiasm. Eusebius composed a memorable *Oration in Praise of Constantine*, which Richard Fletcher describes in *The Conversion of Europe* as 'a prime example of fourth-century rhetoric, a work of oily panegyric that was hugely successful in carefully directing attention to all that was most admirable in its subject while discreetly drawing a veil over the less appealing features of the emperor's character. It is not to Eusebius that we must go to learn that Constantine murdered his father-in-law, his wife and his son.' (p. 22) In propaganda terms, it was a brilliant coup. In his *Ecclesiastical History*, Eusebius explains how the monarchy of Constantine brings the kingdom of God to men. A unified Christian Empire is slotted into the divine plan, Christ and the emperor its mutual supports.

The conversion of Constantine became the pattern for the conversion of pagan monarchs everywhere. We must not forget the role played by his mother, the Empress Helena, who in her old age made a famous pilgrimage to the Holy Land where she 'invented' – that is, discovered – fragments of the True Cross, which she brought home with her. This was the climax of a career of fabulous piety. Eusebius, always concerned to build up Constantine, says that he converted his mother, but it seems much more likely that it was the other way round.

Clovis, the great warlord of the Franks, was nagged by his Catholic wife Clotilde to have their son baptized. Ethelbert of Kent was nudged into Christianity by his wife Bertha. So was Edwin of Northumbria by his wife Ethelburga. Similarly, Queen Olga of Kiev was the driving force in introducing what was to become the Russian royal house to the new faith. Each barbarian nation was carried over by a conversion experience sweeping through the royal family. It was a top-down process almost everywhere, except in one or two places such as Ireland, where Palladius and Patrick do seem to have carried the faith to the people.

The consequence of the process happening this way round was, not surprisingly, that the Church had to adapt to, and to a greater or lesser extent justify, the habits and values of the monarchy, rather than the monarchy transform itself according to the teachings of Jesus. Christianity was, so to speak, parachuted in at the top, without a breathing space to develop a social and economic ethics for the converted nation. The Christians, led by St Paul, had followed the Jews in insisting on being judged by their own people and refusing to melt into the surrounding heathen world. But, as Hans Lietzmann points out in his *History of the Early Church*, 'it is significant that a *corpus juris civilis christianum* was never developed, whereas the Jews codified, in the Talmud, a complete system of civil law'. (I, p. 138) There was an embarrassing gap where other societies had a body of law and practice inherited from their ancestors and modified as time and circumstance required. Nowhere was this absence more glaring than on the ever-pressing question of when it was legitimate to make war.

AUGUSTINE AND THE JUST WAR

How could it possibly be that the spiritual lords of a religion of peace should now be licensed to behave like worldly barons, and fight alongside them? Christian apologists had to think hard and fast, as the empire appeared to be crumbling about them. Nothing more vividly demonstrates the new relations of power than the doctrine of the Just War promulgated by Bishop Augustine of Hippo in the early fifth century, in response to the Fall of Rome and the widespread tendency to blame the recent introduction of Christianity for the collapse in morale. Christian doctrine had to be weaponized for the struggle, and quickly.

Just War theory, as developed by Augustine in his letters and in his great treatise, *The City of God*, lays down a sequence of fair-sounding criteria for determining whether a war is just or not: the gravity of the damage inflicted by the aggressor, the impossibility of alternative remedies short of conflict, the prospects of success in the battle.

Overarching these criteria lies the crucial principle: that a war that is waged in response to a divine command does not infringe the commandment 'Thou shalt not kill'. Moreover, individual Christians must submit themselves to the government and fight as justly as they can, even when the war that has been declared is an immoral one. For Christians have a duty to be obedient citizens and obedient soldiers too. Crucially, it is for the government to decide whether or not the cause for which they are to fight is divinely ordained.

So it's a pretty self-validating sort of theory. Ordinary citizens are given to understand that the ruler would not have embarked on the war unless he was convinced that it was a just war. So the very fact that he has embarked on the project proves that the war must be a just one.

Over a large part of Augustine's argument, 'just' looks suspiciously like a synonym for 'prudent'. It is a prudent king who will refuse to go into a war if its likely costs are out of all proportion to its possible benefits or to the grievance that has sparked it off. Nor will he start a war that he can see he is unlikely to win, or that, even if he does win, will leave him and his state worse off.

In real life, of course, kings (and republics too) often breach these rules of prudence. They may declare war in a fit of myopic rage, or may be prodded into war by the bellowing indignation of their subjects. But even a king who does observe the rules of prudence does not thereby make his war a morally admirable one. All we can say is that he has correctly calculated that the war is likely to turn out well for him and his nation.

So what does make a war just? Even if the king really is setting out to right some identifiable wrong – regaining territory that has been illegally seized or restoring it to its rightful owner, resisting unprovoked aggression, coming to the aid of a weaker, beleaguered power – can he be sure that it might not be better to leave these wrongs unrighted? Is he justified in sacrificing so many lives and so much treasure for what may turn out to be a trumpery gain? May he in reality be driven merely by *amour propre* or by his personal survival as leader? Is there not something to be said, on a national scale as well as a personal one, for turning the other cheek, for forgiving until seventy times seven? Here *raison d'état* comes crashing into the teachings of Jesus. For almost all statesmen and political commentators will respond fiercely: no, no, no, you must always resist evil, by proportionate counter-violence if you can or by massive retaliation if you cannot. Otherwise the evil will spread inexorably.

Very possibly, but that is not what Jesus tells us. He does not say that different rules are to apply in the political sphere. He tells us only that politics is for politicians. But it is a fair deduction that He would expect any politician who claims to be a Christian to follow His teaching in his public as well as in his personal life. Otherwise, he would be surely be identified as a hypocrite, one of those scribes and Pharisees who are so often his butt.

Just War theory is certainly derivable from the classical philosophers of Greece and Rome – indeed, that is where much of it comes from – but it is hard to see that much of it derives from the teaching of Jesus. What is clearly the driver here is the parlous state of the Roman Empire. Augustine is doing his best to rescue some sort of decency in this life-and-death struggle. Christianity has been conscripted into the service of Rome. It has lost its seclusion and its innocence.

Though now the dominant religious force in the empire, the Christian prelates are still hobbled from developing distinctive social, political and economic doctrines of their own. They quarrel and even fight battles, physical as well as verbal, over abstruse points of theology, the nature of the Trinity, for example. But on day-to-day matters, they have little to offer beyond the advice first offered by Peter and Paul: obey the authorities, stay out of trouble.

THE LATE ARRIVAL OF CHRISTIAN DEMOCRACY

You may think this an exaggeration. Surely the Christian Church has played a part, perhaps even a pioneering part, in the development of social thought in general, and modern democracy in particular? It may not have had much success in restraining our violent instincts, but the Christian message of brotherhood must have provided some sort of pattern for how we should live together. But did it?

One of the basic questions confronting any *polis* or nation state is how it should be governed. Yet for the best part of two millennia you will find an embarrassing gap where you might expect to find a Christian blueprint, or at least some fruitful guidelines. Histories of 'Catholic social thought' usually begin in the later nineteenth century with *De Rerum Novarum*, the 1891 encyclical of Pope Leo XIII, which addresses, it seems for the first time, the questions of poverty and injustice in industrial society, and attempts to find a way through that does not amount to state socialism.

From the Reformation onwards, Protestant leaders had appeared to be more worldly, certainly on questions of justice. They fiercely denounced the abuses of papal authority and the widespread corruption in the Catholic Church. But on the whole the successful founders of new sects – Luther, Calvin, Zwingli, Cranmer – believed in civil obedience. The duty of good Christians was to obey their sovereign prince. What mattered was that their sovereign prince should be a Protestant. The terrible civil war that wrecked Europe in the seventeenth century, the Thirty Years War, could only be brought to an end on the basis of *cuius regio, eius religio* – whichever prince the region belongs to, it's his religion the people must follow. Social change or constitutional thought did not come into it. Only the outlandish millennial sects believed in sweeping away wealth and rank and property and giving power to the people. The second wave of dissent, the Nonconformist sects of the eighteenth century, were no different in this respect. They might be theologically radical, although they protested that they were only returning to the purer values of the Early Church, but socially they were mostly quite conformist. The radical Puritans were an exception, and their outcry against injustice and oppression eventually led to emigration and the development of American constitutional thought. But in Europe, the churches tended to be politically quiescent, until the evils of the Industrial Revolution generated 'Christian socialism'. In the twentieth century, fascism and communism eventually provoked a marriage of Christianity and democracy in those Continental countries that had experienced the worst. But with both Christian socialism and Christian democracy, it has to be admitted that the secular doctrine came first and the churches grabbed its coat-tails in a rush to rescue themselves from public disgrace.

By sticking strictly to the instructions of Jesus and Paul, the Church over the centuries had found itself allied to some of the most ghastly authoritarian regimes, up to and including Franco's Spain and Salazar's Portugal. Those regimes had rejoiced in the Church's support as a source of legitimacy. Conversely, the Church had resorted to strong-arm methods to impose its own discipline and retain its monopoly of power, usually with the full approval of the state. Orthodox theology, whether Protestant or Catholic, offered little legitimate space for arguments in favour of democracy, let alone resistance to injustice. Certainly, medieval theologians and lawyers, such as Bracton and Thomas Aquinas, insisted that, be he never so high, the king was under God's law and must rule according to that law. But they were incurably averse to taking the next logical step of endorsing the right to rebel against an unjust sovereign. The duty of civil obedience came first. So, in practical terms, the Church posed no real obstacle to the misuse of power.

Yet if you look back to the early Church, this is not how you might have expected things to turn out. The house-churches (*oikoi* in Greek) of the first few centuries were so clearly little democracies, with a communal, even communistic flavour. St Luke tells us in Acts 4:32–35, repeating what he has already told us two chapters earlier (Acts 2:44): 'The whole body of believers was united in heart and soul. Not a man of them claimed any of his possessions as his own, but everything was held in common ... They were all held in high esteem; for they never had a needy person among them, because all who had property in land or houses sold it, brought the proceeds of the sale, and laid the money at the feet of the apostles; it was then distributed to any who stood in need.' (New English Bible) Luke then gives an example of a Cypriot called Barnabas who does just this, and then of another man called Ananias who keeps back half the proceeds of the sale of his property and drops dead after a dressing-down from Peter.

It is no less clear that the growing flocks proceeded by recognizably democratic methods. The early Christians borrowed from the institutions and practices that were familiar to them: the councils and elections of both the Romans and the Jews. When they called a council to settle a doctrinal dispute or an admin problem, they borrowed the standard drill that obtained throughout the empire. There would be a motion put to the council, a *relatio*, then speeches from either side, followed by a vote, after which a decree would be issued – just the way the Roman Senate did it. The authority of that decree rested solidly, not on any sacred blessing, but on the consent of those present at the council.

Those present would be elected in one way or another by their fellow Christians, not appointed by higher authority. We hear, for example, of a dispute between the Hebrew-speakers and the Greek-speakers in the congregation about the distribution of food to the widows in their respective communities, and a committee of seven reliable men is chosen to sort it out. (Acts 6:1–6) In Acts 15:22, they elect two leading men, Judas Barsabbas and Silas, to accompany Paul and Barnabas to Antioch, bearing a letter setting out the community's views on dietary and sexual abstinence. Sometimes, as in the Greek world if not in the Roman, they draw lots to choose a candidate: in Acts 1:26, Matthias is appointed the twelfth apostle after lots are drawn.

It was not only special commissions that were elected. The early Christians, in the time of the apostles and for some centuries after, chose their own overseers (*episkopoi*, or bishops) and their servants, or ministers (*diakones*, or deacons). Cardinal Daniélou, in his great history of the early Church, says plainly that 'the bishop was elected by the people, and he was ordained by those bishops who were present'. (I, p. 163) The *Didache* (Teaching of the Twelve Apostles), the oldest written catechism and manual of church organization, probably written in the first century AD, tells the faithful: 'Appoint bishops for yourselves, as well as deacons, worthy of the Lord, of meek disposition, unattached to money, truthful and proven; for they also render to you the service of prophets and teachers.' (15, 1)

There was nothing special or separate about these overseers and ministers. Nor was there any requirement for a specially consecrated person to preside over the distribution of bread and wine at the memorial meal: 'As far as eucharistic presidency is concerned, there is no indication anywhere in the New Testament of an explicit link between the Church's office and presiding over the Eucharist ... There is no suggestion that anyone was ordained or appointed to an office which consisted primarily of saying the blessing over the bread and wine.' (House of Bishops of the General Synod of the Church of England, *Eucharistic Presidency*, 1997, p. 41) Or as Herbert Haag, the dissident Swiss priest and defender of Hans Küng, put it more aggressively: 'For nearly 400 years an "ordained" [*Priesterweihe*] was not necessary for the performance of the Eucharist. Why should it be essential today?' (*Worauf es ankommt*, p. 111)

Any local preacher, teacher, prophet or patron of the church could, it seems, preside at the feast. There is unambiguous evidence that all these roles had been filled by women, so it is near certain that women who were apostles, such as Junia in Romans 16:7, or prophets (the four daughters of Philip the Evangelist in Acts 18:26), or church patrons such as Chloe and Phoebe had been known to preside at feasts. St Paul's opposition to uppity women is notorious. He tells us in I Timothy 2:12 that 'I suffer not a woman to preach', which only confirms the impression from the sources that women did in fact preach.

Opponents of women priests are correct in arguing that there were no women priests in the Early Church, but that is because there were no priests at all in our understanding of the office. Priests did not then form a separate caste, with reserved prerogatives. There was merely a swirl of different callings, what St Paul calls 'a cloud of witnesses' (Hebrews 12:1): wandering prophets and charismatic

preachers, elected officials and administrators, helpers and patrons.
Paul wholeheartedly approved of this. He repeatedly rejects the idea
of a single separate priestly caste. (Hebrews, 4:14–15; 8: *passim*)

James Dunn, the trailblazing professor of divinity at Durham, is
indignant at the Church's refusal to listen to Paul:

> It has never ceased to astonish me that a principle so clearly
> formulated could be so blatantly ignored or side-stepped by
> those who insist that, nevertheless, despite Hebrews, an order
> of priesthood is necessary within Christianity. To use Hebrews
> v.1 to justify or explain Christian priesthood, as Vatican II does,
> while ignoring the thrust and argument of the Letter as a whole,
> is a form of eisegesis [reading one's own ideas into the text] which
> ranks more as abuse than as correct use of Scripture. (Dunn and
> Mackay, *New Testament Theology in Dialogue*, pp. 125–6)

My purpose here is not to enter into these theological tussles that
seem to rage as fiercely as they did in the first and second centuries,
but to draw attention to the extraordinary change that transformed
a network of democratic communities into a single, top-down
autocracy. I say single, but of course there were splits aplenty, the
great schism between the Eastern Church and the Western dwarfing
the rest. For present purposes, though, we can leave the splits to one
side, because each of the great Churches came to have the same idea
about itself: that legitimate authority derived from the top, that it
must be undivided, and that it was divinely inspired and therefore
not to be resisted.

Where, how and why did this remarkable shift occur? How did
it come to be pregnant with such consequences for the future of the
Church and for the future of Western humanity? It is not always
easy to trace its course, because historians of the Catholic Church
are not eager to explore it in depth, and even Protestant historians
such as Hans Lietzmann and Henry Chadwick seem sometimes to
underplay its significance.

What is clear is that the beginnings of the shift can be detected
quite early, notably in the first epistle of Bishop Clement of Rome
to the Corinthians, which dates from about AD 100. During one of

those bouts of squabbling that afflicted the Early Church no less
than it afflicts all human organizations, the Christians in Corinth
had ejected several of their bishops (it's not clear whether all at the
same time or one after the other).

Clement's letter is a scorching rebuke. He tells the Corinthians
that their bishops were appointed by succession from the apostles
and were not to be turfed out by a bunch of laymen. His letter is
worth quoting at a little length, because it is the first that lays down
the principle. Largely as a result of it, Clement came to be considered the first Apostolic Father of the Church, and is described by
posterity as Pope Clement I:

> Our Apostles knew through our Lord Jesus Christ that there
> would be strife over the Bishop's office. For this cause therefore,
> having received complete foreknowledge, they appointed the
> aforesaid persons, and afterwards they provided a continuance,
> that if he should fall asleep, other approved men should succeed
> to their ministration. Those therefore who were appointed by
> them, or afterwards by other men of repute with the consent of
> the whole church, and have ministered unblamably to the flock
> of Christ in kindness of mind, peacefully and with all modesty,
> and for long time have borne a good report with all these men
> we consider to be unjustly thrust out from their ministrations.
> (1 Clement, 44:1–2)

Nothing about the people having the right to select and deselect
them. Approval and disapproval now came strictly from the top.

What seems to be happening is that the elected administrators
of the Early Church – the elders and overseers and deacons – had
begun to take over the spiritual mantle of the charismatics, the
supermen to whom God had granted miraculous powers – seeing
visions, healing the sick, exorcizing demons, working miracles.
The elders and overseers carried on with their earthly duties, but
they were now imbued with the special gifts of the Holy Spirit. As
long as they had been mere officials comparable with their Jewish
and Roman counterparts, they could legitimately be turfed out and
replaced if they failed to give satisfaction. But a charismatic had

been chosen by God and so could not be set aside by a popular vote. (Lietzmann, I, pp. 913–14) Gradually, the power of election leaked away from the people. By the fourth century, in theory Christian communities still elected their bishops, but in practice, especially in Rome, the election was in the hands of local clergy, or other bishops. (Daniélou, p. 240) As time went by, the hierarchy crystallized, reinforced by the theory of direct succession from the apostles, and at the pinnacle of the hierarchy sat the pope in Rome. The elders were now ordained by bishops as priests (the word derives from presbyter, *presbuteros*, older man), and the bishops were ordained by other bishops. The principle of submission to higher authority permeated the whole church, and its democratic beginnings were buried under centuries of papal supremacy.

From this obscure theological shift ultimately derive all the conspicuous anti-democratic actions of the papacy over the centuries: Pope Innocent III's Bull annulling Magna Carta, for example, or, six centuries later, Pius IX's excommunicating Garibaldi and the Roman republicans (he forbade Romans to vote in the new elections, which he described as 'a monstrous act of undisguised felony made by the sponsors of anarchic demagogy'). Some popes were better than others. Pius IX had begun as a liberal reformer, after all, before he hardened into the reactionary known to English speakers as 'Pio No-no'. I don't need to go into the ups and downs of the papacy. The point is rather to show how little support the traditions of the later Church offered to those causes of democracy and self-government that had so flourished in its earliest years.

Unfortunately, the truth is that there never was much in the reported teachings of Jesus to help those causes along. Democracy got its belated restart from *secular* traditions: from recollections of popular assemblies, whether in the Greek city states or the Roman Republic or in Anglo-Saxon England; and from legal traditions, whether laid down by Solon of Athens or Alfred of Wessex. No doubt these traditions of ancient common law were partly mythical, as was their founder's part in establishing them. But there was enough reality in the memory of them to make an enduring impact.

In theory, it could all have turned out differently. Jesus could have broadened out his teachings about the equal worth of every human being. He could have indicated, if only in outline, how the ideal of the brotherhood of man could lead, quite logically and naturally, to the ideals of popular assent and of liberation from the rule of alien oppressors. He could have, but he didn't.

And it's not hard to see why he refrained from doing so. What conceivable prospect of success would a Jesus who was politically active have had against the might of the Roman Empire? We have only to look at the suppression by Vespasian and Titus of the great Jewish revolt in AD 70. Jerusalem was torched, and the Jewish historian Josephus tells us that a million people were killed. The spoils of victory are carved on the Arch of Titus in the Roman Forum.

If Christianity had not been a quiet, private faith, it would not have been allowed to survive. As it was, even the non-political Jesus was pursued by accusations that he was setting himself up as King of the Jews. Besides, the quietude of Christianity is one of its greatest attractions. But there is no doubt that the deliberate absence of political engagement left a gap. Over the long term, that gap had consequences for the Church and her people, which were often pernicious and sometimes catastrophic.

THE USES AND ABUSES OF USURY

The ancient philosophers did not think much of commerce. Aristotle called it a *'banausic'* occupation, that is, vulgar, menial, mean-spirited. It smelled of the blacksmith's forge (*baunos* means forge). Of all commercial activities, lending money at interest was the worst. Aristotle says: 'The most hated sort of trade, and with the greatest reason, is usury, which makes a gain out of money itself, and not from the natural use of it.' (*Politics*, I, 10.4) The Old Testament is equally emphatic. Exodus, Leviticus and Deuteronomy all hammer home the same message: 'Thou shalt not lend upon interest to thy brother.' Similar condemnations are to be found in the Vedic texts of India, in Buddhism and in Islam. The medieval theologians, led by Thomas Aquinas, followed the recently rediscovered Aristotle and the Old Testament in denouncing usury as a kind of theft.

The Catholic Church's prohibition on usury lasted through the centuries. Pope Benedict XIV, in his encyclical *Vix pervenit* (1745), condemns usury as a sin in terms that Aristotle would have recognized. The prohibition began to weaken, until the Napoleonic Code allowed the taking of interest throughout the parts of Europe that Napoleon had conquered, and Pope Pius VIII caved in on this as on so much else. Even so, the *New Catholic Dictionary of Social Thought* (1994, pp. 676–8) remarks that 'the words "bank" and "banking" are almost non-existent in the documents of modern Catholic social teaching, perhaps because the medieval teaching was never formally retracted that money was unproductive and therefore moneylending at interest was therefore immoral. Yet the Church itself became an active investor' – and had for centuries borrowed from the great houses, such as Rothschilds.

Besides, even the traditional teaching was always a little fuzzy at the edges. After all, in the next verse after the one in which Deuteronomy tells us that 'thou shalt not lend upon usury to thy brother' (23:19), we are told that 'unto a stranger thou mayest lend upon usury'. Christianity inherited this double standard (and so did much of Islam), all the more reprehensible in a faith that proclaimed that all men were brothers. The ironic result was that, by the Middle Ages, half the monarchs and nobility of Europe were deeply in hock to the Jews, who had taken up moneylending when most other occupations were closed to them. Thus, the double standard of Deuteronomy indirectly led to the persecution and expulsion of these inconveniently successful bankers.

There were other exceptions and loopholes. St Thomas allows that the moneylender could charge for services provided. Profit-sharing too was usually regarded as legitimate; an investor who took a risk had the right to share in the profit. But there had to be a joint venture. To be a lolling rentier who had made no effort for his gain was not a Christian way to live.

Now and then, signs of what we would call 'economic thought' do crop up in the debates of the medieval Church. In the thirteenth century, Cardinal Hostiensis ('of Ostia', where he was bishop) lists thirteen situations in which charging interest was not immoral. The most significant was what he called '*lucrum cessans*' (renouncing

profit): the lender charged interest to compensate him for the profit
he forewent by not investing the money himself. (Rothbard, p. 46)
This is very like what modern economists call 'opportunity cost',
the benefit you might have had if, instead of lending the money, you
had bought a fishing boat or leased a workshop with it. Hostiensis'
argument did not become official doctrine, but it shows how uneasy
and unsure the princes of the Church were in dealing with this
ticklish subject.

This uncertainty does derive in part from the fact that Jesus offers
little clear guidance on usury, or on business generally. Obviously,
the Sermon on the Mount is not a manual for bankers: 'Lay not
up for yourself treasures upon earth' (Matthew 6:19); 'Ye cannot
serve God and Mammon' (6:24); 'Take therefore no thought for the
morrow; for the morrow shall take thought for the things of itself.
Sufficient unto the day is the evil thereof.' (6:34) Postponement of
gratification does not appear to be a building block of the Christian
life (or at least of the Catholic life, for, as Max Weber famously
argued, by contrast, the Protestants believed that they had a duty
to the future and they were much more attuned to the prudential
sacrifices that capitalism demands). According to the Sermon on
the Mount, what is crucial to that life is for Christians to separate
themselves from the grimy business of getting and spending. That
same message underlies the expulsion of the moneychangers from
the temple: the necessary separation between God and Mammon.

Those moneychangers, according to Matthew 21:12, Mark 11:15
and John 2:15, were *kollubistai*, small moneychangers. John adds
the detail that, in overturning their tables, Jesus scattered their
small change, '*ta kermata*'. Luke calls them merely *tous polountas*,
or traders. (19:45) Clearly they were modest currency dealers, offering to change coins for the numerous visitors to the Temple from
other cities, not unlike the forex booths on airport malls today.
Some of them may have chiseled their customers, though competition is thought to have kept their rates down to very low levels,
perhaps as little as 1 per cent – an example to their modern counterparts. The racketeers are more likely to have been the sellers of
doves and other merchandise. The moneychangers were providing
an indispensable service.

The question remains then: how are these benighted money-changers to live their lives? How is day-to-day *'banausic'* business to be carried on? The Parable of the Talents (Matthew 25:14–30) suggests a rather different code of conduct from the carefree injunctions of the Sermon on the Mount. It is one of the longer and more detailed parables, as well as being one of the most vivid. A rich man who is about to make a trip to a distant country calls his servants together and tells them to look after his property. He also gives them tidy sums of cash, each according to his abilities, five talents to the top man, two talents to the next, and one talent to a third. When he returns from his travels, he finds that the first two have doubled their money, while the third, terrified of the displeasure of his master whom he knew to be a hard man 'reaping where he did not sow', simply hid the talent in the ground and now proudly digs it up again and hands it back.

To his horror, the master applauds the first two – 'well done thou good and faithful servant' – but denounces the luckless third servant as wicked and slothful: precisely because the servant knew his master was a hard man, 'thou oughtest therefore to have put my money to the exchangers, and then at my coming I should have received mine own with usury'. That is the King James version. The New English Bible has: 'you should have put my money on deposit, and on my return I should have got it back with interest.' Neither version conveys exactly the word that Matthew uses, which is *trapezitai*, or bankers, that is, moneylenders, not mere moneychangers. The parable is told too in Luke 19:12–26, and there the Authorized Version has, correctly, at verse 23: 'Wherefore then gavest not thou my money into the bank, that at my coming I might have required mine own with usury?' Here the Greek suggests an institution, rather than a bunch of individual traders: *epi trapezan*, into the bank.

Now of course Jesus is not primarily talking about money, but about the use we make of the talents that God has given us. Our modern use of 'talent' derives from this parable; in Greek, a talent is simply a measure of weight, and by extension a coin of great value. But Jesus is also, if incidentally, talking about money too. From the parable, we can clearly see that lending out your money was a routine practice in Jerusalem and entirely legitimate. In using this

extended metaphor, Jesus was confident that the cross-section of
the Jerusalem public who were listening to him would completely
understand the context of it (for the benefit of hardline sceptics, it
is irrelevant for our purposes who actually wrote the two gospels
and even whether Jesus was a partly or wholly mythical figure;
the speaker and the writers, whoever they were, could be sure that
their audiences would know what they were talking about). The
two servants who double their money do so by 'trading'. The word
that Matthew uses here is *ergasato*: the faithful servants make the
money work for them. The point is that trading is what you ought
to do with spare cash, 'idle balances' as we call them today.

We have from the early years of the next century after Jesus a
remarkable secular parallel to the Parable of the Talents. Pliny the
Younger (Pliny *Secundus*) has been sent as governor to the distant
Roman province of Bithynia and Pontus on the Black Sea. It is the
crowning appointment of his career and he dies there two years
later, in about AD 112 (only a few years after the composition of
the Gospels of Matthew and Luke, both dated at AD 80–100). His
careful accounting of the public revenue has produced a healthy
surplus, but he is perplexed what to do with it, and he writes to his
boss in Rome, the Emperor Trajan:

> Public moneys, my lord, through your foresight and my handling
> have already been and are still being levied, but I am fearful that
> they lie unused, for there is no opportunity, or only a most occa-
> sional one, of purchasing estates, and none are found willing to
> become debtors to the state, especially at the rate of twelve per
> cent, the rate at which they borrow from private individuals. So,
> my lord, consider whether you think that this rate of interest
> should be lowered, and suitable debtors enticed by this means.
> (*Letters*, X, 54, p. 261)

Trajan is in no doubt about the right answer: 'I too visualize no
remedy, my dearest Secundus, other than that the level of interest
should be lowered, so that the public money can be more easily lent
out. You must decide on the level, depending on the resources of
those who will borrow.' (X, 55, p. 262)

Not only is there clearly a thriving money market in this remote
province, but even on the shores of the Black Sea it is accepted that
rates of interest should go up and down according to supply of and
demand for money. There is also an assumption that leaving money
to lie idle is a wasteful thing to do. A good steward will seek out
opportunities to find a use for the money. Pliny tells Trajan that if he
cannot find borrowers, even at a lower rate of interest, he proposes
distributing the cash among the city councillors, specifying that
'they safeguard the welfare of the State', we assume by spending
the money on things like roads, drains, baths or food for the poor.
Very much the same argument is used today by those economists
who argue that if borrowers aren't tempted even by near-zero interest rates, then the government ought to kick-start the economy by
increasing public expenditure.

Almost as fascinating as this glimpse of economic policy-making
in AD 110 is the attempt of some modern scholars to prove that
this exchange of letters means something different. The eminent
classicist Sir Moses Finley argues in his seminal work *The Ancient
Economy* (p. 118) that Trajan sees nothing wrong in letting money
lie idle, but this is a total misreading. On the contrary, the emperor
backs Pliny's idea of lowering the interest rate to attract borrowers;
he says only that it would be un-Roman to force them to borrow.
Finley goes on to argue that the Roman Empire 'was a world which
never created fiduciary money in any form or negotiable instruments'. (p. 141) And when criticized by the so-called 'modernists',
who think that Greece and Rome had recognizable banks not unlike
our own, he retorts that 'the absence of credit-creating instruments
and institutions remains as an unshaken foundation of the ancient
economy'. (p. 198) Moneylending, Finley tells us, remained on a
primitive level, carried on mostly between wealthy men who were
temporarily strapped for cash. This 'primitive' view of ancient
commerce was popularized by Karl Marx and is firmly promoted
by many of his followers to this day. For example, Perry Anderson
in *Passages from Antiquity to Feudalism* (1974) asserts roundly that
'apart from the tax-farms and public contracts of the Republican
epoch ... no commercial companies ever developed, and funded
debts did not exist: the credit system remained rudimentary. The

propertied classes maintained their traditional disdain for trade. Merchants were a despised category, frequently recruited from freedmen.' (p. 81) Finley was an American academic who had been forced to flee to England after being denounced by McCarthy and fired from his post at Rutgers University, and while he was unjustly pilloried for his views, his work retains a strong Marxist flavour. It remains an important step in Marx's narrative that Ancient Greece and Rome should be strictly classified as belonging to the 'slave mode of production', in which no hint of the later capitalist mode had begun to emerge. Marxism depends on 'the social newness' of each stage of historical development, as Karl Popper calls it in *The Poverty of Historicism*. In *Lending and Borrowing in Ancient Athens*, Finley's pupil Paul Millett extends Finley's view to Greece. This is not the place to examine the controversy that has raged about the supposedly 'primitive' character of the economy in both cultures. But we do need to get some idea of the extent and sophistication of commerce to assess the relevance of the economic teaching (or lack of it) to be found in the Gospels. If the Marxist view is even half-correct, then Jesus would not have needed to devise rules for a market society simply because he wasn't living in one. But if the commercial spirit was really quite well developed in Jerusalem and other great cities of the empire, then Jesus ought to have said something about how Christians should behave in that sort of society. So what is the reality?

For a start, you cannot help being struck by the sheer number of nouns describing the occupations of Roman money men. There were the *faeneratores* (literally, 'haymakers'), private operators who specialized in banking. Then there were the *numularii*, coin exchangers who also scrutinized coins for their metal content. From Trajan's time onwards, the *numularii* also began to accept deposits and grant credit, functions previously carried out, if on a small scale, by the *argentarii*, who were payment agents as well as lenders. The *argentarii* also acted as wealth managers for rich men and women. Then there were the *coactores*, debt collectors working on commission, usually as low as 1 per cent. Roman bankers copied from the Greeks the system of the bill of exchange, known as a *permutatio*. It was also possible for a banker's client

to draw a cheque on his current account, known as a *praescriptio*.
Our information on exactly how all of this worked is necessarily
fragmentary and sketchy, much of it drawn from the accidental revelations of court cases, which can easily be misinterpreted. But what
does seem undeniable was that the financial sector was not a small
area of life. If anything, historians, especially the Marx-ish ones,
seem to downplay what evidence they come up with. Millett, for
example, argues that 'productive credit', or lending for investment,
was scarcely known in ancient Athens. (Millett, pp. 1, 59) Yet in a
footnote (p. 267) he lists eight interesting examples of such loans: to
set up a perfumery business, to buy a mining concession, to set up a
destitute family as cloth-makers, to buy a mill to process silver ore,
for a freeman to set up as a banker, to buy slaves for a metalworking
business, and two loans to buy real estate. These examples, drawn
mostly from the star cases of the Attic orators, show a spread of
commercial lending not unlike that of a modern investment bank.
It is reasonable to guess that, if we had more evidence, we should
find more such instances.

About the ubiquity of lending money at interest in the ancient
world there can be no doubt at all, not least from the number of
official efforts to regulate the practice and establish fair maximum
rates of interest, and on occasion to decree the forgiving of loans
that had become horrendously burdensome, most famously in the
seisachtheia, or 'shaking off of burdens', decreed by Solon in about
594 BC. The *seisachtheia* cancelled outstanding debts on a huge
scale and swept away the cruel practice by which agricultural debtors who could not repay their mortgages were enslaved and forced
to work the land that had previously been theirs.

What is striking, too, is the antiquity of banking. Heichelheim
(II, p. 2) describes 'The Grandsons of Egibi', a firm that operated in
Babylon between the seventh and fifth centuries BC. Egibi's offered
loans and securities and accepted deposits, providing current
accounts and cheque facilities for their customers. The bank lent on
its capital to buy land, cattle and ships. Banking did develop more
slowly in Greek cities. Even so, in the fifth century BC we have the
names of twenty-three *trapezitai* in Athens alone. Tributes from
other city states that were to be piled up in the Parthenon's inner

sanctum could be paid out of the deposit accounts of aliens resident in the city. The Athenian navy, the source of its imperial power, was often financed out of loans, the high rates of 20–33 per cent acting as a sort of marine insurance necessary in such a hazardous trade.

Depositors had to pay rent in advance for their deposit boxes. They also had to show their ID before gaining access to them. This *symbolon* could take the form of a seal from a signet ring, or the matching half of a broken coin or clay token.

Throughout the ancient world, then, there was a vigorous commercial market, serviced to varying levels of sophistication by a teeming world of money men. Philosophers did not care to admit that this was the reality, and they continued to denounce usury in every form, but as George Grote, himself a banker by trade, put it, 'the feeling against lending money remained in the bosoms of philosophers long after it had ceased to be justified'. (III, pp. 476–83) In the law courts, at the bankers' tables in the *agora* and in the temple complex, Greek and Roman citizens negotiated loans and argued about the terms without any sense of embarrassment or shame.

Any comprehensive theory of civic society needed to confront this sizeable reality and offer some sort of moral guidance. But Jesus didn't. As a result, medieval theologians, and modern ones too, had to grope for a set of viable principles with little or no help from Holy Writ. Business and businessmen accordingly lay under an obscure moral cloud throughout the Christian era. Has that cloud lifted, now that the Church no longer dictates moral principles to society? Curiously, I don't think so.

As Christianity recedes from the moral horizons, it seems to have bequeathed at least its suspicion of commerce. Contrary to Marxist predictions, capitalism has managed to weather its numerous shocks and disgraces. It has survived the recent bank crashes and financial scandals unbowed but even less loved than before. Could a fully articulated code of business ethics have helped capitalism to mend its ways, and gone some way to reduce the public alienation from the society in which we live? That remains a hypothetical question that is hard to answer. What we do know is that Jesus did not give us much help.

Marriage isn't made in heaven

There is one last, and most intimate, part of human life, about which the teaching of Jesus leaves something to be desired: what he has to say about marriage and the family.

Jesus says: 'If any man come to me, and hate not his father, and mother, and wife, and children, and brethren, and sisters, yea, and his own life also, he cannot be my disciple.' (Luke 14:26)

To this day I remember as a child the shock of first coming across this text. The tone is so fierce, so unyielding. It was explained to me that Jesus was merely laying down, in forceful rhetorical terms, the practical conditions of discipleship. He meant only that nobody could hope to be an effective or wholehearted apostle without first giving up family concerns. But this does not really escape the problem. For what the New Testament is stating, and it does so over and over again, is that to be a disciple of Christ is a *higher* calling than to be a loving and devoted member of a family. If the two were alternatives of comparable value, we would expect to find corresponding eulogies of marriage and family life in the Gospels.

There are none. 'Suffer the little children to come unto *me*' – not unto their parents – is the message. It is hard to deny, in the light of these texts, that all those sectarians whose demands and disciplines have caused so many family rifts and human tragedies – the Plymouth Brethren, the Moonies and the Rev. Jim Jones – can claim some sort of scriptural authority, however foully they may have abused it.

The Anglican marriage service contains only two specific references to the Gospels: the Marriage at Cana, and Jesus's remarks in Mark 10:6–9. The party at Cana starts unpromisingly: 'And the third day there was a marriage in Cana of Galilee; and the mother of Jesus was there: both Jesus was called, and his disciples, to the marriage. And when they wanted wine, the mother of Jesus saith unto him, They have no wine. Jesus saith unto her, Woman, what have I to do with thee? Mine hour is not yet come.' The impression is given – indeed, the story would lack point without it – that Jesus is in somewhat irritable mood at being distracted from his work and is annoyed by his mother's request and that he turns the water into wine partly to pacify her and partly to demonstrate that he is who he is (it is his first miracle). The miracle could in no sense be taken to uphold, endorse or glorify the institution of marriage itself.

The only direct quotation from Jesus in the marriage service is the one in Mark: 'But from the beginning of creation God made them male and female. For this cause shall a man leave his father and mother, and cleave to his wife; And they twain shall be one flesh: so then they are no more twain, but one flesh. What therefore God hath joined together, let not man put asunder.'

This is certainly an endorsement of marriage as a biological imperative and a social institution. However, it comes in answer to a trick question from the Pharisees about the legality of divorce. It is hard to read it as a positive assertion of the *spiritual* importance of marriage – something that is absent from the Gospels.

Do the Epistles have a higher opinion of the married state? St Paul does tell husbands to love their wives 'as their own bodies' and 'as Christ loved the Church'. (Colossians 3:19) Men must love their wives and not be bitter against them. Wives are to 'submit yourselves unto your own husbands, as unto the Lord. For the husband is the head of the wife, even as Christ is the head of the Church'(Ephesians 5:22–3); young women are to be taught by the aged women 'to be sober, to love their husbands, to love their children ... To be discreet, chaste, keepers at home, good, obedient to their own husbands, that the word of God be not blasphemed'. (Titus 2:4–5)

What seems to be primarily in question here is decent social behaviour, so as not to disgrace the young Church at a precarious state in its growth. When Paul turns to spiritual priorities, his message is quite different:

It is good for a man not to touch a woman ... I would that all men were even as I myself. But every man hath his proper gift of God, one after this manner, and another after that. I say therefore to the unmarried and widows, It is good for them if they abide even as I. But if they cannot contain, let them marry: for it is better to marry than to burn ... the fashion of this world passeth away. But I would have you without carefulness. He that is unmarried careth for the things that belong to the Lord, how he may please

the Lord: But he that is married careth for the things that are of
the world, how he may please his wife. There is a difference also
between a wife and a virgin. The unmarried woman careth for
the things of the Lord, that she may be holy both in body and in
spirit: but she that is married careth for the things of the world,
how she may please her husband. (I Corinthians 7:1, 7–9, 31–34)

Marriage for St Paul is unquestionably an inferior state, a second
best. Some of the early Christian sects took this view a stage further and taught that sexual abstinence was an obligation for all
good Christians. They admitted to baptism only virgins or married
women who had taken a vow of chastity. Gradually, the Church
yielded to reality in the interests of increasing its flock. In the third
century, Clement of Alexandria wrote a whole book to prove that
marriage was fully compatible with the Christian life. Marriage
began to be sanctified and absorbed into official Christian ritual. In
the fourth century, the custom began of solemnly blessing the bride
and groom as soon as they had been married, accompanied by rites
taken over from pagan custom. In Rome, a veil was placed on the
heads of the married couple, the *velatio conjugalis*.

Yet this accommodation to human weakness (as they saw it)
never quite wiped out the stern code of the desert. Throughout the
third century, apocryphal Acts of the Apostles continued to glorify
both the state of virginity and the separation of married couples in
the service of God. As late as the sixteenth century, the Council of
Trent, the starting point of the Counter-Reformation, denounced
those who claimed that 'the marriage state is to be placed above the
state of virginity, or of celibacy, and that it is not better and more
blessed to remain in virginity, or celibacy, than to be united'.

For centuries, the Church was engaged in a double task: to elaborate a conception of Christian marriage that could survive in the
lay world without sacrificing too much of the Christian reverence
for chastity, and to gain control of the legal and social institutions
governing marriage. This all took a very long time. In England, the
Church did not succeed in its claim to exercise exclusive jurisdiction
in matrimonial cases until the eleventh century. For hundreds of
years after that, poor people continued to marry without 'benefit

of clergy'. For them, marriage remained what it had always been: a private contract involving an exchange of vows between two freely consenting adults, preferably in front of witnesses, not inside the church itself but at the church door, with a blessing to follow afterwards. As for the clergy, celibacy was not effectively enforced in the Roman Church until the Second Lateran Council of 1139, if then.

Looking back, we have to conclude that the Church exercised more or less total control over marriage for only a few centuries out of the 2,000 years of the Christian era, roughly from the thirteenth to the nineteenth century. The undermining of St Paul's teaching began with the Reformation. Calvin, for example: 'As for me, I do not want anyone to think me very virtuous because I am not married. It would rather be a fault in me if I could serve God better in marriage than remaining as I am ... But I know my infirmity, that perhaps a woman might not be happy with me. However that may be, I abstain from marriage in order that I may be more free to serve God. But this is not because I think that I am more virtuous than my brethren. Fie to me if I had that false opinion.' For Calvin, chastity is not self-evidently a superior state, and human happiness is to be taken into account as well as the service of God.

Seventeenth-century radicals like John Milton were fiercely critical of the Church's record. He wrote in *The Doctrine and Discipline of Divorce*: 'It was for many ages that marriage lay in disgrace with most of the ancient doctors, as a work of the flesh, almost a defilement, wholly denied to priests, and the second time dissuaded to all, as he that reads Tertullian or Jerome may see at large. Afterwards it was thought so sacramental, that no adultery or desertion could dissolve it.' Milton looked back to the days before the 'Norman Yoke' had been imposed upon the English people and before the Pope of Rome had dared to 'pluck the power and arbitrament of divorce from the master of the family, into whose hands God and the law of all nations had left it'. (Milton, pp. 255–6) It is not often remembered that Milton's glorious invocation – 'Let not England forget her precedence of teaching nations how to live' – occurs in the introduction to a passionate plea for divorce by consent. For Milton, marriage was a private matter, and the happiness or unhappiness of the couple was the prime consideration. This was intended as a revaluation, not a devaluation of marriage. The married state began to be glorified, not just as another, equally good way of serving but as a better, fuller way. The idea of the sexual life as fulfilling God's purpose permitted the growth of the idea of sex as something good, even sacred, in itself.

The Catholic Church accommodated itself to this new view of marriage with the greatest difficulty. Above all, it stuck to the one part of Jesus's teaching that was quite clear-cut: the prohibition of divorce. Yet this was the part that represented the sharpest and most painful breach with pre-Christian practice almost everywhere. For the most regular and universal feature of non-Christian or pre-Christian marriage is the relative ease of divorce. In Western Europe especially, what marks out the Christian era from earlier and later times is the insistence that marriage should invariably be 'till death us do part'. It is this that makes the most dramatic contrast with the marriage customs of virtually all the peoples who were to be Christianized over the centuries, the Romans no less than the Anglo-Saxons, the Celts in the Dark Ages no less than most of the inhabitants of Africa and Asia who were to be converted by missionaries a thousand years later. Only the Hindus seem to have maintained anything like the strictness of the Catholic Church, or indeed of the Church of England, which in practical terms had often been stricter because it was much less accommodating about annulments.

In many countries, it was often centuries before the Church managed to exert effective control over divorce. In Ireland, for example. In our time, Ireland has been the most uniformly obedient daughter of the Church and did not remove the prohibition on divorce until the Fifteenth Amendment to the Irish Constitution was passed in 1995. Yet, in ancient Ireland, centuries after the conversion to Christianity, a marriage might always be ended by mutual consent. The same in Wales, where the laws stipulated careful arrangements for the division of household goods and the custody of the children. The Anglo-Saxons admitted divorce by mutual consent or even at the will of one party. The penitential of the great Archbishop Theodore in the seventh century offers a string of grounds for divorce, including adultery.

Both the Romans and the barbarians who broke Rome, such as the Visigoths, considered divorce to be a natural part of their civil code. We may go back as far as the Hittites in 1,200 BC and even to the *Code of Hammurabi* in Babylon of c.2,000 BC, and we shall find roughly the same arrangements. Moses sets down at some length in Deuteronomy (22, 24) the conditions under which divorce was permissible. Rabbinic teaching over the centuries refined, and often extended, those conditions, so that being noisy or a bad cook could be grounds for divorce. Jewish law, like other codes in the ancient world, was often brutally unfair to women and usually provided much more restricted grounds, if any, for a woman to sue for divorce. In fact, the Jewish wife had to ask the husband to put her away. But almost everywhere we find elaborate arrangements for the maintenance of divorced women and of the children.

Throughout the centuries of its hegemony, the Church sought to abolish and to blanket out the memory of such traditional humane provisions at every opportunity. This relentless campaign did have clear scriptural authority in Mark 10:9, which prevented the Fathers of the Church and their successors from seriously considering whether such iron rules were consonant with Jesus's message of mercy and forgiveness. Still less did the Church stop to consider whether, in terms of secular society, those rules were sustainable for either the clergy or the laity. In our own times, the sexual backslidings by priests of all denominations have done more than anything to discredit the Church.

Yet if we return once more to the words of Jesus, we shall find that, as with the Church's struggle to arrive at viable doctrines on war, democracy and usury, dogma has had to be constructed out of stray remarks thrown out by Jesus in the course of his disputes with the Pharisees or the Roman authorities. His kingdom was not of this world, as he said himself, and his teachings provide only shreds of guidance for the governance of the world we live in.

III

JEAN-JACQUES ROUSSEAU

and the self supreme

WALKING BACK TO HAPPINESS

On Sundays, the engraver's apprentices would scamper out of the city after morning service. If they were not back by dusk, the gates of Geneva would clang shut, and the boys would have to sleep out, with the prospect of a beating from their bad-tempered master in the morning. This had happened twice to Jean-Jacques and his pals. The third time he had had enough. When the gates opened again at dawn, the others trooped back inside, but he said goodbye to them and to the city of his birth, and at the age of sixteen he set out on the open road. (*Confessions*, I, p. 41) He began adult life as a solitary walker, and that was how he ended it. 'The wandering life is the one for me,' he tells us in his amazing *Confessions* (p. 168), not published in his lifetime because they were so shocking. His last work, *Reveries of a Solitary Stroller*, also not published in his lifetime, extols the delights of walking by yourself and thinking for yourself at the same time. Walking animates his ideas. He can scarcely think when he stays still.

This is how Rousseau wishes to present himself to us, as a wanderer on his own, awkward in company, shy with women, hesitant of speech, perpetually at odds with the world and incurably outspoken about its evils. All this was only part of the truth. You have only to look at Quentin de La Tour's famous pastel of Rousseau at the age of forty – to note the sharp eyes, the sly mouth, the quick, alert look about him – to know that this was not someone the world would easily get the better of.

The *Confessions* are the frankest exercise in self-revealing ever printed, making the *Essays* of Montaigne and the *Confessions* of St Augustine of Hippo seem positively reticent. Rousseau tells us, not without a smidgen of pride: 'I had always laughed at the false naivety of Montaigne, who, while pretending to confess his faults, is very careful to give himself only lovable ones, whereas I, who had always believed myself and who still believe myself to be, all in all, the best of men, felt that there is no human being whose interior, however pure it may be, will not reveal some odious vice.' (p. 505) In his preface, he issues a challenge: 'let each reader imitate me, let him retire within himself, as I have done, and let him, from the depths of his conscience, say to himself if he dares: "I am better than that man was."'

In the early chapters, the reader might feel like conceding Rousseau's point. His youthful misdeeds are pretty commonplace: he pinches some asparagus from a poor man's patch and flogs it in the market (p. 32); he steals a pretty ribbon and blames it on the maid, who gets the sack; he masturbates a lot and exposes himself in dark alleys. (pp. 106, 186) But as time goes by, one begins to notice one or two of his more ingrained faults and to find them more unappealing than most people's. Jean-Jacques continues to insist that he is the most loving and loveable of men, but his own testimony shows him to be malicious, jealous, paranoid and ruthless. He is taken under the wing of his first open-hearted patroness, Madame de Warens, and tells us how much he dreads having sex with her. She has another lover, an admirable young herbalist, Claude Anet, who befriends Rousseau. When Anet dies of pleurisy after botanizing in the Alps, Rousseau immediately asks Madame de Warens if he can inherit Anet's smart black suit. In his bestselling novel, *Julie, or the New Heloise*, Rousseau gives the name of Claude Anet to a treacherous servant.

But it is when he takes up with the laundry maid in his Paris lodgings, Thérèse Levasseur, that even the most besotted fan of Rousseau must feel a qualm or two. He is thirty-three years old, and they stay together for another thirty-three years until his death. They even go through a form of marriage, though not a legal one. His loyalty to her might seem touching, if it were not

combined with such a searing contempt. She can scarcely read, he
tells us, and she certainly cannot tell the time, despite his efforts
to teach her. She doesn't know the order of the months and can't
recognize numerals. She mangles her words, and Rousseau hurries
off to regale his aristocratic friends with her latest malapropisms.
(pp. 322–3) When she becomes pregnant, he persuades her 'blithely
and without scruple' to send the baby to the foundling hospital.
He does this because the ribald company he keeps in the local
hostelry compete in boasting who has sent the most children to
the orphanage. The baby has a token tucked into his swaddling
clothes, the standard procedure that allows the mother, if her
circumstances improve, to reclaim the child by presenting a
matching token.

'The following year, the same inconvenience presented itself,
except that the card with the cipher was overlooked. I reflected no
more deeply on the subject, the mother agreed no more readily; she
groaned, but obeyed.' (p. 335) In this way, Rousseau dispatched all
five children he had by Thérèse to the foundling hospital. In later
years, he claimed to be greatly distressed by the thought of his
actions, but this was only because the news had got out and had
been broadcast to the world by Voltaire, whom he never forgave.
Rousseau's belief in his own innate benevolence remains undented:
'Never for a single moment in his life could Jean-Jacques have been
without sentiment, without pity, an unnatural father.' (p. 347) By
handing his children over to be educated at the public expense,
he was acting as a good citizen and father because he had not the
money to educate them. He even claimed that he would like to have
been brought up that way himself, and looked upon himself as a
model citizen of Plato's imaginary Republic, where the children
were brought up communally. This rationale came to look a bit
thin twelve years later, when his patronne of the moment, Madame
de Luxembourg, tried to reclaim the first child by presenting the
matching token that Rousseau had handed to her. Alas, the hospital register was so chaotic that no trace of the child could be
found. Edmund Burke's wisecrack that Rousseau was 'a lover of his
kind but a hater of his kindred' echoed round the drawing rooms
of Europe.

THE FIRST CELEBRITY

Jean-Jacques had had an unpromising start in life. His mother had died giving birth to him. His elder brother had gone to the bad and disappeared. His father, Isaac, as prickly as his son, had been expelled from Geneva for challenging a man of higher rank to a duel and, when told he was no gentleman, brandishing his sword and refusing to climb down. Isaac Rousseau started a second family outside Geneva and never lifted a finger to help Jean-Jacques, who none the less remained fond of him and visited him from time to time.

So, without money, skills or connections to speak of, Jean-Jacques strode off into the wider world and never looked back. For all his proclaimed awkwardness, he never lacked for patrons of either sex, often at the highest social levels: after Mme de Warens, there came Mme Dupin, the Duc and Duchesse de Luxembourg, Mme d'Épinay, the Marquis de Girardin, not to mention Lord Keith, the retired Scottish general settled in Neuchâtel who had become a favourite of Frederick the Great. All found something irresistible about this gawky young Swiss and fixed him up with a hermitage or a pavilion somewhere on their estates where he could write his subversive books in peace. His last patron, the extremely progressive M. de Girardin, under whose wing he spent the final months of his life at Ermenonville, just north of Paris, saw to the publication of Rousseau's posthumous works, above all the *Confessions*, which made him still more famous in the 1780s and 1790s. Already in his lifetime he had become so celebrated that he complained that fans would traipse hundreds of miles to see him without having read a single one of his books.

Even when dwelling out in the country, he was seldom as far from civilization as he pretended. He tells us in the *Reveries* that when he was plant-hunting in the hills, he came to a spot that seemed so remote that he fancied himself a new Columbus treading where no man had ever trod, when he suddenly heard the clacking from a stocking factory hidden in a hollow a few yards away. In his famous promenades round his beloved Lac de Bienne, you begin to notice that this solitary rambler is often accompanied by his wife Thérèse and by the intendant, the island's governor, and the intendant's family as well.

He wasn't left alone much in his grace-and-favour residences either. He moaned about having to dance attendance on his patrons. Madame d'Épinay, in particular, insisted on soulful literary conversations whenever she found that she was going to be on her own. Yet most of these patrons were remarkably long-suffering. The Luxembourgs even forgave him for the stinker he wrote them in October 1760: 'How cruel your kindness is ... You are merely playing at friendship ... How I detest all your titles, how I pity you for possessing them!' (p. 521)

In Paris, too, he was immediately swept up by the cream of intellectual society, above all by the circle of *illuminati* who were putting together the great *Encyclopédie* that was to revolutionize public knowledge, and to which Rousseau was soon a contributor. For a time, he was friends with them all: Diderot, Voltaire, d'Alembert, Helvétius, d'Holbach, Condillac. They were mostly to become his deadly enemies – or rather he thought they were, after paranoia took its terminal hold on him – but nobody could deny the warmth of their initial welcome.

He swam effortlessly upwards. He played chess with Philidor, the greatest player of the century; he collaborated, rather scratchily, with Rameau, the greatest composer. In music, as in most things, Rousseau was mostly self-taught. He never went to any college. Yet his operetta, *Le devin du village* (*The Village Soothsayer*), was an instant hit. Its catchy melodies entranced Louis XV: 'all day long ... His Majesty does nothing but sing, in the least tuneful voice in his whole realm, *I have lost my suitor, I have lost all my joy?*' (p. 371) Jean-Jacques could have had a royal pension without having to beg for it, but he was too shy and surly to appear before the king and deliberately turned up at the theatre in ordinary clothes, unshaven and with his wig unbrushed. His play *Narcisse* went down well too. When in his late thirties he won an essay prize offered by the Dijon Academy, he found himself unmistakably 'a celebrity'. He is the first person to use the word in our modern sense, just as he was the first to use the word 'perfectibility'. Indeed, he was also the first to imbue the word 'bourgeois' with the modern, derisive meaning it carries today. The originality of his thought shows up in the originality of his vocabulary.

At quite an early stage in his career we can, I think, catch sight of him manipulating his public persona. Where other writers took refuge in pseudonyms, 'Monsieur de ... ', or 'A Nobleman', Rousseau stamped the Jean-Jacques label on everything he wrote. He never missed an opportunity to give the reader a more pungent sense of his personality. On several occasions, he defended himself from his critics by writing dialogues between 'Jean-Jacques' and imaginary interlocutors, the most bizarre being the three-way dialogue called *Rousseau, Juge de Jean-Jacques* (*Rousseau, Judge of Jean-Jacques*), in which 'Rousseau', his alter ego 'Jean-Jacques' and 'A Frenchman' debate the merits of the great man's work. At the same time, he continues to insist on his poverty and obscurity and his distance from the great world. All the time, he is backing into the limelight.

What he had in abundance, whatever his detractors might think, was the gift of popularity, as much as, say, Andrew Lloyd Webber has it today. Everything he turned his hand to was instantly adored by the public. His vast sentimental novel (a genre he had hitherto sneered at) was the greatest bestseller of the century. *Julie* went through seventy editions in France and dozens in England. His long semi-novelistic treatise on education, *Emile*, was scarcely less popular. His political writings – the two *Discourses*, on the progress of the arts and sciences and on the origins of inequality, and above all *The Social Contract* – were the founding texts of the French Revolution.

Far from Rousseau falling out of favour after his death, the Jacobins gave his reputation a second wind. He was elevated to a national sage. Jean-Paul Marat gave readings from his work at street corners. Robespierre read out long extracts at the National Convention. His ashes were transported from the shrine that M. de Girardin had built for them at Ermenonville to the new secular Valhalla in Paris, the Pantheon. The little town of Montmorency, where he had basked in the favour of the Luxembourgs, was renamed Emile in his honour, at least for the duration of the Revolution. This allure has never faded. Again and again, you can

see how many ideas Karl Marx soaked up from Rousseau, not the
least of them being the idea of religion as 'the opium of the masses'
(of the soul, Rousseau said). Che Guevara took Rousseau's works
with him up into the Cuban hills.

Nor has the distrust faded either. 'He makes me uneasy,' Diderot
wrote on the evening before he and Rousseau broke irrevocably, 'and
I feel as if a damned soul stood beside me. I never want to see that
man again.' (December 1757, *Oeuvres*, ed. Assézat, XIX, p. 446;
Cassirer, p. 91) After Rousseau fell out with David Hume, who had
tried so hard to help him, even that amiable philosopher could not
contain his baffled resentment. To Adam Smith, he summed up
Rousseau as a 'Composition of Whim, Affectation, Wickedness,
Vanity, and Inquietude, with a small, if any Ingredient of Madness',
plus, at the end of the same paragraph, 'Ingratitude, Ferocity, and
Lying, I need not mention, Eloquence and Invention'. (Smith, *Works
and Correspondence*, No. 109) As for his legacy, later critics have
been damning. Bertrand Russell blamed the totalitarian ills of the
modern age on the teachings of Rousseau, as did J. L. Talmon in
The Origins of Totalitarian Democracy.

Above all, Jean-Jacques told his age and thousands of readers
in succeeding ages something that they wished to hear but didn't
know how to express. Not unlike Donald Trump, he purported to
tell them important truths that were being kept from them by 'the
elite'. But what were these truths?

THE MESSAGE

In the nineteenth and twentieth centuries, critics often confessed to
being nonplussed by Rousseau. They couldn't quite make him out.
Was he a rationalist or an irrationalist, a collectivist or an individualist? If he was a socialist, he seemed an odd sort of one, being so
keen on his privacy and his independence. He was born a Geneva
Protestant, then, in a painful conversion of convenience, became a
Catholic after he fled to France, then reverted to his original faith
when he fled from France. He never ceased to proclaim himself a
Christian, but with so many reservations that you had to wonder
whether he really believed in God at all.

Some critics claimed to trace some sort of intellectual progress. First, he had been one thing, then another, and so on throughout his life. The great Rousseau scholar Charles Edwyn Vaughan argued that 'the political work of Rousseau, when taken as a whole, presents an unbroken movement from one position almost to its opposite'. He had started as the prophet of freedom and ended in 'total surrender to the service of the State'. With this final shift, 'the long journey is at last ended. And Rousseau now stands at the opposite point of the compass from that at which he started.'

But it wasn't a very long journey. Only twelve years separates the publication of his first *Discourse* from *Emile*, the last major publication in his lifetime. Rousseau himself stoutly denied any such shift. On the contrary, he had been saying the same thing all along. 'Everything that is daring in the *Social Contract* was already to be found in the *Discourse on Inequality*. Everything that is daring in *Emile* was already to be found in *Julie*.' (*Confessions*, p. 397)

I think that Rousseau was right about this. By and large, so do most modern scholars. Whatever you may think about what Rousseau is telling us, he does seem to be telling us pretty much the same thing from his first publication to his last. His posthumous works say the same thing too. Perhaps this should not surprise us, since he didn't publish anything to speak of until he was nearly forty, by which age you might expect his views to have crystallized. You may be blown away by Rousseau's daring, or you may detect glaring flaws or contradictions in his argument, but whether you find him inspiring or repugnant, what I don't think can be denied is that it is always basically the same argument.

The question that the Academy of Dijon proposed for the first prize essay that Rousseau went in for was: 'whether the Restoration of the Sciences and Arts contributed to the Purification of "Moeurs"' [an amalgam of what we would call 'morals' or 'culture']. And Rousseau wins the prize by answering the question with a resounding No. The arts and sciences, including technology and crafts, have corrupted our morals and our manners. They owe their birth to our vices, not our virtues. They teach us to 'sneer contemptuously at such old-fashioned words as "homeland" and "religion" and dedicate their talents and their philosophy to destroying and degrading all that is sacred among men'. (Rousseau, *Basic Political Writings*, p. 15) The printing press had already caused frightful disorders throughout Europe. How wise Socrates had been to praise 'the happy ignorance where eternal wisdom had placed us'. In the old days, before the arts had fashioned our manners and taught our passions to speak an affected language, our *moeurs* were rustic but natural. Men could see through each other. But now the demands of politeness and propriety mean that 'one no longer dares to seem what one really is'. Under the much-vaunted urbanity that we owe to the enlightenment of our century, we hide suspicion, hatred and betrayal. We are no longer capable of sincere friendships and genuine esteem.

Here is the germ of all Rousseau's thought: hatred of the falseness that society forces upon us, a longing for the natural, uncorrupted state of man. And he wins the prize. So, this is the hot mustard that the notables of Dijon and, it turns out, much of Europe are longing for. Rousseau did not win the prize for the second essay competition he went in for (perhaps because he had already become too well-known), though his second *Discourse* was to prove far more influential in the history of ideas. Once again, look at the question that the Academy is asking: 'What is the origin of the inequality among men, and is it authorized by natural law?' We cannot help feeling that the *illuminati* were looking for a rousing denunciation of inequality and a biting analysis of its causes. The mere asking of the question suggests that by 1750 inequality had climbed to the top of the political agenda. We can see a similar phenomenon today: inequality took a back seat in the last decades of the twentieth century and has only recently become a real talking point again.

Once again, Rousseau did not disappoint his audience. Hobbes had argued that in the state of nature life had been 'solitary, poor, nasty, brutish and short'. Not a bit, says Rousseau: 'Nothing is more peaceable than man in his natural state.' (*A Discourse on Inequality*, p. 115) The early stages of human society must have been 'the happiest epoch and most long lasting ... The example of savages who have almost always been found at this point of development [for all his praise of ignorance, Rousseau had read a huge amount of what then passed for anthropology, as he had of almost everything else] appears to confirm that the human race was made to remain there always; to confirm that this state was the true youth of the world.' (p. 115) As long as men were content with their huts and their bows and arrows, they 'lived as free, healthy, good and happy men ... and they continued to enjoy among themselves the sweetness of independent intercourse'. (p. 116)

So what went wrong in this easy-going paradise? What are Rousseau's equivalent of the serpent and the apple? In a crucial passage, he makes it clear that the division of labour was the root of all evil: 'from the instant one man needed the help of another, and it was useful for one man to have provisions enough for two, equality disappeared, property was introduced, work became necessary, and vast forests were transformed into pleasant fields which had to be watered with the sweat of men, and where slavery and misery were soon seen to germinate and flourish with the crops.' (p. 116) It was iron and wheat – industry and agriculture –which first 'civilized men and ruined the human race'. For the first time, men had to think ahead, to sow that they might in due course reap, to resign themselves to an immediate loss for the sake of a greater gain in the future. This is, more or less, what we now call capitalism (the word itself first occurs in *The Newcomes*, which Thackeray published in 1854). And the life it generates is quite unlike that led by the leisurely savage, who, Rousseau says, 'is hard pressed to imagine in the morning the needs he will have in the evening'.

With the division of labour comes co-operation, the need to rely on others. And what comes next is property. 'The demon of property infects everything it touches,' we are told in *Emile*. (p. 354) In the second *Discourse*, Rousseau lays it out hot and strong:

The first man who, having enclosed a piece of land, thought of saying 'This is mine' and found people simple enough to believe him, was the true founder of civil society. How many crimes, wars, murders, how much misery and horror the human race would have been spared if someone had pulled up the stakes and filled in the ditch and cried out to his fellow men: 'Beware of listening to this impostor. You are lost if you forget that the fruits of the earth belong to everyone and that the earth itself belongs to no one.' (p. 109)

The most thrilling opening sentence in all political writing is often said to be the opening sentence of Rousseau's *Social Contract*: 'Man is born free, but everywhere he is in chains.' But it is really the argument in the *Discourse on Inequality* that does the spadework; for it is here that we learn where our chains came from and how we learnt to love them. It is the *Discourse* that explains how man is naturally good and why men in society are bad.

Education in existing society is 'fit only for making double men. By removing the contradictions of men, a great obstacle to his happiness would be removed.' (*Emile*, p. 41) By entering society, man becomes alienated from his true self. In fact, it is estrangement more than actual inequality that is Rousseau's target in the second *Discourse*, as it was in the first. Rousseau never actually uses the phrase 'noble savage' with which he has so often been linked. What the savage possesses is not so much nobility as genuine freedom: 'the savage man breathes only peace and freedom; he desires only to live and stay idle ... Civil man, on the contrary, being always active, sweating and restless, torments himself endlessly in search of ever more laborious occupations; he works himself to death, he even runs towards the grave to put himself into shape to live.' Rousseau would not, I think, have approved of jogging. The crucial difference is that 'the savage man lives within himself; social man lives always outside himself. He knows how to live only in the opinion of others; it is, so to speak, from their judgement alone that he derives the sense of his own existence.' (p. 136) Here we have the first framing of the modern distinction between the inner-directed and the outer-directed man. To survive in society, man had to become devious and artful: 'it was necessary in one's own interest to be other than one was in reality.' (p. 119)

Rousseau tells us several times that the happiest moment in his life was when he sold his watch (e.g. *Confessions*, p. 354). Having to know what time it is is an essential element in working with others. In that sense, Thérèse's inability to tell the time was a blessing to her. The happy man dwells in the present, untroubled by regrets for the past or hopes and plans for the future. Emile is taught that 'foresight is the true source of all our miseries'. (p. 82) Rousseau's recipe has something in common with the carefree attitude of the

Sermon on the Mount. It has even more in common with modern therapies such as mindfulness. More significantly still, his critique of the lifestyle of the fretful bourgeois anticipates much that we shall find in Karl Marx, especially the more idealistic texts of the younger Marx. In fact, there is not much in Marx's doctrine of alienation, or indeed in *Das Kapital* as a whole, that does not owe a lot to Jean-Jacques' helping hand.

We need to pause here to catch our breath and take in quite how sweeping is Rousseau's condemnation of society. It starts with a few conventional swipes at the politesses, the hypocrisy and the corruption of the *ancien régime*, with the court as the rotten core. But the condemnation goes much deeper and wider, to embrace all organized co-operation, all private institutions and commercial associations. Behind the wigs and paniers of the aristos, we begin to discern Rousseau's real target – the money-grubbing commercial classes, or the bourgeoisie.

This hatred of social connection runs through all Rousseau's works, nowhere more so than in *Emile*, where we are told that 'dependence on men ... engenders all the vices and by it master and slave are mutually corrupted'. (p. 85) In a footnote, the Tutor presses home the crucial argument: 'The precept of never hurting another carries with it that of being attached to human society as little as possible, for in the social state the good of one necessarily constitutes the harm of another.' (p. 105fn) An illustrious author, by whom he means Diderot, says that it is only the wicked man who is alone. Rousseau never forgave Diderot for that dig, which he thought, not wrongly, was aimed personally at him. And he fires back: 'I say that it is only the good man who is alone.'

Leaving aside this personal spat, this footnote contains a central contention of Rousseau's: that society is a zero-sum game. In any of its transactions, there are no mutual benefits. Either *A* screws *B*, or *B* screws *A*. On this, Karl Marx and Donald Trump agree with Rousseau. That is why in the *Confessions* Rousseau congratulates himself on his withdrawal from society: 'Having experienced the disadvantages of dependence on others I was determined never to expose myself to it again.' (p. 320) As we have seen, this was not how Rousseau actually lived his life. Till the day he died under the devoted care of M. de Girardin at Ermenonville, he continued, most of the time, to rely on the kindness of others. But whatever his personal practice, the theory remained intact: private association and connection were demeaning and corrupting. By contrast, if you look forward to Burke's defence of liberty and property – and the intimate connection between the two – in *Reflections on the Revolution in France*, you will see a warm endorsement of how tenderly the British Parliament treats 'the tenant right of a cabbage garden, a year's interest in a hovel, the goodwill of an ale-house or a baker's shop'. (p. 277) For Burke, all these little private contracts and legal rights are the lifeblood of a civilized society. For Rousseau, they are squalid stitch-ups by which one man cheats and oppresses another.

There has to be a better, purer guide to human relations, and where else can we take such guidance than from the unblemished inner self? To find out what to do, all we have to do is look inside our selves. The voice of conscience never lies.

FORCED TO BE FREE

How then are men to live together? (For Rousseau does not pretend that we can go back to the state of nature, however alluring that prospect may be to him.) Already for a century, if not longer, political philosophers had been fond of a particular thought experiment, the 'social contract'. We were to imagine that, at some point in the misty past, men had agreed to come together, whether for prosperity or for mutual protection, and they had signed a pact to form a society. The versions of this contract differed. John Locke's was more amiable than Thomas Hobbes's, less idealistic perhaps than that of Hugo Grotius. But what they had in common was that they were constructs located at some indistinct moment in prehistory. They offered only a faint claim to describe what had actually happened; they merely put forward a vivid and concrete way of describing a process that, if it happened at all, must have evolved over centuries. At the same time, they offered a convenient model for imagining how a just society might be organized. That is how modern social-contractors like John Rawls and Philip Pettit use the device. For them, it's a handy way of describing the sort of society we would like to build if we were starting from scratch.

Jean-Jacques' social contract is not like that. It's much more a blueprint for action than an explanation of the past, or of how the past generated the foundations of the society we now live in. It is prescriptive, not descriptive. Rousseau asserts that all previous philosophers have dealt in sophisms and fantasies. Only the admirable Montesquieu had taken a scientific approach. 'But he was careful not to discuss the principles of political right. He was content to discuss the positive right of established governments.' (*Emile*, p. 458) That was not good enough. 'It is necessary to know what ought to be in order to judge soundly about what is.'

And so Jean-Jacques tells us, in his *Social Contract*, what ought to be. It is a vision dazzling in its daring and aspiration, overwhelming in the demands it makes on us, and was to prove terrifying in its consequences over the next two centuries.

The pact that he proposes is really quite simple: its 'clauses, rightly understood, are reducible to one only, *viz.* the total alienation to the whole community of each associate with all his rights . . . Each of us puts in common his person and his whole power under the supreme direction of the general will and in return we receive every member as an indivisible part of the whole.' (p. 15) There were to be no exceptions: 'whoever refuses to obey the general will shall be constrained to do so by the whole body; which means nothing else than that he shall be forced to be free.' (p. 18)

This social pact gives the body politic an absolute and unlimited power over all its members. The sovereign alone is to be the judge of everything. At first sight, this sounds not unlike Hobbes's *Leviathan*. There too we are told that absolute power, undivided and unquestioned, is the only basis for a successful and enduring state. But Hobbes does not say that every citizen has to give up everything to the state. He has only to obey the commands of the sovereign. In matters where the sovereign is silent, he can carry on his old life and associations. By contrast, in Rousseau's ideal state there must be 'no partial associations', no factions or parties, and not much in the way of private opinions either: individuals 'must be compelled to conform their wills to their reason; the people must be taught to know what they require'. (p. 39) The enlightenment of the public will bring their minds and their wills into alignment. And who is to do the enlightening? 'Hence arises the need of a legislator,' Rousseau tells us airily.

Who is this legislator to be? Rousseau concedes that he faces a tough task: 'a superior intelligence would be necessary who could see all the passions of men without experiencing any of them; who would have no affinity with our nature and yet know it thoroughly'. (p. 39) It's not just a question of dictating wise laws: 'he who dares undertake to give institutions to a nation ought to feel himself capable, as it were, of changing human nature ... of transforming every individual ... into part of a greater whole'. (p. 40) The legislator has the task that Stalin allotted to writers under socialism: to be 'an engineer of human souls'. Jean-Jacques sighs as he goes through this daunting job description: 'Gods would be necessary to give laws to men.'

Yet, we are told, such a superman did emerge, in the Greek cities of old and in Rousseau's own Geneva too. It is only a footnote on the same page, but I think it gives us the key, not only to what type of man the mysterious legislator is to be, but to the underlying origin and drift of Rousseau's thought: 'Those who consider Calvin only as a theologian are but little acquainted with the extent of his genius. The preparation of our wise edicts, in which he had a large share, does him as much credit as his *Institutes*. Whatever revolution time may bring about in our religion, so long as love of country and of liberty is not extinct among us, the memory of that great man will not cease to be revered.'

Geneva, and Jean Calvin. That is the ideal city he has in mind, and that is the legislator. Later on, in his *Letters Written from the Mountain*, Rousseau explicitly tells the people of Geneva that 'I took your constitution, which I considered good, as my model for political institutions'. When he thinks of the ideal republic, he thinks of Geneva, not of Switzerland as a whole, with its jumbled federation of peoples speaking different languages and following different faiths. His ideal is a small, enclosed, homogeneous republic. When he comes to edit the Abbé de St-Pierre's *Project for Perpetual Peace* – a blueprint for a sort of European Union – he can scarcely conceal his dislike; such a mongrel combo can never last. What he values in a state, above all, is total cohesion – civic, moral and religious.

Towards the end of *The Social Contract*, he makes this even clearer. He criticizes Jesus for establishing a spiritual kingdom only. By separating religion from the political system, Jesus destroyed the unity of the state and caused the divisions that have never ceased to plague Asian nations. (p. 131) In contrast, 'Muhammad had very sound views; he thoroughly unified his political system; and so long as his form of government subsisted under his successors, the khalifs, the government was quite undivided, and in that respect good.' (pp. 131–2)

Indulgent readers have played up Rousseau's democratic inclinations. But his is a cramped and cramping sort of democracy. He denounces all private associations and interests and complains that when 'unanimity no longer reigns in the voting, the general will is no longer the will of all'. (p. 106) It is also pointed out, in Rousseau's favour, that what he recommends is direct democracy of the ancient Greek variety, as opposed to representative government as practised in England and the American colonies. Yet any such endorsement slides over the purpose behind this direct democracy, which is to sign up every citizen to a collective *nem. con.* society, with no right of silence or dissent. Everyone has a vote in the assembly, and attendance is compulsory, and everyone is expected to vote the same way. Malcontents or backsliders are to be re-educated, and, if still recalcitrant, expelled or even executed. The echoes of *Nineteen Eighty-Four* and Pol Pot are unmistakable.

Yes, Rousseau does call for a national assembly chosen by periodic and fair elections, but he wishes to discourage argument and debate in its proceedings: 'long discussions, dissensions, and uproar proclaim the ascendancy of private interests and the decline of the state'. (p. 107) This sounds like the sort of parliament that, though impeccably democratic in theory, in practice rubberstamps the decisions of the legislator, aka the Politburo, as under Stalin's 1936 Constitution.

Or as in Rousseau's home town. What, after all, was the Geneva that Calvin transformed from a medieval bishopric into a thriving independent republic? It was not a tolerant place. Calvin expelled from the city all those native Genevans who refused to convert to the Reformed Faith. There were occasional burnings at the stake for heresy or atheism. There was a general council of all the citizens and an executive council of twenty-five aristocrats, not unlike a typical democracy in ancient Greece – but on top of these there was the element that Calvin regarded as the most important, a set of religious institutions: the Consistory, which controlled people's morals by elaborate surveillance; the Company of Pastors; and the Academy, which guided culture and opinion. In other words, Calvin's Geneva could better be described as a quasi-democratic theocracy, not unlike the Iran of the Ayatollahs. A prosperous place, no doubt, for its numerous bankers and merchants, but a gloomy prison for those who couldn't stand the enforced conformity. Isaac Rousseau and both his sons had fled from it. Yet Jean-Jacques retained a sentimental affection for Geneva and an idealized picture of its politics. He proudly announces himself as 'Jean-Jacques Rousseau, Citizen of Geneva' on the title page of his second *Discourse* and follows it up with a long and fulsome preface addressed to the city's rulers: 'the more I reflect on your civil and political arrangements, the less can I imagine that the nature of human contrivance could produce anything better'. (p. 61) He remains keen to preserve Geneva as he thought he had known it. His famous *Letter to M. D'Alembert on Spectacles* denounces the project to open a theatre in the city, as this would infallibly corrupt local morals – a peculiar stance from one who had known some success in the theatre, but then Jean-Jacques had little time for consistency.

Geneva had in fact already gone downhill since Calvin's day – at least Calvin would have thought so – and was beginning to look rather like other cities, a placed of mixed morals and civil unrest. But Calvinism was to show that it was by no means dead. On 19 June 1762, both *Emile* and *The Social Contract* were publicly burnt in Geneva by order of the Council, as *Emile* already had been in Paris. It was a double hit: *Emile* was burnt because it was sacrilegious; *The Social Contract* because it was subversive. Thus, on both counts, Geneva had demonstrated that it was still the sort of city that Jean-Jacques dreamed of; one that tolerated no opinions contrary to those approved by its democratic assemblies. Yet only a week earlier, Rousseau had fled for sanctuary from Paris to Switzerland, and on reaching Swiss soil, he had ordered the postilion to stop the coach, climbed down and kissed the ground, crying aloud: 'I have reached the land of freedom.'

The irony is perhaps even greater in the case of *Emile*, because what that book does is to set out at enormous length a programme for manufacturing precisely the sort of citizen that Jean-Jacques has in mind for his New Geneva.

Educating Emile

The subtitle of *Emile* is *On Education*, and it remains probably the most famous treatise on the subject ever published. As Rousseau does so often, he subverts the genre, because the book is not a textbook but a sort of semi-novel: the anonymous Governor takes charge of the young Emile and guides him through childhood and adolescence, until he is ready for the adult world and for marriage to Sophie, who has been reared with equal care and forethought. Typically, every now and then Jean-Jacques comes out from behind the shadow of the Tutor or Governor to address the reader. Thus, we have a double dose of admonition.

What we must notice from the start is Rousseau's assumption that a re-education project of this reach can be carried through only by removing Emile from his father and mother. Not a new thought for Rousseau: in his *Discourse on Political Economy* (a contribution to the *Encyclopédie*), he first enunciates the assumptions of the kibbutz: 'the education of children should not be abandoned to the lights and prejudices of their fathers, since it is of even more importance to the state than it is to their fathers'. (*Basic Political Writings*, p. 138) Why is this? Because 'if children are raised in common and in the bosom of equality, if they are imbued with the laws of the state and the maxims of the general will ... undoubtedly they will thus learn to cherish one another as brothers, never to want anything but what the society wants'. It is a dream that goes back to Plato's *Republic*, but Rousseau gives it an extra impetus that is both fresh and sinister.

Since he so often foreshadows the future of social thought and since *Emile* is such a classic, we would expect its teachings to anticipate the mantras of modern educationists. So very often they do. The advice is child-centred and concentrates on learning by discovery. 'Our didactic and pedantic craze is always to teach children what they would learn much better by themselves,' (p. 78) such as learning to walk. 'I do not intend to teach geometry to Emile; it is he who will teach it to me' (p. 145) – by drawing a circle with a piece of string on a pivot, for example. All in all, 'we want to teach Emile nothing which he could not learn by himself'. (p. 260) We must allow children to enjoy themselves: 'Love childhood, promote its games, its pleasures, its amiable instincts ... Why do you want to deprive these little innocents of the enjoyment of a time so short which escapes them ... ' (p. 79) Emile will not be tortured by exam league tables or compulsory sport: 'Let there never be any comparisons with other children, no rivals, no competitors, not even in running.' (p. 184)

We can see a stream of thought here proceeding from Rousseau to Dr Spock. His ideal schooling would also find strong echoes in Maria Montessori's emphasis on physical discovery and in the freedom from discipline at Dartington and A. S. Neill's Summerhill. The tradition of learning by practice is parodied by Dickens in the unspeakable Wackford Squeers in *Nicholas Nickleby*. Rousseau builds on earlier pedagogues such as Plato and Locke but adds his own characteristic verve and freedom. Even conventional schools and teacher training colleges today retain marks of *Emile*'s influence. The anti-competitive bias of some British comprehensive secondary schools comes straight from Jean-Jacques. At first sight, he does appear to be the grandfather of modern progressive education.

Except for one thing. Emile is in a class of one. He is, we are vaguely told, an orphan, or becomes one: 'it makes no difference whether he has his father and mother'. What matters is that he is to be reared entirely by himself, removed from the corrupting influences of society, which include the corrupting influences of other minds. 'Exercise his body, his organs, his senses, his strength, but keep his soul idle for as long as possible.' (p. 94) 'Reading is the plague of childhood.' The Governor doesn't care if Emile doesn't learn to read before the age of fifteen. (pp. 116–17) Rousseau, who has read so many books, proclaims: 'I hate books. They only teach one to talk about what one does not know.' (p. 184) The first book – perhaps the only book – that Emile is to read will be *Robinson Crusoe*, that gospel of solitude, because it will teach him how to deal with his physical surroundings. As part of this process, Emile learns how to handle a spade and a hoe, how to use a hammer, a plane, a lathe. He is to learn a useful trade, the carpenter's for preference. No book learning.

What he is also not to learn is how to play with others. 'Socialization' – so prominent in modern educational talk – is off the agenda. Emile knows that his first duty is to himself. (p. 250) 'Indifferent to everything outside of himself like all other children, he takes an interest in no one. All that distinguishes him is his not caring to appear interested and his not being false like them.' (p. 222) And he will be happy that way, because 'a truly happy being is a solitary being'. (p. 221) He has less need of others than others have of him. Of course, when he grows up, he will come into contact with other men, but he won't think much of them. The Governor will have taught him that 'man is naturally good' (p. 237), but when he looks around him, he will realize how corrupted these actual existing men have been by the depravities of society. 'He will say to himself, "I am wise, and men are mad."' (p. 245)

Not surprisingly, 'he will not be celebrated as a likeable man'. (p. 339) In our terms, Emile sounds like a prize prig, insufferably smug and with more than a touch of Asperger's syndrome about him. His inability, or his unwillingness, to interact with others has been deliberately fostered, but he doesn't know it, because the Governor's maxim has always been 'Let him always believe he is the master, and let it always be you who are. There is no subjection so perfect as that which keeps the appearance of freedom.' (p. 120) In other words, Emile has been brainwashed.

He has been taught to be selfish, one might almost say 'self-ist', because his focus on himself amounts to an ideology. We have come to the opposite pole from Pascal's dictum that '*le moi est haïssable*'. For Emile, the self-centred life is the nobler path, the only way of really living. When Saint-Preux, the hero of Rousseau's novel *Julie*, reports back to the idyllic Swiss countryside about his stay in Paris, his principal complaint about the French theatre is that 'the "I" is almost as scrupulously banished from the stage as from the writings of Port-Royal [the Jansenist monastery where Pascal wrote his greatest work], and human passions, as modest as Christian humility, are never expressed except by "one"'. (*Julie*, Book II, XVII, p. 180) From now on, in Rousseau's human drama, the 'I' is to take centre stage.

When presented so baldly, this unvarnished, purposeful egoism may shock us. But as Allan Bloom points out in his introduction to his translation of *Emile*, it is the underlying drive behind the sublimation projects of Schopenhauer, Nietzsche and Freud. The spiritual exhaustion of bourgeois society teaches me, or ought to teach me, to turn inward and concentrate upon raising myself into a 'real man', if not a superman. We are no longer to find our fulfilment in life with others (though the Governor and Emile do some rather improbable good deeds to help the underprivileged). Nor are we to derive our principles from each other, and certainly not from books, except the Great Book of Nature. What we must do is look inward, look into our selves.

THE SAVOYARD SERMON

Nowhere is this clearer than in the interpolation in Book IV of *Emile*, fifty pages long, which is known as the 'Profession of Faith of the Savoyard Vicar'. The fictional speaker is an amalgam of two free-thinking priests who were warm friends of Rousseau: Jean-Claude Gaime, who actually was an abbé from Savoy (*Confessions*, pp. 88–9); and Jean-Baptiste Gâtier, a handsome priest also from Savoy who was disgraced and jailed for making a girl pregnant. (*Confessions*, pp. 116–17) The views of these two men greatly appealed to Rousseau, but such views were not unusual at the time. In fact, he interrupts the Vicar to say that such views are not as novel as the Vicar thinks: 'I see in them pretty nearly the theism or the natural religion that the Christians pretend to confound with atheism or irreligiousness, which is the directly contrary doctrine.' (*Emile*, p. 294) Many of Rousseau's Encyclopedist friends thought along these lines, and so did quite a few of the liberal aristos. Malesherbes, who was in effect the chief censor in Paris, wrote to Rousseau in his own hand 'arguing that the Savoyard Vicar's profession of faith was precisely the kind of composition likely to win the approbation of humankind everywhere, as well as that of the court under present circumstances'. (*Confessions*, p. 523) But Malesherbes turned out to be hopelessly wrong, for these advanced views had not percolated to the broader population, let alone to the religious hierarchy. Hence the trouble that the Vicar's words were to cause Rousseau all over Europe, not least in Geneva. In fact, the Profession of Faith became the most notorious portion of *Emile* and a standard text in the history of religion (or irreligion) in France.

What is this religious doctrine doing in the middle of an educational treatise? Well, Rousseau says, we have got three-quarters of the way through Emile's education, and we have still not explored what sort of religion he is to be taught. Which is fair enough, but it does not quite reveal, or indeed justify, what we are in for: namely, a fierce and unrelenting assault on revealed religion, its hierarchies, its rituals and shibboleths, above all its authority over the minds of men. Although Rousseau continues to profess himself a Christian, it is here that he makes plain that the Church – or, rather, all Churches – is the last enemy.

In the light of the teachings of Jesus, how can the Church justify its intolerance? Is it not iniquitous to reward or punish men for being born in the wrong country? How can you judge one religion to be superior to another? Can it really be true that the wicked are condemned to torment throughout eternity? Why should God require our genuflexions? 'You proclaim to me a God born and dead 2,000 years ago at the other end of the world in some little town, and you tell me that whoever has not believed in this mystery will be damned. These are very strange things to believe so quickly on the sole authority of a man whom I do not know.' (p. 305) Why should we believe the revelations of sacred books written in languages unknown to the men who follow them? There is one book open to all eyes: the Great Book of Nature. It is the unalterable order of nature that best shows the Supreme Being, rather than those dodgy little miracles that convince only gullible peasants. Conscience never deceives: it is man's true guide. It is to the soul what instinct is to the body. What other religion is needed but what is called natural religion? 'View the spectacle of nature; hear the inner voice. Has not God told everything to our eyes, to our conscience, to our judgement? What more will men tell us? Their revelations have only the effect of degrading God by giving Him human passions.' (p. 295)

This appeal to the inner voice is of course an intrinsic part of the Protestant tradition, and the Calvinist tradition in particular. But the Savoyard Vicar carries it a whole stage further: for him the inner voice is the *only* guide. External forces – sermons, Church diktats, rituals – are trivial and fallible adjuncts of the true faith. The Vicar tells us that he follows the practices of his own Church punctiliously: 'one must not disturb peaceful souls or alarm the faith of simple people' (p. 310), but these practices are outward shells. The heart and soul of faith lie within our selves.

Thus, the Vicar's Profession, far from being a cumbersome intrusion into Rousseau's project, is a crucial element in it. The place to look for answers, even to the deepest questions of life, is within myself. Religious contemplation is the ultimate selfie. *Emile* is as subversive a book as *The Satanic Verses*, and it was burned for much the same reasons.

SEPARATE SPHERES

But it would be a mistake to assume from all this that *Emile* foreshadows our modern world views in every respect. Far from it. Rousseau was never reliable as a *bien pensant* or as anything else, and in one respect he was the very reverse of a progressive thinker.

In the last book of *Emile*, we are introduced to Emile's intended, Sophie. As a character, she is little more than a flawless doll. It is what Rousseau has to say about the upbringing he proposes for her that is so startling. It is another tempting but mistaken assumption that the revolutionary atmosphere of the second half of the eighteenth century must have brought with it an advance in women's rights. In general, Rousseau certainly believes that 'we are approaching a state of crisis and the age of revolutions'. He holds it to be impossible that the great monarchies of Europe have much longer to last. (p. 194) Yet if we are coming into a new era of human equality, Rousseau does not believe in extending that equality to women. The odd thing is, he was by no means alone in this belief. The new emphasis on domesticity, on the sacred duties of marriage, motherhood and home, brought with it a doctrine that, if it was not exactly new, was now enunciated with fresh enthusiasm: the doctrine of 'separate spheres'. A woman's place was now explicitly in the home, no longer working alongside men in the fields or on the factory floor. For the working classes, this separation was a long way from being a reality. Women went on working in the mills throughout the nineteenth century and were conscripted into the munitions factories in both world wars. But the idea of women having a separate, nurturing, supportive, home-making destiny gained a new impetus.

Very few opinion-formers, though, took this view quite as far as Rousseau does in *Emile*. His estimation of the inferior intellect of women is almost as fervent as his relegation of them to their separate sphere – a sacred sphere but certainly not an equal one. Men, he says, ought to be active and strong, women ought to be passive and weak. The inequality of the sexes was not unjust or manmade, but in accordance with the dictates of nature.

For this reason, men and women ought not to have the same education. Women should learn only those things that are suitable for them to know. (p. 364) They should be taught sewing and embroidery; a little painting, but landscapes and flowers only, no human figures. Even less than Emile is Sophie to be taught to read at an early age, though some light arithmetic will help her with the household accounts in years to come. In fact, Sophie has read only two books, Fénelon's improving romance *Telemachus*, which she adores, and Barrême's book on accounting. (p. 410) According to Jean-Jacques, a brilliant wife is a plague; a woman's true dignity consists not in shining in society but in managing to be ignored. In any case, abstract works are out of women's reach; their minds lack enough precision to succeed in the sciences. The art of thinking is not completely foreign to women, but they ought only to skim. 'Sophie gets a conception of everything and does not remember very much.' (p. 426) In fact, she is thick, just about as thick as Rousseau tells us his Thérèse is thick. Emile thinks she is the perfect wife for him.

How does Rousseau land in this breathtaking position, extreme even for his time? There are perhaps two elements to it. In thinking about women, Rousseau thinks mostly about biological differences, in particular about the physical and psychological strains of mother-hood. So, if we are to shift society to a more natural existence, then that must involve attaching women closer to their biological destiny. They must stop wittering on in drawing rooms, giving themselves airs and writing silly books. Rousseau hates women writers and bluestockings of every description, from Ninon de Lenclos to Madame du Deffand.

The second element, which intertwines with the first and perhaps nags at Rousseau's brain more insistently, is the fear that gender equality might actually lead to female superiority: 'For to leave her above us in the qualities proper to her sex and to make her our equal in all the rest is to transfer to the wife the primacy that nature gives to the husband.' (p. 382) In other words, the equalized woman might manage to Have It All.

You slowly begin to realize as the Governor unveils his plans, with the assistance of the Savoy Vicar, just how radical this project is and how much of the familiar furniture of life has to be cleared away to make room for it: kings and princes, commerce and indus-try, party politics, organized religion and uppity women – all have to give way to the Supreme Self.

JULIE AND THE NEW SENTIMENTALITY

But how is this self to be generated? Where does it come from? When I look inside myself, much of what I see is created by the culture and traditions in which I have been immersed. The language in which my inner voice talks to me is the outcome of centuries of linguistic evolution. The allegiances, ideals and revulsions that shape my reactions to events are the outcome of my history – personal, social and national. What creates this precious self is the interplay between all these influences and my genetically given temperament. As a result, the self is partly stable and partly mutable, both continuing and changeable. But how can it be *reliable*, as a source of moral and spiritual guidance? Jean-Jacques himself seems to be an unreliable narrator, in the tradition of Cervantes and Sterne, the forerunner of all those untrustworthy tale-tellers of modern fiction. Why should we trust the self alone, and disregard any counsel from that outside world that has done so much to shape that self?

Now and then, Rousseau does suggest that there might be a problem here, for example when he concedes, if only in a footnote, the softening influence of Christianity upon society: 'How many works of mercy are the result of the Gospel! Among the Catholics, how many restitutions, how many reparations are caused by the confession! Among us [he means the Protestants], how many reconciliations and deeds of charity are fostered by the approach of Communion time. How much less greedy usurers were made by the Jubilee of the Hebrews and how many miseries it prevented!' (*Emile*, p. 313fn) The Turks, too, he tells us, had innumerable pious institutions. So it cannot be true that everything good in us comes from nature, everything bad from our institutions.

Jean-Jacques does not confront this difficulty, because he doesn't confront *any* difficulty. With his marvellous agility, he simply dances off on a new tack. Having denounced 'effeminate', sentimental novels, he himself produced the most sentimental, effeminate novel ever written – and one of the most successful. The *comédie larmoyante*, the convention that light literature should bring tears rather than laughter, was nearly a century old when Rousseau brought out *Julie* in 1761, a year before *Emile*. It leaves its predecessors trailing far behind in its relentless lachrymosity.

Julie, her tutor and later lover, Saint-Preux, her best friend, Claire, and their friend the English milord with the improbable name of Lord Bomston are all in tears from start to finish. They weep when they meet, they weep when they say goodbye, they weep when they are happy, they weep when they are sad, they weep when they have sex, they weep even more when they don't have sex. All the characters are intrinsically good by nature. Even Julie's father, the crotchety Baron whose snobbishness prevents her from marrying the humbly born Saint-Preux, turns out at the end to be a loveable old codger. It is only the *convenances* and *bienséances* of society that make them unhappy. The one man who does not weep is the imperturbable M. de Wolmar, who eventually marries

Julie. He too believes that 'all characters are good and healthy in themselves; there are no errors in nature'. (Book IV, III, p. 426) According to Wolmar, every criminal would have followed the path of virtue, if only he had been better directed. By the end, even M. de Wolmar is in tears too. No book has ever tugged more shamelessly at the heartstrings. As Saint-Preux warbles to Edward Bomston: 'O sentiment, sentiment! Sweet life of the soul, what heart of iron have you not touched! From what unfortunate mortal have you never torn tears?' (Book V, VI, p. 453)

The Niagara of tears that *Julie* squeezed from its readers all over Europe cannot disguise the reality that the book is a deliberate, if not cynical, attempt to catch the popular market, unique only in its unbridled effusiveness, but also borrowing shamelessly from earlier successful models, most obviously the *Clarissa* of Samuel Richardson (long as *Julie* is, *Clarissa* is three times as long). The interminable laments of all the characters borrow from classical French drama too. I lost count of the echoes of Racine, especially from *Phèdre* and *Bérénice*. The novelist Anthony Powell observed that 'an immense self-pity is an almost essential ingredient of all bestsellers'. There is scarcely a page of *Julie* that is not drenched in the stuff. The style, too, is quite unlike that of the finer passages of the *Confessions* or the *Reveries*, which are genuinely lyrical or poignant. With *Julie*, it is as though Philip Roth had knocked out a vast romantic saga in the style of Barbara Cartland.

Nor is Rousseau blind to the defects of the book. As so often, he is almost post-modern in his readiness to subvert himself. In a puckish preface, he anticipates all the criticisms that might be made of the book. There's not a single evil deed or bad man in it, he says. It's full of exclamations, and overflowing with verbosity and sentiment. Nobody's going to like it, certainly not the libertines or the society ladies. Also, it's full of commonplaces and flat language, because the people in it are not witty academicians or philosophers but provincial folk – solitaries, young people, almost children – with a romantic imagination. In fact, he tells us, it's a girly sort of book, the kind of effeminate novel for which previously he had nothing but scorn.

So, this vast hymn to nature and the natural goodness of man is admitted by the author to be a deeply artificial production, conceived with Rousseau's usual amazing fertility and energy (he seems to have written it in not much more than a year) but with no ambition to reflect the real world.

Just as the political reformation that Rousseau envisions demands a completely artificial remoulding of society from top to bottom, so *Julie* makes no effort to confront the world as it is but prefers to conjure an imaginary universe of unblemished sentiment and virtue. It is a bleached-out fantasy in which all the men and women are good but unlucky. Compare its interminable vapourings with Rousseau's *Confessions*, that salty, venomous, deceitful, salacious but also gloriously vivid and occasionally warm and touching masterpiece. When Rousseau speaks kindly there of some ill-used abbé or wretched prostitute, you feel he means it.

What is ultimately wrong with Rousseau is not that he loves nature too much, but that he loves it too little. In seeking to detach man from the society of which he is part-creator and part-inheritor, he is not renaturing but denaturing him. The revolutions that Rousseau was to have such a hand in inspiring all share the same ambition of starting with a blank sheet of paper and inventing a new race of men, and they mostly end in tears far more bitter than any shed in *Julie*.

It was the devoted M. de Girardin who saw the *Confessions* and the *Reveries* through the printing presses of Geneva after Rousseau's death and so cemented his European fame. As well as his extreme liberal views, M. de Girardin was a masterly landscape gardener, very much in the natural English taste, which Rousseau shared, though he wouldn't have called it English, because he didn't like England or the English. On an island in the little river Aurette, M. de Girardin built for Rousseau a thatched cottage surrounded by rocks, based on the wild garden, the so-called Elysium, that Julie builds in Rousseau's novel. There Rousseau lived his last few months, literally dwelling in the landscape of his own imagination. An apt end for a master illusionist.

Ermenonville became a place of pilgrimage, and the visitor list was extraordinary: Joseph II of Austria, Gustav III of Sweden, the future Czar of Russia and even Queen Marie Antoinette on the one hand, Thomas Jefferson, Benjamin Franklin, Danton and Robespierre on the other. Some of those who were guillotined and those who did some of the guillotining had all fallen under Jean-Jacques' spell. But the last word should go to the greatest of all the visitors to Ermenonville.

Napoleon Bonaparte, when First Consul, came to pay tribute and was shown round by the elderly M. de Girardin, who despite his support for the Revolution had been placed under house arrest during the Terror. Gazing at Rousseau's tomb (now emptied of its ashes), Napoleon remarked to his host: 'It would have been better for the peace of France if that man had never existed. He prepared the way for the French Revolution.'

'It seems to me, Citizen Consul,' M. de Girardin responded tartly, 'that it's not for you to complain about the Revolution.' (Which had, after all, prepared the way for Napoleon.)

'Well,' said Napoleon, 'the future will decide if it would not have been better for the peace of the earth if neither I nor Rousseau had ever existed.'

ADAM SMITH

and the invisible hand

How well he looks in his bag-wig with a quiet smile playing around his lips, all in purple on the £20 note. 'Sonsy' is, I think, the Scots word for it, meaning something like 'comfortable in his good fortune'. What I hadn't noticed before is that beside his profile and his name and dates – 'Adam Smith 1723–1790' – the bank note also has an engraving captioned 'the division of labour in pin manufacturing (and the great increase in the quantity of work that results)'. The engraving shows several little men – some possibly children – in floppy, old-style hats who are tending a cat's cradle of pulleys, platforms, vats and treadles. So, Smith not merely has his beguiling profile on the 'score', as punters call the twenty-pounder, he has also the whole basis of his economic theory etched upon it. There's glory for you.

Adam's master work, *The Wealth of Nations*, opens with a chapter on the benefits of the division of labour, and he spells out the message in pins:

One man draws out the wire, another straights it, a third cuts it, a fourth points it, a fifth grinds it at the top for receiving the head; to make the head requires two or three distinct operations; to put it on is a peculiar business, to whiten the pins is another . . . I have seen a small manufactory where ten men only were employed . . . though they were very poor and therefore but indifferently accommodated with the necessary machinery, those ten persons could make among them upwards of forty-eight thousands pins in a day . . . But if they had all wrought separately and independently . . . they certainly could not each of them have made twenty, perhaps not one pin in a day. (I, p. 5)

I can think of no other economist who has enjoyed such fame all over the world, both in his own lifetime and in ours. There are Adam Smith societies everywhere. Every self-respecting university and business school in the United States has its Adam Smith Institute. Anyone who has the faintest interest in how the economy works has a rough idea of what he thought: leave the market free, let people do their own thing, in short, laissez-faire. Actually, Smith never used that last phrase. It seems to originate in a conversation between Colbert, the great French minister of Louis XIV's reign, and a merchant called Le Gendre, who reassured the interfering minister '*laissez-nous faire*' or 'leave it to us' – a slightly different idea, suggesting something of a stitch-up between government and business, the sort of arrangement that Smith hated. It's also worth noting that the illustration on the £20 note is a montage of the illustration accompanying '*L'épingle*', the article on pin-manufacturing in the *Encyclopédie* of Voltaire and Diderot, which spelled out the same message about the wonders of the division of labour in 1755, twenty years before the publication of *The Wealth of Nations* in 1776. So, Smith's opening salvo was not exactly original, but it would be a mistake to imagine that he borrowed his ideas from his French counterparts, although he had affection and respect for them when he visited France in his early forties as tutor to the son and heir of the Duke of Buccleuch and got to know most of them. Smith was the quintessential product of the Scottish rather than the French Enlightenment, and he drew his stock of ideas from the gurus of Glasgow and Edinburgh, notably Francis Hutcheson and David Hume.

When he became celebrated on the Continent, it was for his earlier work, *The Theory of Moral Sentiments* – 'Adam Smith's other book' – which provoked Voltaire to say: 'We have nothing to compare with him, and I am embarrassed for my dear compatriots.' A generation later, Immanuel Kant asked: 'Where in Germany is the man who can write so well about the moral character?' (Ross,

p. 194) In England, by contrast, it was *The Wealth of Nations* that won him a national reputation. Chancellors of the Exchequer asked for his advice, and quite often took it. When he came south to visit Henry Dundas, the all-powerful Lord Advocate who was nick-named 'the Grand Manager of Scotland', in his villa at Wimbledon, the company of assembled ministers, including Prime Minister William Pitt the Younger, rose to greet him. When he asked them to sit down, Pitt said: 'No, we will stand till you are seated, for we are all your scholars.' (Ross, p. 376)

It was an unlikely apotheosis for such an oddball. In person, Adam was not very prepossessing. He had big teeth and a harsh, thick voice, but it was his personality that was so unnerving. His friend Alexander Carlyle of Inveresk said: 'He was the most absent man in Company that I ever saw, Moving his lips and talking to himself and Smiling in the midst of large Company's. If you awak'd him from his Reverie, and made him attend to the Subject of Conversation, he immediately began a Harangue and never stop'd till he told you all he knew about it, with the utmost Philosophical Ingenuity.' (Ross, p. 142) His table manners were unpredictable too. He once spread a piece of bread and butter, put it into a teapot and poured the boiling water on it, and when he had tasted it declared it was the worst tea he had ever met with. (Ross, p. 226) He found handwriting difficult and took to dictating most of his output, a habit shared with other original minds such as Dostoevsky and Henry James. Once, when he took a long time to sign a customs document, it emerged that he had taken so long because he had been imitating the signature of the colleague signing before him. (Ross, p. 317)

He was a peculiar sight, going up Edinburgh High Street to the Customs House from his fine old seventeenth-century house on the north side of the Canongate, with his swaying gait, described as 'vermicular' or wormlike by a naturalist friend, as if with each step he meant to alter his direction, or even to turn back, his lips moving and occasionally breaking into a smile, apparently deep in conversation with an unseen friend.

His eminence in London as well as Edinburgh brought him coun-try membership of The Club, that unrivalled gathering of talent, which included Sir Joshua Reynolds, Goldsmith, Garrick, Gibbon and Burke, as well as Dr Johnson and Boswell (who had studied under Smith in Glasgow). Not surprisingly, Smith turned out not to be 'clubbable', at least not in the sense approved by Johnson, who declared him 'as dull a dog as he had ever met with' (Ross, p. 251) and thought him 'a most disagreeable fellow after he had drank wine which bubbled in his mouth'. Clearly Smith's breaking abruptly into one of his unstoppable harangues did not suit the Great Doctor, who preferred a more cut-and-thrust style of conversation, with him doing most of the cutting and thrusting.

There was a deeper disagreement too. Smith was a typical eighteenth-century deist, a man of science who abhorred superstition and religious enthusiasm. He thought Johnson as peculiar as Johnson thought him. 'I have seen that creature,' he said of Johnson, 'bolt up in the midst of mixed company; and, without any previous notice, fall upon his knees behind a chair, repeat the Lord's Prayer, and then resume his seat at table – He has played this freak over and over, perhaps five or six times in the course of an evening. It is not hypocrisy but madness.' (Ross, p. 335)

For all his own oddities, Adam was intensely sociable. He belonged to every society in Glasgow and Edinburgh that was worth belonging to. He managed the business of Glasgow University and later of the Customs Board in Edinburgh with assiduous and incisive efficiency. He became deeply attached to his old pupils and his numerous young cousins. Over his life, he had earned a fair amount, but little remained after his death because of his numberless acts of secret charity. He never married, though he had several yearning *tendresses* that came to nothing. He certainly liked pretty women and thought the Irish prostitutes the loveliest women in the country, attributing their beauty to a healthy diet of potatoes. (*Wealth of Nations*, I, p. 147)

Adam was the son of another Adam Smith who died before he was born. Adam Senior had been a highly regarded customs officer in Kirkcaldy on the Fife coast. Most of the Smiths were in the customs, and many of them were called Adam. It was a rewarding profession then, and an exciting one. Smuggling was big business in Scotland, as it was in England, because of the crippling import duties and excise taxes on inland trade. The smugglers were often prosperous merchants and farmers who deployed sizeable vessels of up to 300 tons carrying twelve-pounder guns. Adam was so accustomed that in later life, when he was already famous, he was happy to join the Customs Board, although the work took up much of the time that he might have devoted to the great works he planned but never finished. He was even invited to give evidence to the House of Commons on how to reduce smuggling.

Like most of the Edinburgh literati, he adored the poetry of Robert Burns, and it is thought that one of his last acts as head of the Customs Board was to find a place for Burns as a salt officer at £30 per annum (salt duties were especially stiff, and salt smuggling was rife). It is a piquant thought that the two greatest liberators of the Scottish mind should both have served as tax collectors.

His earlier life had been spent entirely in academe, apart from the two years he spent travelling on the Continent as tutor to Buccleuch's son. He and the lordling got on well, but he had no time for the Grand Tour. The young man 'commonly returns home more conceited, more unprincipled, more dissipated and more incapable of any serious application either to study or to business than he could well have become in so short a time had he lived at home'. (WN, II, p. 257)

Adam was no more impressed by the six years he had spent down south as a Snell Exhibitioner at Balliol. Like Edward Gibbon at Magdalen, he was contemptuous of the idle, port-swilling dons. 'In the university of Oxford, the greater part of the public professors have, for these many years, given up altogether even the pretence of teaching.' (WN, II, p. 247) There were books to read in the libraries of Oxford, and he read thousands of them, but from the company of his fellow scholars he seems to have derived little more than an English accent that he kept for the rest of his life.

His happiest years, he said later, had been the thirteen he spent on his return to Scotland, as professor of logic and then of moral philosophy at Glasgow. When he left, he retired back to Kirkcaldy to live with his mother, the formidable Margaret Douglas, and their cousin Janet Douglas. There, in relative solitude, over a total period of seventeen years, he wrote *The Wealth of Nations*. It is an extraordinary book, not only for its length (nearly nine hundred pages in the Everyman edition) and its unflagging intellectual energy but also for its huge sweep. Smith darts back into the primeval mists and the origins of human society, then swoops forward to engage with yesterday's news – the collapse of the Ayr Bank and the ruin of its customers, the impending collapse of Britain's empire in America, the scandalous mismanagement of the East India Company. The book is relentless, sometimes prolix, sometimes repetitive, but often witty and sardonic, amazingly sharp and prophetic in its grasp of future consequences. Adam Smith is quite unembarrassed by the hurdles he asks the reader to jump: 'I am always willing to run some hazard of being tedious, in order to be sure that I am perspicuous.' (I, p. 25)

THE GREAT METAPHOR

He plunges us straight in. The opening words are: 'The greatest improvement in the productive powers of labour, and the greater part of the skill, dexterity, and judgement with which it is anywhere directed or applied, seem to have been the effects of the division of labour.' (I, p. 4)

It's not just a question of pins. Take an ordinary thing like a labourer's woollen coat. 'The shepherd, the sorter of the wool, the wool-comber or carder, the dyer, the scribbler, the spinner, the weaver, the fuller, the dresser, with many others, must all join their different arts in order to complete even this homely production.' (I, p. 10) Think too of the merchants and carriers who shift the raw and semi-finished materials, the ships that have brought the dyestuffs from all over, then the tools and the energy sources employed: the miners, the furnace-builders, the smelters, the blacksmiths and tool-makers, and so on ad infinitum.

And the social consequences are enormous. See how 'the separation is generally carried furthest in those countries which enjoy the highest degree of industry and improvement'. (I, p. 6) Improvement generates and spreads affluence. 'It is the great multiplication of the productions of all the different arts, in consequence of the division of labour, which occasions, in a well-governed society, that universal opulence which extends itself to the lowest ranks of the people.' (I, p. 10)

How does this remarkable process start? What makes it happen? Smith tells us: 'This division of labour, from which so many advantages are derived, is not originally the effect of any human wisdom, which foresees and intends that general opulence to which it gives occasion.' (I, p. 12) Here, for the first time, we encounter what is to be a running theme in the book: the benign role of unintended consequences in human affairs. 'It is the necessary, though very slow and gradual consequence of a certain propensity in human nature which has in view no such extensive utility; the propensity to truck, barter, and exchange one thing for another.' (I, p. 12)

Exchanging stuff and swapping services come naturally to us. That is what civilized society means. Man 'stands at all times in the need of the co-operation and assistance of great multitudes'. (I, p. 12) These networks of co-operation offer an endless series of mutual benefits. The exchanges they promote are never zero-sum games. This is true of co-operation on the larger scale too. The country supplies the town with food and raw materials. The town sends back its manufactured goods. 'We must not, however, upon this account, imagine that the gain of the town is the loss of the country. The gains of both are mutual and reciprocal, and the division of labour is in this, as in all other cases, advantageous to all the different persons employed in the various occupations into which it is subdivided.' (I, p. 337) The same is true of trade between nations. Free trade benefits all the players, and the freer the conditions of trade, the more all sides benefit.

So far, any half-awake reader may be nodding a sleepy half-assent. All this is easy enough to take on board. Nothing very surprising about the argument, certainly nothing shocking. But then – and we are still only on page thirteen – Smith introduces the insight that later generations have found so unsettling. Yes, man has constant need of the assistance of his fellow men, but, Smith says, it is in vain for him to expect this help from their benevolence alone. Certainly, other people have their benevolent side; we hope we have too. But that benevolence is not to be depended on. It is not a reliable driver of their actions. What we have to do instead is to enlist the 'self-love' of our neighbours. They will regularly help us out, but there has to be something in it for them: 'It is not from the benevolence of the butcher, the brewer, or the baker that we expect our dinner, but from their regard to their own interest. We address ourselves, not to their humanity but to their self-love.' (I, p. 13)

I have always wondered whether 'self-love' was quite the right word to use. Of course, it makes Smith's point more dramatically. But really all that he is saying is that other people have their own agendas just as we have ours. They are doing their own thing just as we are. That agenda may include all sorts of purposes which would count as charitable on any valuation. The butcher may wish to earn some extra cash to pay for treatment for a sick child; the baker may wish to sell a few more loaves so that he can contribute to the appeal for the church roof. The point is that these purposes, no less than their intention to buy a new car or book a fancy holiday, are their purposes, not ours. They may or may not be selfish, in the pejorative sense with which 'self-love' is undoubtedly tinged. In any case, the daily tasks of self-maintenance – keeping yourself and your family well fed and in decent health, keeping your house in good repair, paying your taxes – are generally reckoned as moral responsibilities. They may not be heroic acts of self-forgetting, like rescuing a baby from a burning house or going over the top in a war, but they certainly form part of the spectrum of moral actions.

We will return to the 'self-love' question, but for the moment let us accept that the term is deployed simply to remind us that we are all independent, self-moving beings. What Smith calls 'the man of system' finds this reality hard to grasp: 'he seems to imagine that he can arrange the different members of a great society with as much ease as the hand arranges the different pieces upon a chess-board; he does not consider that . . . in the great chess-board of human society, every single piece has a principle of motion of its own'. (*Theory of Moral Sentiments*, p. 343)

What happens if you leave the human chess pieces to their own devices? Well, Smith declares that, by and large, and with hugely important qualifications that we'll also come to, good things happen. The unguided system tends towards benign outcomes.

Adam Smith is an optimist. What he calls 'the System of Natural Liberty' is the path to follow.

It is not until halfway through *The Wealth of Nations* that he unleashes the immortal metaphor that is to explain more fully what he means. We have to recognize that the individual neither intends to promote the public interest, nor knows how much he is promoting it: 'He intends only his own gain, and he is in this, as in many other cases, led by an invisible hand to promote an end which was no part of his intention. Nor is it always the worse for the society that it was no part of it. By pursuing his own interest he frequently promotes that of the society more effectually than when he really intends to promote it.' (I, p. 400)

Now this really is a shocking thought. From classical antiquity through the Christian era, political philosophers had spent most of their time exploring what constituted good behaviour and what the good man must do to promote the good society. Now Adam Smith, in setting out what purports to be a scientific enquiry into human society, tells us that goodness has nothing to do with it. Self-sacrifice, self-denial, altruism – none of these qualities is essential for a society to grow and prosper.

This is the only mention of the 'invisible hand' in *The Wealth of Nations*, but it is not the first time he has used the term. In *The Theory of Moral Sentiments*, he claims that because the rich employ so many thousands of poor people, they 'are led by an invisible hand to make nearly the same distribution of the necessaries of life which would have been made had the earth been distributed into equal portions among its inhabitants; and thus, without intending, without knowing it, advance the interest of the society, and afford means to the multiplication of the species'. (*TMS*, p. 264) So here the invisible hand not only promotes prosperity but, as a further result, encourages population growth. This will in turn promote further prosperity, for, unlike Parson Malthus, Smith believes that an enlarged market will be a richer one.

Earlier still, in his less-known 'History of Astronomy' essay, Smith uses the invisible hand as a metaphor for the underlying causal mechanisms that generate the patterns and regularities that we see in nature. Thus, the invisible hand seems to be his go-to metaphor for describing how natural systems work, whether in social or physical science. But, of course, it is far more disquieting to see it used in a book that set out to be the founding text of economics, and has indeed become so. As Professor William Letwin says in his introduction to *The Wealth of Nations*: 'The book opens as a treatise in pure science, and indeed it is the foundation of theoretical economics; but about midway it seems to turn into a work of advocacy, a sort of lawyer's brief in favour of capitalism ... This conjunction of science and polemic strikes the modern reader as uncomfortable.' (*WN*, p. v)

There are more unsettling thoughts to come. Smith's metaphor leads on to another related thought: if the hand is invisible, its operations must also be, to a large extent, unknowable. The millions of transactions that make up human life every day are beyond the scope of any human mind to comprehend in their entirety. Government simply does not and cannot know enough. Accordingly, 'the sovereign is completely discharged from a duty, in the attempting to perform which he must always be exposed to innumerable delusions, and for the proper performance of which no human wisdom or knowledge could ever be sufficient; the duty of superintending the industry of private people, and of directing it towards the employments most suitable to the interest of the society'. (II, p. 180)

This insight is crucial to the work of the early twentieth-century 'Austrian school' of economics, led by Ludwig von Mises and Friedrich von Hayek. In their view, the myriad transactions and interactions of independent human beings produce optimum results when left to themselves; governments interfere at their peril. Apparent malfunctions of the free market ought to be tweaked or repaired in the most modest fashion, for the likelihood is that the best intentions will unleash unforeseeable and often unwelcome consequences. Grand industrial strategies, national plans and root-and-branch reforms are likely to lead to the misallocation of resources and all too often end in tears. The first thing for politicians to understand is how little they understand.

For the followers of Adam Smith, who are probably more numerous today than at any time in the past, he is the founder of economic science. What he founded could not be described as 'the dismal science', as Thomas Carlyle dubbed economics. It would be better called 'the gay science'. Long before Nietzsche pinched it, that lovely phrase was first applied to the art of the Provençal troubadours of the later Middle Ages. The troubadours' ballads combine great technical skill with a joyful message of liberation. That is what *The Wealth of Nations* is like: it is rigorous (sometimes exhaustingly rigorous, as Smith goes through all the possible permutations and combinations), but it is also unfailingly cheerful. Adam wants people to have a good time. 'Science is the great antidote to the poison of enthusiasm and superstition.' (II, p. 278) But along with science, the second remedy is 'the frequency and gaiety of public diversions'. Painting, poetry, music, dancing, the theatre – these all inspired a public good humour that dissipated that melancholy and gloomy humour that was almost always the nurse of fanaticism. For Adam, there is an answer to every question, a corrective remedy to every economic ailment or folly, and it is usually an agreeable answer. If governments do the right thing or, more often, abstain from doing the wrong thing, the future will be bright.

In person, I have noticed, the followers of Adam Smith tend themselves to be rather serene, sweet-natured, almost innocent creatures. This was certainly true of Ludwig von Mises and of Sir Alan Walters, Margaret Thatcher's economic adviser. For them, the world was always a friendly place, if it was allowed to be.

JEAN-JACQUES AND ADAM

What a contrast all this makes with the outlook of our last Mover. Jean-Jacques Rousseau and Adam Smith take exactly the same starting point for the history of modern man: the division of labour. What is so remarkable is that they reach exactly opposite conclusions. For Rousseau, as we have seen, the division of labour is the root of all evil. From the moment one man needed the help of another, the fields were watered with the sweat of man and all his slavery and misery began. Society is a zero-sum game. There are no mutual benefits to be had from human exchanges. On the contrary, 'the good of one necessarily constitutes the harm of another'. (*Emile*, p. 105fn) These acts of exploitation are cumulatively degenerative for society as a whole. 'Dependence on men', we are told in *Emile*, 'engenders all the vices and by it master and slave are mutually corrupted.' (p. 85) Society is irredeemably fouled up. Each of us is frustrated and constrained into an unnatural existence by the demands of so-called polite society. 'One no longer dares to seem what one really is.'

Rousseau was almost the only one of the *Encyclopédie* crowd whom Smith never met when he was in Paris, but he knew Rousseau's work well. In fact, Smith's second appearance in print (an article in the second issue of the *Edinburgh Review*, January 1756) was an essay on foreign writers, which focused on Rousseau and quoted long chunks of the *Discourse on Inequality* that had come out the year before. Although Smith's conclusions were to be so different, his public writings were always respectful. In *The Theory of Moral Sentiments*, he refers to 'the ingenious and eloquent M. Rousseau of Geneva'. He even begged Hume not to publish his side of his quarrel with the ungrateful Jean-Jacques. He should not 'unmask before the public this hypocritical Pedant', because that would disturb 'the tranquillity of your whole life'. In any case, 'to write against him is, you may depend upon it, the very thing he wishes you to do'. (Ross, pp. 210–11) Shrewd advice, and Hume took it.

The cleavage between Rousseau and Smith is one of the great forks in the political roadmap. For Rousseau, all the little accommodations that we make to fit in with other people are the vilest humbug. They rob us of our natural freedom to be ourselves, those true selves from which society estranges us. All the modern discourse about alienation, from Marx down to the present day, derives ultimately from Rousseau. Only by a huge wrench of the collective will can we liberate ourselves from this estrangement. We must be 'forced to be free', Rousseau tells us, or we shall never be free at all.

Nothing could be more repugnant to Adam Smith than this approach to life. For him, to be fully human is to be with others, to engage with our fellow men. He would regard the solitary education prescribed for Emile as pernicious and intolerable. For it is not only our material lives that we make in co-operation with others, but our moral lives too. Our selves are socially created.

Adam had a penchant for the searing maxims of the seventeenth-century moralist La Rochefoucauld, often regarded as a bitter cynic for such bons mots as 'hypocrisy is the homage that vice pays to virtue' and 'virtues join with self-interest as the rivers join with the sea'. Smith quoted that second maxim in early editions of *The Theory of Moral Sentiments* but dropped it from the final 1790 edition, completed just before his death. Perhaps he thought it too risqué for the revolutionary times. But Smith certainly did endorse La Rochefoucauld's message that morality and insincerity are not incompatible. Sometimes it is right to tell a white lie. Self-driven behaviour can produce socially desirable outcomes. Smith also expresses guarded approval of the Dutch-English physician Bernard Mandeville and his notorious *Fable of the Bees* (1714), with its shocking subtitle 'Private Vices, Publick Benefits'. In this poetic-political satire, the hive thrives, until the bees are suddenly made honest and virtuous. No longer buzzing busily in the pursuit of honey, their economy collapses, and they fly off to lead simple but impoverished lives in a hollow tree. In *The Theory of Moral Sentiments*, Smith describes Mandeville's system as 'in almost every respect erroneous' (p. 451), but he clearly has a soft spot for the argument and admits at the end that it 'in some respects bordered upon the truth'. (p. 459) He borrows several of Mandeville's illustrations of the division of labour, such as the number of small specializations that had vastly improved the quality and lowered the price of clocks and watches. A watch that in the 1650s would have cost £20 could now be had for 20 shillings: 'It is the natural effect of improvement to diminish gradually the real price of almost all manufactures.' (WN, I, pp. 224–5) Smith doesn't agree with Mandeville's other contention, that the economy needs to be regulated to ensure that the actions of individuals benefit society. But he does garner from Mandeville the crucial insight that non-moral, amoral and immoral behaviour can be socially beneficial just as much as actions dictated by the highest principles.

Rousseau finds the thought nauseating. Good can only come out of a good heart. One's own conscience is the only true guide to doing the right thing. To pay any attention to the opinions of others is to become enmeshed in the foul hypocrisy of the bourgeoisie.

The irony is that societies remade as moral dictatorships, along Rousseau's lines, are just the ones in which you have to pay the most careful attention to the opinions of your neighbours. In Rousseau's Geneva, no less than in the totalitarian regimes of the twentieth century, fitting in was not just a matter of *convenance* or *bienséance*. It could be, literally, a matter of life and death. Just as in Smith's commercial society every man 'becomes in some measure a merchant', so in Stalin's Russia or Hitler's Germany every man becomes in some measure a spy.

With deepest sympathy

Thus, there are two ways in which Smith sharply disagrees with Rousseau. The first is that our motives do not always need to be pure and unselfish for our actions to be beneficial to society. The second is that, even when our motives are unselfish, they are largely shaped by the moral opinions of other people. You cannot elude this fact by appealing to your conscience as the only reliable guide, as Rousseau persistently does, for that conscience is itself only the mirror of other people's moral feelings.

This is what Smith's 'other book' is largely about. *The Theory of Moral Sentiments* arose originally out of his lectures on ethics in Glasgow. That is no disadvantage, because Smith tells us quite a bit about the other philosophers he has been lecturing on, and about how his opinions differ from theirs. The book is just as meticulous and thoughtful as *The Wealth of Nations*, though not quite so enjoyable to read. But its many merits have not prevented it from being misunderstood by those who have not read it or have not progressed much further than the opening chapter, 'Of Sympathy', and the first sentence: 'How selfish soever man may be supposed, there are evidently some principles in his nature, which interest him in the fortune of others, and render their happiness necessary to him, though he derives nothing from it, except the pleasure of seeing it. Of this kind is pity or compassion.' (*TMS*, p. 3)

At first blush then, it seems as if we are in for a treatise on Sympathy, in the rather limp sense in which we sign off a letter of condolence 'with deepest sympathy'. This leads on to the quite understandable inference that there is some kind of contradiction between Adam Smith's two great works. This inference has had a long innings in the nineteenth and twentieth centuries, especially in Germany, where much ink has been spilt on *Das Adam Smith Problem*. It looks as if Smith first wrote one big book about being nice to each other, then another big book, twice as long, about looking after Number One. Isn't there an insuperable conflict between other-love and self-love, between sympathy and self-interest?

In reality, the problem is not so hard to resolve, especially if you read *The Theory of Moral Sentiments* before *The Wealth of Nations*, as most of Smith's eighteenth-century readers would have done, because it was published seventeen years earlier and it was a bestseller.

What the earlier book sets out to establish is that our moral world is based on our imagination of what other people think is admirable or deplorable. This has to be an effort of the imagination. 'As we have no immediate experience of what other men feel, we can form no idea of the manner in which they are affected, but by conceiving what we ourselves should feel in the like situation.' (*TMS*, p. 3) We cannot see inside other minds, a problem that continues to vex philosophers with nothing better to think about.

What if we differ, perhaps violently, from our neighbours on some question? Where can we find a reliable alternative guide on how to behave or not to behave? Smith says that we can imagine 'an impartial spectator', someone who is level-headed and well-informed about the case. What would he or she think? Would he or she be horrified or tolerant or even approving? Approbation (and disapprobation) is the name of Smith's game. He insists from the outset that this is ultimately and originally a matter of feeling, of our gut reaction. That is where our moral sentiments come from, not from rational thought, or social utility, or some mysterious indwelling 'moral sense', or from God who supposedly implanted it. Smith derived this idea from his hero and friend David Hume, but he carries the line of thought much further, to denounce all the alternative explanations offered by Plato and Aristotle, by Epictetus and the Stoics, by Hobbes and even by his immediate Scots predecessors such as Francis Hutcheson. The Christian casuists are just as far off the mark, Smith says, because 'they attempted, to no purpose, to direct by precise rules, what it belongs to feeling and sentiment only to judge of'. (p. 499) For Smith, as for Goethe: '*Gefühl ist alles.*' ('Feeling is everything.')

We can and do work up fancy arguments to justify our moral feelings for or against, let's say, homosexuality or alcohol, but ultimately our feelings will be shaped by our feelings of revulsion or approval, and those feelings will in turn be shaped by the sea we and our contemporaries are swimming in. As David Raphael sums up in his little book on Smith: 'Sympathy and imagination in the *Moral Sentiments* are the cement of human society in forming socializing attitudes.' (p. 93) They generate approbation and disapprobation, and induce conformity to social norms both in behaviour and in attitude.

Sympathy and imagination create a social bond. It's different from the social bonds of mutual dependence that are described in *The Wealth of Nations* as resulting from the division of labour and the workings of the market. But the two sorts of bond are not inconsistent with one another. They may overlap and dovetail, according to context. I may dispose of my extra rubbish by taking it to the recycling centre myself (self-love and good citizenship), or the dustman may take it if I give him a few quid (market forces), or I may take my housebound elderly neighbour's rubbish as well as my own (altruism). All of these actions have their place in the great scheme of waste disposal. I may buy Wimbledon tickets from a tout and give one of the tickets to a friend. Altruism mingles with market forces. There's no contradiction. Do I approve of the ticket tout as a useful middleman for the efficient distribution of tickets, or do I deplore his existence as a knavish profiteer? There's something to be said for both views. My position may depend on whether I am a committee member of the Lawn Tennis Association or a desperate tennis fan.

Smith insists that our moral feelings of admiration or disgust are just that: feelings, not rational deductions from some overarching philosophical system. When we put those feelings together into an ethical code, we are constructing what Smith calls 'an imaginary machine', or as academics say today: 'a model'. To get a sharper sense of what Smith is up to, it may help to refer to his

earlier 'History of Astronomy' essay – a pioneer document in the
history and philosophy of science. What Smith says there is that
when we are uncomfortable with a scientific orthodoxy that no
longer seems to fit the facts of observation – Ptolemy's account
of the cosmos, for example, or centuries later, the system of
Copernicus – we grope around for a new 'paradigm', as Thomas
Kuhn calls it in *The Structure of Scientific Revolutions* (1962).
We quickly come to think of the new paradigm as the last word,
when it is only the latest word, the best that our imaginations can
devise to fit the facts as we presently know them. Smith brilliantly
describes how we gradually come to think of our imaginative
theories as substantial realities: 'Even we, while we have been
endeavouring to represent all philosophical systems as mere inventions of the imagination . . . have insensibly been drawn in to make
use of language expressing the connecting principles of this one,
as if they were the real chains which Nature makes use of to bind
together her several operations.' Newton's system had gained 'the
general and complete approbation of mankind' and it was now
considered 'not as an attempt to connect in the imagination the
phaenomena of the Heavens, but as the greatest discovery that ever
was made by man, the discovery of an immense chain of the most
important and sublime truths'. (quoted Raphael, p. 111)

Smith is an outstanding figure in the chain of thinkers who have
taught us that scientific truth is provisional – not relative, but provisional. A hypothesis is valid so long as – and only so long as – it
stands up to the most rigorous tests that are available to us. Much
the same line of thinking is set out by Karl Popper in his *Logic of
Scientific Discovery* (1959; originally published in 1934 as *Logik der
Forschung*): science progresses by a series of falsifiable hypotheses.
If a thesis cannot be falsified, then it cannot be counted as part of
scientific knowledge – Popper offers Freud and Marx as ripe examples of pseudo-scientific thinkers who fail this test.

Similarly, in constructing our moral codes, we may find that the
old shibboleths no longer fit the world as we see it today. We are no
longer disgusted by homosexuality or abortion as we once were, and
so we construct a new moral code to fit our feelings. 'The general
rules of morality are . . . ultimately founded upon experience of what,

in particular instances, our moral faculties, our natural sense of merit and propriety, approve or disapprove of. We do not originally approve or condemn certain actions, because, upon examination, they appear to be agreeable or inconsistent with a certain general rule.' (*TMS*, p. 224)

The Theory of Moral Sentiments went into numerous editions and drew warm praise from the great men of the day. Edmund Burke described it as 'one of the most beautiful fabrics of moral theory, that has perhaps ever appeared'. He was convinced of the 'Solidity and Truth' of Smith's theory, because it was based on 'the whole of Human Nature'. (Ross, p. 181) The appeal to what Burke often called 'prejudice' rather than abstract theory was very much in line with Burke's own psychological approach to political thought.

But perhaps the most memorable reaction from an early reader came not from a reviewer but from a poet. Robert Burns had been reading a copy of the first edition, perhaps belonging to his father. There's a quatrain in 'To a Louse' which is a vivid paraphrase of Smith's argument:

> O wad some Pow'er the giftie gie us
> To see oursels as others see us!
> It wad frae monie a blunder free us
> An' foolish notion.

THE UNACCEPTABLE FACES OF CAPITALISM

So far, you might perhaps think there appears to be a certain guile-less quality about Adam Smith, perhaps even a naivety about the wicked ways of the real world, an excessive willingness to focus on the benign face of the free market. His optimism may even have reminded you of Dr Pangloss in Voltaire's fable *Candide*, published in the same year as *The Theory of Moral Sentiments*, with his appalling maxim: 'Everything is for the best in the best of all possible worlds.'

If I have given any such impression, it is high time to correct it. Adam was no academic innocent. It is a mistake to dwell on the absent-minded professor zigzagging his way up Canongate. Think rather of the hard-headed Customs boss, immersed in his work (to the detriment, he thought, as did others, of his literary and scholarly pursuits), sharp as a ferret, eager as a beaver.

The Wealth of Nations is no goofy hymn to the free market. It is, among many other things, one of the fiercest polemics ever against the greed and duplicity of businessmen, and in particular against the way they manage to pervert and manipulate governments in their favour. 'The capricious ambition of kings and ministers has not, during the present and the preceding century, been more fatal to the repose of Europe than the impertinent jealousy of merchants and manufacturers.' (WN, I, p. 436) Smith is determined that 'the mean rapacity, the monopolising spirit of merchants and manufacturers' must be prevented from ruling the roost. Left to themselves, the business class is usually up to no good. Famously, Smith tells us: 'People of the same trade seldom meet together, even for merriment and diversion, but the conversation ends in a conspiracy against the public, or in some contrivance to raise prices.' (I, p. 117)

Employers will put forward the most bogus arguments to bolster their own positions. They always have the edge over their employees: 'The masters, being fewer in number, can combine much more easily; and the law, besides, authorises, or at least does not prohibit their combinations, while it prohibits those of the workmen. We have no acts of parliament against combining to lower the price of work; but many against combining to raise it.' (I, p. 59) Trade unions were not to be legalized until 1824, as a concession after the persistent unrest of the Napoleonic years. Businessmen blamed everyone but themselves. 'Our merchants and master-manufacturers complain much of the bad effects of high wages in raising the price, and thereby lessening the sale of their goods, both at home and abroad. They say nothing of the bad effects of high profits.' (I, p. 88) Ever since Edward III's Statute of Labourers, merchants had pressed Parliament to pass laws imposing a maximum wage. There was no record of any law imposing a minimum wage – and there would be none until Winston Churchill's Trade Boards Act of 1909, which applied only to certain industries where wages were notoriously low, such as tailoring and lace-making. For a national minimum wage, the low-paid had to wait more than two centuries, until the 1998 Act.

Smith points out that exceptions are made for the professional classes: 'the law has upon many occasions attempted to raise the wages of curates'. (I, p. 119) The point is, though, that none of these laws have succeeded in bucking the market: 'in both cases, the law seems to have been equally ineffectual, and has never either been able to raise the wages of curates, or to sink those of labourers to the degree that was intended'. (I, p. 119) The curates were too poor to refuse any pittance, and the employers were so desperate for labour that they had to offer the going rate.

Merchants, then as now, took every opportunity to shut out competition by restricting entry to their trades. Monopoly was always the aim: 'A monopoly granted either to an individual or to a trading company has the same effect as a secret in trade or manufactures.' (I, p. 54) By keeping the market understocked, the monopolist kept up prices. Restricting the number of apprentices allowed had the same effect. In Sheffield, no master cutler could have more than one apprentice at a time. Any weaver or hatter in Norfolk who took on more than two apprentices at a time had to pay a fine. Such restrictions were always defended on the grounds of maintaining quality, just as they are today by the black cabs. Smith is having none of it. 'The pretence that corporations are necessary for the better government of the trade is without any foundation. The real and effectual discipline which is exercised over a workman is not that of his corporation, but that of his customers.' (I, p. 117) All over, then and now, the aim was always to keep out rivals and keep up prices. Already in Smith's day, the *vignerons* of France were doing their damnedest to prevent the planting of new vines, as they still are today. (I, p. 140) Woollen manufacturers in Abbeville insisted on what we would call 'non-compete agreements' within a radius of thirty miles. (I, p. 406)

Again and again, Smith's comments on the business practices of his day twang a twenty-first-century chord. Apothecaries' profits were already a byword, but Smith defends the pharmacists; the price of their drugs was no more than was owed to their dispensing skills. (I, p. 100) By contrast, he was less indulgent to the promoters of the state lotteries. The tickets were not worth the price, and the more tickets you bought, the more certain you were to end up a loser. (I, p. 96)

Anyone who thinks that the restlessness of global capital is a twenty-first-century problem should read *The Wealth of Nations*. 'A merchant . . . is not necessarily the citizen of any particular country. It is in a great measure indifferent to him from what place he carries on his trade; and a very trifling disgust will make him remove his capital, and together with it, all the industry which it supports, from one country to another.' (I, p. 373) Then as now, capital was footloose, and the tax funk was no slouch: 'the proprietor of stock is properly a citizen of the world, and is not necessarily attached to any particular country. He would be apt to abandon the country in which he was exposed to a vexatious inquisition, in order to be assessed to a burdensome tax, and would remove his stock to some other country where he could either carry on his business, or enjoy his fortune more at his ease.' (II, p. 331) Monte Carlo, here we come.

Smith was in no sense hostile to financial innovation. Any device that expanded trade and made the economy function more smoothly was worth a look. He believed in the much-maligned middleman, corn merchants, for example, who far from exploiting a dearth, did more to smooth out prices and forestall famine than the bungling intrusions of governments. It was not the Indian merchants but the ham-fisted regulations of the East India Company that had turned the recent drought in Bengal and consequent rice shortage into a terrible famine.

The great thing, he thought, was always to try to increase the size of the market as far as prudence would allow. Since the founding of the two great banks in Scotland, the Royal Bank and the Bank of Scotland, trade in the kingdom had more than quadrupled. He was intrigued, too, by the practice of the Royal Bank, under its founder Archibald Campbell, Lord Ilay (later the third Duke of Argyll), of granting its customers what they called 'cash accounts' – what we call overdrafts. (I, p. 263) This device, another of the great inventions that Scotland gave the world, enabled the merchant to expand his trade without risk, so long as he was prudent. Lord Ilay, a cynical and ingenious fellow, fully deserved the place he occupied for many years on the RBS ten-pound note in a splendid full-bottomed wig that put Adam's bag-wig to shame.

But Smith was equally alert to the congenital recklessness of bankers. He gives a brilliant account of the rise and fall of the Ayr Bank, which had played out over the last years of his work on *The Wealth of Nations*. (I, pp. 278–82) This new bank had been established only recently, with the best intentions of relieving the current distress of Scotland. The existing banks, it was claimed, had been too ignorant and pusillanimous 'to give a sufficiently liberal aid to the spirited undertakings of those who exerted themselves in order to beautify, improve and enrich the country'. The Ayr Bank had no such qualms. It 'was more liberal than any other had ever been, both in granting cash accounts, and in discounting bills of exchange'. In short, it was overtrading like crazy, and in no time began to run out of cash and to borrow and reborrow far and wide from anyone who would lend money to it. In a glorious simile, Smith says: 'The project of replenishing their coffers in this manner may be compared to that of a man who had a water-pond from which a stream was continually running out, and into which no stream was continually running, but who proposed to keep it always equally full by employing a number of people to go continually with buckets to a well at some miles distance in order to bring water to replenish it.'

The bank went bust and took twenty years to wind up. Many of the lairds who had subscribed to it were partially or totally ruined, although even a collapse on this scale could not quite sink Smith's plutocratic old pupil, now the Duke of Buccleuch. The ripples of the crash were felt as far away as London and Calcutta. Work stopped for a time on Robert Adam's New Town and his sister project, the Adelphi by the Thames. The manner of the bank's rise and fall mirrored almost exactly that of the Royal Bank of Scotland two centuries later. The signature of the Chief Cashier under Lord Ilay's wig is that of Fred Goodwin.

The report into the bank's collapse blamed the managers for 'open disregard, not only of the principles of the co-partnery, but of the express and positive rules and regulations laid down for the conduct of Managers'. Even so, Smith doubted whether the existing regulations were enough to deter this reckless 'roundabout trading', which had piled up such a tangled heap of bills that nobody could be sure how much the bank owed or who were the ultimate creditors. Smith was prepared to intervene to prevent banks from gambling with their customers' money. There had to be a separation between the two types of banking: the sober retail business and the chancier investment banking. 'The obligation of building party walls, in order to prevent the communication of fire, is a violation of natural liberty exactly of the same kind with the regulations of the banking trade which are here proposed.' (I, p. 289) It has taken two centuries to rediscover this simple truth and start rebuilding those party walls.

Smith is anything but naive in his attitude towards managers. The joint stock company was the corporation of the future. In its refined limited-liability form, by the twentieth century it had virtually obliterated all the rival forms of governance. Yet Smith saw very early on an intrinsic weakness in it: 'The directors of such companies, however, being the managers rather of other people's money than of their own, it cannot well be expected that they should watch over it with the same anxious vigilance with which the partners in a private copartnery frequently watch over their own.' (II, p. 229) This is what we call today 'the problem of agency', and the outcome is very frequently just as Smith diagnosed: 'Negligence and profusion, therefore, must always prevail, more or less, in the management of the affairs of such a company.' When we deplore the spectacle of the fat cats in the boardroom helping themselves to millions in return for a decidedly mediocre performance, we are deploring nothing new.

THE CLUMSY HAND

But if Smith had few illusions about businessmen, he had even fewer about politicians. The world was directed, he said, not by the science of high-minded legislators acting from general principles but by 'the skill of that insidious and crafty animal, vulgarly called a statesman or politician, whose councils are directed by the momentary fluctuation of affairs'. (I, p. 412) It was in the continuous, often secret negotiation between the businessman and the politician that the damage was done to the interests and welfare of the public. As a result of this relentless lobbying and these devious deals, the commerce of Britain and Ireland in Smith's day – and for many decades before – was a jungle of taxes and regulations: inland excise duties and external customs duties of all shapes and sizes – import taxes, export taxes and rebates ('drawbacks' as they called them then), and export subsidies, or 'bounties', not to mention actual embargoes on the export or import of certain commodities. All these imposts were designed to make trade flow in directions in which it would not naturally have flowed.

These rules were often of fantastic complexity and, sometimes, of a ferocity so extreme that they were never fully enforced. One Elizabethan statute completely prohibited the export of sheep. For the first offence, the exporter was to forfeit all his goods and have his hand cut off and nailed up in the market place; for the second offence, he was to suffer the death penalty. (II, p. 143) To prevent any such export, the whole inland traffic in wool was severely policed; wool could only be transported in daylight in specially marked leather packs. Sheep farmers near the coast were kept under constant surveillance. In order to justify their demand for these extraordinary restrictions, the manufacturers claimed that 'English wool was of a peculiar quality, superior to that of any other country ... that fine cloth could not be made without it; that England, therefore, if the exportation of it could be totally prevented, could monopolise to herself almost the whole woollen trade of the world; and thus, having no rivals, could sell at what price she pleased'. (II, p. 146) This claim, Smith tells us, was utter tosh: 'It is, however, so perfectly false that English wool is in any respect necessary for the making of fine cloth that it is altogether unfit for it.' Fine cloth was made entirely of Spanish wool, and if English wool was mixed in, it would actually degrade the fabric. Making exports illegal benefited only the smuggler.

Smith's attitude to all these subsidies and embargoes was unwavering. In the same passage where he praises the invisible hand of the market, he denounces the all too visible and clumsy hand of government: 'To give the monopoly of the home market to the produce of domestic industry, in any particular art or manufacture, is in some measure to direct private people in what manner they ought to employ their capital, and must, in almost all cases, be either a useless or a hurtful regulation. If the produce of domestic can be bought there as cheap as that of foreign industry, the regulation is evidently useless. If it cannot, it must generally be hurtful.' (I, p. 401)

It is of course always possible to warp the terms of trade in favour of your domestic suppliers, but only at horrendous cost: 'By means of glasses, hotbeds and hot walls, very good grapes can be raised in Scotland, and very good wine too can be made of them at about thirty times the expense for which at least equally good can be bought from foreign countries. Would it be a reasonable law to prohibit the importation of foreign wines merely to encourage the making of claret and burgundy in Scotland?' (I, p. 402)

The most damaging of all interferences with the operations of the free market were those relating to corn. Unfortunately, these were also the most prevalent. 'The laws concerning corn may everywhere be compared to the laws concerning religion. The people feel themselves so much interested in what relates either to their subsistence in this life, or to their happiness in the life to come, that government must yield to their prejudices.' (II, p. 39) The corn laws were all too often not the result of overmighty governments but of misguided popular clamour. It was to take another seventy years before the Free Traders managed to abolish the corn laws and give the British public access to the cheaper corn from the great American prairies.

In extreme cases, the subsidies were so juicy that traders would enter the business just to qualify for the bounty. In the white-herring fishery, Smith tells us, 'it has, I am afraid, been all too common for vessels to fit out for the sole purpose of catching, not the fish, but the bounty'. (II, p. 19) We have seen such episodes in our own time, for example, when the government has offered irresistible incentives to farmers and landowners to build wind farms and solar farms.

Smith is never an ultra-dogmatist. He freely concedes that nations can make progress even under a regime of harmful tariffs. Perfect liberty and perfect justice were not essential for progress (in any case, they were not attainable in the real world). The natural effort that men were constantly making to improve their own condition outweighed the retarding effects of bad regulations. Smith accepts, too, that the transition to free trade often needs to be gradual. 'Humanity may require ... that the freedom of trade should be restored only by slow gradations, and with a good deal of reserve and circumspection. Were those high duties and prohibitions taken away all at once, cheaper foreign goods of the same kind might be poured so fast into the home market as to deprive all at once many thousands of our people of their ordinary employment and means of subsistence.' (I, p. 412) Such distress would be only temporary, as people found other jobs, but the shock ought to be cushioned. There was a case, too, for 'start-up' protection for new experimental businesses: 'A temporary monopoly of this kind may be vindicated upon the same principles upon which a like monopoly of a new machine is granted to an inventor, and that of a new book to its author.' (II, p. 241)

But in general, the mercantile system of subsidies and duties tended to help only the rich and powerful, and not the general public, let alone the poor. What we now call 'producer capture' was always harmful to the consumer. And the consumer must always come first, for 'Consumption is the sole end and purpose of all production; and the interest of the producer ought to be attended to only so far as it may be necessary for promoting that of the consumer.' (II, p. 155) This bold statement is to us a commonplace, but until Adam Smith came along, that order of priorities was generally reversed. Preachers and statesmen tended to deplore consumption – 'luxury' was a favourite pejorative term – while applauding the worthy producer.

THE COLONIAL ILLUSION

Least of all should governments listen to merchants when they are promoting great imperial ventures, mostly in order to line their own pockets by securing exclusive rights. Smith was a globalist. He wanted to see free trade everywhere. He was as opposed to monopolies abroad as at home. By giving the colonial merchants the monopoly on supplying goods to Britain's colonies, 'the interest of the colonies was sacrificed to the interest of those merchants'. (II, p. 81) By drawing away British manufactures to her distant possessions, 'like all other mean and malignant expedients of the mercantile system' (II, p. 107), the monopoly depressed the manufactures of all other countries without helping Britain's domestic economy. In fact, 'Britain derived nothing but loss from the dominion which she assumes over her colonies'. (II, p. 112) The whole enterprise was based on an illusion. 'To found a great empire for the sole purpose of raising up a people of customers may at first sight appear to be a project fit only for a nation of shopkeepers.' (II, p. 110) (This is the first known use of that phrase; Napoleon, to whom it is so often attributed, never used it, so far as we know.) But in fact the project was quite unfit for a nation of shopkeepers, only for a nation influenced by shopkeepers. All the benefits flowed to the merchants and nabobs.

Adam Smith forecasts a splendid future for the American colonists. Their empire was likely to become 'one of the greatest and most formidable that ever was in the world' (II, p. 119) – but not under British rule. The Continental Congress would never submit to Britain. The coming rupture would be as final as it was inevitable. *The Wealth of Nations* ends with an extraordinary passage. Smith calls for a graceful surrender. The defence of the colonies was unbearably expensive. If the mother country could no longer support 'this splendid and showy equipage', she should give it up. The rulers of Great Britain should wake up from 'this golden dream' of empire and 'endeavour to accommodate her future views and designs to the real mediocrity of her circumstances'. (II, pp. 429–30) A daring defeatism to urge in the middle of a huge conflict that had aroused every patriot's passion.

Smith was no less forthright in his condemnation of the East India Company and its monopolies. Its administration was 'essentially and perhaps incurably faulty'. (II, p. 134) A company of merchants was utterly unsuitable to govern a great country. 'Such exclusive companies, therefore, are nuisances in every respect; always more or less inconvenient to the countries in which they are established, and destructive to those which have the misfortune to fall under their government.' (II, p. 137)

For one thing, all the officers of the Company were trading upon their own account, and it was hopeless to try to prevent such abuses. (II, p. 135) For another, they were all anxious to sail home to Britain as soon as they had made their pile. 'It is a very singular government in which every member of the administration wishes to get out of the country, and consequently to have done with the government as soon as he can, and to whose interest, the day after he has left it and carried his whole fortune with him, it is perfectly indifferent though the whole country was swallowed up by an earthquake.' (II, p. 136)

The greed and corruption of the East India Company were a public scandal by the time *The Wealth of Nations* came out, and Fox's India Bill and Pitt's India Act would soon attempt to introduce some control over the private speculators and some decent adminis-tration. Smith's point, though, was that trading and governing could never mix. 'If the trading spirit of the English East India Company renders them very bad sovereigns, the spirit of sovereignty seems to have rendered them very bad traders.' (II, p. 301) Despite enjoying a revenue of more than three million sterling, they had been obliged to beg government help to avoid immediate bankruptcy. In India, as in Britain, government undermined commerce, just as commerce undermined government.

THE DUTIES OF GOVERNMENT

Smith's careless modern admirers tend to undervalue or ignore the close attention he paid to the proper scope and quality of gov-ernment. In his improved state, the role of government was to be limited, but it was also crucial. In the later sections of *The Wealth of Nations*, he sets out government's three main tasks: the defence of the realm, the defence of justice and the promotion of educa-tion. The free market could operate only within a secure political system, where the rule of law was paramount and unquestioned. He endorses Montesquieu's view that to secure our rights, it was necessary to separate the judicial power from the executive. It is

commonly said that Montesquieu misunderstood the British constitution and overestimated the extent of the separation of powers
prevailing there in his day. I'm not so sure. I think he got through
to an essential reality: that although in Britain there might be no
formal separation such as there was to be in the Constitution of
the United States, for practical purposes, Parliament, the Crown
and the judges did consider that they possessed certain independent functions and rights. And Adam Smith takes it for granted
that this is how they do in practice operate.

Perhaps the most surprising duty that Smith allots to government
is the education of the labouring poor, who needed to be raised
from their ignorant stupor. State-financed schools should be set up
in every parish, plus examinations for school leavers to invigilate
standards. The state ought also to support works of public benefit
such as roads and canals.

This is a far more extensive programme of public expenditure
than the conventional picture of Adam Smith might suggest. To
pay for it, Smith has a substantial section on good and bad ways
to tax. In England, for example, 'the different poll-taxes never
produced the sum which had been expected from them, or which,
it was supposed, they might have produced, had they been exactly
levied'. (II, p. 350) Many people either could not, or would not, pay.
Margaret Thatcher might have saved herself a good deal of trouble
by reading this passage.

Rather than laying equal rates of taxes on all classes in society,
taxes should always be related to the ability to pay. (II, p. 307) A
commonplace idea to us, but a relatively new one then. On the
whole, Smith favours moderate taxes (otherwise there will be a
lot of smuggling) and suggests they be concentrated on articles
of consumption, such as salt, leather, soap, candles and coal. Yes,
consumption taxes do put up the cost of living and hence put up
wages too, but 'they afford a considerable revenue to government
which it might not be easy to find in any other way' (II, p. 356) – as
Chancellors of the Exchequer then and now have discovered. About
taxation as about most other subjects, Adam Smith was unfailingly
hard-headed.

POOR HEARING

Hard-headed certainly, but was Adam Smith also ultimately a little hard-hearted? How closely does he listen to the voice of the poor, the dispossessed, the marginal citizens? The picture that he paints of Georgian England and Scotland is striking. He talks of 'the great, and almost universal prosperity of the country' and 'its peculiarly happy circumstances'. (I, p. 183) In tracing the progress of Britain since the invasion of Julius Caesar, he describes the present as 'the happiest and most fortunate period of them all, that which has passed since the Restoration'. (I, p. 308) There is no suggestion that the poor have been left behind or left out of this great accession of affluence. On the contrary, the division of labour in a well-governed society (such as he thought on the whole Britain was) produces 'that universal opulence which extends itself to the lowest ranks of the people'. (I, p. 10) In fact, it was now 'a common complaint that luxury extends itself even to the lowest ranks of the people'. (I, p. 70) Personally, Smith is delighted to see this state of affairs: 'No society can surely be flourishing and happy, of which the far greater part of the members are poor and miserable.' (I, p. 70) In *The Theory of Moral Sentiments*, he expands this optimism to cover the globe, rebuking 'those whining and melancholy moralists who are perpetually reproaching us with our happiness, while so many of our brethren are in misery'. (p. 194) 'Take the whole earth as an average, for one man who suffers pain or misery, you will find twenty in prosperity and joy, or at least in tolerable circumstances.' (p. 197)

But was Georgian Britain, let alone the rest of the world, really such a wonderful place to be at the bottom of the heap? True, the average expectation of life did climb slowly during the eighteenth century to reach about forty years, and the population increased too. But unemployment and underemployment remained endemic. Even respectable journeymen such as bricklayers and plasterers could expect to be out of work for months on end. And below them lay a whole underclass living off scraps, surviving by scrounging, thieving and selling their bodies. Smith does refer once or twice to the 'distress' caused to the poor by the rapacity of merchants or the mistaken policies of governments. But only once, so far as I can see, does he refer in detail to any particular dilemma or hardship faced by the labouring poor.

He spends several pages on the obstruction to the free movement of labour posed by the system of parish poor relief, which derived from the Elizabethan poor laws. (*WN*, I, pp. 124–8) The parish officers had a duty to provide relief for their own resident poor. Naturally, they were reluctant to admit new poor families to settle within the parish boundaries. An in-migrant would be allowed to settle and so entitled to draw welfare only if he had paid rent and parish rates and held down a job for a year. Obviously it was hell-ishly hard to secure a job in advance of settlement, and how could you rent a place with no money coming in? Various solutions were devised to overcome this chicken-and-egg problem, none of them, Smith says, very satisfactory. In these pages, we see for a moment the hideous difficulties faced by the vagrant poor displaced by agri-cultural and industrial improvements. But that is almost all he has to say in 800-plus pages.

Absent-minded Adam might be, but as he zigzagged up Canon-gate or stepped out of his carriage to dine with The Club at the Turk's Head in Soho, he would have been jostled by beggars and those handsome Irish prostitutes he admired so much. He would have seen the gin-sodden human wrecks lying in the Edinburgh wynds and the alleys of Covent Garden, would have been familiar with Hogarth's famous print 'Gin Lane' (1751), with its scenes of infanticide, starvation, suicide and madness. He would have known a lot, too, about the system of workhouses, 2,000 of them all over the country, following Sir Edward Knatchbull's Workhouse Test Act of 1723. Smith does refer to the high rate of mortality in the found-ling hospitals (so much for Rousseau's plea that his babes would be better looked after there), but with the exception of the parish relief question, he has little to say on the relief of poverty. It is not as if the subject was not high on the public agenda at the time. All sorts of initiatives, both official and private charitable ones, were under way. But all Smith likes to tell us is that the general opulence now extends to the lowest classes in society.

Yet it is, after all, Adam Smith who first alerted us to what Joseph Schumpeter nearly two centuries later was to call 'the gale of creative destruction' that capitalism blew through traditional society. Smith repeatedly brings home to us the restlessness of merchants, their relentless search for new techniques to develop and new markets to conquer. It is largely from Smith, whom he read with great attention, that Marx derives his unforgettable picture of the bourgeoisie in *The Communist Manifesto*. But Smith never dwells on the casualties of that restlessness. True, in his day, many of the greatest technical innovations lay a few decades in the future. But by the time *The Wealth of Nations* was published, the spinning jenny was already patented and Arkwright had built his first spinning factory. The defeated Highlanders were beginning to pour into Glasgow to take up work in the cotton mills of Renfrewshire. Right from the first pages of the book, we are made aware of the shape of the future and the explosive potential of the division of labour. In the modern pin factory, ten men turn out as many pins in a day as 240 men used to. What is to become of the other 230 men? In a productive economy they will, sooner or later, find other work, perhaps work just as good if not better. But in the meantime? What economists so blandly describe as 'frictional unemployment', the churning of the labour force between one job and another, can bring desperate families close to starvation as they roam the country for months, sometimes years, looking for a fresh situation.

Modern followers of Adam Smith have sometimes shown a similar unconcern, for example the 'Chicago Boys' who recommended such drastic reforms for the poorly performing economies of South America in the 1980s, and later on in Russia and Eastern Europe after the fall of the Berlin Wall. In the long term, the result was usually a far more prosperous and dynamic economy. But the transition often brought with it an appalling toll in destitution, alcoholism, suicide and even falling life expectancy (as it did in Yeltsin's Russia). Critics queried whether all this was a price worth paying, whether a more careful 'gradation' – to use Adam Smith's own word – could not have reached the same destination at a lesser human cost.

It would be hard to criticize Smith for not having foreseen or devised something like our welfare state. But he can be criticized for failing to see that, as capitalism speeded up – 'turbo-capitalism' as we now call it – far greater institutional protection would be required to shelter those who were blown off their feet by the gale. Undeniably his worst legacy was a certain indifference to the victims of change. You can find that indifference in the mindsets of the most brilliant neoclassical economists today. I have myself listened to their persuasive arguments, basked in their optimism about the sunny future in front of us. But I have always felt that there is something missing. They seem to lack the imaginative capacity to think themselves into other men's shoes, or rather shoelessness. They lack – now, what was Adam Smith's word for it? – they lack sympathy.

V

EDMUND BURKE

and the stickiness of society

'You could not stand five minutes with that man beneath a shed while it rained, but you must be convinced you had been standing with the greatest man you had ever yet seen.'

Dr Johnson's remark on Edmund Burke, related in one of Hester Thrale's anecdotes, is unforgettable. The greatest Tory of the eighteenth century takes off his hat and makes the lowest possible bow to the much younger Irish Whig (Burke's dates are 1729–97, Johnson's 1709–84). Johnson's veneration started a fashion that lasted long after Burke's death. Karl Marx himself denounced Burke as a sycophant and 'out-and-out vulgar bourgeois', but also told the readers of the *New York Daily Tribune* in 1856 that he was 'the man who is held by every party in England as the paragon of British statesmen'. Burke was revered by Tories and Liberals alike, if with rather different motives, not just for his torrential eloquence but as a politician who somehow transcended politics and as a philosopher who uniquely immersed himself in the world.

Then, quite suddenly, it all changed. For the next century or so, Burke was reviled with the same enthusiasm as he had been praised: he was a corrupt placeman, a party hack, a coward and a stick-in-the-mud, a reactionary mystagogue, his speeches and writings irredeemably tainted by his personal corruption and his superstitiousness. In his quirky but compelling book on Burke, *The Great Melody*, Conor Cruise O'Brien fingers James Mill in his *History of British India* as one of the first to put the knife in. On the question of India, Mill says, Burke 'neither stretched his eye to the whole of the subject, nor did he carry its vision to the bottom. He was afraid. He was not a man to explore a new and dangerous path without associates. Edmund Burke lived upon applause ... In the case of public institutions, Mr Burke had also worked himself into an artificial admiration of the bare fact of existence; especially ancient existence. Every thing was to be protected, not because it was good, but because it existed.'

Such a tirade might be expected from Utilitarians, suspicious of Burke's romantic eloquence. Jeremy Bentham dismisses Burke as 'a madman, an incendiary, a caster of verbal filth'. But it is surprising more recently to find Isaiah Berlin lumping Burke in with 'reactionary thinkers' such as Joseph de Maistre. Berlin's friend Stuart Hampshire is contemptuous not simply of Burke's views but of the quality of his thought: 'Burke's rhetoric was mere assertion. It was not proof or even argument. He was not clear and he was not consistent. He saw less far into the future than the philosophical radicals and the men of the Enlightenment, less far certainly than Condorcet ... He was often merely reactionary and frightened.'(Hampshire, p 165)

The continuity between James Mill's critique and Hampshire's is striking. Either these liberal thinkers have detected some essentially meretricious qualities in Burke, something bogus and inflated in his earlier reputation, or they are missing something. Is it possible that such critiques may rest on not having actually read much of Burke? Certainly Berlin, in his generous way, conceded in a correspondence with O'Brien that 'I really should not argue with you about Burke. I know virtually nothing about him except what most people know – the image handed down in history books and conversation, which is plainly not good enough.'

Let us start by saying something very simple – the only wonder is that it's not the first thing that everyone notices. Burke was on the side of the underdog. That is a pallid way of putting what must be an overwhelming impression to anyone who reviews his career. There were at least seven great issues on which he defended the victims of mistreatment with a steely vigour and an unhesitating sympathy. These seven issues deserve to be listed, if only to dispel once and for all the illusion that Burke was the lackey of the rich and powerful.

They are, roughly in the order in which they dominated Burke's life: Wilkes and liberty; the American war; Irish rights; the treatment of debtors; the black slave trade; the treatment of Jews in the West Indies; and – the grand finale – the misdeeds of Warren Hastings and the East India Company.

THE PEOPLE'S FRIEND?

From first to last, he stuck up for John Wilkes and the cause of liberty. He drily recognized Wilkes's failings: 'There has been no hero of the mob but Wilkes'; 'He is not ours, and if he were, is little to be trusted. He is a lively agreeable man, but of no prudence and no principles.' (Letter to Charles O'Hara, 9 June 1768, quoted Bromwich, *Burke*, p. 136) That was putting it mildly. Wilkes was a lecherous scoundrel, as well as a free spirit genuinely dedicated to liberty. But the important thing was that the electors of Middlesex had chosen him. Burke defended Wilkes throughout his struggle to be elected to a House of Commons that repeatedly refused to recognize his election. It was a sacrosanct principle that in a free country the people must be allowed to choose their own representatives. 'Carry the principle on, by which you expelled Mr Wilkes, there is not a man in the House, hardly a man in the Nation, who may not be disqualified,' Burke told his fellow MPs with characteristic hyperbole. (7 February 1771, *Works*, X, p. 63) 'That the people should not choose their own representative is a saying that shakes the Constitution.'

Burke's first major initiative in Parliament was to call for a committee to enquire into the St George's Fields Massacre. There had been a largely peaceful demo to welcome Wilkes on his return from prison to attend the first day of Parliament's sitting (10 May 1768). The soldiers had fired on the unarmed crowd, and between six and eleven people had been killed. In his speech, Burke had warned the government against the increasingly high-handed attitude the authorities were taking towards Wilkes and his supporters: 'If you lay down a Rule that because the people are absurd, their grievances are not to be redressed, then in plain Terms, it is impossible that popular grievances should receive any redress at all, because the people when they are injured will be violent; when they are violent, they will be absurd – and their absurdity will in general be proportioned to the greatness of their Grievances.' (*Writings and Speeches*, II, p. 24)

Burke was passionate about the liberties of the people. And he was passionate about the House of Commons. In his *Representation to His Majesty* (14 June 1784, *Works*, IV, p. 133), he fiercely resisted the insidious claim that the three leading elements in the Constitution – the Crown, the House of Commons and the House of Lords – were equal. Between them, they provided the Constitution with its valuable checks and balances, but the Commons was ultimately supreme. That was why, for example, the Lords ought not to have any power to alter, amend or reject a money bill, as Lord Shelburne was demanding. The Commons was supreme because its authority came from the people.

This does not mean that Burke was a democrat in our modern sense. What he believed in was government for the people, not by the people, and he stubbornly opposed the proposed reforms of Parliament – wider suffrage, more frequent elections, the end of rotten boroughs – on the grounds that, though the British constitution might be imperfect, it worked, and its faults should be corrected only over time and with great caution.

Three times Pitt the Younger tried in vain to persuade the House of Commons to accept a moderate measure of reform. In his last great speech on the subject on 18 April 1785, he argued that representation should always keep pace with changes in population and wealth; it was in fact an ancient part of the law of the land that 'the state of representation was to be changed with change of circumstances'. To remove seats from thirty-six 'decayed boroughs' and make room for seventy-two new MPs in counties where the population was growing was not a reckless innovation, but part of a continuous natural process of reform.

You might have expected Burke to be sympathetic. Did he not believe that 'a state without the means of some change is without the means of its conservation'? (*Reflections*, *Works*, V, pp. 29–438) Had he not mocked the unpeopled borough of Old Sarum, whose only manufacture was the manufacture of MPs? Yet each time Pitt brought forward what may seem to us his mild and incremental proposals, Burke resisted them. Why?

Let's take his first effort, on 7 May 1782. (*Works*, X, pp. 92–108) What Burke says is that the Constitution of England had for ages been the admiration and envy of wise and learned men in every other nation. Now they were told that it was 'infested by the dry rot and ready to tumble about their ears'. But, Burke argues: 'It is a presumption in favour of any settled scheme of government against any untried project, that a nation has long existed and flourished under it.' This continuity was 'a choice not of one day, or one set of people, not a tumultuary and giddy choice; it is a deliberate election of ages and of generations'. To those who said it was a bad and degenerate constitution, Burke says, look to the effects. 'I do not vilify theory and speculation – no, because that would be to vilify reason itself,' he protests. 'No, whenever I speak against theory, I mean always a weak, erroneous, fallacious, unfounded or imperfect theory; and one of the ways of discovering that it is a false theory, is by comparing it with practice.' The question was, did the status quo suit the people? 'I went through most of the Northern parts – the Yorkshire election was then raging; the year before, through most of the Western counties – Bath, Bristol, Gloucester – not one word, either in the towns or country, on the subject of representation; much on the receipt tax, something on Mr Fox's ambition; much greater apprehension of danger from thence than from want of representation.'

The proposers of the reform claimed to be moderate and temperate, but in reality there would be no end to the clamour until exact 'arithmetical' equality of representation was reached. 'The Constitution of England is never to have a quietus; it is to be continually vilified, attacked, reproached, resisted: instead of being the hope and sure anchor in all storms.' In other words, if it ain't broke, don't fix it.

Besides, the existing system offered an invaluable diversity of members: the country seats represented the landed interest, while the so-called rotten boroughs offered convenient access for talented men like Burke, who was now sitting for Lord Rockingham's borough of Malton, and Pitt himself, who sat for Appleby, one of the many seats controlled by Sir James Lowther, the great boroughmonger of the north. As for the unrepresented places, were Warwick and Stafford, which had plenty of members, 'more opulent, happy or free' than Newcastle and Birmingham, which had none? In reality, 'you have an equality of representation, because you have men equally interested in the prosperity of the whole, who are involved in the general interest and the general sympathy'. Not much of an argument when you think about it. If it was good to have the landed interest represented by the country members, why wasn't it equally good to have the manufacturers of Manchester and Newcastle, not to mention the middle and working classes of those great cities, represented too?

Pitt failed, and the cause of reform was lost for a generation, in the upheaval and panic of the Napoleonic Wars. But Burke was wrong, absurdly and totally wrong. Postponing reform, far from quietening the underlying discontent, made it even more unappeasable when it resurfaced, and much of the next century was to be taken up with gradual progress towards that 'arithmetical' equality of representation he feared so much, including the half of the British population nobody in Burke's time even thought about.

At each stage in the broadening of the suffrage, the constitutional sages of the day were just as fearful as Burke had been. After Disraeli's 1867 Reform Act, Walter Bagehot confessed that 'I am exceedingly afraid of the ignorant multitude of the new constituencies'. Twenty years later, A. V. Dicey was scared stiff by the thought of votes for women. Yet we now regard that gradual – and timely – broadening of the right to vote as a key element in the civil peace we have been lucky enough to enjoy ever since. In this crucial respect, Burke *was* frightened, as Stuart Hampshire says, and he was mistaken. He was frightened of the multitudes, and he believed that in a happy society the poor knew their place. For this he was roasted, and rightly roasted by Tom Paine and, as we shall see, reduced to toast by Mary Wollstonecraft. No honest admirer of Burke can overlook this consistent and culpable blindness.

When we come to his famous attack on the French Revolution, we can never quite forget how doggedly he opposed the English evolution. He could and should have followed his own maxim that 'a state without the means of some change is without the means of its conservation'. But he didn't.

THE INVENTION OF AMERICANS

Almost simultaneously, Burke was defending the American colonists in their struggle not to be taxed by a parliament 3,000 miles away. Here we see, perhaps for the first time, Burke's crucially socio-historical bent. It was not simply a sound principle that the people should choose their own governors. In the historical situation of the American colonies, they were going to choose them whether George III and Lord North liked it or not. The colonists had grown away from their mother country, grown too 'Whiggish', become in fact a separate people. There was no point in arguing with that political fact: 'I do not know the method of drawing up an indictment against an whole people.'

In his famous speeches on the American question, on taxation in 1774 and on conciliation in 1775, Burke gives us, with his usual over-flowing eloquence, the standard argument the colonists were putting for 'no taxation without representation'. He points out, too, that direct representation of the American colonists at Westminster is a physical impossibility: 'three thousand miles of ocean lie between you and them. No contrivance can prevent the effect of this distance, in weakening government. Seas roll, months pass, between the order and the execution.' (*Works*, III, p. 56) The only practicable and just solution was to allow the colonists in their popular assemblies to tax themselves in the name of King George – the equivalent of what we would call Dominion status.

These were not unfamiliar arguments, but Burke adds to the strength of them by vividly evoking the extraordinary achievement of the Americans: 'Nothing in the history of mankind is like their progress. For my part, I never cast an eye on their flourishing commerce, and their cultivated and commodious life, but they seem to me rather ancient nations grown to perfection through a long series of fortunate events, and a train of successful industry, accumulating wealth in many centuries, than the colonies of yesterday; than a set of miserable out-casts, a few years ago, not so much sent as thrown out, on the bleak and barren shore of a desolate wilderness three thousand miles from all civilized intercourse.' (*Works*, II, p. 384)

Burke has himself never crossed the Atlantic, but he boldly says; 'I think I know America.' (*Works*, III, p. 160) I think he does. He grasps the spirit of independence and the pride shared by the otherwise painfully different Yankee Puritans and Southern slave-owners. There was no point in trying to prescribe the way they were to be governed. He famously told his constituents in Bristol: 'If any ask me what a free government is, I answer that for any practical purpose, it is what the people think so; and that they, and not I, are the natural, lawful and competent judges of this matter.' (*Works*, III, p. 176)

People accused him of being 'an American'. And he was ready to admit a warm affection for those he still thought of as fellow Englishmen. (III, p. 176) But he knew they weren't, not any more. They were Americans. The term itself as applied to those of European descent rather than to American Indians, or as we would say 'native Americans', is first recorded by the *Oxford English Dictionary* in 1765, only ten years earlier. Burke uses the word as if he had been using it all his life. It was another decade before the United States was to be born, but he could see it coming. And he could see something of the further future too. What would happen if the Crown tried to squash the growth of the American population by refusing to make any more land grants?

The people would occupy without grants. They have already so occupied in many places. You cannot station garrisons in every part of these deserts. If you drive the people from one place, they will carry on their annual tillage, and remove with their flocks and herds to another. Many of the people in the back settlements are already little attached to particular situations. Already they have topped the Appalachian mountains. From thence they behold before them an immense, one vast, rich, level meadow; a square of five hundred miles. Over this they would wander, with-out a possibility of restraint; they would change their manners with the habits of their life; would soon forget a government, by which they were disowned. . . (*Works*, III, pp. 63–4)

In short, the Americans would Go West. And they did.

UNDER IRISH EYES

Burke also strenuously opposed any effort to bring the Americans
to heel, and he remained a steadfast enemy of the war, refusing to
rejoice in any of the several British victories in its early stages. His
loathing of the American war has a further dimension that comes
close to a blanket opposition to war itself. He had been educated
at Abraham Shackleton's Quaker school outside Dublin. In his
prospectus, Shackleton declared that he declined 'to teach that
part of the academic course which he conceives injurious to morals
and subversive of sound principles, particularly those authors who
recommend, in seducing language, the illusions of love and the
abominable trade of war'. Abraham's son Richard became Burke's
best friend (Burke wrote sixty letters to him over five years), and the
Quaker and Huguenot connections, both in Dublin and in Co. Cork
(where Burke's mother originally came from), are not to be under-
estimated. As for his Catholic connections, there was no danger of
those being overlooked. Edmund's mother and his wife were both
Catholics of Irish stock. His father may have converted in order to
pursue his successful legal career. Certainly, the cartoonists kept his
origins in public sight; he was typically portrayed in cassock and
biretta as well as his trademark specs.

From the beginning of his public life to the end of it, Burke
was concerned for the rights of his fellow Irishmen. Among all
his other preoccupations, he never ceased agitating for relief from
their disqualifications and miseries. In the early 1760s, he put
together an elaborate analysis of the penal laws against the Irish,
which he claimed amounted to a deliberate system of persecution.
(*Tracts Relating to Popery Laws*, 1761–65, *Works*, IX, pp. 323–96)
Everywhere you looked in the Irish system – the tenure of property,
the laws of inheritance, education, marriage, the practice of religion, to say nothing of the right to vote – the laws were designed
to degrade and impoverish the Catholics. Since they formed the
large majority of the population (Burke thought 1,600,500; modern
estimates say three million out of a total of four million; Bourke,
p. 409), the Popery laws could be regarded as directed against a
whole nation. (Bourke, pp. 218–22)

In the 1770s, Burke took aim at the cruel restrictions on Irish trade with Britain. Some of these, such as the Cattle Acts of Charles II, banning the sale of Irish livestock in Britain, dated back a century. In one of his letters on Irish trade to his stroppy merchant-constituents in Bristol, he ridiculed the claims of those who opposed the proposed reliefs on Irish trade that they were merely standing up for equality: 'What equality? Do they forget, that the whole woollen manufacture of Ireland, the most extensive and profitable of any, and the natural staple of that kingdom, has been in a manner so destroyed by restrictive laws of ours, and (at our persuasion, and on our promises) by restrictive laws of *their own* [he means laws passed by the Irish Parliament] that in a few years, it is probable, they will not be able to wear a coat of their own fabric? Is this equality?' (*Works*, III, p. 226) Similar restrictions applied to linen, beer and agricultural products. Ireland was being ruined by British laws.

As fans of free trade always discover, he had to persuade his sceptical opponents that trade is not a zero-sum game: 'I know, that it is but too natural for us to see our own certain ruin, in the *possible* prosperity of other people. It is hard to persuade us, that every thing which is *got* by another is not *taken* from ourselves.' (*Works*, III, pp. 223–4) But 'trade is not a limited thing'. 'The prosperity arising from an enlarged and liberal system improves all its objects; and the participation of a trade with flourishing Countries is much better than the monopoly of want and penury.' (Letter to Samuel Span, 9 April 1778, *Corr.* III, p. 426) Besides, some of these fears were 'blind terrors'. The petitioners were alarmed by proposals to legalize the export of sailcloth, cordage and iron from Ireland, but Burke pointed out that these commodities could already be freely imported into Britain. (Speech on Irish trade, 6 May 1778, Bourke, p. 399) Burke was so fluent in economic argument that Adam Smith said 'he was the only man I ever knew who thinks on economic subjects exactly as I do, without any previous communication having passed between us.' (E. G. West, *Adam Smith*, 1969, p. 201)

Then Burke turned his attention to the civil disabilities that Irishmen suffered and 'the Gigantick Prejudice' against them that made them 'aliens in their own country'. (Letter to Sexton Perry, June 16, 1778, *Corr.* III, p. 145) Some progress was being made. In

1782, Catholics gained the right to purchase and bequeath land on the same terms as Protestants. Burke turned to the struggle for recognition by the Catholic clergy, and to a more general agitation for toleration, that 'new virtue' as he called it. (Bourke, pp. 410–19) By the 1790s, his last decade, Burke was exuberantly warning anyone who would listen that Catholic emancipation in the broadest sense was coming: 'They *will* have it, because the nature of things *will* do it.' (Bourke, p. 790) In his widely published 1792 letter to Sir Hercules Langrishe, a prominent member of the Irish House of Commons, who was still unwilling to go the whole way to emancipation, he declared that 'our Constitution is not made for great, general, proscriptive exclusions; sooner or later, it will destroy them, or they will destroy the constitution'. (*Works*, VI, pp. 310–11)

The Penal Laws were responsible for much Irish misery and Irish unrest:

> Their declared object was to reduce the Catholicks of Ireland to a miserable populace, without property, without estimation, without education ... They divided the nation into two distinct bodies, without common interest, sympathy or connexion. One of these bodies was to possess *all* the franchises, *all* the property, *all* the education: the other was to be composed of drawers of waters and cutters of turf for them. Are we to be astonished, when by the effects of so much violence in conquest, and so much policy in regulation, continued without intermission for near an hundred years, we had reduced them to a mob; that whenever they came to act at all, many of them would act exactly like a mob, without temper, measure or foresight? (*Works*, VI, pp. 303–4)

It was to be another thirty years after Burke's death that Catholic emancipation finally arrived through the unlikely agency of the Duke of Wellington and Sir Robert Peel, both previously stern opponents (as Chief Secretary for Ireland, Peel had been known as 'Orange Peel'). But Burke had lit the fuse, and kept on relighting it whenever it spluttered out.

Not Bristol fashion

When the parliamentary session of 1774 ended, Burke's patron Lord Verney was strapped for cash, and so Burke would have to abandon Verney's pocket borough of Wendover, Bucks, and look elsewhere for a seat. Reluctantly, he approached Lord Rockingham, who had first employed Burke as his secretary and then found him the Wendover billet. Rockingham admired Burke almost as much as Burke admired him, and he managed to get him elected for Malton, Yorkshire.

At the very moment of his election, an opening came up for the great city of Bristol, a far more prestigious place to represent. Some local merchants hurried up to London to make Burke an offer, but he was already gone north. They followed him up to Malton and persuaded him to gallop back to Bristol post-haste, at six in the evening of Tuesday 11 October. He arrived in Bristol at 2.30 p.m. on the Thursday, not having slept for two nights. The lord mayor was not at home, and they hurried on to the Guildhall where Burke clambered up onto the hustings, 'reposed himself for a few minutes', then said yes to Bristol. Three weeks later, he was elected, and to the same audience made what was to become the most famous of all his speeches. In terms both uncompromising and crystalline, he set out his vision of an MP's duty to his constituents. Parliament, he said, was not a congress of ambassadors from different and hostile interests. It was a deliberative assembly of one nation, with the whole nation's interests at its heart.

'You choose a member indeed; but when you have chosen him, he is not member of Bristol but member of Parliament.' (*Works*, III, p. 20)

> Certainly, gentleman, it ought to be the happiness and glory of a representative, to live in the strictest union, the closest correspondence, and the most unreserved communication with his constituents. Their wishes ought to have great weight with him; their opinion high respect; their business unremitted attention ... But, his unbiased opinion, his mature judgement, his enlightened conscience, he ought not to sacrifice to you; to any man, or to any

set of men living ... Your representative owes, not his industry
only, but his judgement; and he betrays, instead of serving you, if
he sacrifices it to your opinion. (*Works*, III, pp. 18–19)

Burke's doctrine of representation has become a classic, much
quoted to this day, not only in constitutional textbooks but by many
an MP who finds himself defying his constituents' wishes. Less often
quoted, though no less remarkable, is the last speech he made to
those same Bristol merchants six years later.

His arrival at Bristol was just as hasty and frenetic as it had
been on his first visit. He had got wind of energetic moves in the
city to 'deselect' him, as we now say. He was well aware of how
unpopular he had become among the prosperous merchants, and
their fury at their MP's unpatriotic, 'treasonous' support for the
American rebels, at his pleas on behalf of his fellow Irishmen, and
much else besides.

He resolved to take them head-on. In fact, it is hard to think of
a more magnificently contemptuous speech made by any politician
to his constituents. He had no intention of apologizing for any part
of his record: 'I come to claim your approbation, not to amuse you
with vain apologies, or with professions still more vain and sense-
less.' (*Works*, III, p. 357)

They claimed that he had not visited Bristol often enough (in
fact he had come down only a couple of times, and not at all in
the past four years). Well, he said, he had been knocking himself
out on their behalf up in London. What's more, a visit to Bristol
was no fun at all: 'Gentlemen, I live at an hundred miles distance
from Bristol; and at the end of a session I come to my own house,
fatigued in body and mind, to a little repose, and to a very little
attention to my family and my private concerns. A visit to Bristol
is always a sort of canvas; else it will do more harm than good. To
pass from the toils of a session to the toils of a canvas is the furthest
thing in the world from repose. I could hardly serve you *as I have
done*, and court you too.' (*Works*, III, p. 362) What's more, 'while
I watched, and fasted and sweated in the house of commons', his
constituents were intriguing to quietly move him out of his seat,
'as if I were dead'.

As if all this wasn't offensive enough, he told them plainly that there were times during the American war when they were so inflamed with war fever that 'I should have sooner fled to the extremities of the earth than have shewn myself here'. (*Works*, III, p. 365) Even when the war had come to the disastrous end that he had predicted, he still stayed away from Bristol because he didn't want to look as if he was telling them 'I told you so'. 'I did not wish to have the least appearance of insulting you with that show of superiority, which though it may not be assumed, is generally suspected in a time of calamity, from those whose previous warnings have been despised.' (*Works*, III, p. 366)

They complained too that, on Irish trade, 'I did not consult the interest of my constituents; or, to speak out strongly, that I rather acted as a native of Ireland, than as an English member of parliament.' Well, he had much affection for the country of his birth, but he was no more acting as an Irishman than he had acted as an American when he pleaded for concession and conciliation in the war: 'I did not obey your instructions. No. I conformed to the instructions of truth and nature, and maintained your interest, against your opinions, with a constancy that became me ... I am to look, indeed, to your opinions; but to such opinions as you and I *must* have five years hence. I was not to look to the flash of the day.' That was what he was there for, to take the long view. 'I knew that you chose me, in my place, along with others, to be a pillar of the state, and not a weathercock on top of the edifice, exalted for my levity and versatility, and of no use but to indicate the shiftings of every fashionable gale.' (*Works*, III, p. 374)

They complained, too, that he had given enthusiastic support to Lord Beauchamp's Bill for the relief of debtors in the previous session. They alleged that he had treated their petition against the Bill with indecent contempt. No, he hadn't, he said. On the contrary, he had pushed their petition in front of the Solicitor-General and brought it before the Committee on the Bill too. In fact, it was due to Burke's efforts that the Bill was lost.

Which, he thought, was a great pity. Lord Beauchamp's Bill was 'a law of justice and policy, as far as it went'. It was a scandal that 'in all cases of civil insolvency, without a pardon from his creditors, the debtor is to be imprisoned for life – and thus a miserable mistaken invention of artificial science, operates to change a civil into a criminal judgement, and to scourge misfortune or indiscretion with a punishment which the law does not inflict on the greatest crimes.' (*Works*, III, p. 377) Worse still, this punishment was inflicted, not by a professional, impartial judge but at 'the individual discretion of a private, nay interested, and irritated, individual'. (*Works*, III, p. 377) When John Howard, the great penal reformer, visited Rotterdam, he found only one man imprisoned for debt in the whole city; in England, there were 3,000. All this, says Burke with magnificent scorn, to appease the fears of the Bristol burghers that credit might be weakened if debtors were not punished with the utmost severity.

It was a magnificent performance but politically suicidal. Though his remaining supporters dragged him to the poll, it soon became clear that he was done for, and he withdrew from the contest three days later. For the rest of his political career, he sat in Lord Rockingham's lap, as MP for Malton, the seat from which he had withdrawn in such haste six years earlier.

He had concluded from his Bristol years, not only that it was the MP's duty 'to look the people in the face whenever our instruction is greater than theirs', but also that, when stirred up, the people 'are naturally proud, tyrannical and ignorant, bad scholars and worse masters'. (Bourke, p. 388) At the same time, ultimately if unfortunately, the people *were* the masters. They were more often right than wrong, and, if they did not like their MP, it was up to them to remove and replace him.

Bitter experience had turned Burke into what might be called a disillusioned democrat, or a democratic elitist. He acknowledged the contradictions of his position, without showing any inclination to shift it in either direction – forward towards support for full-blown democracy or backward to aristocratic oligarchy. The contradictions recurred throughout his life: if the country landowners deserved to be directly represented in Parliament, why not the urban manufacturers? If Irish Catholics deserved a share of government, why not the English lower orders? But in those tumultuous and often terrifying times, Burke thought it was better to live with these imperfections. For him, civil peace came a long way before constitutional improvement. Only very occasionally, as in Ireland, was he ready to concede that improving the constitution might be the only way to keep the peace.

For Burke personally, though, it would be impossible to sit again for a populous city. He could enjoy the freedom of speech and conscience that he cherished above everything else only in the tranquillity of a pocket borough, where there were no voters to annoy, or none that dared gainsay their noble patron.

THE WRETCHED OF THE EARTH

Edmund Burke had always loathed the slave trade. With his friend William Burke (no relation), he had published in 1757 *An Account of European Settlements in America*, which denounced the British slave trade as more ferocious than any other. (*Accounts*, II, pp. 128–9; Bourke, p. 596) The horrific treatment of British slaves was scarcely excused by the fact that they had been African slaves first. When he was still MP for Bristol, he had publicly condemned the trade as being 'of the most inhuman nature, a traffic for human bodies'. (Speeches on slave trade, 5 June 1777 and 14 May 1778; quoted Bourke, p. 596)

That was bad enough in the eyes of the Bristol merchants, who were the prime profiteers from the traffic. They would have been even keener to get rid of Edmund if they had known that in 1780 he was already hard at work on a scheme to gradually abolish the trade altogether. It was, he said, 'the most shameful trade that ever the hardened heart of man could bear' and 'rather than suffer it to continue as it is, I heartily wish it at an end'. But he recognized the interests of the slave merchants and the economic dislocation that would be caused by immediate abolition. So he devised a detailed blueprint for its slow strangulation, his *Sketch of a Negro Code* (*Writings and Speeches*, III, pp. 568–80), which he allowed to be sent to Pitt's home secretary Henry Dundas in 1792. Under the *Code*, there would be strict controls over the transport of slaves: breathing room, diet, medical treatment. On arrival, there were to be severe criminal sanctions against maltreatment or the seizure of their property; plantations were to have churches and schools; brighter pupils would be sent to the Bishop of London for further education, where they would automatically become free, though Burke does not spell this out. Above all, families were not to be separated, and slave-owners would have to offer proper support to pregnant and nursing mothers and their children. Blacks over the age of thirty with three children or more would be entitled to purchase their freedom at half their market value. All this would make slave-holding so costly as to become ultimately unviable.

But what should also be noted is how Burke goes beyond sloganizing for abolition and sets himself to work out a more tolerable way of life for slave families during the transition.

I must mention here another, far smaller group of wretched and dispossessed victims in the New World, whose cause Burke also championed. During the American war, the British invaded the Dutch-owned Caribbean island of Sint Eustatius and roughed up the inhabitants. The brutality was all the more callous because the tiny volcanic island had recently been flattened by a hurricane. The people who came off worst were the little band of Jewish merchants who resided there. They were banished from Sint Eustatius, leaving behind not only their houses and merchandise but their wives and children. They were confined in a makeshift jail, where they were stripped and robbed of every shilling, before being thrown off the island.

Their plight might have been utterly forgotten except for Burke's speech of 14 May 1781, which lasted just short of three hours:

> The persecution was begun with the people, whom of all others it ought to be the care and the wish of humane nations to protect, the Jews. Having no fixed settlement in any part of the world, no kingdom nor country in which they have a government, a community, and a system of laws, they are thrown upon the benevolence of nations, and claim protection and civility from their weakness, as well as from their utility ... Their abandoned state and their defenceless situation calls most forcibly for the protection of civilised nations. (Bromwich, pp. 429–30; Bourke, pp. 435–9)

Burke wheels on the big guns of international law to support his argument: Pufendorf, Vattel, Grotius, Gentili. Whether you invoked the law of nations or the natural law or the laws of war, conquerors had a duty of clemency. They had a duty to acquit themselves, as Montesquieu had put it, 'in the eye of humanity'. Wherever possible, Burke invokes philosophical theory to support his case for humane conduct. But you can always see that at the back of his mind he has the duties of a Christian.

THE DISHONOURABLE COMPANY

Then finally comes the greatest of all Burke's campaigns against injustice: his crusade against the East India Company that consumed a whole decade of his life. He was a slow convert to the cause. In the late 1760s, he had been suspicious of the Crown's attempts to intervene in the Company's affairs. It was only in the mid-1770s that humanitarian concern for the welfare of the Indian population began to overwhelm him. His real obsession took hold when he joined the new Select Committee on Indian Affairs, himself writing the Committee's incisive Ninth and Eleventh Reports that came out in 1783. (Bourke, p. 517)

Fox's Bill to regulate the so-called Honourable Company fell when the Fox–North coalition fell, but Burke had nailed his colours to that mast. In his marvellous speech on Fox's Bill, delivered on 1 December 1783, he took aim at the basic premise of the existing system: 'Magna charta is a charter to restrain power, and to destroy monopoly. The East India charter is a charter to establish monopoly and to create power.' (Works, IV, p. 9) The rule of this private company over a huge nation had led to despotism, beggary and famine for the millions of Indians it was supposed to protect.

Burke was eager to remind the House exactly who the Indians were: 'This multitude of men does not consist of an abject and barbarous populace; much less of gangs of savages, like the Guaraníes and Chiquitos, who wander on the waste borders of the river of Amazons, or the Plate; but a people for ages civilized and cultivated; cultivated by all the arts of polished life, whilst we were yet in the woods.' (Works, IV, p. 18)

And how had the Company treated them? 'There is not a *single* prince, state or potentate, great or small, in India, with whom they have come into contact, whom they have not sold ... there is not a *single treaty* they have ever made, which they have not broken ... there is not a single prince or state, who ever put any trust in the company, who is not utterly ruined.' (*Works*, IV, p. 21) The motives of the Company were uniformly mercenary, and its conduct cynical. Its servants stayed in India only long enough to pile up a fortune in rupees or pagodas (the currency of southern India): 'The natives scarcely know what it is to see the grey head of an Englishman. Young men (boys almost) govern there, without society, and without sympathy with the natives. They have no more social habits with the people, than if they still resided in England; nor indeed any species of intercourse but that which is necessary to making a sudden fortune.' (*Works*, IV, p. 40) Every rupee of profit made by an Englishman was lost for ever to India. England had erected no churches or schools or hospitals, dug no roads or canals, built no bridges. The reservoirs that fed the paddy fields were broken down, the rivers silted up, the people in once prosperous districts now starving.

Here, for the first time, he launches the catalogue of charges directly aimed at the long-serving Governor-General from 1773 to 1785, Warren Hastings. For Burke, Hastings is to become 'the Captain-General of Iniquity'. Here he lists some of the major charges against him: the stripping and violation of the Princesses of Oude; the maltreatment of the Rajah of Benares; the failure to relieve the dreadful famine in Bengal.

All these charges and many more were to be repeated in Burke's relentless and interminable impeachment of Hastings, which lasted seven years from 1788 to 1795 and ended in acquittal by an exhausted and death-depleted House of Lords. Like many great orators, Fidel Castro and Mr Gladstone for example, Burke was inclined to go on and on. His critics in the House of Commons dubbed him 'the dinner bell' – you could go off to dine in the certainty that he would still be on his feet when you came back. It may be that the sheer unstoppable volume of his indictment eventually proved counter-productive, evoking a spasm of sympathy for

Hastings, not to mention an uneasy feeling among the directors of the Company that he probably had not done anything much worse than they themselves had done in their Indian days.

Was Hastings guilty as charged? He was certainly high-handed, and anyone who gazes today on his vast palace at Alipore, Kolkata, or on his great English country house, Daylesford in the Cotswolds, will not be surprised that he made a huge fortune out of India. But his level of personal corruption was probably not much above the average, and he had an above-average interest in Indian language, art and culture, and had helped found several colleges and the Bengal Asiatic Society. He did try, too, to cut out the more out-rageous practices of British traders and middlemen, such as the appalling Paul Benfield who seduced the Nawab of Arcot, himself a nasty piece of work, into penury and gained hold of the tax revenues of the Nawab's richest provinces. (Speech on the Nawab of Arcot's debts, February 1785, *Works*, IV, pp. 185–444)

What we need to do is look beyond Burke's blunderbuss attacks on Hastings personally and take in his more acute dissection of the system that turned both high-ups like Hastings and lowlifes like Benfield into millionaires. Burke puts his finger on the particular set of fraudulent practices by which the British authorities got a grip on province after province:

> The invariable course of the company's policy is this: either they set up some prince too odious to maintain himself without the necessity of their assistance; or they soon render him odious by making him the instrument of their government. In that case troops are bountifully sent to him to maintain his authority. That he should have no want of assistance, a civil gentleman, called a resident, is kept at his court, who under pretence of providing duly for the pay of these troops, gets assignments on the revenue into his hands. Under his provident management, debts soon accumulate; new assignments are made for these debts; until, step by step, the whole revenue, and with it the whole power of the country, is delivered into his hands. (Speech on the Nawab of Arcot's debts, February 1785, *Works*, IV, pp. 49–50)

In theory, Pitt's Act of 1784, which succeeded Fox's Bill, was supposed to put a stop to these insidious land-grabs. The Act said explicitly that Britain had no further territorial ambitions in India: 'To pursue schemes of conquest and extension of dominion in India are measures repugnant to the wish, the honour and the policy of the nation.' As the nineteenth century wore on, the British Raj, as it now began to be called, did begin to build churches and colleges, and to dig canals and eventually railways. Yet the seizure of native territory went on remorselessly. One Governor-General after another pursued precisely the same greedy manoeuvres right up to the great Mutiny of 1857. My own great-great-grandfather John Low, as Resident of Hyderabad, acting on the orders of the egregious Lord Dalhousie, pulled off the same trick in 1853, strong-arming the Nizam into surrendering his cotton-rich provinces to the British Crown. The most notorious of the grabbers before Dalhousie was Richard Wellesley, whose conduct managed to shock his own brother, the future Duke of Wellington, then a young commander in India.

Burke's impeachment of the man might have failed. His grand critique of the system was irrefutable – and unheeded.

The party spirit

Now this is a remarkable record: these seven staunch defences of very different peoples and communities, ranging from the millions in India to a handful of Jews on an obscure West Indian island, each of them oppressed in one way or another by a more powerful nation, Burke's own adopted nation. In defending them, he was utterly undeterred by his own political interests and patrons. He stood as defiant against the merchants of Bristol when he was their MP as against the plutocrats of London to whom he owed or from whom he hoped advancement. Nor was he influenced by the near-ness or remoteness of the people he was speaking up for: he was as careful of the rights of voters in Middlesex as of those Jews on a faraway island.

We can, I think, separate his motives into two categories, though the two categories overlap. The first was his sense of the moral duty we owe to all our fellow men, to treat them with kindness and respect, to treat them as equals. These principles come direct to us through the Christian tradition, straight from the Gospels. They are historically derived in Burke's eyes as well as divinely derived. There can be no arguing with them.

The second, overlapping motive is Burke's insistence that we must respect the arrangements of other societies, including their political and religious beliefs and their social traditions and customs. This was a much more unusual belief at the time, unusual at any time in recorded history in fact. It was from Montesquieu that Burke had derived his understanding of the huge diversity of human society, and of the factors that had shaped their differences – their history, their climate, their economic resources, their language. But it was Burke who coloured this understanding with an intense moral warmth.

Britain, he said, had to respect the wishes of the American colonists because they had grown into a separate society with its own values and political system. They had become different. In the case of Ireland, the faith and culture of the Catholic majority had always been stubbornly different. However alien it might seem to the settlers of the Protestant ascendancy, that was no excuse for denying the Catholic Irish their civil rights or for cutting off their textile trade to protect their competitors in Great Britain.

Most spectacularly of all, Burke threw himself wholeheartedly into the defence of the culture, religion and commerce of India – a country he never visited and knew only from books. True, he was not alone in his scorn for the returning British Nabobs or for the officially approved exploitation of the natives. But for someone who never left Europe, he had an amazing sympathy for the rajas and their world, with all its glaring faults.

We would today describe Burke's sympathy for ancient alien cultures that others thought backward and barbaric as coming close to 'relativism'. Burke, though, would have argued – and did argue – that his sympathy was grounded in principles derived from our common human nature. If you were tender about the lives and liberties of other peoples, you had a duty to respect their cultures too.

You can see why Burke might have been mocked and loathed in

his own day, and why he was caricatured as an Irish bumpkin or as a tool of the Catholic Church. What is puzzling at first sight, though, is that he should be loathed by so many modern liberal-minded writers who, you would imagine, must surely share his tolerance and sympathy. What is it about Burke that gets their goat?

The first thing that inflames this aversion, I think, is the way Burke plunged headlong into party politics. His speeches and writings are so immersed in political negotiation as often to be inaccessible to modern readers, and also for that reason rather off-putting. He deliberately avoids the marmoreal detachment from the fray that we are accustomed to in political thinkers. Worse still, Burke refuses to regard parties as a grubby tactical necessity. On the contrary, he presents party affiliation as a noble aspect of political life. David Bromwich, in his fine study of Burke's intellectual life, reminds us that Burke never uttered those famous words attributed to him: 'The only thing necessary for the triumph of evil is for good men to do nothing.' What he did say was: 'When bad men combine, the good must associate; else they will fall, one by one, an unpitied sacrifice in a contemptible struggle.' Burke was proud to be a leader of the Rockingham Whigs, who have a claim to be the first ongoing political party in British history, for 'Commonwealths are made of families, free commonwealths of parties also; and we may as well affirm that our natural regards and ties of blood tend inevitably to make men bad citizens as that the bonds of our party weaken those by which we are held to our country'. (quoted Bromwich, p. 2)

In his well-turned account of Burke's thought, which makes up the second half of his *Edmund Burke* (2013), the Conservative MP Jesse Norman sets out the reasons for seeing parties as indispensable to politics: they bring stability, they bring openness (collectively agreed principles cannot be kept dark), they tend to moderate and control headstrong governments, and if a party fails to represent the people as they wish to be represented, another party will come along to replace it. Parties do not need great men like Lord Chatham to lead them; they can be managed by ordinary people who may well have a better idea of what other ordinary men and women actually want.

None of these reasons has tickled the fashionable fancy, then or now. Intellectual opinion has been more inclined to lament with Oliver Goldsmith that his friend Burke,

> Who, born for the universe, narrow'd his mind
> And to party gave up what was meant for mankind.
> Though fraught with all learning, yet straining his throat
> To persuade Tommy Townshend to lend him a vote.

Goldsmith and Burke were both clubbable men and members of Dr Johnson's famous dining fraternity, The Club. Burke could not imagine life without such associations, out of Parliament or in it:

> How men can proceed without any connexion at all, is to me utterly incomprehensible. Of what sort of materials must that man be made, how must he be tempered and put together, who can sit whole years in Parliament, with five hundred and fifty of his fellow citizens, amidst the storm of such tempestuous passions, in the sharp conflict of so many wits, and tempers, and characters, in the discussion of such vast and ponderous interests, without seeing any one sort of men, whose character, conduct, or disposition would lead him to associate himself with them, to aid and be aided, in any one system of public utility? (*Works*, II, p. 340)

Yet of course, there have been many such loners, both in politics and in academic life, who find association irksome. Rousseau and Marx, for example, shared a preference for solitary enquiry; Marx and Engels wrote to each other, congratulating themselves on belonging to a party of two. Much political philosophy bears the stamp of such men, tending to concentrate on the individual on the one hand and the mass movement on the other. To intellectuals in general, party is seen more as a means of asserting discipline than of a pleasurable association. Party loyalty is seen as a loss of intellectual integrity rather than an admirable human quality. Burke, by contrast, does not see the conflict between conscience and party as much of a problem: 'A man must be peculiarly unfortunate in his choice of political company if he does not agree with them at least nine times in ten. If he does not concur in these general principles upon which the party is founded, and which necessarily draw on a concurrence in their application, he ought from the beginning to have chosen some other, more conformable to his opinions.' (*Works*, II, p. 339)

More off-putting still is the thought that the arguments in defence of party might be deployed in the service of *any* party, including a party you regard as deplorable or disgusting. In Burke's case, it remains hotly disputed which party is entitled to claim his legacy. Even the admirable Professor Bromwich seems to lose his cool for a moment when he declares that 'no serious historian today would repeat the commonplace that Burke was the father of modern conservatism'. The load-bearing word in that sentence is 'historian'. Of course, Burke was a Whig all his life until he backed Pitt in the French war, and he had little or nothing in common with the Tories of the day. But modern conservatives, especially in the United States, claim Burke as their ancestor, not on account of his political programme in the 1770s and 1780s, but rather because of his disposition to 'slow politics', to an inching forward on the secure foundation of inherited settlements and loyalties – a claim based on political *philosophy* rather than on political *history*.

As for being an 'irrationalist', as his enemies then and now claim, Burke repeatedly denied that he was any such thing. On the contrary, Burke declares himself a thoroughgoing empiricist: 'The science of constructing a commonwealth, or renovating it, or reforming it, is, like every other experimental science, not to be taught *a priori* ... We must look to the evidence ... Circumstances (which with some gentlemen pass for nothing) give in reality to every political principle its distinguishing colour and discriminating effect.'

The attention to circumstance must be close and unremitting, for society is 'a dense medium', never easy to penetrate or get the hang of. 'I must see with my own eyes,' Burke insists. 'I must, in a manner, touch with my own hands, not only the fixed but the momentary circumstances before I could venture to suggest any political project whatsoever ... I must see all the aids, and all the obstacles. I must see the means of correcting the plan, where correctives would be wanted. I must see the things; I must see the men.' As policy wonks have discovered time and again, even the best evidence-based policies stand or fall by the context into which they are introduced.

If politics is a science, then it is a kind of geology. As J. W. Burrow puts it: 'The common law is not a creation of heroic judges but the slow, anonymous sedimentation of immemorial custom; the constitution is no gift but the continuous self-defining public activity of the nation.' Burke is a sedimentalist, just as he is, in a non-pejorative sense, a sentimentalist. The sentiments of the people, himself included, are political facts accreted over time, which cannot be ignored or easily overridden in the interests of abstract principles, however desirable. The thought experiment so beloved of philosophers from Hobbes and Locke to John Rawls, of men in the state of nature coming together to conclude a social contract, would have seemed to Burke a sophistical fantasy. Burke foreshadows the nineteenth century in seeing everything – law, morality, solidarity – as historically evolved, the outcome of experience rather than design.

Conservatives claiming a share of Burke need to understand that they are adopting a demanding ancestor. For Burke insists that much of our inheritance, from classical antiquity, from the Christian Fathers and from the great lawyers of the Renaissance, requires that we cannot be indifferent to the sufferings of our fellow men anywhere in the world. Hard-hearted pseudo-realism is incompatible with Burkean sympathies. For again and again, he declares that 'the principles of true politics are those of morality enlarged'. None of which ought to put off the *bien pensants*, for they too subscribe to those same moral principles.

No theatricks

So what is it that still nags them about Burke? The answer, I think, is to do with culture, even with aesthetics. It is worth spending a fair bit of time on Burke's two earliest works, written in his twenties: *A Vindication of Natural Society* and *A Philosophical Enquiry into the Origin of Our Ideas of the Sublime and Beautiful*. The first is a

parody intended to explode the myth that man in the state of nature
was happier than when he fell under the control of artificial governments that had brought so much misery and slaughter. The trouble
with the *Vindication* is that Burke carries the parody off with such
gusto that innocent readers such as William Godwin took it literally
and were convinced by the myth that it was intended to demolish;
some even believed that it might be the work of Bolingbroke, who
was actually Burke's target.

The second edition had to be rescued by a new preface that
revealed something of what Burke was really up to. This preface
identified Bolingbroke as the target, referring to 'the inaccuracies
in calculation, in reasoning, or in method' for which that great
statesman-philosopher was notorious.

Despite this warning, only the wideawake reader is likely to
appreciate fully that the institutions that the supposed author, an
anonymous Noble Lord, is attacking with such gusto are precisely
those institutions Edmund Burke cherished: the Established Church
and revealed religion, British parliamentary government, the Nation
State and, of course, political parties, which he regards as an essential ingredient of healthy politics and good government. You can
feel Burke getting carried away by the rhetoric he is supposed to
be parodying. For example, the *Vindication* lays into the famous
democracy of Athens with all guns blazing: 'The whole history of
this celebrated republic is but one tissue of rashness, folly, ingratitude, injustice, tumult, violence and tyranny. This was the city
which banished Themistocles, starved Aristides, forced into exile
Miltiades, drove out Anaxagoras and poisoned Socrates.' (*Works*,
I, pp. 50–1)

All of which has enough truth in it to make the reader pause and
think: 'Well, perhaps Athens wasn't so great after all.'

So, if the *Vindication* is a brilliant squib, it is also a squib that
backfires. For us, I think, its importance is that, right at the outset
of his career, this 25-year-old Irishman without wealth or connections to speak of announces himself not only as a writer of dazzling
eloquence, but also as a reasoned and impassioned defender of all
the things that the brilliant savants of the eighteenth century were
so gleefully attacking. The *Vindication* is not just an assault on the

homegrown *illuminati* like Bolingbroke. Behind Bolingbroke and his like, Burke is taking aim at the great European figures: Voltaire and Rousseau. His life is to be devoted to rebuilding much of what they have sought to demolish. The *Vindication* may in a sense be a flop, but it is a resonant flop.

The *Enquiry*, by contrast, is an excursion of daring and originality that defines the Sublime and Beautiful in recognizably modernist terms. Burke begins by asserting that 'the first and the simplest emotion that we discover in the human mind is curiosity. By curiosity, I mean whatever desire we have for, or whatever pleasure we take in, novelty.' The quest for the Sublime drags us away from 'those things which a daily vulgar use have brought into a stale, unaffecting familiarity'. (ibid., pp. 121–22) The quest is driven by our restless desire to be astonished, if possible to be frightened out of our wits. 'Whatever is fitted in any sort to excite the ideas of pain and danger ... is a source of the Sublime.'(ibid., p. 133)

The ideal of the Beautiful, by contrast, is associated with warmth, smoothness and delicacy, in fact with loveableness. Burke refers with approval to Hogarth's 'serpentine line of beauty', and he gives us the most sensuous example possible: 'Consider that part of a beautiful woman where she is perhaps the most beautiful, about the neck and breasts; the smoothness; the softness; the easy and insensible swell.' (ibid., pp. 239–40) Yet Burke leaves us with the half-spoken impression that the Beautiful is somehow a less great, if more seductive, ideal than the Sublime. In parts of his treatment, the Beautiful sounds uncomfortably like what a stern modern critic might mock as *kitsch* or *gemütlich*.

The Sublime is something else. Sublime art, Burke tells us, is not a school of morals; it has little to do with good breeding or good taste, and nothing to do with proportion or fitness of purpose as previous art critics had asserted. At bottom, the Sublime is a quest for sensation. Both in nature and in art, the principal passion that it causes is terror. All sorts of things can intensify the terror – darkness, loudness, piercing shrieks, thunder. The Sublime – and this is almost Burke's most interesting point – is quite consistent with *ugliness*. Burke would have been quick to see how the distortion of a Picasso head was another route of access to the Sublime. Art shocks and awes; it is only by accident that modernism's great mantra, 'the shock of the new', does not crop up somewhere in the text. Burke would certainly agree that art ought to be 'edgy', its jagged outlines not worn down by habit or familiarity. Art is meant to be uncomfortable, to be 'disturbing', to use another favourite epithet of the modern critic.

The *Enquiry*'s definitions of the Sublime and the Beautiful were to be influential in the evolution of the romantic movement. For aestheticians, the *Enquiry* has never lost its importance. Yet it was Burke's only excursion into pure aesthetics. For the rest of his life, what he wrote and spoke about was politics – to be sure, politics in its broadest sense, taking in religion and society and a lot else, but all conceived in a political framework. That is, he was concerned with the well-being of the nation, not the nature of art.

So the *Enquiry* might seem like something of a deviation in Burke's life, even a dead end. But it isn't. It left a mark on his thought that, if anything, became more and more important to him as he grew older. What the *Enquiry* taught him was the difference between art and politics. Burke came to see politics as everything that art is not: politics is about preserving the familiar and the hum-drum, about gradual and cautious change, about keeping people safe, about not frightening people. For those purposes, politics requires a steady, undistracted mind, not a raving genius. Often a second-class mind is what the situation requires. Thirty years later, he wrote in his masterwork, *Reflections on the Revolution in France*: 'I have never yet seen any plan which has not been mended by the observations of those who were much inferior in under-standing to the person who took the lead in the business.' Burke's own rhetoric is often soaring and memorable, but in thrilling to his cadences we should never forget that the things he is defending are the small, the unremarkable, the familiar places and customs, whose beauty – he would not be ashamed to use the word – lies in their ordinariness, even their banality.

For Burke then, the crucial point is that art is the opposite of politics as it ought to be practised, that is, as a down-to-earth man-agement of life with all its everyday needs and hackneyed hopes. It was to be Burke's key criticism of the French revolutionaries thirty-five years later that they sought to aestheticize politics; they titillated their public by a series of sensational tableaux:

> Statesmen, like your present rulers, exist by everything which is spurious, fictitious and false; by everything which takes the man from his house, and sets him on a stage, which makes him up an artificial creature, with painted theatrick sentiments, fit to be seen by the glare of candle-light, and formed to be contemplated at a due distance ... If the system of institution recommended by the assembly is false and theatrick it is because their system of government is of the same character. (*Letter to a Memeber of the National Assembly*, *Works*, VI, pp. 34–5)

The aim of the revolutionaries was to make politics irresistibly exciting and to make political life all-consuming. In a revolutionary state, the citizen is expected to be politically alert and involved all day long. This approach is dogmatically opposed to the more relaxed mode of politics, one that aspires only to devise and maintain the arrangements that are necessary for the citizen to get on with his own life. That is Burke's mode.

We need to remind ourselves that *Reflections on the Revolution in France* was published in November 1790, before the September Massacres and the Terror and the execution of the king and queen. At that point, it was not only the radicals who were still exclaiming with Charles James Fox that the Revolution was the greatest and the best event that had ever happened to the world. Pitt himself had declared a few months earlier that 'the present convulsions of France must, sooner or later, terminate in general harmony ... thus circumstanced, France ... will enjoy just that kind of liberty which I venerate'. At such a moment, it required an amazing jump of the imagination for a Whig like Burke to forecast all the horrors to come, up to and including the rise of Napoleon:

> In the weakness of one kind of authority, and in the fluctuation of all, the officers of an army will remain for some time mutinous and full of faction, until some popular general, who understands the art of conciliating the soldiery, and who possesses the true

> spirit of command, shall draw the eyes of all men upon him-
> self ... the moment in which that event shall happen, the person
> who really commands the army is your master; the master (that
> is little) of your king, the master of your Assembly, the master of
> your whole republic. (*Works*, V, pp. 390–1)

So much for seeing less far into the future than Condorcet (who, we
may presume, did not see as far as his own suicide when on the run
from Robespierre). If Burke was frightened, well, it turned out that
there was plenty to be frightened of, most immediately a world war
that was destined to last more than twenty years.

What Burke also foresaw, as Pitt did not, was that this brutal
rupture with the past would not easily settle down into a new nor-
mality. It was to take a century and a half and four more French
Republics before the wounds of 1789 were finally healed. Yet Burke
was not to be forgiven by his old friends for his clairvoyance. His
attitude seemed to them a baffling betrayal. As a good Whig, he
had endorsed the Glorious Revolution in England. The American
revolutionaries had had no more loyal friend. Why then did he draw
back in horror from this third and greatest revolution? Not merely
the Foxites in his own day but a good part of liberal posterity have
refused to recognize the distinction he sought to make: that in
England in 1688, as in the American colonies in 1776, the aim was
to continue an existing political culture, and to strengthen it by
careful and restricted reforms. In France in 1789, the aim was utterly
different. In the words of Rabaut Saint-Étienne, quoted by Burke in
the *Reflections*: 'All the institutions in France reinforce the misery
of the people. To make the people happy, it is necessary to renew
them completely: change their ideas, change their laws, change their
morals; change the men, change the things, change the words ...
destroy everything, yes, destroy everything, since everything has to
be re-created.' Begin again from scratch; *tabula rasa*, Year Zero,
Chairman Mao, Pol Pot. Rabaut was a Protestant pastor and a
relatively moderate revolutionary, swept along by the giddy times
and guillotined in 1793 along with the other Girondins. There were
great men caught up in the American Revolution who thought a bit
like that at the time. Such is the drift of Jefferson's famous letter,

'The Earth belongs to the living', in which he suggests that it ought to be possible for each generation of men to begin anew, cleared of ancestral debts and antiquated laws. But America did not turn out that way. On the contrary, the United States was to become a living monument of constitutional conservatism, uniquely reverent towards precedent and towards its Founding Fathers. The rhetoric of novelty remained, but the practice of politics became decidedly Burkean, which is why Burke is today revered more in the United States than anywhere else.

MUD, MUD, GLORIOUS MUD

We have seen that Burke can justly be criticized as a stick-in-the-mud, as someone overly frightened of political change in general and of democracy in particular, fearful of upheaval and terrified of the damage the mob could do when it is roused. This is in fact the principal indictment against him, and there is undeniably something in it.

At the same time, though, Burke is worth listening to when he declares in effect that the mud is not a bad place to stick in. To talk of Burke as 'a defender of tradition' is certainly not inaccurate, but it is a rather thin description. What Burke is really on about is what today we call 'cultural identity'.

Let us recall those most famous passages in the *Reflections*:

To be attached to the subdivision, to love the little platoon we belong to in society, is the first principle, the germ as it were, of public affections. It is the first link in the series by which we proceed towards a love to our country and to mankind ... No man ever was attached by a sense of pride, partiality, or real affection, to a description of square measurement. He never will glory in belonging to the Chequer No. 71, or to any other badge-ticket. We begin our public affections in our families. No cold relation is a zealous citizen. We pass on to our neighbours and our habitual provincial connections. These are inns and resting places. Such divisions of our country as have been forced by habit and not by a sudden jerk of authority, are so many little images of that great

country in which the heart found something which it could fill.
(*Works*, V, pp. 100, 352–3)

Notice the repetition of certain words: attached ... love ...
belong ... affection ... connection ... association ... link. You will
find these words everywhere in Burke, for everywhere, whatever his
immediate concern, he is celebrating the *stickiness* of human society. For Burke, we are formed by our adhesions. While Rousseau
starts off with that dazzling declaration that man is born free but
is everywhere in chains, Burke glorifies those chains that link us
together and define who we are.

David Bromwich, the most acute modern critic of Burke, draws
on him for the title of his collections of essays on culture and politics, *Moral Imagination*. That phrase is drawn from the passage in
Reflections where Burke declares that he thought 10,000 swords must
have leapt from their scabbards to avenge the mob's assault on Marie
Antoinette, but the age of chivalry is gone: 'All the decent drapery of
life is to be rudely torn off. All the superadded ideas, furnished from
the wardrobe of a moral imagination, which the heart owns, and the
understanding ratifies, as necessary to cover the defects of our naked
shivering nature, and to raise it to a dignity in our own estimation,
are to be exploded as a ridiculous, absurd, and antiquated fashion.'
Bromwich justly points out that this wardrobe 'furnishes habitual
ideas' which are the product of culture and custom. What do the
contents of this wardrobe amount to? Our cultural identity.

But Bromwich does not think that cultural identity is therefore
intrinsically valuable. On the contrary, he regards it as potentially
harmful. In 'A Dissent on Cultural Identity', he sets out his position
with brutal candour: 'That cultural identity is "a permanent feature
of human life" is trivially true. We all come from somewhere ...
But why must each of us be more than matter-of-fact in committing
our lives to our history, our culture, our identity? They – culture,
history, identity – have done many things for us and many things
to us. What makes us affect gratitude instead of anger in return?'

We are perfectly entitled to junk our cultural identity if we don't
like it, Bromwich thinks. We can stand outside it and start afresh
tomorrow if we fancy, as several writers whom Bromwich admires

have done. Is that what Jefferson meant? Is that what being an American means? If so, Bromwich muses, 'one might choose to treat America as the rare case of normal humanity and not therefore eccentric'. He does not conceal his hope that somehow cultural identity – including religious identity – will disappear from the public square: 'The thing to do with a cultural identity is to keep it to yourself.' The sooner the lot of us are detribalized, the better.

In today's world, Burke would argue just as vigorously as he did in his own day that cultural identity is both an abiding consolation and a stubborn political fact. Witness the harsh collision across the world between secular urban elites and pious rural peasantries. The costs of these collisions show little sign so far of melting away under the benign rays of modernization and globalization. Look at the triumphs of Donald Trump and Narendra Modi, look at Brexit. In America, India and the UK, those three great countries to whose welfare Burke devoted so much of his life, wallowing in the old mud still retains its charms. These recent reversions to type have startled political commentators everywhere. They would not have surprised Edmund Burke.

VI

THOMAS JEFFERSON

and the endless revolution

THE AUTHOR – OR THE DRAUGHTSMAN?

There are two stories about how Thomas Jefferson came to write the Declaration of Independence. The first is Jefferson's own account: 'The committee of five met; no such thing as a sub-committee was proposed, but they unanimously pressed on myself alone to undertake the draught.' (Jefferson to James Madison, 30 August 1823, *Writings*, I, p. 27fn) The other comes from John Adams, Jefferson's grumpy, brilliant predecessor both as vice-president and as president of the United States:

> The sub-committee met. Jefferson proposed to me to make the draft. I said: 'I will not.' 'You should do it.' 'Oh! no.' 'Why will you not? You ought to do it.' 'I will not.' 'Why?' 'Reasons enough.' 'What can be your reasons?' 'Reason first – You are a Virginian, and a Virginian ought to appear at the head of this business. Reason second – I am obnoxious, suspected and unpopular. You are very much otherwise. Reason third – you can write ten times better than I can.' 'Well,' said Jefferson, 'If you are decided, I will do as well as I can.' (Adams to Timothy Pickering, 22 August 1822, *Writings*, I, p. 26fn)

Both men were writing nearly fifty years after the event, but I prefer Adams's version, which brings back the anxious, chaotic days of July 1776. 'We were all in haste, Congress was impatient,' Adams recalled, 'and the instrument was reported, as I believe, in Jefferson's handwriting as he first drew it' – no time for a fair copy. Adams and Pickering agreed that the Declaration, for all its subsequent fame, 'contained no new ideas, that it is a commonplace compilation, its sentiments hacknied in Congress for two years before'. (Ibid., p. 27fn) The equally aged Jefferson retorted that 'I did not consider it as any part of my charge to invent new ideas altogether, and to offer no sentiments which had ever been expressed before'. (Ibid.)

Just how true that was you can see from the opening words of the Virginia Declaration of Rights signed and sealed a couple of weeks earlier. Though Jefferson was the greatest of Virginians after George Washington, he was away in Philadelphia at the Continental Congress and had no hand in the drafting of this other Declaration. This is how it starts: 'That all men are by nature equally free and independent and have certain inherent rights, of which, when they enter into a state of society, they cannot, by any compact, deprive or divest their posterity; namely the enjoyment of life and liberty, with the means of acquiring and possessing property, and pursuing and obtaining happiness and safety.'

The Virginia Declaration was mostly written by the under-sung George Mason. As you can see, it is very similar to and in some ways clearer, if less resonant, than the Declaration Jefferson drafted a few weeks later in Philadelphia. For one thing, it dispels the slight fog around 'the pursuit of happiness', whether happiness was to be thought of as a pursuit like backgammon or badminton, or as an unending search for contentment.

The source of that ever-alluring phrase, like so much else in both Declarations, is John Locke. In his *Essay Concerning Human Understanding* (1690), Locke tells us: 'The necessity of pursuing happiness is the foundation of liberty.' In his *Two Treatises of Government*, Locke links 'goods', 'estate' or 'possessions' with life and liberty as the natural rights of man. Mason introduces a more nuanced formulation, in which the means of getting property and hanging on to it are, as it were, a secondary right to be secured by the best possible government. Jefferson leaves out property altogether and goes for happiness instead. Twenty years later, the French revolutionary Saint-Just was to declare that 'happiness is a new idea in Europe'. In America, it was already entrenched in the founding documents of the new nation.

When the Congress went through Jefferson's draft, they struck out quite a bit of the high-flown, near-hysterical language about blood and tyranny, though leaving in a long enough catalogue of George III's crimes against the colonies. What they most conspicuously took out was Jefferson's fierce denunciation of the king for having 'waged cruel war against human nature itself, violating it's [sic] most sacred rights of life and liberty in the persons of a distant people who never offended him, captivating & carrying them into slavery in another hemisphere, or to incur miserable death in their transportation thither'. (*Writings*, I, p. 34) It was outrageous humbug to blame George III for the slave trade, since it was the colonists who had so enthusiastically imported the slaves. In fact, Lord Dunmore, the last British Governor of Virginia, had freed any slave who was willing to fight for the British, and it was the first business of the victorious American rebels to recapture and re-enslave as many as they could. The same issue of the *Virginia Gazette* (20 July 1776) that printed Jefferson's Declaration also carried ads offering rewards for the recapture of runaway slaves. (Kranish, p. 90)

We are told that Thomas Jefferson listened in silence as his draft was reported to Congress. In fact, he seems to have remained silent throughout the proceedings. He was always an awkward speaker, though unstoppable when he got started. Senator William Maclay, a not uncritical supporter of Jefferson's, describes how he looked when he first appeared before a senate committee as Secretary of State in 1790:

Jefferson is a slender man. He has rather the air of Stiffness in his manner. His clothes seem too small for him. He sits in a lounging Manner on one hip, and with one of his shoulders elevated much above the other. His face has a scrany [sic] aspect. His whole figure has a loose shackling Air. He had a rambling Vacant look and nothing of that firm collected deportment which I expected would dignify the presence of a secretary or Minister. I looked for Gravity, but a laxity of Manner, seemed shed about him. He spoke almost without ceasing. But even his discourse partook of his personal demeanour. It was loose and rambling and yet he scattered information wherever he went, and some even brilliant Sentiments sparkled from him. (*Journal of William Maclay*, 24 May 1790, 1927 edn, pp. 265–6)

On the whole, though, Congress was pleased with Jefferson's draft. Even the acidulous Adams confessed: 'I was delighted with its high tone and the flights of oratory with which it abounded.' (*Writings*, I, p. 26fn) Posterity has been delighted too. It is primarily because he composed the Declaration that Jefferson has been acclaimed as one of the Founding Fathers of the Republic. It is for that reason, rather than the achievements of his two-term presidency, that he is one of the four presidents whose head is sculpted on Mount Rushmore in the Black Hills of Dakota – though it is because of his other great achievement, the Louisiana Purchase, that Dakota today forms part of the territory of the United States. In a canyon behind the heads, there is a chamber cut into the rock containing the texts of the Declaration and the Constitution on porcelain enamel panels. The head of Jefferson was originally intended for the rock face to Washington's right, but the stone turned out to be too crumbly, and so Jefferson was moved to a narrow space on the general's other shoulder.

In other ways, too, it has been a struggle to fit Jefferson into the national pantheon and keep him there. Throughout the standard six-volume biography of him, Dumas Malone repeatedly magnifies his hero beyond all the evidence, downplays his debacles, declines to offer direct quotation from his more embarrassing outbursts and badmouths or ignores his rivals. For example, he does mention George Mason's Virginia Declaration, but only in passing, and does not quote from it, fearing that it would make the Jefferson version seem less trailblazing and original. How, after all, can you glorify a mere draughtsman?

THE FLIGHT FROM MONTICELLO

At least Jefferson did actually write the Declaration. Malone has a harder time glorifying Jefferson's role during the War of Independence. The reality is that, having issued such a clarion call to arms, Jefferson did nothing very much during the fighting and didn't do even that very well. Lord Botetourt, the genial British governor of Virginia, who had tried his utmost to keep the colonists sweet, had appointed the 27-year-old squire as chief commander of the militia in his native Albemarle County, where he had inherited 5,000 acres (he acquired another 5,000 on his marriage to Martha Wayles), entitling him to the rank of colonel. By the time the war reached Virginia, Jefferson was governor of the state, or Commonwealth as it was and is officially called.

Dumas Malone describes his performance in that role with some delicacy: 'It did not fall to his own lot to go to the battlefield to learn how to fight by fighting.' (I, p. 326) Nor did he make much visible effort to raise extra troops or to find better kit for the ill-armed militiamen, who were suffering severe losses. He failed to requisition horses from the jealous Virginia squires or to post look-outs or fortify the bluffs on the James river. On the morale front, he was no great shakes either. Malone concedes that 'he made no spectacular efforts to inspire his people'. (I, p. 327)

Civilian governors often have little aptitude for or experience of military matters, but at least they can be expected to move in the general direction of the battlefront to see how they can help. But when the renegade Benedict Arnold launched a raid on Richmond, the state capital, Thomas Jefferson speedily retreated upriver to his home at Fine Creek, leaving the command of the militia to General Steuben. After Arnold had burnt down the town, then made mostly of wood, Jefferson returned to make his report to General Washington. Malone hurries to explain: 'This was not a precipitate flight but a dignified, if discouraged, retirement before a new alignment of superior forces.' (I, p. 350) That's not how most people saw it then, or for years afterwards.

More unforgivable still, the governor then refused Steuben's request to summon in militiamen from neighbouring counties. Jefferson refused on the pettifogging grounds that 'the executives have not by the laws of this state any power to call a freeman to labor even for the public without his consent, nor a slave without that of his master'. (I, p. 343) He spoke as a slave-owning squire, rather than as the commander whose country was in danger. If the governor lacked the necessary powers, it was he himself who had insisted that the governor's office should be weak, and he admitted afterwards that he had been wrong.

Worse was to come. There were now 7,000 enemy troops in

Virginia. A strong detachment of them under Lt-Col Banastre Tarleton was heading up the fork of the James river towards Jefferson, who had taken refuge at his beloved Monticello. From the top of his little mountain, he could actually see the British dragoons coming. Tarleton reported: 'the attempt to secure Mr Jefferson was ineffectual. He discovered the British dragoons from his house . . . before they could approach him, and he provided for his personal safety with a precipitate retreat.' Or as Betsy Ambler, the daughter of his old flame Rebecca Burwell, put it: 'Such terror and confusion you have no idea of. Governor, Council, every-body scampering.' (I, pp. 357–9) Having sent off his family in a carriage, Jefferson scarpered through the woods to the next emi-nence known as Carter's Mountain, from where he escaped to yet another of his estates, Poplar Forest. Once again, Malone does his best: 'his whole procedure was as dignified as that of any wartime fugitive, but the circumstances did not lend themselves to heroic legend'. (I, p. 358)

No, indeed. The Tarleton Raid was just as ignominious for Jefferson as Benedict Arnold's had been, and his reputation took years to recover. His conduct contrasted painfully with that of his successor Thomas Nelson, who stayed with his troops throughout the fighting. Jefferson might well have been censured by the Virginia Assembly if the glorious victory at Yorktown had not erased the earlier humiliations.

A CURIOUS MAN

If Thomas Jefferson was never going to win fame as a soldier, he was already a celebrated public intellectual, rivalled in that field only by Benjamin Franklin, and like Franklin conjoining the new idea of 'Americanness' to a restless spirit of scientific enquiry. This is one reputation he never lost. President Kennedy, welcoming a party of Nobel Prize-winners in April 1962, told them that 'this is the most extraordinary collection of talent, of human knowledge, that has ever been gathered together at the White House, with the possible exception of when Thomas Jefferson dined alone'.

Certainly, Jefferson was a curious man. But his curiosity was overwhelmingly technological. He was a tepid sort of deist, and had no interest in religion at all, except to insist on complete freedom of worship. He had little interest in history either. He told John Adams in August 1816 that he had always liked 'the dream of the future better than the history of the past'. The historian Gordon Wood says that he lacked any sense of 'man's capacity for evil' and had 'no tragic sense whatsoever'. (*Jeffersonian Legacies*, ed. Peter S. Onuf, 1993, p. 413) He was not really an original political thinker. Like his fellow Virginians, he derived most of his ideas from the Anglo-Scottish Enlightenment of Locke and Francis Hutcheson, which he had sucked up from his charismatic teacher at the College of William & Mary, the visiting Scots professor of natural philosophy, William Small.

Jefferson's prime interest was in how things worked and how they could be made to work better, often to his own designs, such as the swivel chair he designed for himself and in which he sat while drafting the Declaration of Independence. He was later much mocked for this by those who thought that his principles were liable to swivel too, but his technological bent was in tune with his fellow Americans. Alexis de Tocqueville on his famous visit to America wondered at how the bookshops were full of how-to books rather than history or poetry. Jefferson's love of gadgets was inexhaustible. He had an odometer strapped to his phaeton to record his progress. Striding around Paris before and during the Revolution, he wore a pedometer to record his daily mileage. On his trip through the Rhineland, he made notes on the designs of folding ladders and wheelbarrows rather than the Gothic cathedrals. He hated the Gothic style anyway, regarding Milan Cathedral as a ridiculous waste of money. His love of regularity drew him to classical colonnades. In Champagne, while pursuing his obsessive enquiries into which varieties of grape could be persuaded to flourish back in Virginia, he watched men ploughing and noticed the awkward movement of the moldboard – the wooden part that lifts and turns the sod – and designed an improved 'moldboard of least resistance'. He was much interested in agricultural improvement of all sorts, and even while desperately busy as Washington's Secretary of State, served on the American Philosophical Society's committee on a pest called the Hessian fly. He brought back from France a huge variety of plants and a shedload of instruments for American workshops to copy – theodolite, solar microscope, thermometer, telescope and Hawkins' polygraph, for making copies by moving two pens at once.

He was an amateur architect and town planner too, drawing up designs for the Capitol in Virginia, based on the Maison Carrée at Nîmes, and for the Capitol in the new city of Washington DC. He much admired the arcades that the Duc d'Orléans had developed at the Palais-Royal, and thought that the large underground hall could be copied back home as an indoor mall for shopping in the harsh American winters.

Jefferson was a great standardizer. He thought that all weights and measures ought to be decimalized. The miles on his odometer were divided into cents. He devoted a great deal of time in achieving an agreed standard length for the foot, and he was instrumental in getting the dollar adopted as a universal, standardized and, of course, decimal currency.

The same standardizing itch shows up in his far-reaching plans for expanding the territory of the United States when he was chairman of Congress's Western Lands Committee in 1783–84. In his Northwest Ordinance, he lays out a blueprint and draws a map for no less than fourteen new states to be established to the west of the mountains. The names he gave them were classical versions of Indian names or geographical features. Some never caught on – Cherronesus, Assenisipia, Metropotamia – but there is a Michigania and an Illinoia. But his most lasting legacy is the chequerboard pattern of the 'flyover states' that persists to this day.

He was obsessive, too, about measurements of climate and temperature. On the day he took his draft of the Declaration of Independence down to Congress, he studiously noted that the temperature had risen from 68°F at 6 a.m. to 76°F. He was strongly of the belief that 'A change in our climate, however, is taking place very sensibly. Both heats and colds are become much more moderate within the memory even of the middle-aged. Snows are less frequent and less deep ... The rivers, which then seldom failed to freeze over in the course of the winter, scarcely ever do so now.'

(*Writings*, VIII, p. 327) In fact, the so-called Little Ice Age was still going on, though there were intervals of more moderate weather and Jefferson may have identified one such. In general, his scientific observations are admirably cautious, often superior to those of the French *philosophes*, such as Buffon and Voltaire. In his *Encyclopédie* article on *coquilles*, for example, Voltaire claims that the mystery of seashells being found on the top of mountains can be explained by the water forming calcareous shell-shaped drops (like stalactites and stalagmites). Jefferson rejects this as implausible. He mentions the alternative possibility of geological upheaval raising the sea bed to these heights, but he says frankly that he doesn't know the answer, adding that 'ignorance is preferable to error; and he is less remote from the truth who believes nothing, than he who believes what is wrong'. (*Notes on Virginia*, *Writings*, VIII, pp. 276–7)

Towards a white America

Many of Thomas Jefferson's scientific observations were collected in the only full-length book he ever published, *Notes on Virginia*. The book bears the marks of its odd genesis, as a prolonged 200-page response to a questionnaire from a French minister, the Marquis de Barbé-Marbois. His government didn't know much about the infant United States, and wanted to know more. This explains why it is such a compendium of information about the rivers and mountains, flora and fauna of the state, and the religion, customs and manufactures of its inhabitants. For this reason, too, it was first published in Paris and soon became a bestseller on both sides of the Atlantic.

Even so, it is a very odd book and in many places a repellent one. The author sets out as a scientifically minded philosopher surveying the beauties of his native country – for Thomas in these early years and always in his heart, 'my country' was the Commonwealth of Virginia and not the United States of America. But as the *Notes* billows forth, it mutates into a very peculiar vision of the American destiny.

In the Declaration of Independence, one of the charges against

George III was that: 'He has endeavoured to prevent the population of these states; for that purpose obstructing the laws for naturalization of foreigners, refusing to pass others to encourage their migrations hither, & raising the conditions of new appropriations of land.' But now it is Jefferson who is worried about the country being 'swamped'.

'The present desire of America is to produce rapid population by as great importations of foreigners as possible. But is this founded in good policy?' (*Writings*, VIII, p. 330) At present, Virginia had only just over half a million inhabitants. If immigration went on at its present rate, in seventy or eighty years the Commonwealth would contain four and a half million people. 'I am persuaded it is a greater number than the country spoken of, considering how much inarable land it contains, can clothe and feed without a material change in the quality of their diet.' (Ibid., p. 331) And it wasn't just a question of food. 'It is for the happiness of those united in society to harmonize as much as possible in matters which they must of necessity transact together.' (Ibid.)

The danger was not simply of more foreigners, but the wrong kind of foreigners. The country could expect the greatest number of new immigrants to be fleeing from the absolute monarchies: 'they will bring with them the principles of the governments they leave, imbibed in their early youth; or, if able to throw them off, it will be in exchange for an unbounded licentiousness, passing, as is usual, from one extreme to another. It would be a miracle were they to stop precisely at the point of temperate liberty.' (Ibid.) Under the influence of these degenerates, the legislature of the Commonwealth would be warped into 'a heterogeneous, distracted, incoherent mass'.

Worse still, these immigrants would inevitably urbanize Virginia, turning a sylvan paradise into a grimy industrial state. Jefferson shudders at the prospect: 'While we have land to labour then, let us never wish to see our citizens occupied at a work-bench, or twirling a distaff. Carpenters, masons, smiths, are wanting in husbandry; but, for the general operations of manufacture, let our workshops remain in Europe. It is better to carry provisions and materials to workmen there, than bring them to the provisions and materials, and with them their manners and principles. The loss by the transportation of commodities across the Atlantic will be made up in happiness and permanence of government.' (Ibid., pp. 405–6) What Jefferson calls 'the mobs of great cities' were like sores on the human body.

It is not simply that Jefferson wants a purely agricultural future for his country. He insists, too, and with even greater passion, that the future shall be white. The most notorious passage in the book starts innocently enough as a description of Jefferson's new legislative programme for Virginia: to abolish primogeniture, to establish religious freedom in the state, to emancipate all slaves born after the act is passed. All sound measures in the liberal spirit.

But then, after being brought up at the public expense, the freed slave-children would be 'colonized to such place as the circumstances of the time should render most proper', and at the same time vessels would be sent 'to other parts of the world for an equal number of white inhabitants'. (Ibid., p. 380) In other words, a progressive racial exchange of populations.

Why not retain and incorporate the freed blacks into the state and save the expense of this huge exercise in inhuman engineering? Jefferson starts off his reasons in seemingly liberal style by instancing the 'deep-rooted prejudices entertained by the whites' and the 'ten thousand recollections by the blacks, of the injuries they have sustained'. But then he switches unnervingly into claiming that 'the real distinctions which nature has made; and many other circumstances, will divide us into parties, and produce convulsions, which will probably never end but in the termination of the one or the other race'. (Ibid., pp. 380–1)

And what are these natural distinctions that will infallibly end in all-out war between the races? Well, blacks are uglier. Is skin colour 'not the foundation of a greater or less share of beauty in the two races? Are not the fine mixtures of red and white, the expressions of every passion by greater or less suffusions of color in the one, preferable to that eternal monotony, which reigns in the countenances, that immovable veil of black which covers the emotions of the other race?' (Ibid.) Even the blacks think that the whites are more beautiful. Look at 'their own judgement in favor of the whites, declared by their preference of them, as uniformly as is the preference of the Oranootan for the black woman over those of his own species'.

Besides, blacks smell. 'They secrete less by the kidneys, and more by the glands of the skin, which gives them a very strong and disagreeable odor.' (Ibid.)

They are lustful, but they are incapable of the deeper feelings. 'They are more ardent after their female; but love seems with them to be more an eager desire, than a tender delicate mixture of sentiment and sensation. Their griefs are transient.' (Ibid., p. 382)

Blacks are stupid. 'Comparing them by their faculties of memory, reason and imagination, it appears to me that in memory they are equal to the whites; in reason much inferior, as I think one could scarcely be found capable of and tracing and comprehending the investigations of Euclid; and that in imagination they are dull, tasteless and anomalous.' But they do have a superior sense of rhythm: 'in music they are more generally gifted than the whites with accurate ears for tune and time; and they have been found capable of imagining a small catch'. (Ibid., p. 383)

Jefferson is at pains to make it clear that 'their inferiority is not the effect merely of their conditions of life'. (Ibid., p. 384) Roman slaves had a much worse time, yet there were great scientists and artists among them, such as Terence and Epictetus – but they were all white.

Perhaps the worst thing of all is their moral effect upon the whites: 'There must doubtless be an unhappy influence on the manners of our people produced by the existence of slavery among us. The whole commerce between master and slave is a perpetual exercise of the most boisterous passions, the most unremitting despotism on the one part, and degrading submissions on the other.' (Ibid., p. 403)

The usual indictment of Jefferson is that he was a large slaveholder – he had more than 200 slaves at one time or another – and that, unlike other Virginia squires such as George Washington, he freed almost none of them, even in his will. Nor was he a notably kindly master; he was not slow to punish offending slaves or to take measures to recapture his runaways, of whom there were plenty. But what he actually thought about the blacks is, to our eyes, almost more repellent than his treatment of them.

At the end of this breathtakingly racist riff, Jefferson tiptoes backwards, claiming that he hazards these opinions with great diffidence, and that it's 'a suspicion only, that the blacks, whether originally a distinct race, or made distinct by time and circumstances, are inferior to the whites in the endowments both of body and mind'. (Ibid., p. 386) Dumas Malone seizes, with an almost audible gasp of relief, upon these qualifications and, without quoting a single word of the horrific sentiments that his hero has just expressed, says merely that 'dubious of the natural equality of endowment of the blacks with their masters, he was keeping his mind open about them'. (Malone, II, p. 101) But the damage was already done, the poison already fed deep into the veins of Jefferson's readers.

We also know that Jefferson was not 'keeping his mind open', because he was still saying the same thing forty years later. In his *Autobiography* written in his late seventies, he asserts no less plainly that the blacks must be emancipated and then got rid of: 'Nothing is more certainly written in the book of fate than that these people are to be free. Nor is it less certain that the two races, equally free, cannot live in the same government. Nature, habit, opinion has drawn indelible lines of distinction between them. It is still in our power to direct the process of emancipation and deportation peaceably and in such slow degree as that the evil will wear off insensibly, and their place be pari passu filled up by free white laborers.' If this is not done, human nature must shudder at the carnage that will follow, which will be far worse than 'the Spanish deportation or deletion of the Moors'. (*Writings*, I, p. 68) 'Deletion' – now there's a word.

Go to the Jefferson Memorial in Washington DC, dedicated by FDR in 1943, on the bicentenary of Jefferson's birth, and you will see the last words of the inscription: 'Nothing is more certainly written in the book of fate than that these people are to be free.' The inscription stops there. The lie that hides Jefferson's vision of an all-white America is graven in stone at the heart of the American pantheon.

THE PARIS YEARS

In 1784, Jefferson, now entering his forties and still grieving after the death of his beloved wife Martha, sailed to Paris to become the minister at the court of Versailles. He spent the next five years there, long enough to witness the Fall of the Bastille and the first head-spinning days of the Revolution. With him he took his eldest daughter Martha, known as Patsy, and left the younger two in Virginia with their uncle and aunt. The youngest, Lucy, died soon after he reached Paris – Lafayette brought the sad news. The middle daughter Polly joined him later, accompanied by a 14-year-old slave, Sally Hemings, a bright, mixed-race girl who seemed rather disoriented by the voyage. Also in the little household at the rented Hôtel de Langeac (near where the Arc de Triomphe now stands) was Jefferson's sharp young kinsman and protégé, William Short, who acted as secretary to the legation.

According to Dumas Malone and some of his other American biographers, the 'empty bustle' of Paris made little impression on the virtuous Virginian. 'The chief effect of Jefferson's stay in France upon his fundamental political ideas was to confirm him in the ones he held before he went there.' (Malone, II, p. 153) The fashionable French thinkers didn't teach him anything he didn't already know – in fact, they were eager to learn from the already famous author of the Declaration. Apart from John and Abigail Adams, he didn't have any real friends in the city, and he was desolate when they left: 'The departure of your family has left me in the dumps. My afternoons hang heavily on me.' (25 May 1785, Boyd, VIII, pp. 163–4) Malone warns us in his introduction that 'highly exaggerated statements about his personal part in the preliminaries and first stages of the French Revolution were afterwards made by his political foes. In reality this personal part was slight ... despite certain stock quotations which keep reappearing in the history books, what he advocated can be much better described as "reformation" rather than "revolution".' (Malone, II, pp. xvi-xvii)

We are left with a rather poignant picture of the lonely widower stalking the streets of Paris, clocking up the miles on his pedometer, recoiling from the licentious world of the salons with their affected hostesses and their punning chatter, his only amusements the contemplation of vineyards and shopping malls. *The Paris Years of Thomas Jefferson*, William Howard Adams's vivid account, tells a different story. Jefferson might write home to his folks in Virginia, moaning about how he longed to be back home, but like other great letter-writers, he was adept at telling his correspondents what they might like to hear. In fact, he was a regular in the leading drawing rooms of the day, of Mme de Tessé above all, but also of Mme de Corny, Mme de Bréhan and Rousseau's old love, Mme d'Houdetot. He had a delicious walk-out with Maria Cosway, the miniature painter and sparky wife of Richard Cosway. It was when trying to impress Maria with his youthful agility that he tried to vault over a low railing in the Tuileries and broke his wrist. Jefferson had an equally pleasurable flirtation with Angelica Schuyler Church, who when back in America had a comparable dalliance with her brother-in-law Alexander Hamilton (the hit musical *Hamilton* focuses on this relationship). He was also an intimate of the multi-talented Baron von Grimm, against whom Rousseau had taken such a vicious dislike. In short, the minister got around.

But it is his French political friends who are of the greatest interest to us, above all: Lafayette, the youthful hero of the American Revolution, the marquis de Condorcet, the most advanced political theorist in Paris and, like Jefferson, an enthusiast for gadgets and ingenious schemes (he devised a pioneer system of proportional representation), and the duc de La Rochefoucauld, who had married his much younger niece, known as Rosalie. La Rochefoucauld's group of liberal aristocrats was known as 'les Américains', and their interest in the American Revolution was serious and sustained. The year before Jefferson arrived, La Rochefoucauld and Franklin had together published *Constitutions des treize États-Unis de l'Amérique*, a careful examination of the constitution of each colony, with the texts of the Declaration and the Virginia Bill of Rights thrown in, all designed as future models for France.

All of them were also members of La Société des Amis des Noirs, founded by Brissot de Warville, an ambitious lawyer who was to take a prominent part in the early phases of the Revolution. William Short accepted membership with alacrity. Thomas Jefferson declined on the grounds that it would do him no good back home if his member-ship became public knowledge.

When Lafayette set about drafting his *Declaration of the Rights of Man*, he repeatedly consulted Jefferson for his thoughts. We cannot be sure which bits he contributed to, though we do know that, as with his own Declaration, he advised them to leave out the right to property (Malone, II, p. 223), but they didn't. After the National Assembly had adopted the Declaration in August 1789, Lafayette became alarmed that the two wings of the Patriotic or popular party were beginning to split apart, and he asked Jefferson to host a dinner for the leaders at the Hôtel de Langeac. (Malone, II, p. 230; *Writings*, I, pp. 145–6) Jefferson was ecstatic about the quality of the after-dinner debate:

> The discussions began at the hour of four, and were continued till ten o'clock in the evening; during which time I was a silent witness to a coolness and candor of argument unusual in the conflicts of political opinion; to a logical reasoning, and chaste eloquence, disfigured by no gaudy tinsel of rhetoric or declamation, and truly worthy of being placed in parallel with the finest dialogues of antiquity, as handed to us by Xenophon, by Plato and Cicero. (*Writings*, ibid.)

So much for Jefferson's detachment from the political scene. He was up to his neck in the campaigns of the liberal revolutionaries. He cared passionately that they should succeed. Moreover, he earn-estly hoped and believed that there would be a peaceful outcome: 'I think it probable, this country will, within two or three years, be in the enjoyment of a tolerably free constitution, and that without its having cost them a drop of blood.' (Jefferson to Monroe, 9 August 1788, Boyd, XVIII, p. 489) As he left Paris on leave in September 1789, he expected to return 'to see the end of the Revolution, which, I then thought, would be certainly and happily closed in less than a year'. (*Writings*, I, p. 149) He left with regret and affection for a country whose society had 'a charm to be found nowhere else'. Like any traveller, he said, he would rather live in his own country, but 'Which would be your second choice? France.' (Ibid.)

He had a farewell dinner with his three closest political friends, Lafayette, Condorcet and La Rochefoucauld. During the Terror,

Lafayette had to flee for his life, La Rochefoucauld was torn to pieces by the mob in front of his wife and mother, and Condorcet took poison while on the run from Robespierre's police. Brissot perished on the guillotine with the other Girondin leaders. Rosalie's brother died in prison during the September Massacres of 1792. Rosalie wrote to Jefferson reporting these calamities. She received no answer.

Jefferson had left William Short as *chargé d'affaires* at the legation in his absence. Short wrote frequent dispatches to his master. He was vivid and unsparing in his analysis of events. Even before the September Massacres, Short was deeply pessimistic: 'Robespierre & others of that atrocious and cruel cast compose the tribunal, named by popular election. We may expect, therefore, to hear of such proceedings under the cloak of *égalité* & patriotism as would disgrace any *chambre ardente* that ever existed. Humanity shudders at the idea.' (24 August 1792, Shackelford, p. 67)

Jefferson responded with uncontrollable fury: 'The tone of your letters had for some time given me pain, on account of the extreme warmth with which they censured the proceedings of the Jacobins of France.' On the contrary, Robespierre and the Jacobins were doing the right thing. They saw that 'the expunging that officer [he means executing the king] was of absolute necessity'. As euphemisms go, 'expunging' is every bit as ripe as 'deleting'. Then he goes on, in words that continue to chill the blood and must be quoted in full:

In the struggle which was necessary, many guilty persons fell without the forms of trial, and with them some innocent. These I deplore as much as any body, and shall deplore some of them to the day of my death. But I deplore them as I should have done had they fallen in battle. It was necessary to use the arm of the people, a machine not quite so blind as balls and bombs, but blind to a certain degree. A few of their cordial friends met at their hands the fate of enemies. But time and truth will rescue and embalm their memories, while their posterity will be enjoying that very liberty for which they would never have hesitated to offer up their lives. The liberty of the whole earth was depending on the issue of the contest, and was ever such a prize won with so little innocent

blood? My own affections have been deeply wounded by some
of the martyrs to this cause, but rather than that it should have
failed, I would have seen half the earth desolated. Were there but
an Adam and an Eve left in every country, and left free, it would
be better than as it now is. (3 January 1793, O'Brien, p. 145)

Never was the doctrine of what W. H. Auden called 'the necessary
murder' hymned with such zeal. Dumas Malone does not quote
a single word of the 'Adam and Eve letter', merely referring to
it as the most 'fervid' comment that Jefferson ever made on the
French Revolution.

THE TREE OF LIBERTY

It won't do either to dismiss his letter to William Short as a one-off
explosion or as applying only to French affairs. Six years earlier,
writing to his old friend Abigail Adams about Shays' Rebellion, a
rising of small farmers in Massachusetts, he had declared that 'the
spirit of resistance to government is so valuable on certain occasions, that I wish it always to be kept alive. It will often be exercised
when wrong, but better so than not to be exercised at all. I like a
little rebellion now and then. It is like a storm in the Atmosphere.'
(12 February 1787, O'Brien, p. 40)

Writing to William Smith about the same rebellion a few months
later, he went further: 'God forbid we should ever be 20 years without such a rebellion ... What signify a few lives lost in a century or
two? The tree of liberty must be refreshed from time to time with
the blood of patriots and tyrants. It is it's [sic] natural manure.'
(13 November 1787, O'Brien, pp. 41–2)

Famously, the 'tree of liberty' phrase was emblazoned on the
T-shirt of Timothy McVeigh, the Oklahoma City bomber. Conor
Cruise O'Brien points out that McVeigh's co-bomber, Terry Lynn
Nichols, was also a disciple of Jefferson's and fond of 'the tree of
liberty' maxim. Oklahoma is part of the United States only because
it was included in the huge tract of land that President Jefferson
bought from Napoleon in 1803, the so-called Louisiana Purchase.
The territory stretched far from Louisiana to the Canadian border

in the north and the Rocky Mountains in the west, comprising large
stretches of fifteen modern American states. It is thus to Jefferson
more than any other man that Americans today owe both their
limitless chequerboard prairies and their inveterate distrust of the
Federal government.

Certainly, Jefferson's repeated praises of violent rebellion cannot
be dismissed as 'stock quotations' wrenched out of context. They
represent a clear, passionate and settled belief in the ongoing uses
of violence as a threat. It is the sharp end of a more general doctrine. In America, that doctrine is politely described as 'Jeffersonian
democracy'. In other, less happier lands, it is more usually called
'permanent revolution'. The outline of such doctrines is fuzzy,
often deliberately so, but their core is roughly as follows: legitimate
authority flows directly from the people, and only from the people.
It is merely on temporary loan to political institutions and leaders, and may be recalled at any time, by violent means if need be,
whenever the people believe that the institution is betraying them.
Thus, the mandate that any government enjoys is strictly provisional. By contrast, those individuals or groups whom the people
have chosen to carry out their wishes, the 'democratic vanguard',
are equipped with an absolute authority that is not to be resisted.
A permanent revolution of this kind is also exportable. The French
and Russian Revolutions both claimed the right to operate beyond
bourgeois national boundaries in order to further worldwide revolution. Arriving in the United States in April 1793, the charismatic
Citizen-Consul Edmond-Charles Genêt claimed exactly the same
right to spread the revolution as any agent of the Comintern would
have asserted 150 years later. For a time, Jefferson eagerly supported
Genêt, until his antics made him too unpopular with American
public opinion.

The Jefferson industry has persistently tried to anchor their man
in the mainstream of the American political tradition, to make him
look much like his three neighbours on Mount Rushmore. Yet it is
clear that his views about the proper nature of government place
him in a different tradition altogether.

We must remember that he had little or no part in the making
of the Constitution of the United States, because he was in Paris

throughout the process. When he eventually received a copy of the text, he claimed to have read it 'with great satisfaction'. (*Autobiography*, *Writings*, I, p. 109) But even at that first reading he raised substantial objections: to the eligibility of the president for re-election, for example, which he thought smacked too much of 'an elective despotism', which 'was not the government we fought for'. (*Writings*, VIII, p. 361) Then he didn't like the way the judges were to be virtually irremovable and so 'effectually independent of the nation'. Instead, they should be 'submitted to some practical and impartial control', by which he appears to mean that it should be possible to vote them out. (*Writings*, I, p. 112) Thirdly, he wants a Bill of Rights to entrench the rights of individuals against an over-mighty state.

You might call these the respectable demands of Jeffersonian democracy, calculated to give the people more immediate and frequent access to the levers of power. But he goes further, much further. Jefferson is suspicious of the very idea of a constitution in the sense of a document with special status. He proposes that 'the ordinary legislators may alter the Constitution itself'. Why should the Constitution be anything superior to an ordinary statute law? 'To get rid of the magic supposed to be in the word *constitution* . . . let us suppose the convention, instead of saying "We the ordinary legislature, establish a *constitution*," had said, "we the ordinary legislature, establish an act *above the power of the ordinary legislature*." Does not this expose the absurdity of the attempt?' (Ibid., VIII, p. 366)

So no arrangements are to be considered as permanent or un-alterable. Everything is up for question all the time, everything is reformable at will. The revolution is never over. This doctrine is set out most memorably in Jefferson's long letter to his disciple James Madison of 6 September 1789 (*Writings*, V, p. 121): 'I set out on this ground which I suppose to be self-evident, "that the earth belongs in usufruct to the living", that the dead have neither powers nor rights over it.' Usufruct means temporary enjoyment of the earth and its fruits, rather than outright ownership. What Jefferson wants us to believe is that 'no society can make a perpetual constitution, or even a perpetual law. The earth belongs always to the living generation.

They may manage it then, and what proceeds from them, as they please, during their usufruct. They are masters too of their own persons, and consequently may govern them as they please ... Every constitution then, and every law naturally expires at the end of 19 years. If it be enforced longer, it is an act of force and not of right.' (Jefferson had done his usual painstaking calculations to work out the average length of a generation as nineteen years.)

It follows then that 'between society and society, or generation and generation there is no municipal obligation, no umpire but the law of nature. We seem not to have perceived that, by the law of nature, one generation is to another as one independent nation is to another.'

Now of course some people don't think this is self-evident at all. Edmund Burke, writing only a few months after Jefferson, declares that, on the contrary, society is a contract between the generations: 'It is a partnership in all science; a partnership in all art, a partnership in every virtue, and in all perfection. As the ends of such a partnership cannot be obtained in many generations, it becomes a partnership not only between those who are living, but between those who are living, those who are dead, and those who have yet to be born.'

These two views of society are utterly opposed: on the one hand, the idea of culture with all its obligations, accumulated data and learning curves as maturing over generations: and on the other, the view that it is we *now* who make our own culture as we go along, and that we owe nothing to our forefathers or to our descendants. These remain the two magnetic poles of political thought.

For our present purposes, though, we need to investigate where the doctrine was to lead Jefferson himself and, after him, the Jeffersonian tradition. Its impact was immediate, the challenge to traditional ways of thinking posed almost as soon as Jefferson returned from Paris. After his usual fine show of reluctance, Jefferson accepted Washington's offer of the secretaryship of state and abandoned his plans to go back to France. He soon found himself embroiled in a cat fight with the secretary of the Treasury, Alexander Hamilton. It was both a turf war and a profound doctrinal dispute that was to last through most of the 1790s. Both sides deployed the seediest hired hacks and resorted to some of the bitchiest abuse in political history. Malone does his best to suggest that all the foulest vituperation came from the Hamilton camp. That just isn't true. Jefferson and his fans were equally trigger-happy with their insults: 'covert monarchists', 'anglomanes', 'tools of corruption', and so on.

Hamilton believed that the nation could not progress until it had a central bank to expand credit and that individual states, especially the poorer southern states, could not advance unless the nation assumed their considerable debts. Hamilton justified the necessary measures under Article I, Section 8 of the Constitution: 'the Congress shall have power to lay and collect Taxes, Duties, Imposts and Excises, to pay the Debts and Provide for the common Defence and general Welfare'.

The southern states, led not so covertly by Jefferson, argued that there was nothing in the Constitution about a central bank or the assumption of states' debts. Hamilton retorted, in essence, that any fool could see that if you wanted to provide for the general welfare, this was what you had to do: they were 'implied Powers'. Jefferson and the 'strict constructionists' relied on the Tenth Amendment, which reserved to the states all powers not delegated and 'enumerated' to the United States. So the row went on, to be resolved, in practical if not doctrinal terms, by what was called the 'Residence-Assumption' bargain. The northern states would agree to a southerly site for the new capital on the banks of the Potomac, and in return the South would agree to the United States assuming their debts.

But like any self-respecting ideologue, Jefferson did not give up. He continued to denounce what he called 'the Hamilton system' as a boondoggle for the speculators and stockjobbers who infested Congress and who were all in the pocket of the Treasury secretary. He even made a private list of their names to show how pervasive their influence was. His populist indignation was reinforced by his revulsion against the tightening grip of the Federal government. The Hamilton system would not only chain successive generations to the debts of their fathers; it would also see the progressive extinguishing of the people's freedom.

His vision of a looser union in which the people could call the
shots and where the states did not have to dance to Washington's
tune took a further turn only eight years later when he and his protégé Madison secretly wrote the Kentucky and Virginia Resolutions.
These 'Principles of '98', as they became known, claimed that the
states had the right to judge whether or not a proposed federal law
or decree was 'constitutional'. The immediate provocation for the
Resolutions was the Alien and Sedition Acts, a panicky measure
triggered by the Napoleonic Wars (there were similar laws passed
in England too). But the point was a general one. Any power that
the Federal government claimed which was not 'enumerated' in the
text was a breach of the Constitution. Any state court therefore
had the right to strike it down or 'nullify' it. This was a recipe for
unravelling the Union step by step, as one state after another might
choose to nullify any federal law it disliked.

The text of the Resolutions as originally written, entirely in
secret, by Jefferson was so extreme that the alarmed Kentucky legislature watered it down. But Jefferson was keen to make it clear
to his co-conspirator James Madison just how far he wanted to
go: 'where powers are assumed, which have not been delegated, a
nullification of the act is the rightful remedy'. (Malone, III, p. 405)
Every state had this natural right to strike down any federal act
that exceeded its powers under the US Constitution; and it was
the individual state that was to be the judge of whether the Federal
government had exceeded those powers. He and his friends were
'determined, were we to be disappointed in this, to sever ourselves
from the union we so much value, rather than give up the rights of
self-government which we have reserved; and in which alone we see
liberty, safety and happiness'. (Ibid., p. 421) Thus Jefferson uses
the language of his own famous Declaration to justify the threat to
break up the Union.

In practice, the other states were reluctant to follow the lead given
by Kentucky and Virginia. The Resolutions fizzled out, though not
before Hamilton had threatened to send in the army, of which he
was now the commander.

But the states-rights theory lingered on, erupting at intervals
throughout the early nineteenth century, and gathering final and

catastrophic force as the pretext for the breakaway of the South, although the driving force was the defence of the 'peculiar institution', better known as slavery. At the close of the Civil War, President Garfield said that 'Jefferson's Kentucky Resolution contained the germ of nullification and secession, and we are today reaping the fruits'. From first to last, Jeffersonian democracy and Jeffersonian racism remained hopelessly, tragically, intertwined.

What is even more remarkable was that Jefferson was vice-president at the time of the Kentucky Resolutions and the administration that he was undermining was his own. Even the ever-charitable Dumas Malone admits that 'the Vice President of the United States could have been charged with sedition and perhaps impeached for treason' if it had got out that he was the author of the Kentucky Resolutions. (Ibid., p. 400) Malone also points out that 'the doctrine which Jefferson was presenting here ... could have paralyzed the general government if carried to its logical conclusion. It was not in character with the basic practicality he manifested when actually engaged in the conduct of the affairs of the Republic.' (Ibid., p. 404) You couldn't run a government if any state could strike down a federal law whenever it fancied. And Jefferson never dreamed of doing so.

Among the keenest supporters of the Principles of '98 was Jefferson's squeaky-voiced cousin, John Randolph of Roanoke. During his thirty years in Congress, Randolph vehemently opposed almost any measure that came out of Washington. Like Jefferson, he also had mixed feelings about slavery, and freed all his own slaves in his will, as Jefferson conspicuously did not. But like Jefferson, Randolph's driving concern was to ship as many blacks out of Virginia as he could. He dispatched no less than 385 of his own slaves to settle on land he had bought for them in the free state of Ohio. At the same time, in 1816, he helped found the American Colonization Society, a weird coalition of slave-owners and abolitionists, which set about transporting blacks back to Africa, and resettling them in the territory that was to become Liberia. Thus, the pipe dream of *Notes on Virginia* became a reality.

It is difficult not to agree with Conor Cruise O'Brien that as the twenty-first century progresses, we will increasingly find Jefferson's

influence flourishing, not on the Left where he has traditionally
been placed, but on the libertarian, gun-toting, not-so-crypto-racist
right. You want to 'drain the swamp' of Washington, you want to
build a wall to keep the Mexicans out, you want to ban immigrants
from countries that have nasty regimes, you want to keep out foreign goods? What you get is President Donald J. Trump. President
Thomas Jefferson would have done the job for you so much better,
and with a lot more class.

Maria and Betsey and Sally

James T. Callender, a whisky-sodden journalist of strong republican views, had cut his teeth in his native Scotland with a series of
venomous attacks on Dr Samuel Johnson. After further scurrilous
pasquinades, he fled to Ireland and then to Philadelphia in the
early 1790s, where he quickly made a name as a Congressional
reporter. He hit the headlines with his exposé in 1796 of Alexander
Hamilton's affair with a married woman, Maria Reynolds. The
affair was made murkier by her husband having blackmailed
Hamilton for several years.

Impressed by this successful assault on the reputation of his
hated rival, Jefferson took on Callender as a verbal hitman, directing his fire on John Adams and the corruption within the Federal
government. Once again, we need to recall that Jefferson was
vice-president at the time, and Adams was his president and long-
time friend. In retaliation, the Adams administration prosecuted
Callender under the Sedition Act and he was jailed – only to be
pardoned by the incoming president, Thomas Jefferson. His patron
could do no less, as it was widely reckoned that Jefferson owed his
victory over Adams to Callender's smears.

Callender demanded as a reward to be appointed postmaster in
Richmond. Jefferson refused, terrified of unleashing this loosest of
cannons. Callender, now in desperate straits, turned on his patron
and revealed in print that the president had been paying him for
his scurvy services. But that was only the beginning. Callender
reached back into Jefferson's past and in the *Richmond Recorder*
(27 October 1802) told the story of Jefferson's improper advances

to Betsey, the wife of his old friend John Walker. Later, Walker made a full statement to Betsey's nephew by marriage, 'Light-Horse Harry' Lee (the father of General Robert E. Lee). John Walker had left his wife and infant daughter at home, relying on his 'neighbour and fast friend' Mr Jefferson to look after them. When he returned four months later, Betsey complained that Mr J had made improper advances to her, and wondered that John had so much confidence in him. On a later visit to Mr J's home at Shadwell, he had renewed his caresses and 'placed in Mrs W's gown sleeve cuff a paper tending to convince her of the innocence of promiscuous love. This Mrs W on the first glance tore up.'

Then on a visit to Colonel Coles, a mutual acquaintance, after the ladies had retired, Mr J complained of a headache, but instead of going to bed he stole into the Walkers' room where Mrs W was undressing or in bed. Again, she fended him off. These assaults continued even after Mr J was married in 1771. On a later occasion, he waylaid her in his nightshirt in an indecent manner. 'All this time I believed him to be my best *frd*.' (Malone, I, p. 449)

Was any of this true? Yes, some of it was. Speaking to friends three years later in the spring of 1805, Jefferson said that he wished 'to stand with them on the ground of truth', and referring to the attacks of his enemies, explained: 'You will perceive that I plead guilty to one of their charges, that when young and single I offered love to a handsome lady. I acknowledge its incorrectness [that is, the incorrectness of his own conduct]. It is the only one founded in truth among all their allegations against me.' (Malone, I, p. 448)

So, what were all the other allegations?

Two months earlier, on 1 September, Callender published in the *Recorder* another article about the president. 'It is well-known', the article began, 'that the man whom it *delighted the people to honor* keeps and for many years has kept, as his concubine, one of his own slaves.'

Her name is SALLY. The name of her eldest son is Tom. His features are said to bear a striking though sable resemblance to those of the President himself. The boy is ten or twelve years of age. His mother went to France in the same vessel with Mr Jefferson and

his two daughters. The delicacy of this arrangement must strike
every portion of common sensibility. What a sublime pattern for
an American ambassador to place before the eyes of two young
ladies ... By this wench Sally, our President has had several children ... The African Venus is said to officiate as housekeeper
at Monticello.

Knowing that a good scandal needs repetition and embroidery,
Callender followed the tale up with further reports on 15, 22 and 29
September. The coverage spread across the country, so that a couple
of months later, on 14 November, the *Recorder* was able to reprint
a jingle first published in the *Boston Gazette*:

> Yankee Doodle, who's the noodle,
> What wife were half so handy?
> To breed a flock of slaves for stock,
> A blackamoor's the dandy.

So began the media history of the Sally Hemings saga. Two hundred
years later, it is still running hot and strong, having already inspired
a shelf-ful of biographies, essays, reviews, historical novels, not to
mention a feature film. For many years, there was little or no actual
evidence for any liaison beyond the rumours fomented by Jefferson's
enemies in the usual robust style of the times.

Then, in 1873, Sally's son Madison Hemings (1805–77) told his
local paper in Ohio, the *Pike County Republican* (13 March), that

> Maria [Polly] was left at home, but was afterwards ordered to
> accompany him to France. She was three years or so younger than
> Martha [Patsy]. My mother accompanied her as her body serv-
> ant ... Their stay (my mother's and Maria's) was about eighteen
> months. But during that time my mother became Mr Jefferson's
> concubine and when he was called home she was 'enciente'
> [enceinte] by him ... Soon after their arrival she gave birth to a
> child of whom Thomas Jefferson was the father. It lived but a
> short time. She gave birth to four others, and Jefferson was the
> father of all of them.

That essentially is the testimony that has persuaded several of
Jefferson's modern biographers that he fathered some or all of
Sally's children over a period of twenty years, though not of course
the faithful Dumas Malone, who pooh-poohs the idea as 'distinctly
out of character, being virtually unthinkable in a man of Jefferson's
moral standards and habitual conduct'. (IV, p. 214) Those who
were already critical of Jefferson's ambiguous attitude towards
slavery have found in this clandestine spawning the most damning
condemnation of his humbug, racism and exploitation. Garry Wills,
for example, while pouring scorn on the 'hint-and-run' method of
Fawn Brodie's *Intimate History* of Jefferson, goes along with the
thesis of more respectable historians such as Winthrop Jordan and
Richard B. Morris that Jefferson did father most or all of Sally's
children but that he was in no way in love with her, regarding her as
little more than 'a healthy and obliging prostitute'. ('Uncle Thomas's
Cabin', *New York Review of Books*, 18 April 1974) Conor Cruise
O'Brien argues (p. 22) that Jefferson felt no horror at the idea of
miscegenation between white masters and black female slaves
(although we have seen passages in *Notes on Virginia* that give the
opposite impression). If Jefferson's father-in-law, John Wayles, had
sired Sally with his slave Betty Hemings, as was widely rumoured,
why should he do not do the same with Sally? O'Brien wonders if
genetics might soon be able to prove through DNA comparisons
whether or not Jefferson was the father of Madison and the others.

Only two years later, just such an experiment was made and its
results reported in *Nature*. (5 November 1998, p. 27) Since Jefferson
had no legitimate male descendants, the results were obtained by
comparing the DNA of the male descendants of his father's brother,
Field Jefferson, with the DNA of the male descendants of Sally's
three sons. This ruled out the dark-skinned Madison himself,
because his male-line descendants did not survive the Civil War. But
the other two, Thomas Woodson (1790–1879) and Eston Hemings
Jefferson (1808–52), did have male-line descendants.

The results in both cases were emphatic. Four out of five male-
line descendants of Thomas Woodson showed a haplotype (one
with MSYi variant) that was not similar to the Y chromosome
of the Field Jefferson male line but one that was characteristic of

Europeans. So Thomas Woodson was definitely not the son of Thomas Jefferson, though he probably did have a white father.

By contrast, the single male descendant of Eston who was tested did have the Field Jefferson haplotype, so any one of Field Jefferson's twelve descendants or Thomas Jefferson or one of his brothers could have been Eston's father.

This verdict was seized on with halloos by those who were out to smash the idol of American rectitude. Gore Vidal, in *Inventing a Nation* (2003), exulted: 'The fact that Jefferson would have six children by Sally (half-sister to his beloved wife, another Martha) has been a source of despair to many old-guard historians, but unhappily for them, recent DNA testings establish consanguinity between the Hemingses and their master, whose ambivalences about slavery (not venery) are still of central concern to us.' (p. 77) The Thomas Jefferson Memorial Foundation blithely claimed (26 January 2000) a 'high probability that Thomas Jefferson fathered Eston and most likely was the father of all six of Sally Hemings's children'. Some time later, troubled by the furore its hasty verdict had aroused, the foundation revised its conclusions in a more agnostic direction, but the damage had been done.

Before we examine the DNA evidence a little more closely, let us go back to the deposition that Madison Hemings gave in old age. He says that Sally came back from Paris pregnant by Jefferson but that the child lived only a little while. Yet in reality Thomas lived to a ripe old age and he is the one child of Sally's whom DNA evidence confirms was not Jefferson's. It was Thomas's parentage, too, that provoked Callender's original allegation, which sparked off the whole scandal. Madison and Eston were not yet born at the time of the article in the *Recorder*. Faced with this difficulty, Jefferson's more entrenched enemies assert that Sally did not become pregnant until some time after her return to Monticello and that therefore Thomas Woodson was not her son and indeed was never at Monticello because his name does not appear in Jefferson's carefully kept records. But Callender in 1802 specifically names Tom as Jefferson's son, clearly insinuates that the affair began in Paris and states that Tom is still alive.

Apart from casting doubt both on Callender's veracity and

According to Plutarch, 'Squill-headed' Pericles was always shown wearing a helmet in statues and paintings.

Jesus drives out the money-changers, by Giotto.

The Vision of the Cross, by Raphael's assistants, shows the Cross appearing to the Emperor Constantine just before his decisive victory at the battle of the Milvian Bridge. Beside the Cross streams a banner proclaiming in Greek, '*En touto nika*', usually rendered in Latin as '*In hoc signo vinces*' – 'by this sign you shall conquer'.

Rousseau the wanderer – Jean-Jacques as he liked to see himself.

Quentin de La Tour's famous pastel of Rousseau in his early forties.

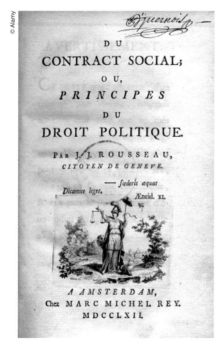

DU

CONTRACT SOCIAL;

OU,

PRINCIPES

DU

DROIT POLITIQUE.

PAR J. J. ROUSSEAU,
CITOYEN DE GENEVE.

—— fœderis æquas
Dicamus leges.
Æneid. XI.

A AMSTERDAM,
Chez MARC MICHEL REY.
MDCCLXII.

The first edition of *Du Contrat Social* proudly proclaims Rousseau as 'Citizen of Geneva'.

Adam Smith on the British £20 note, with the little figures of pin-makers illustrating the benefits of the division of labour.

Edmund Burke, 1774, watercolour on ivory after a painting by Burke's protégé James Barry.

A fanciful reconstruction of the committee drafting the American Declaration of Independence. Thomas Jefferson is far left, John Adams far right, Benjamin Franklin in the middle.

Jeremy Bentham on a nineteenth-century commercial postcard, already celebrated as the promoter of 'the greatest happiness of the greatest number'.

Bentham's head, still preserved at University College London as part of his 'Auto-Icon' but not normally on display.

Mary Wollstonecraft in her bloom, by John Opie.

Wollstonecraft's tombstone, erected by her husband William Godwin, in Old St Pancras churchyard, where Shelley courted her daughter Mary.

Citizens being shot for reading Mazzini's journals.

Photograph of
Mazzini in later
life.

Statue of Karl Marx and Friedrich Engels in Berlin.

The young Marx, 'the democratic dictator incarnate'.

Marx as Moses with his tablets, *Das Kapital* and *The Communist Manifesto*.

Gandhi in India, circa 1942, 'the half-naked fakir'.

God is Truth
The way to Truth
lies through Ahimsa
(non violence)
sabarmati
13 3/127   MKgandhi

Gandhi's simple recipe.

Muhammad Iqbal in his beloved fez after receiving an honorary D.Litt at the University of the Punjab in 1933.

Iqbal at Cambridge in 1932 with young Muslim activists, including Choudhary Rahmat Ali (front row, left), who is credited with inventing the name of Pakistan.

Madison's, this latest version of the increasingly tortuous accusation makes Jefferson's next moves rather peculiar, if we are to believe his slanderers. There he is, well into his sixties and by now president of the United States, already *wrongly* accused in the public prints of having fathered a bastard by his teenage slave some twelve years earlier in Paris. What does he do? He goes and repeatedly has sex with this same slave, by now a mature woman and the target of what we would today call 'intense media speculation'. And she bears him several more children.

This is surely a strange course of behaviour for one who, as O'Brien himself points out, was always painfully solicitous for his public reputation and did not disdain the arts of spin to maintain the purity of his image. Yet such is the logical position of those commentators such as William Safire (and indeed Professor Eugene Foster and the other geneticists who carried out the DNA tests). For what they are saying is that Callender was wrong about Thomas Woodson but was right about the parentage of Eston, who was born eighteen years after Thomas and six years after Callender's accusation was published. I find that assertion frankly incredible.

So, if Jefferson was not the father of either Thomas Woodson or Eston – who was? Well, the historians who were hastily assembled to form the Jefferson–Hemings Scholars Commission to rebut the even hastier judgements of the TJ Memorial Foundation concluded (12 April 2001) that there was insufficient evidence to link Thomas Jefferson with any of Sally's children but that the most likely candidate for Eston's father was TJ's much younger brother Randolph (1755–1815), who was notorious for hanging around with the slaves at Monticello, singing and playing the fiddle – and so why not other malarkey too? This would, among other things, explain why Jefferson himself never issued any formal public denial of the Sally stories. What would be the use if his denial only exposed Randolph as the culprit? Then as now, the revelation of scandalous behaviour by a president's brother would be an embarrassment, especially if it revealed him as belonging to a family who routinely abused their slaves.

But what about Thomas Woodson? If he was Sally's son, then

he was conceived in Paris. And his mother, barely sixteen years old at the time, is known to have been in two places only during the period, either waiting on Polly and Patsy at their convent school, where the girls were under strict supervision, or at the Hôtel de Langeac, which was a surprisingly small house and, so far as we know, contained at the time only two young men: Sally's brother James, the minister's cook, and the minister's secretary, William Short – the only European around. So William becomes the obvious candidate for father of Thomas. For two centuries he has escaped being so fingered, I believe, only because he is not one-hundredth as famous as his master.

If William was indeed Thomas's father, then again Jefferson would have wished to keep the matter dark and avoid any scandal that would damage the life chances of his protégé, of whom he was extremely fond. So would William, assuming that he ever knew Sally had borne him a child. Neither man would have dreamed of mentioning the matter in their letters when Jefferson was back in America, since the mails were so avidly read by spies and censors.

If you want any further pointers, consider the strong and sur-prising tradition that Sally had been reluctant to return to the United States with her master. She was pregnant, unmarried, very young and, as far as we can tell, knew little or no French. Why on earth would she wish to stay behind in Paris, rather than go back to her mother in Virginia, unless it was to be with the father of her child? And who else was remaining at the legation but William Short?

Finally, and rather sadly, why should William be so reluctant for the rest of his life to visit his ageing patron and adopted father at Monticello? Yes, the older he became, the more this lifelong *ami des noirs* kept to the Northern States, hating to see the despicable institution of slavery in action. But how much more sickened might he have been to be reminded of the consequences of his own actions?

For what it's worth, I tend to believe Jefferson's denial, given indirectly in his admission of misbehaviour with Betsey Walker. His revulsion against black bodies, even perhaps that of a 'bright mulatto' such as Sally, seems so visceral as to rule out anything more than the briefest of flings, if that. Or was his description of 'boisterous passion' and 'degrading submissions' a secret, self-loathing admission?

What is undeniable is Jefferson's unscrupulous and unpleasant behaviour in the matter of James T. Callender, first hiring him to abuse his old friend John Adams, then ratting on him and getting his comeuppance as a result. The following year, Callender, no doubt pre-soaked in whisky, drowned or drowned himself in the James river. There must have been sighs of relief all over Virginia, not least at Monticello.

Anyone who still sees the Founding Fathers as a choir of angels singing from the same hymn sheet needs a new pair of lenses.

VII

JEREMY BENTHAM

and the management of happiness

THE RESURRECTION MAN

Bentham is with us still, literally. He is the only political thinker of the eighteenth or any other century who remains visible in the flesh. Impishly mocking organized religion to the last, he left instructions in his will that he should be bodily resurrected by his physician and friend Dr Thomas Southwood Smith. And there he sits in his old straw hat, lace jabot and plain black coat and white stockings, his skeleton stuffed with straw and tow, at the south end of the cloisters of University College, London, the non-religious establishment of which he is the founding spirit.

Well, at least that's the idea. In reality, of his fleshly envelope only the strands of sandy hair are genuine. The head is a wax model by the distinguished French medical modeller Jacques Talrich. Bentham had hoped that his actual head would be part of the display when his disciples met together on high days and holidays 'for the purpose of commemorating the Founder of the Greatest Happiness system of morals and legislation'. Unfortunately, despite his efforts to get hold of someone else's head to practise on, the preserving method that Southwood Smith employed, of placing the head under an air pump over sulphuric acid and drawing off the fluids, did not work out as hoped. Far from preserving the great man as his friends had known him in all his serenity, the result was a death's head that might have turned up in the rubble of a concentration camp. For many years, this macabre object was displayed between Bentham's boots, rather like a football between the legs of the team captain. But it became the target of student pranks, being stolen by students from the rival King's College and allegedly also being used for football kickabouts in the quad. So much for Bentham's hope that the sight of his remains would show that 'the human body when dissected, instead of being an object of disgust is as much more beautiful than any other piece of mechanism as it is more curious and wonderful'. (Schofield, p. 337)

Nor did the 'Auto-Icon', as he called it, with his incurable fondness for coining new compounds from Greek, succeed in dispersing the superstitious reverence paid to dead bodies, as Bentham had hoped. In 2005, the head was relocated to the Conservation Safe in the UCL Institute of Archaeology, and you now need special permission from the curator to see it. Why? Because, as with pickled Maori heads (from which Bentham and Southwood Smith had hoped to learn the art of mummification), modern susceptibilities deem it 'inappropriate' to put 'human remains' on display. How furious Bentham would have been.

Bentham laid down careful instructions for the inauguration of the Auto-Icon, and these were scrupulously followed. Three days after his death, Southwood Smith delivered a long oration over the corpse at the Webb Street School of Anatomy and Medicine, after which it was publicly dissected in front of the students and the soft parts removed for them to experiment on. The obsequies took place during a heavy thunderstorm with lightning flashing through the windows of the lecture room, and Southwood Smith delivering the homily 'with a clear, unfaltering voice, but with a face as white as that of the dead philosopher before him'. (Marmoy, p. 81)

This was no last-minute octogenarian whim. Bentham had been thinking about his Auto-Icon for years. He was said to jingle in his pocket the glass eyes he had bought for it. Bentham was not the first *philosophe* to leave his body for dissection. Denis Diderot had done the same, but the wry, self-aware Diderot would never have turned the whole performance into such a giant ego trip.

The Auto-Icon did of course have the respectable purpose of furthering medical education. Only four years earlier, Burke and Hare had committed their notorious murders in Edinburgh and sold the bodies for dissection, to add to the dead bodies they had dug up from graves. The 'Resurrection Men', as the bodysnatchers were known, had fascinated and scandalized the nation. The outcry led to the passing of Warburton's Anatomy Act of 1832, just before Bentham's death, which allowed people to leave their bodies to medical science. Always alert to the possibilities of publicity, Jeremy Bentham now became his own Resurrection Man.

He also left behind a playful pamphlet of no less than 13,000 words to accompany the event, entitled *Auto-Icon: or, Farther Uses of the Dead for the Living.* The 'Farther' refers to an earlier pamphlet by Southwood Smith arguing that people should leave their bodies for dissection and that this should be made legal. (Marmoy, p. 78) But Bentham went way beyond his friend's sober brief. His pamphlet was so jocular, so irreverent, that his acolyte Sir John Bowring, who was at his deathbed, refused to include it in the *Collected Works* he edited, along with many other anti-religious pieces, 'so bold and adventurous were some of his writings'. (Marmoy, p. 79) In fact, the letter accompanying the British Library's copy, one of the few surviving, says that Bowring wanted the pamphlet destroyed.

Mere medicine was only the beginning of the possible uses of the Auto-Icon. It could, for example, be deployed in theatrical performances:

> By means of strings or wires, by persons under the stage, or if the Auto-Icon were clothed in a robe, by a boy stationed within, and hidden by the robe ... the eyelids might be made to move, and in so far as needful or conducive to keeping up the illusion, the hands and feet, one, more, or all. As to voice, by well-known contrivances, it may, without difficulty, be made to appear to proceed from the vocal organs of the body; the body, if necessary, might, by obvious contrivances, be made to appear to breathe. (British Library copy, p. 13, quoted Schofield, p. 339)

Bentham imagined Auto-Icons staging public discussions about philosophy, himself going hammer and tongs with Plato, whom he regarded as 'the grand original manufacturer of moral unintelligibles', in whose 'vast wilderness of words' not a single clear idea was to be found. (Mack, p. 110) Auto-Icons of deceased lords could be put on display among live peers in the Upper House. Bentham's own Auto-Icon might become an object of pilgrimage, a 'Quasi-Hadj' made by votaries of his Greatest Happiness principle. 'Why not to this receptacle as well as to Mahomet's? Is not Bentham as good as Mahomet was? In this or that, however distant, age will he not have done as much good as Mahomet will have done evil to mankind?' (British Library copy, p. 15, quoted Schofield, p. 341)

At all ages, Jeremy Bentham had a strong sense of his own importance. He had an ego to match his brain, which was as huge as his frame was tiny. He always seemed frail, yet lived to the age of eighty-four, jogging, or 'trotting', as he called his favourite pastime, from Fleet Street to St James's Park in his late seventies. He was a child prodigy, writing Latin and Greek at the age of five or six. At the age of twelve, he was entered as a commoner at Queen's College, Oxford – the youngest in the history of the university – and graduated by the time he was fifteen. All this delighted his father, a pushy property magnate, but Jeremy refused to be pushed, at least not in the conventional way his father wanted, ending up as, say, Lord Chancellor. He did qualify as a lawyer but hated the law and despised lawyers. In fact, he never took a job, living modestly on a small allowance until his father died, when he took over the family home, 2 Queen's Square Place (where Petty France now runs), and also rented the beautiful Forde Abbey in Somerset for a number of years. He was liberal and enthusiastic about sex, but never had much experience in that line, though he did once propose to a niece of Lady Shelburne's who turned him down politely. He called his house the Hermitage and devised strange domestic customs, such as serving the dessert first and having his desk and armchair built on an elevated platform, surrounded by a sunken passage or 'vibratory ditch' for indoor jogging round. He kept up an endless chatter of facetious fancies and songs, which he composed impromptu. He would also break out into an involuntary laugh at unexpected moments.

A recent study by two psychologists, Philip Lucas and Anne Sheeran, suggests that Bentham may have suffered from Asperger's syndrome. Psychiatric diagnoses across a distance of two centuries

need to be treated with suspicion, but Bentham's contemporaries
did detect a certain human absence in him, and record foibles that
sound not unlike what today we might call 'typical Asperger's'.

William Hazlitt had been one of Bentham's tenants until he fell
behind with the rent. He said of his landlord that

> in general habits and in all but his professional pursuits, he is
> a mere child. He has lived for the last forty years in a house in
> Westminster, overlooking the Park, like an anchoret in his cell,
> reducing law to a system, and the mind of man to a machine. He
> scarcely ever goes out, and sees very little company. The favoured
> few, who have the privilege of the *entrée*, are always admitted
> one by one. He does not like to have witnesses to his conversa-
> tion. He talks a great deal and listens to nothing but facts . . . He
> regards the people about him no more than the flies of a summer.
> (Hazlitt, 'Jeremy Bentham')

John Stuart Mill, who knew Bentham even better than Hazlitt,
wrote of 'the incompleteness of his own mind as representative of
universal human nature. In many of the most natural and strong-
est feelings of human nature he had no sympathy; from many of
its graver experiences he was altogether cut off; and the faculty
by which one mind understands a mind different from itself and
throws itself into the feelings of that other mind, was denied him
by his deficiency of imagination.' (Ryan, p. 148) Which is certainly
classic Asperger's and testimony all the more impressive because it
was written long before Dr Hans Asperger was born or his theory
thought of.

Several Bentham scholars have noted the oddity that there is no
full-length modern biography covering all his life (though there are
plenty of books about this or that aspect of his thought). At the
same time, none of them seems eager to take on the job. It is as if
they dreaded finding an empty space at the end of what would be
a mountainous task. Certainly, as we have already seen, Bentham
had no doubt that he would be remembered, and deserved to be.
In that, he succeeded so well that his admirers have often forgotten
or played down how deliciously silly he could be. One or two have

refused to accept the Auto-Icon pamphlet as Bentham's own work, fearing that it might be a malicious parody of his style. Even those who do acknowledge this extravaganza as authentic have tended to sideline it as a mere *jeu d'esprit*. But it seems to me as deadly serious as any of Voltaire's satires, for it does embody Bentham's driving purpose: to dissolve reverence for the icons of organized religion and to dispel the superstitious dread of death.

THE NON-ENTITY OF GOD

From an early age, he had hated religion of any kind, especially the Church of England in which he was reared. He refused to believe that any of it was true; he disliked its gloomy rituals; and he was contemptuous of the dishonesty, both worldly and intellectual, of its priests. He laid elaborate plans for what he called the 'euthanasia of the Church', by which all the C of E's property and income would be gradually handed over to the state as bishops and vicars retired or died. He never recovered from his distress at having to subscribe to the Thirty-nine Articles in order to qualify for Oxford. He became increasingly convinced that the grounds for inferring the existence of God were so weak to non-existent that He ought rather to be regarded as a 'Non-Entity'. (Dinwiddy, p. 113)

He was, besides, utterly indifferent to any spiritual dimension in life, except possibly in relation to music (he was proficient on the violin). He deeply distrusted poetry as lending false colours to reality. He once defined it as the stuff where the lines did not reach the margin of the page. (Dinwiddy, p. 114) All he would concede was that doggerel might be a useful aid for 'lodging facts more effectually in the mind'. (Atkins, p. 205) As reported by John Stuart Mill, he thought that pushpin (a form of shove-halfpenny) was as good as poetry, at least 'for the purposes of ethical theory and law'. (Letwin, p. 139)

At the same time, Bentham was anxious that his scandalous religious views should not prejudice the reception of his political nostrums. There were sheaves of anti-religious pages that he never published. Bowring was even less anxious to publish them, as he did not share his master's secular views. Among his intimates, though,

Bentham was happy to pass round his anti-clerical squibs. He referred to orthodox Christianity under the alias of 'the Juggernaut' or 'Jug' for short, with facetious derivatives such as 'juggical' or 'anti-jug'. (Atkins, p. 211) In a prefiguring of Margaret Thatcher, he would refer to fellow agnostics as 'one of us'.

Bentham's interpreters and fans tend not to spend much time on his dislike of religion. Since so little of his published work is on this area, they reason that this side of Bentham can have had little influence on his contemporaries or posterity. Yet I think that this is where we need to start. For Bentham sets out with a passionate desire to desacralize the world. It is a desire shared by many modern spokesmen for atheism. We can discredit the idea of the sacred by rational argument, or we can make fun of it, as Bentham does in *Auto-Icon*. Either way, this anti-crusade is a point of departure for Bentham, not a mere sideline. And the Auto-Icon itself is not a jokey prank but a parting salvo in a long campaign, even though one waged largely below the public radar.

THE WRONGNESS OF RIGHTS

Bentham does not stop at religion. His mission is to cleanse the world of all metaphysics, not just religious metaphysics. He is out to expose the emptiness of all fancy talk, to debag the windbags, to debunk their bunkum wherever it comes from. Here he parts company with the progressive radicals with whom he seems at first to belong. He is as hot against the airy visions of secular progressives as against the humbug of the clergy. The American Declaration of Independence, for example, he describes as 'a hodge-podge of confusion and absurdity, in which the thing to be proved is all along taken for granted'. (*Works*, X, p. 63, quoted Letwin, p. 142) Surprisingly, he sided with Lord North, not because he admired North (he didn't) but because the Americans had founded their rebellion on 'natural rights', which he thought was meaningless twaddle. All the vehemence and passion of these declarations was merely 'bawling upon paper'. ('*Rights, Representation and Reform*', *Works*, ed. Philip Scofield, 2002, pp. 186–7) The rebels claimed that men were born with these rights and they wanted to institute a government in order to secure them, but: 'They see not ... that nothing that was ever called Government ever was or ever could be exercised but at the expence [sic] of one or other of those rights.' (Mack, p. 186) As for equality, 'What is it they mean when they say all men are created equal ... Do they know of any other way in which men are created ... in which they themselves were created, than by being *born*? ... Is the child born equal to his parents, born equal to the Magistrates of his country? In what sense is he their equal?' (Ibid.) Well, in the sense that he's a human being like they are, so in what initial sense is he not equal? The believer in human rights is saying no more that all laws and inequalities have to be justified against that initial endowment conferred by God or Nature. One may or may not wish to use the language of rights, but it's a stretch to argue that it's all nonsense, and Bentham, as so often, does not really argue the case but waves it away with a fine dismissive phrase.

Besides, only a few years later, when the American experiment was going along swimmingly, Bentham began to applaud the new system and compared it favourably with the encrusted British status quo. He was to perform much the same reverse ferret when the French Revolution came along. He was horrified by the French *Declaration of the Rights of Man*. In a work entitled *Anarchical Fallacies*, written at a time in the mid-1790s when he was scared of the threat to property, he wrote that the *Declaration* was 'a perpetual vein of nonsense, flowing from a perpetual abuse of words', written with the same inaccuracy, the same inattention 'as if it had been an oriental tale, or an allegory for a magazine'. (Dinwiddy, p. 40) Such claims to natural, imprescriptible rights were 'nonsense upon stilts', the most famous phrase he ever coined.

Yet, years later, he became a radical democrat and came round at least to the practical implications of that Declaration. In fact, this was a return to his initial sympathy for the Revolution, shared in the early days by many if not most liberal minds in Britain. He had even drafted a set of rules of procedure for the benefit of the French National Assembly, which he called *An Essay on Political Tactics*, and he was so eager to get it adopted that he wrote to his Paris contact, the abbé Morellet: 'I could wish that these sheets were translated and sent off to be printed sheet by sheet that no time may be lost in getting out this part before the meeting.' (Mack,

p. 414) He wanted to station people at the door with copies to sell to the members as they went in, with free copies for poor *curés* and labourers. As so often, alas, the Assembly was not disposed to take advice from foreign policy wonks.

Bentham never passed up an opportunity to fast-track his latest wheeze straight to the people who mattered. He wrote to Benjamin Franklin, for example, proposing to send him a copy of his *Introduction to the Principles of Morals and Legislation* as this book 'was written for the use of leading men: nor to any but leading men has it been sent' (Mack, p. 363) – the standard pitch of investment advisors through the ages. In 1811, he wrote at great length to President Madison offering to draw up a comprehensive legal code for the United States. Three years later, he made the same offer to Alexander I of Russia. Similar offers were made to the parliaments of Portugal and Spain, to President Rivadavia of Argentina, to Simón Bolívar in Colombia, to the grand duke of Tuscany, to the prime minister of the Two Sicilies, to Gustavus of Sweden and to Frederick of Prussia. He privately exulted in the existence of so many absolute rulers who had such power to do good for their countries. The comprehensive legal code, or *Pannomion*, that he offered these supermen was not actually written, or only fragments of it were, but he was confident that, if given 'encouragement' by any 'competent authority', he could knock it out in no time, for any country anywhere. He differed sharply from Montesquieu in regarding as trivial the differences in climate, religion and population between one country and another. His first work, *A Fragment on Government*, written when he was only twenty-eight, argued that once set out in codified statutes, the laws of one country could serve any other, with only modest variation, and, what's more, would not need serious revision more than once in a hundred years. For on the 'grand principle of utility', one could form a 'precise notion of a perfect system of legislation'. (*Works*, I, p. 194; quoted Letwin, p. 166) 'A natural arrangement, governed as it is by a principle which is recognized by all men, will serve alike for the jurisprudence of all nations.' (*Morals and Legislation*, p. cclv)

The first thing to do was to get rid of that rickety old thing known as the common law. English lawyers like Sir William Blackstone were absurdly reverential towards this heap of ancient rubbish. In fact, Blackstone and his like were as bad as the medieval school-men, with delusions that their airy abstractions corresponded to real objects. The common law was not only an excuse for lawyers to deny and delay justice, contrary to Magna Carta, but an excuse to line their pockets.

LOST FOR WORDS

The language of law had to be transformed. 'All questions of Law are no more than questions concerning the import of words.' (Steintrager, p. 23) The only way to clear up the confusion and make it possible to deliver justice was 'to lay aside the old phraseology and invent a new one'. (Letwin, p. 158; *Principles of Morals*, p. 221) Or as Bentham put it in a sort of memo to himself: 'Postulate: that all new words and phrases necessary to the substitution of truth to error – of clearness to obscurity – conciseness to verbosity – be coined, uttered, and received.' (Mack, p. 151) And the way to achieve this was to show that all our complex ideas originally arose in simple ideas and could be broken back down into simple words. At one moment, he even mused that we could do away with words altogether: 'why should not all intellectual ideas be communicated by figures – as musical ideas are by notes, and arithmetical by cyphers?' (Mack, p. 271) Here we see foreshadowed the linguistic preoccupations of Russell and Wittgenstein and the algebraic pre-tensions of modern logicians too.

Bentham certainly did his bit as far as minting new words goes. He is the Olympic champion of neologism. Quite a few of his coinings have stuck: maximize, minimize, international, forthcom-ingness, codify and codification, eulogistic. There are dozens more that have got no further than Bentham's voluminous sheets of folio paper: phraseoplerosis, thelematology, pothography, contrectation, phthano-parenomic.

He also thought that you could make the English language con-crete and simple by getting rid of verbs as far as possible, because nouns were the only *things*: 'substantives are the only real entities; situations, motions are imaginary entities'. So he began to eliminate all but a few basic verbs like 'give' and 'take'. The trouble is that this is not how we speak, and so it is actually harder to understand someone who says 'give extension to' rather than 'extend', or 'give denomination to' rather than 'denominate'. But once again, we find an echo of Bentham's method in twentieth-century plain-language advocates such as C. K. Ogden, whose Basic English claimed to use a minimal vocabulary of 850 words to do the work of 20,000, thus offering an alternative international language that anyone could learn in no time. The richness and flexibility of English as she is actually spoken was of no interest to these linguistic puritans.

The combination of these quirks and quiddities, together with his determination to leave no qualification or clarification unvoiced, makes huge tracts of Bentham's later work almost unreadable. The more exhaustively he tried to show the truth beyond any doubt, the more exhausting his work became, the less easy to penetrate. The puckish brilliance of his journalistic pasquinades disappears under a load of redundant verbiage. The new edition of his *Collected Works* will fill fifty volumes. Many great men have written a huge amount; the complete Voltaire is reckoned to run out at two hundred volumes. But Bentham is surely unique among great thinkers in the way so much of his output repels even the most willing boarders. Even his modern admirers and editors confess with Frederick Rosen: 'The long, often obscure sentences, the technical language, the numerous digressions, and the legalistic framework act as strong deterrents to both Bentham scholars and students of political ideas.' (Rosen, pp. 1–2) His brief squibs and polemics are as sparky as any tabloid columnist's, but his longer theoretical stuff can be unendurable.

Part of the trouble is that Bentham left so much of his work unfinished. As his friend George Wilson said in a letter to Bentham's brother Sam: 'The reason is that he does too many things at once, not that he is lazy. He begins to write about the Code, but within an hour he's writing about twenty other subjects, so as not to lose the ideas which would no doubt present themselves again, and which he perhaps already has in papers which he wrote a long time ago and has forgotten.' (18 January 1780, quoted Atkinson, p. 40, original in French, my translation) Even the works that were published had often been left for years before he got around to them again. In the case of his central work, *An Introduction to the Principles of Morals and Legislation*, he confesses to having 'found himself unexpectedly entangled in an unsuspected corner of the metaphysical maze'. But after leaving the text for eight years, he found the task of reworking it so irksome that he published it just as it was, along with the imperfections of which he was painfully aware.

There is a deeper difficulty in getting to grips with Bentham. For all his finicky elaborations and qualifications, the quality of the argument often seems thin, consisting of a series of brief assertions followed by pages and pages of examples, not all of them obviously relevant. He was a great list-maker, but was he always a great thinker? Bentham scholars have noted too how, as he grew older, he read fewer books and engaged with fewer of his critics. His admiring first editor, John Bowring, tells us: 'He paid little regard to the attacks of which he was sometimes the object, and, in fact, was scarcely ever known to read a criticism upon his own writings. "Why should I be put out of my way? – I have much to do – I have little time to do it in."' (*Works*, X, Part XIX, p. 78)

Gertrude Himmelfarb notes in his letters as well as in his formal writings,

a pronounced insularity, self-containment, and self-satisfaction. It is as if, very early in his life, he had committed himself to a system of thought which he found entirely persuasive, totally comprehensive, and, not the least of its merits, uniquely his. Because that system was, for him, so unproblematic, so evidently true and sufficient for all purposes, he felt little need, in his public presentations of it, to take special note of either his forebears or his contemporaries. ('On Reading Bentham Seriously', pp. 185–6)

There is no mystery about what he was setting out to do. He wanted to introduce scientific method into political theory. More broadly, he planned to import the restless, inquisitive and innovative spirit of the natural sciences into the new social sciences of law, politics and economics. And he was hugely optimistic about the prospects. He prefaces his first work, *A Fragment on Government*, with the words: 'the age we live in is a busy age; in which knowledge is rapidly

advancing towards perfection ... if there be room for making, and
if there be use in publishing, *discoveries* in the *natural* world, surely
there is not much less room for making, nor much less use in proposing, *reformation* in the *moral*.' He was diametrically opposed to
Burke's view that there were no new discoveries to be made in morals.

HAPPINESS IS ALL

In that same preface, he offers what he calls 'a fundamental axiom'
for making these discoveries: 'it is the greatest happiness of the
greatest number that is the measure of right and wrong'. (*Fragment*,
pp. 3–4) All his life he remained thrilled by the moment when he
stumbled upon this key to everything. He was browsing in the
library of Harper's coffee house near his Oxford college when he
found in a pamphlet by Dr Priestley the phrase 'the greatest happiness of the greatest number'. Years later, writing of himself in the
third person, he remembered: 'At the sight of it he cried out, as it
were in an inward ecstasy like Archimedes on the discovery of the
fundamental principles of hydrostatics, *Eureka*.' (Mack, p. 103)
As with several of Bentham's later memories of his early career,
this was not quite accurate, as the actual phrase does not occur in
Priestley's pamphlet.

   This was the principle that was to bring political theory down
to earth, to ground it securely in physical reality, to make its conclusions verifiable and, where possible, quantifiable, by means of a
'felicific calculus'. To make headway, he needed to reduce his subject
matter to the simplest factor: the individual. In this sense, Bentham
was always an individualist. Concepts such as 'the community'
were fictitious, and not innocent fictions either, for if such words
had any practical purpose, it was to cloak oppression and manipulation. 'The interest of the community then is, what? – The sum
of the interests of the several members who compose it.' (*Morals
and Legislation*, I, IV) So Bentham might even have agreed with
Margaret Thatcher that 'there is no such thing as society – there are
only individual men and women and their families' – for the family
was in Bentham's view a social fact, whatever its faults. The only
scientific way to benefit society as a whole was through improving

the happiness of its individual members. The technical name for it is 'psychological egoism'.

How was that happiness to be measured and defined? Here too Bentham hopes to simplify, to reduce the problem to the basic physical level. He begins the *Introduction to the Principles of Morals and Legislation* with the resounding claim that 'Nature has placed mankind under the governance of two sovereign masters, *pain* and *pleasure*. It is for them to point out what we ought to do, as well as to determine what we shall do. On the one hand the standard of right and wrong, on the other the chain of causes and effects are fastened to their throne.' (I, p. 1) No man needed to go to a lawyer to know the meaning of pain and pleasure. (*Fragment*, p. 415–18)

That's all there is to life. Human beings set out to 'maximise' (copyright J. Bentham) pleasure and 'minimise' (also copyright J. Bentham) pain. And they are morally right to do so. That is what politics and law and economics are ultimately for. In his *Rationale of Judicial Evidence*, he tells us that 'in morals, as in legislation, the *principle of utility* is that which holds up to view as the only sources and tests of right and wrong, human suffering and enjoyment – pain and pleasure'. (Dinwiddy, p. 21; *Rationale*, VI, p. 238)

Of course, it didn't escape Bentham's critics – and it didn't escape him either – that he has yoked together here a supposed statement of fact, about how humans do behave, to a recommendation of how they *ought* to behave. He has himself committed the fault that he criticizes so fiercely in others, such as Sir William Blackstone: jammed together an 'is' statement and an 'ought' statement. He recognizes, if only in a footnote, that this sleight of hand puts off a lot of readers: 'This want of a sufficiently manifest connection between the ideas of *happiness* and *pleasure* on the one hand and the idea of *utility* on the other, I have every now and then found operating, and with but too much efficiency, as a bar to the acceptance, that might otherwise have been given, to this principle.' (*Fragment*, p. 58fn)

But Bentham does not bother to dwell on this snag. In all the thousands of pages he wrote, only those four pages at the beginning of the *Introduction* give an explicit account of the foundation of his whole system. (Steintrager, p. 28) He is too eager to press on and demonstrate that his pain–pleasure principle did in fact cover pretty much everything human beings did or avoided doing. 'If it be through the happiness of another, or others, in whatsoever number, that a man pursues his own happiness, still the direct and immediate object is not the less his own happiness.' (Dinwiddy, p. 22; *Introduction*, X, p. 532)

One may wonder whether this is a satisfactory way to describe all our actions. What about situations in which we have to choose between two options that are both repulsive? What about all those actions that we take out of habit or duty or by miscalculation or without expectation of any material benefit or the slightest flicker of pleasure, like obeying a traffic signal or filling in a tax form? What about the decisions that we regret, even as we are taking them, because we cannot think of a practicable alternative? Are not human motives in reality a good deal more complex than the pain–pleasure spectrum allows? And are not some of the most intense pleasures experienced communally, in church or mosque, say, or at patriotic demos or football matches – none of them occasions at which Bentham would have cared to be present? Yes, of course the pleasure is felt by individuals, but the community is its precondition.

Extended as far as Bentham needs to extend it, the principle becomes almost invisibly thin. At the extreme, it amounts to saying no more than that in some etiolated sense we must have a positive attitude to every decision we take, or we would not have taken it. Ultimately the principle is empty if not circular. The decision that we have taken has to be accounted a pleasure-driven or pain-avoiding one, because it is the decision we have taken, and not another one. If we had taken the opposite decision, that too would have counted as pleasure-driven or pain-avoiding, for the same reason.

Bentham's link between 'is' and 'ought' begins to look shaky too. A suicide bomber looking forward to his reward in heaven may be maximizing his own pleasure, but we would not therefore consider his action to be morally good. Yet if he is deluded, what becomes of the principle, essential for Bentham's argument, that each man is the best judge of his own actions, because he is the best assessor of his own pleasure/pain? 'No man can be so good a judge as the man himself, what it is gives him pleasure or displeasure.'

(*Introduction*, p. cxlix) If he isn't, then it's the dreaded community that is to be the arbiter of what is to count as legitimate pleasure and what isn't. And it must be the community, too, in the shape of the government or the legislator, as Bentham likes to call him, who will have to do the sums in order to calculate the greatest happiness of the greatest number. When a man is mistaken about his interest, it is the legislator's duty to sort him out on the happiness principle, 'the sole standard, in conformity to which each individual ought, as far as depends upon the Legislator, to be *made* to fashion his behaviour'. (*Introduction*, p. 34, italics are Bentham's) So, willy-nilly, we are driven off the Benthamite individual physical criterion and back on to communally determined standards of right and wrong.

But let us assume for a moment that we are agreed on Bentham's guiding principle. How are we to evaluate, let alone achieve 'the greatest happiness of the greatest number'? How are we to maximize that happiness? Here we come to what, I think, is a genuine discovery of Bentham's – or at least a more precise working out of something of which his predecessors were only dimly aware. This is the principle of 'marginal utility', a key element in his felicific calculus, and one that continues to bear fruit today, especially in economics.

Why was it fair, for example, to redistribute some of the wealth of the rich man to his poorer neighbours? Because £10 was worth much more to the poor man than to the millionaire. Money had a diminishing marginal utility as you travelled up the income scale: 'The effect of wealth in the production of happiness goes on diminishing, as the quantity by which the wealth of one man exceeds that of another goes on increasing: in other words, the quantity of happiness produced by a particle of wealth ... will be less and less at every particle.' (Dinwiddy, p. 52; *Works*, III, p. 229) This idea of marginal utility can be applied not just to income distribution, but to almost any practical decision we take or refrain from taking: to work more hours, or to take on more debt, for example. In that sense, we are all calculators of our own marginal felicity. It is from Bentham's calculus that is born the modern economist's model man who seeks always to maximize his satisfactions.

In this field, Bentham had a sharper sense of reality even than Adam Smith. His best known economic writing, *Defence of Usury* (1787), criticizes Smith for supporting the legal maximum on interest rates (which Pitt was thinking of reducing from 5 per cent to 4 per cent at the time). Bentham thought that lenders and borrowers had a better sense of the risks and rewards involved than any government official could have. Those who justified such restrictions as necessary 'to restrain projects and projectors' ought to remember that economic progress depended on risk-taking: 'for think, Sir, let me beg of you [he was addressing Adam Smith, normally his economic mentor], whether whatever is now the *routine* of trade, was not, at its commencement, *project*? whether whatever is now *establishment* was not, at one time, innovation?' (*Defence of Usury*, 1818 edn, p. 145)

Bentham was just as emphatic in defence of free trade and against subsidies and tariffs. Individuals were far more likely than government agents to know in which branches of trade to put their money: 'Nor let it be forgotten, that on the side of the individual in this strange competition, there is the most perfect and minute knowledge and information, which interest, the whole interest of a man's reputation and fortune, can ensure: on the side of the legislator, the most perfect ignorance.' (p. 164) Hayek could not have put it better. Smith praises as socially beneficial two sorts of conventional villain: exporters and corn merchants. Bentham adds two more to the list: usurers (vilified ever since Aristotle) and 'projectors', or as we would say entrepreneurs. If Adam Smith is the father of classical economics, Bentham is the godfather.

When Bentham argues in favour of redistribution, it is not on grounds of social justice or Christian charity or human rights but on the grounds of what he takes to be observable, quantifiable facts. 'The question is put, as every political and moral question ought to be, upon the issue of fact; and mankind are directed into the only true track of investigation which can afford instruction or hope of rational argument, the track of experiment and observation.' (Dinwiddy, p. 35)

That was what Bentham really did contribute not only to Utilarianism as a doctrine but to modern social science generally.

John Stuart Mill had many criticisms to make of Bentham, but he was swift to concede his overwhelming merit: 'It was not his *opinions*, in short, but his *method*, that constituted the novelty and value of what he did.' (Atkinson, p. 31)

SEX AND THE SINGLE MAN

The utility principle carried in its armoury an even more potent depth charge that was, in the long term, to explode the conventional moral standards of his time, and ours. If we were to judge actions strictly by the pain and pleasure that they afford ourselves and others, how could we justify punishing behaviour that caused no visible damage to other parties? Could there be crimes that had no victims and no public consequences? So why was it right to criminalize sexual conduct that mostly took place in private between consenting adults? Bentham's most radical deductions remained mostly unpublished for fear of staining his name and the repute of his published work. But he was indefatigable on this as on everything. Between 1814 and 1816, he wrote two hundred pages on sex and penal reform.

For Bentham, sex was a strong and natural pleasure, although one of which, as we have said, he seems to have had little, if any, personal experience. There was no rational justification for limiting its expression, no reason for the laws against homosexuality or incest. Blackstone had placed sodomy under the heading of 'Offences against the safety of individuals', but 'how a voluntary act of this sort by two individuals can be said to have any thing to do with the safety of them or any other individual whatever, is somewhat difficult to be conceived', according to Bentham. (Dinwiddy, pp. 110–11) Such laws were a pernicious encouragement to blackmail: 'how easy it is to fabricate out of the dread of an accusation of this nature an instrument of extortion is but too obvious.' (Ibid.) Men should be allowed to do as they wished with their bodies if they did no harm to others. For the same reason, it was equally irrational to make suicide a crime.

All this applied to women too, for they could hardly be excluded from 'the greatest number'. If he had not feared public ridicule, he would have added votes for women to his call for universal male suffrage: 'on the ground of the greatest happiness principle, the claim of this sex is, if not still better, at least altogether as good as that of the other'. (p. 110)

Thus, by his own route, Bentham manages to reach the same policy conclusions as those modern liberal reformers who have started out from theories of human rights and natural law. In one specific respect, he is in an easier position. Bentham is just about the first writer to call strongly and consistently for the humane treatment of animals. He was fiercely opposed to all blood sports – fox-hunting, shooting, fishing, as well as bull-baiting and cock-fighting. He derived this view, not from any theory of animal rights – which he would have thought nonsensical – but from the principle that the law ought to protect any being capable of feeling pain.

As we have seen, Bentham had been trained as a lawyer, though he hated the trade. He had begun his polemical, pamphleteering life as a critic of lawyers and their self-seeking obfuscations. From there he had branched out into economics, where we see him at his incisive best. But in one department of the social sciences, this intellectual dynamo had been largely silent until quite late in his career: political theory. His patron, Lord Shelburne, twitted him with this neglect. Bentham replied, in effect, that as far as the people's happiness went, constitutional theory was of secondary importance, standing 'the farthest from that mark in the chain of causes and effects'. (Schofield, p. 223)

If anything, he looked like a somewhat unthinking reactionary. He had come out against the American Revolution. At the outset of the French Revolution, he had briefly shared in the general enthusiasm for the new dawn, but soon retreated, motivated by the fear of violence and the threat to property. On political reform, he had nothing much to say. In fact, he even began a pamphlet in defence of rotten boroughs, to be entitled 'Rottenness No Corruption', rather in the style of Edmund Burke whom he detested; the argument would have been that pocket boroughs provided an opportunity to promote young men of talent (Bentham had hoped that Shelburne would offer him the seat of Calne or Chipping Wycombe).

(Schofield, p. 104) He was certainly not choosy about who he offered his half-written Civil Code to. Dictators and democratic assemblies alike were the target of his importunings.

A PECULIAR DEMOCRAT

Then, in the last two decades of his life, he came out hot and strong as a full-blown radical democrat, or so it seemed. No longer was it imprudent to meddle with the British constitution, whose excellence outweighed its obvious faults. Opinions differ about exactly when he was converted to the cause of reform, but by 1822 he was declaring that the penal and civil codes of law were 'unavoidably dependent in principle & even in tenor' on the Constitutional Code. (Schofield, p. 249) The system was riddled with 'sinister interest'. Enraged by the failure of George III and his corrupt ministers to implement his brilliant ideas, he came to the conclusion that only in a democracy, where ultimate power was in the hands of everyone, could the government be trusted to seek the happiness of the greatest number. That meant universal male suffrage (and secretly votes for women too), annual parliaments, the secret ballot, no king, no House of Lords, and an elected prime minister. In short, the full democratic package.

Excited as he always was by his latest craze, Bentham dashed off hundreds of pages on how the new system was to work in every detail. The editors of the new *Collected Works*, as they have come across more and more previously unlogged material, have themselves invested much time and energy on charting Bentham's late U-turn, or perhaps S-turn (see in particular, Frederick Rosen's *Jeremy Bentham and Representative Democracy*, and Philip Schofield's *Utility and Democracy*).

So, on the face of it, late in both his life and his afterlife, Bentham has become a fully paid-up radical democrat. But if we look a little closer, Bentham's version of democracy seems rather different, certainly different from the Constitution of the United States, or even from the imperfect British democracy of the nineteenth century. To start with, there was to be no upper house to restrain the popular chamber. There were to be no juries of ordinary citizens to protect innocent defendants from rabid judges. The most that Bentham would concede were what he called 'Quasi-Juries', panels of three lay assessors selected for aptitude and intelligence who would assist the judge and comment on his findings. And this jury did not operate in courts of first instance, but only in cases where the verdict was disputed. Rather than the corrupt and bumbling civil courts, Bentham preferred 'the simplicity, the honesty, the straightforwardness of courts-martial'. (Atkinson, p. 203) He was in no doubt what courts were for: 'The end of procedure is the conviction of the guilty ... The Jury trial is a bad means to the end of procedure. The Star-Chamber trial was a good one. A better can not be devised.' (Mack, p. 425) He strongly disagreed with Blackstone's view that 'delays and little inconveniences in the forms of justice, are the price that all free nations must pay for their liberty in more substantial matters'. (Letwin, p. 163) Bentham was in favour of simplicity and speed. He recoiled from any complicating factor, such as the separation of powers. In fact, he thought everything about the Constitution of the United States was far too complicated – the federal system, the Bill of Rights, the Senate, the right of judicial review (although, if we look closer, we see that even under Bentham's system judges would still have power to interpret and so remake the law in certain circumstances). All these things were an 'unreflecting imitation' of the British system, which he now thought hopelessly flawed. Curious then that he also admired the way the United States had turned out.

Bentham had always hated all the talk of liberty in the American arrangements. 'As to the word liberty, it is a word, the import of which is of so loose a texture, that, in studied discourses on political subjects, I am not (I must confess) very fond of employing it, or of seeing it employed.' (Rosen, p. 69) He much preferred 'security' as a substitute. Now in some cases, say, the protection of your property against intrusion by your neighbour or by the state, 'security' can be seen as more or less a synonym for 'liberty', but in other cases it has a more authoritarian ring. And in many respects, Bentham's Code does seem to put authority first. He advocated a centralized, permanent Ministry of Police that would be able to draw on the resources of the army and the Royal Navy and would operate nationwide. The country would be split up into districts administered by 'local headmen', who sound rather like the French *intendants* of *départements* (Bentham admired Napoleon and his code). He had no qualms about deploying an army of paid informers across the country: 'To the word espionage, a stigma is attached: let us substitute the word inspection which is unconnected'. (Letwin, p. 175; *Works*, II, p. 222) – always watch out when Bentham uses the word 'inspection'. To help catch criminals, everyone should have his or her full name tattooed on the wrist, as English sailors did.

We begin to glimpse a chasm separating Bentham from those democrats who base their system on human rights of some sort. For the latter, democracy was (and is) the way to let the people breathe and speak and act, to exercise their inborn liberties as they please. For Bentham, democracy is the civilized way to *improve* the people. It is the business of the legislator to endeavour to correct the ill-founded prejudices of the people. And it is the sign of indolence or weakness in a legislator when he allows the people, 'for the want of some instruction, which ought to be and might be given them, to quarrel with their own interest,' Bentham tells us in the *Introduction*. 'Every nation is liable to have its prejudices and its caprices which it is the business of the legislator to look out for, to study, and to cure.' (*Introduction*, p. clxxiv) 'Cure' – the legislator is, if you like, a People Doctor. The legislator's task is to make the greatest number happier in a higher, more moral sense, by what Bentham called 'Indirect Legislation': that is, a system of carefully targeted rewards and punishments, and by official cajoling and persuading, often by what we today call 'subliminal' means (the word did not exist then, though Bentham would have been fully capable of devising it). The phrase 'guided democracy' has more often been applied to Communist regimes or semi-democratic autocracies, such as Soekarno's Indonesia. It would certainly do nicely for Bentham's late-life blueprint.

As early as 1794, Bentham explained that 'Vulgar legislation drags men to its purpose in chains, from which thanks to the bungling clumsiness of the grimgibber man at the anvil who forges them, the captives break loose in crowds: transcendental legislation leads men by silken threads, entwined round their affections, and makes them its own forever'. (Mack, p. 293) Indirect legislation could be made virtually painless and imperceptible. Bentham's *Limits of Jurisprudence Defined* began as a mere chapter (XVII) of the *Introduction to the Principles of Morals and Legislation* and swelled into hundreds of unpublished pages describing 'expedients for adjusting the propensities of men to the standard of utility'. (Mack, p. 295) Bentham says 'adjusting the propensities'; Chairman Mao would have called it 're-educating' them. He would have liked the idea of silken threads, though.

Bentham makes it startlingly clear exactly how he proposes to guide the people towards their best interests. Before taking his seat, and after passing a demanding series of exams to prove his 'aptitude', the incoming MP has to make a lengthy declaration, which would be made under oath if Bentham believed in oaths, which he doesn't. It's called the 'Legislator's Inaugural Declaration', and it was printed in Volume I of the Constitutional Code in 1830, and separately in 1831 (as *Parliamentary Candidates' Proposed Declaration of Principles*), shortly before Bentham's death. He called it 'a sort of moral code' and 'a map of the field of legislation', but the best way of describing it is as a compendium of all Bentham's loves and hates.

The incoming Assembly member has to subscribe, first and foremost, to the greatest-happiness principle. Then he has to promise to maximize security and minimize expense, or as we would say, public expenditure. He has to refuse to accept or confer any honours or pensions, and to be uncorrupt. So far perhaps, nothing very odd, if you go along with Bentham's basic principle. But then the new MP has to promise not to offer any public encouragement 'to piety, to arts, to sciences, and in particular to the fine arts, or merely curious sciences or literary pursuits'. The amusements of the opulent few are not to be subsidized by the taxes of the indigent many. Then the Declaration launches into a long rant, promising useful knowledge to all and denouncing by comparison all sports and games as useless and socially pernicious. Useful knowledge would be the most effectual preservative 'against the most productive sources of human misery such as gluttony, drunkenness, gaming and quarrelsomeness'. Bentham is especially critical of competitive games that place 'the parties in a state of constant opposition'. So no money for the British Museum or the Olympics, or indeed for sport in school. Like Rousseau, Bentham would have approved of the anti-competitive bias of some comprehensive schools.

But that is by no means the end of all the things the new MP has to subscribe to. He has to promise not to put any taxes upon the press; not to support any declaration of offensive war; not to support the acquisition of any colonies, even if the natives wish to be colonized; not to place any restrictions upon immigration or emigration, not to seek any advantage in commerce over other countries.

One may or may not agree with these policies, but what on earth are they all doing in a document setting out constitutional duties? What is clear is that the scope of action allowed to Bentham's democratic assembly is severely limited. The Assembly's ground rules are constructed to encourage good behaviour and discourage life's simpler pleasures, and it is not free to alter those ground rules. No wonder Bentham dislikes using or hearing the word 'liberty'. He knows perfectly well what it means, and he does not like its anarchic implications. At bottom, he is a control freak, and his utopia, like most utopias, is a controlled state.

And he knows what he is doing. There remains in an earlier draft a revealing admission that, in the eyes of the people, all these restrictions to secure the aptitude of their MP 'may be too great a liberty taken with their power of choice'. He brushes this worry aside. In his future ideal state, it would be hard to justify that the possession of these aptitudes should 'be left to chance'. (Rosen, p. 199) But 'chance' in this context is only another word for 'freedom'. Democracy, as most of us understand it, is an open-ended thing in which the people must be allowed to choose their representatives, whatever their views and qualifications or lack of them. That is not how Bentham sees it.

THE INSPECTOR CALLS

One must concede, though, the irrepressible fertility of Bentham's improving mind, whether expressed in legislative codes or in cunning gadgets. Some of Bentham's gadgets seem harmless enough. He had installed in Queen's Square Place a system of 'conversation tubes', made of thin airtight pipes to 'maximize the promptitude of oral intercourse'. These would be installed in the offices of ministers, as would a secure system of ropes and pulleys to send documents from one office to another, not unlike the money cylinders that used to whizz your change round old-fashioned department stores. He devised his own 'teasmade' machine, installed a system of steam-powered central heating and planned a frigidarium, an igloo-shaped ice-house in his garden for storing perishables. Before refrigeration, food prices fluctuated wildly according to the season, from two shillings to fifteen shillings for a hundredweight of herrings for example, from a shilling a pound for peaches and peas in season to a guinea out of it. The frig would smooth out prices round the year, yet another example of Bentham's desire to make men more 'secure' – something he rated far higher than liberty.

At other times, his inventions had a more authoritarian ring to them. None more so than the one he described so vividly in his pamphlet *Panopticon; or, the Inspection-House* (1787). The Panopticon is the most notorious, the most memorable of all Bentham's creations. The story of how it came about shows this extraordinary man at his most touching and vulnerable, also at his craziest.

In his essentially solitary life, the one person to whom Jeremy was unfailingly devoted was his only surviving sibling, Sam, who was nine years younger. Samuel Johnson Bentham, as he was christened (their crotchety old father shared all Dr Johnson's prejudices), was everything that Jeremy was not: tall, handsome, jovial, athletic and a trifle dyslexic. Jeremy adored him: 'O my Sam, my child, the only child I shall ever have, my second self, could you bear to part with me?' Jeremy moaned in 1779 when Sam was thinking of emigrating to the East Indies.

Despite Jeremy's best efforts, Sam found it difficult to get a job after being apprenticed to the naval dockyard at Woolwich, and took off to Russia to try his skills as a naval architect and engineer, which turned out to be considerable, for though no great shakes at his books, he had his brother's bump of ingenuity. Jeremy was desperate to follow Sam to Russia, both to see his brother again and to persuade the Empress Catherine to adopt his Criminal Code. Of all the enlightened despots of his day, she was the one he admired most, and he had his Code translated into her native German, by among others Rudolf Raspe, the author of the Munchausen tales, who was a rogue. Raspe couldn't make head nor tail of Bentham's impenetrable prose and anyway was soon carted off to jail for debt.

By the time Jeremy got to Russia in 1786, Sam had wearied of court life in St Petersburg and had become estate manager, down at Krichev in what is now Belarus, for Catherine's mega-rich favourite, Prince Potemkin, who was establishing a shipyard there, though Krichev was miles inland.

Potemkin was to become famous to posterity, not merely for the battleship named after him, which played a prominent part in the 1905 Revolution and for Eisenstein's film, often nominated as the greatest film ever, but also for the 'Potemkin villages', fake portable villages erected along the banks of the Dnieper, allegedly to fool the Empress on her progress down to the Black Sea. After she had passed, the structures would be dismantled and reassembled further downstream. The idea was to impress the foreign ambassadors accompanying Catherine with the wealth and power of Russia's southern provinces. Certainly, later Russian regimes did go in for all sorts of fakery, but Potemkin's recent biographer Simon Montefiore says that the Potemkin village itself was more or less a myth. The Prince might have tarted up the villages she passed through, but he could not have deceived her. There's no doubt, though, that Potemkin was a fertile and energetic fellow who, with Sam's aid, built all sorts of ships, fortresses, dockyards and breweries on his vast estates.

So it should have been an epic meeting between these two great innovators. Unfortunately, Jeremy seems to have been overcome by shyness when he got there. Even when the empress passed through, he hid away and never saw her. Nor did he ever meet Potemkin, who was in Petersburg most of the eighteen months that Jeremy was in Russia.

But his time at Krichev was not wasted. He wrote the *Defence of Usury* there and worked on his various Codes. More importantly, he was witness to the huge upheavals taking place in Russia under Catherine's impatient patronage and Potemkin's drive. The Czars had been hoovering up Church property ever since Peter the Great's day, and in 1764 Catherine had decreed that all of it had to be handed over to the state. Through the 1770s and 1780s, churches and monasteries were being secularized and converted into hospitals, prisons, schools and asylums (not so very different from what was to happen under communism). Jeremy noted gleefully: 'we are dissolving monasteries as you would lumps of sugar'.

It was the ingenious Sam who was designing many of these massive new institutions that were to civilize the unruly serfs. And it was from Sam's designs that Jeremy borrowed the celebrated panopticon that was to intrigue and scandalize posterity. What Jeremy brought to the project was the hype of a PR genius. On the title page of the pamphlet he published after he got back to England, he advertises the multiple purposes of the panopticon: it contained 'the idea of a new principle of construction applicable to any sort of establishment, in which persons of any description are to be kept under inspection; and in particular to penitentiary-houses, prisons, houses of industry, work-houses, poor-houses, lazarettos, manufactories, hospitals, mad-houses and schools: with a plan of management adapted to the principle'.

If that wasn't thrilling enough, he led off with a string of breathless slogans in italics: '*Morals reformed – health preserved – industry invigorated – instruction diffused – public burthens lightened – Economy seated, as it were, upon a rock – the gordian knot of the Poor-Laws not cut, but untied – all by a simple idea in Architecture!*'

It was, he claimed without fear of exaggeration, 'a new mode of obtaining power of mind over mind'. The main aim of the Inspection-House, or Elaboratory as he could not resist also calling it, was what it said on the tin: to keep as many people as possible under inspection all the time, whether the purpose was punishing the incorrigible, guarding the insane, confining the suspected, employing the idle, curing the sick, or training the rising race in the path of education. Ideally, every inmate should be under inspection 24/7. The next best thing was that the inmate 'should conceive himself to be so'.

The institution was to be called the Panopticon, after Argos Panoptes, the many-eyed giant of Greek legend, who had so many eyes that some of them were always watching while others slept. It would be a large circular building. The inmates' cells would occupy the circumference, each secluded from any communication with the others. In the middle would be the Inspector's lodge – 'at the heart of the spider's web', as a disenchanted Burke put it when he was shown the design. Each cell would have an iron grating on the inside, providing enough light for the inspector to see every part of the cell. A small tin tube would run from each cell to the lodge. If the Inspector put his ear to it, he would hear the slightest whisper. So those 'conversation tubes' in Queen's Square Place were not so innocent after all.

Think of the beauties of the thing. No danger of infection because the cells were separate, no danger of riot because each prisoner was in solitary confinement. No irons needed. Even 'the most boisterous malefactor' could vent his rage only by beating his head against the wall. Noise coming down the tubes might be a problem, but recalcitrant lags could be gagged. Visitors – and Bentham intended that there should be plenty of paying visitors – would be saved the 'disgust' of having to visit individual cells. They could simply watch and listen from the lodge. A decent income could be extracted from these visitors. The extreme economy of operation – one Inspector could oversee forty prisoners or more – could make the Panopticon self-supporting. Certainly, it would be far cheaper than maintaining convicts on the hulks, let alone transporting them to Botany Bay, as Lord Sydney proposed – Bentham argues repeatedly against the Australian option. The Inspector's contract would be open to tender, and you could rely on the contractor to run a tight ship. To prevent him starving the inmates to death: 'I would make him pay so much for every one that died, without troubling myself whether any care of his could have kept the man alive.' (*Panopticon*, p. 37)

And how perfectly the Panopticon was adapted for purposes beyond the incarceration of criminals. 'The melancholy abodes for the reception of the insane' would be far better run on pan-optical lines, which rendered unnecessary 'the use of chains and other corporal sufferances' – think of the saving on straitjackets. Hospitals too: the desperately sick patient could communicate his wants to the lodge, 'though he were equal to no more than a whisper'. Better still for a school: 'all play, all chattering in short, all distraction of every kind, is effectually banished by the central and covered situation of the master, seconded by partitions or screens between the scholars ... That species of fraud at Westminster [which Bentham had briefly attended and hated] called cribbing, a vice thought hitherto congenial to schools, will never creep in here.' (p. 64)

When he thought about it, Bentham says at the end, 'my wonder is, not only that this plan should never have hitherto been put in practice, but how any other should ever have been thought of'. (p. 72) He was desperate to see his (or rather Sam's) brainchild built in London, and he poured his own money into the project and for years buttonholed MPs relentlessly, even managing to secure parliamentary approval for the purchase of a site on Battersea Rise. The scheme finally miscarried in 1811, when the government decided to build its own more conventional prison. Bentham was awarded compensation of £23,000 for the heavy losses he had sustained.

The only person who ever did build Panopticons, several of them to Sam's designs, was, not surprisingly, the Czar. For all Jeremy's advocacy, the Panopticon was really better suited to an autocrat with serf problems. That, after all, was where it had originated.

Even today, the Panopticon has its fans. Janet Semple, in *Bentham's Prison*, excuses Jeremy as 'a realistic, kindly man looking for ways to ameliorate the lot of the poor'. But most of us would, I suspect, lean more to the view of Michel Foucault that the Panopticon was 'a diabolical piece of machinery for social control'. It seems to us to fore-shadow our darkest nightmares of *Brave New World* and Big Brother, not to mention the terrible realities of the Gulag and the Stasi.

Nudge, nudge

Yet many of the devices and practices on which Bentham prides himself as having invented are commonplace in modern societies. And I don't just mean the telephone. CCTV is everywhere, in all public institutions and outdoor urban spaces. The authorities have wide powers to listen in to our conversations and to hack into our emails. Bentham would have thoroughly approved. He thought that transparency and publicity were indispensable for the improvement of public morals. If he had thought of the phrase 'the surveillance society', he would have said, 'bring it on'. An ideal Benthamite society would be one big Panopticon.

What he called 'Indirect Legislation' is a routine part of the modern government's armoury: the breathalyzer, the speed camera, the sugar tax, the warnings on cigarette packets. Modern government often resorts to Bentham-sounding devices to improve moral conduct: the Anti-Social Behaviour Order, the Social Exclusion Unit, Neighbourhood Watch. More recently, there has been a willingness to learn from the insights of behaviourism, as developed by B. F. Skinner and J. B. Watson in the first half of the twentieth century. Human behaviour, like the behaviour of our nearest relatives in the animal kingdom, can be explained in terms of response to external stimuli and can be modified for the better by framing a suitable set of stimuli. We can be 'nudged' into being healthier, more responsible, less wasteful citizens. Cass Sunstein's bestselling books have popularized Nudge Theory, and President Obama gave him a job in his administration. In Britain, under the guidance of Sunstein's co-author Richard Thaler, the coalition government set up a Behavioural Insights Team in the Cabinet Office, which was immediately nicknamed the Nudge Unit. In 2017, Thaler was awarded the Nobel Prize for Economics. It was the apotheosis of Nudge, or you could call it a posthumous Nobel for Jeremy Bentham and his silken threads.

Critics have denounced such operations as covert psychological manipulation, which ought to have no place in a true democracy, especially as they are often not subject to parliamentary approval. Others have wondered how many of these techniques actually work over the long term, though some do seem to, such as the campaign to make people stop smoking by a combination of horrendous taxes and horrendous health warnings. But the point is that governments today feel duty-bound to consider such options, whenever they can see a worthwhile goal in view.

Often without being fully aware of it, governments today regard themselves as *managers* of society rather than simply as servants of the voters. They see their duty as governing *for* the people rather than *by* the people. We live, whether we intended it or not, and whether we like it or not, in a Benthamite world. The Auto-Icon of UCL is calling the shots today more than he ever did when he was really alive.

VIII

MARY WOLLSTONECRAFT

and the rights of woman – and men too

She was a blazer. She led the way and she left a fiery trail behind her. There had been no woman quite like her before, and the women who came after, a long way after, though considered firebrands in their day, often look like mere reflections of her afterglow. From her unpromising beginnings to her tragic early end, Mary Wollstonecraft was always herself. As a schoolgirl of fourteen, she wrote after a spat to her friend Jane Arden (Mary had attended her father's lectures on electricity in Beverley): 'I have a heart that scorns disguise, and a countenance which will not dissemble. I am a little singular in my thoughts of love and friendship. I must have the first place or none. I own your behaviour is more according to the opinion of the world, but I would break such bounds.' (Tomalin, pp. 19–20)

Break such bounds she did, again and again. And the opinion of the world did not care for it and determined to break her back. One of the many bitter accusations hurled at her during her life, and after her death too, was that she was a 'utopian projector' or 'philosopheress' who had not enough experience of the world to know what she was talking about. But she did. She had lived every inch of the terrain. Her hypersensitive, prickly, alert personality and her effortless eloquence made her a superb absorber and retailer of experience. When she spoke of the wrongs of woman, she spoke of the wrongs she had herself suffered or witnessed. She was never slow to let everyone know when she was being mistreated, tossing aside any suggestion that she should contain herself, as women were supposed to. In the words of her most recent biographer, Janet Todd: 'As thoroughly as any American of the 1970s, Mary was caught in the sentimental myth that it was good to express every emotion, to let everything hang out.' (Todd, p. 19)

She was tall with auburn hair and light-brown eyes. One of her eyelids was slightly paralysed, which could give her a mocking gaze, though not half as mocking as her conversation or her letters when she was in full flow – and when was she not? Her best friends, the Blood family (descended from the Colonel Thomas Blood who attempted to steal the Crown Jewels in the reign of Charles II), nicknamed her The Princess and she took it as a compliment. At the age of fifteen, a century before Virginia Woolf, she began to ask for a room of her own.

THE ELDEST DAUGHTER

There was nothing like being an eldest daughter for teaching you the injustice of male primogeniture. Why should her elder brother Ned have all the love, all the schooling and all the money, 'to carry the empty family-name down to posterity'? as she put it bitterly in her novel-fragment *Maria: Or, the Wrongs of Woman* (her other novel was entitled *Mary*, and the lead character in her moral fables for children, *Original Stories*, was called Mary too, which tells you something). Her grandfather, Edward, a prosperous silk-weaver of Spitalfields, had left considerable legacies to all his descendants, except Mary. The unfairness might have rankled less if her father, Edward Jr, had been a loving parent. But he was a feckless drunken brute who dragged his seven children all over the country, from Spitalfields to Barking, then to the handsome Yorkshire town of Beverley, where he scattered his cash at the local race meetings, down again to Hoxton, then west to the little Welsh port of Laugharne, where he must have been the most disagreeable incomer before Dylan Thomas. Sometimes he farmed, sometimes he dabbled in mysterious other businesses, but always he failed. He was often violent. Mary remembered sleeping on the landing and shielding her mother from his blows when he came home. After her mother's death, he was a nuisance to her and her sisters all his life.

Her brother Ned was set up in style as a lawyer, and the girls were left to their own scant devices. Mary tried all the options: companion to a crotchety widow in Bath, governess to the simpering Lady Kingsborough in Mitchelstown Castle, Co. Cork, keeping a school in Newington Green with her sister Eliza and Fanny Blood. She was sacked as a governess for being too uppity, and after a promising start the school failed, because there was so much competition from other unmarried young women.

It was a bold enterprise anyway, for a girl who was virtually self-taught, and never stopped improving herself. She went on to teach herself French, German and passable Italian, as well as giving herself a decent grounding in the histories of England and France. In her early twenties, she was already guying herself as a spinster bluestocking and claiming to relish the prospect: 'I will not marry, for I don't want to be tied to this nasty world, and old maids are of little consequence – that "let them live or die, nobody will laugh or cry" – It is a happy thing to be a mere blank, and to be able to pursue one's own whims, where they lead, without having a husband and half a hundred children at hand to teaze and controul [sic] a poor woman who wishes to be free.' (Todd, p. 44) Yet she craved affection. When the Blood family – whom she sometimes thought of as her real family – scattered, she wrote 'without some one to love, this world is a desert [sic] to me'. (Todd, p. 66)

At her worst, she could be intolerably bossy, and her forceful character had already declared itself in unmistakable fashion. Her sister Eliza had married a young boat-builder from Bermondsey called Meredith Bishop. After giving birth to a daughter, Eliza had depression, and Meredith summoned Mary across the river to help – which he must soon have regretted. Mary quickly gathered the impression that Meredith had been roughing up Eliza, perhaps sexually – 'he cant [sic] look beyond the present gratification', she told their sister Everina – and decided, in typical peremptory style, that she must rescue Eliza from this horrible marriage. So she whisked her away from Bermondsey to Hackney, where the two sisters installed themselves in lodgings under false names. It is not clear that Eliza really wanted to end the marriage, but she never went back to Bermondsey and never saw her daughter again (the baby died just before her first birthday). She never forgave Mary either.

Mary's forcefulness sometimes had more beneficial results. On her way back from Lisbon, where she had been tending her beloved Fanny Blood, who died in childbirth there, the boat came up with a storm-tossed French vessel. The French captain wanted to abandon ship and bring his crew aboard. The British captain refused on the ground that he had only enough provisions for his own passengers and crew. Mary pleaded on behalf of the distressed Frenchmen. The captain still refused. Mary threatened to give a full public account of the shameful episode. The captain caved in and the Frenchmen were taken aboard. A lifesaving achievement for a young Englishwoman without a penny.

She was aware of her willpower. 'I never yet resolved to do any thing of consequence, that I did not adhere resolutely to it.' (Todd, p. 120) She had a firm sense of her own destiny too. After she had published her first book, a modest manual on the education of daughters, she boasted to the long-suffering Everina: 'I am then going to be the first of a new genus ... You know I am not born to tread in the beaten track – the peculiar bent of my nature pushes me on.' (Todd, p. 124)

The school on Newington Green had one fortunate aspect, literally. Across the green lay the little Unitarian Chapel with its famous radical minister, Dr Richard Price. Friend of the American rebels, correspondent of Benjamin Franklin, Thomas Jefferson and the marquis de Condorcet, this kindly old gentleman had friends in all quarters. Not only had he just turned down one invitation from the new American government to settle over there, he had also declined another from the new British prime minister, Lord Shelburne, to act as his private secretary. He preferred to spend his days on long country walks, where he would free netted birds and set upturned beetles back on their legs. (Tomalin, p. 47) Although still an Anglican of sorts, Mary suddenly found herself part of that extraordinary local congregation of forward-thinking Dissenters.

Through them she had an introduction to the great radical publisher Joseph Johnson, who was to be her loyal supporter and affectionate correspondent. Like Dr Price, he became a father figure.

When on the verge of breakdown, she always relied on this benevolent old bachelor: 'You are my only friend – the only person I am
intimate with. – I never had a father, or a brother – you have been
both to me, ever since I knew you.' (Todd, p. 142)

Johnson's shop was a hub for all the reformers and radicals – Tom
Paine, William Godwin, William Blake, and the young Wordsworth
and Coleridge, before they turned away from the cause of revolution. He had quite a few bestselling women writers on his list too,
such as Anna Letitia Barbauld and, later, Maria Edgeworth, who
wasn't radical at all. So, Mary's first book fitted in nicely. By comparison with the books she was to write over the next five years,
Thoughts on the Education of Daughters (1787) is a timid affair. She
even preaches a dose of Christian resignation, in a chapter entitled
'The Benefits of Disappointments'. But already the real Mary is
beginning to peep through. She points out how the scales are loaded
against women: 'few are the modes of earning substance, and those
very humiliating' – listing the ones she had tried herself.

Mary was not only painfully aware of the dangers of destitution
and prostitution that unattached women might fall into; she was
also alive to the general depths of poverty and disease pervading
Georgian England. She had visited the workhouse in Beverley, and
had noticed the squalor in which servants lived. Her next book was
for children rather than about them. *Original Stories* is a series of
improving episodes in which Mrs Mason guides her wards Mary
and Caroline along the paths of virtue. Mrs Mason may strike the
modern reader as too smug to be bearable, and her advice to belong
to the conventional tradition of late-Georgian and Victorian moral
manuals. But it has some unusual features. There is great emphasis
on being kind to animals, from dogs and donkeys down to snails
and caterpillars, and on our duties to treat the deformed as normal
people. There are no punches pulled either. The stories are full of
beauty destroyed by smallpox, deaths in childbirth, the horrors of
debtors' prisons. There are some hard economic lessons, too: an
honest tradesman is jailed for debt, because his rich customers pay
late or not at all; a family is starving in a garret, because 'the master
who had formerly given him work, lost gradually the great part of
his business; for his best customers were grown so fond of foreign

articles, that his goods grew old in the warehouse'. (Chapter XXIV) So Adam Smith's invisible hand is anything but a helping hand to the poor. These issues are of course current today: small suppliers still suffer from late payments by the supermarket chains, and cheap imports still wipe out domestic firms. It is an austere book, made a good deal more austere by the six harrowing engravings by Mary's new acquaintance William Blake, which Johnson put in the second edition. *Original Stories* is down on baby talk, cosmetics, the theatre and flirtatiousness of any sort; it was sufficient for women to receive caresses, not to bestow them. But in among the standard puritanical injunctions, a more radical sort of politics is beginning to show through.

Mary had already developed a visceral dislike of anything posh. On her way to take up her governess job in Co. Cork, she stopped off at Eton to pick up a master and his wife who were to escort her to the west of Ireland. She hated the school: 'I could not lead the life they lead at Eton – nothing but dress and ridicule going forward.' (Todd, p. 82) Her heart sank when she arrived at Mitchelstown Castle: 'There was such a solemn kind of stupidity about this place as froze my very blood – I entered the great gates with the same kind of feeling as I should have if I was going into the Bastille.' (Todd, p. 87) Lady Kingsborough was every bit as ghastly as she had imagined, more attached to her pets than her children: 'I endeavoured to amuse them while she lavished awkward fondness on her dogs – I think now I hear her infantine lisp – She rouges – and in short is a fine Lady without fancy or sensibility. I am almost tormented to death by dogs.' (Todd, p. 88) It's amazing Mary lasted as long at Mitchelstown as she did, but then she had no place else to go, and Lady K did do her best to be kind.

A FAREWELL TO CHIVALRY

Along with her critique of the unequal treatment of women, Mary is beginning to develop a critique of inequality more generally. And it is this more general onslaught that she unleashes in her first great work, *A Vindication of the Rights of Men*, written as a reply to Burke's *Reflections on the Revolution in France*. Thus, both in order of publication and in her head, the rights of mankind generally preceded the rights of women, something that sets her apart from many feminists, then and now. The intrinsic equality of all human beings was the driving principle behind her argument, and the intrinsic equality of women followed from this.

It's important, too, to notice the dazzling rapidity of Mary's response to Burke. She was the first out of the blocks among the forty ripostes from the radicals. *Reflections* came out in November 1790. Only four weeks later, Mary's boiling, vituperative retort was on the bookstalls, anonymously at first but in January Johnson brought out a second edition with her name on it. Mary was famous, as she would remain for the rest of her short life.

She had briefly flagged and lost heart halfway through her brainstorming, barnstorming tirade. The ever kindly and ingenious Johnson said, not to worry, he'd cheerfully throw aside the sheets already printed if she wanted to start afresh. Which of course pricked her on to sit down and finish the thing.

Posterity has preferred the far longer and more systematic treatment by Tom Paine, which came out two years later and quickly gained a greater celebrity. But though Paine's *Rights of Man* remains a landmark in radical thought, there is something about Mary's unstoppable blast, with its unashamedly personal, come-off-it, you-can-do-better-than-that derision, that makes me love it more.

Most Movers are great vituperators. It is, to quite an extent, their ability to tear their opponents to shreds that heartens and confirms their supporters and leaves bystanders gasping. It is in her *Rights of Men* that Mary discovers and displays a matchless talent in that department. She wades straight in. There is no pretence of coolness, no show of respect for the elder statesman who is twice her age (thirty-one plays sixty): 'My indignation was roused by the sophistical arguments that every moment crossed me.' She confesses her impatience with Burke's 'turgid bombast' and 'your slavish paradoxes, in which I can find no fixed first principle to refute'. Her first complaint – an especially impudent line for a mere woman to take – is Burke's lack of intellectual system and rigour. 'I know that a lively imagination renders a man particularly calculated to shine in conversation, and in those desultory productions where method is disregarded; and the instantaneous applause which his eloquence extorts is at once a reward and a spur.' (p. 5) Burke is simply showing off and concealing the threadbare nature of his argument with rhetorical fireworks. The *Reflections* are pervaded by 'a mortal antipathy to Reason'. (p. 8)

If there is anything like an argument, or principle, running through Burke's book, it is that 'we are to reverence the rust of antiquity'. If we do come across some errors in our constitutional arrangements, 'our feelings should lead us to excuse, with blind love or unprincipled filial affection, the venerable vestiges of ancient days'. We should preserve our existing laws and customs simply because they are old. This is a Gothic notion of beauty: the ivy may be beautiful, but when it begins to destroy the trunk, should we not dig it up?

Mary goes on to assert that Burke's idea of the historical process is bogus and sentimental. He claims that the constitution of our Church and state was formed 'under the auspices and confirmed by the sanctions of religion and piety'. (p. 34) But this was not how it happened at all. 'You must know that private cabals and public feuds, private virtues and vices, religion and superstition, have all concurred to foment the mass and swell it to its present form; nay more, that it in part owes its sightly appearance to bold rebellion and insidious innovation. Factions, Sir, have been the leaven, and private interest has produced public good.' (p. 34) Burke's soppy religiose historiography simply does not correspond to the facts. Mary is a fan of the British constitution, with all its remediable faults, and she will not have it travestied. The foundation of our liberty was established, not by a high-minded moral effort, but 'chiefly through the pressing necessities of the king, who was more intent on being supplied for the moment, in order to carry on his wars and ambitious projects'. (p. 10)

Burke knows perfectly well, too, that the present system is riddled with corruption, because he is an insider, part of the Westminster Bubble. 'You have been behind the curtain . . . you must have seen the clogged wheels of corruption continually oiled by the sweat of the laborious poor, squeezed out of them by unceasing taxation.

You must have discovered that the majority in the House of Commons was often purchased by the crown, and that the people were oppressed by the influence of their own money, extorted by the venal voice of a packed representation.' (p. 20) As for parliamentary election, where was the spirit of reverence in 'the thoughtless extravagance of an electioneering frolic'?

Mary detects humbug in Burke's rhetoric. How could he ever have defended the independence of the America colonies, or campaigned for the abolition of slavery? Surely on his principles of 'implicit submission to authority', he should have been on the other side? Did he recommend to the deluded French every last bit of the British system – the press gang, for example, or the game laws? She suggests that he has only 'deserted his post' as a defender of liberty because he has been losing his audience. 'You have lately lost a great part of your popularity: members were tired of listening to declamation, or had not sufficient taste to be amused when you ingeniously wandered from the question.' (p. 44) This was a wicked thrust, for MPs had indeed been wearying of Burke's unstoppable flow. She even puckishly hazards that, had he been a Frenchman, his romantic enthusiasm would have made him 'a violent revolutionist'. (Ibid.) His veneration for the French royal family seemed inconsistent, considering how he had treated King George III in his illness, 'when you, with unfeeling disrespect and indecent haste, wished to strip him of all his hereditary honours. You were so eager to taste the sweets of power, that you could not wait till time had determined, whether a dreadful illness would settle into a confirmed madness.' (p. 26) And indeed, it had not been the Whigs' noblest hour, when they pressed for a regency with full powers, in the justified hope that this would get them back into government – with Burke as Paymaster-General.

As for Dr Price's sermon in Old Jewry in praise of the Revolution, even if you granted that it was a utopian reverie, did it really deserve Burke's venomous tirade, especially when the mere thought of the French queen made him go weak at the knees? 'Tottering on the edge of the grave, that worthy man in his whole life never dreamt of struggling for power or riches; and if a glimpse of the glad dawn of liberty rekindled the fire of youth in his veins, you, who could not stand the fascinating glance of a great lady's eyes, when neither virtue nor sense beamed in them, might have pardoned his unseemly transport.' (p. 17) Burke's rhapsody on the memory of seeing Marie Antoinette at Versailles is one of the great set pieces of English rhetoric. But Mary's defence of her old mentor is pretty hot stuff too.

By any objective criterion, Wollstonecraft's view of Marie Antoinette is far more clear-eyed than Burke's. The queen had not been nicknamed *Madame Déficit* for nothing. Her extravagance, her quarrelling with Louis' more sensible ministers, her warmongering, to say nothing of her playacting the milkmaid at her rustic *cottage orné*, make her personally at least a contributory cause of the Revolution. And her reluctance to compromise afterwards led her and her family to the guillotine.

Moreover, Wollstonecraft's analysis has a strong argument running through it. She begins by setting out her first principle, derived from John Locke, that 'the birthright of man, to give you, Sir, a short definition of this disputed right, is such a degree of liberty, civil and religious, as is compatible with the liberty of every other individual with whom he is united in a social compact.' (p. 7) She ends by sketching out some possible consequence of carrying that principle into practice: by dividing large estates into small farms, by reforming our method of electing our representatives, by regulating society on a more enlarged plan to provide employment for mechanics thrown out of work by a flux of trade or fashion. These foreglimpses of some sort of welfare state are not intended as a detailed or comprehensive programme, merely as an indication of how a reformed government, acting on rational first principles and in a benevolent sprit, might start work.

Burke seems to suggest that 'any attempt to civilize the heart, to make it humane by implanting reasonable principles, is a mere philosophic dream'. She admits that time only would show whether his contempt for the French National Assembly would turn out to be founded on reason, or spawned by envy. (p. 40) But at least the Assembly was trying to act on the right lines. By contrast, Burke seemed to be motivated above all by the need to protect property against the lower orders. 'Among all your plausible arguments, and witty illustrations, your contempt for the poor always appears conspicuous and rouses my indignation.' (p. 56) One paragraph of Burke's in particular stokes her fury, and it is worth quoting in full, as she does:

> Good order is the foundation of all good things. To be enabled to acquire, the people, without being servile, must be tractable and obedient. The magistrate must have his reverence, the laws their authority. The body of the people must not find the principles of natural subordination by art rooted out of their minds. They *must* respect that property of which they *cannot* partake. *They must labour to obtain what by labour can be obtained; and when they find, as they commonly do, the success disproportioned to the endeavour, they must be taught their consolation in the final proportions of eternal justice.* (pp. 56–7, italics are Mary's)

Mary responds with searing force: 'This is contemptible hard-hearted sophistry, in the specious form of humility, and submission to the will of Heaven. – It is, Sir, *possible* to render the poor happier in this world, without depriving them of the consolation which you gratuitously grant them in the next.' (p. 57) As for Christian charity, Mary waspishly remarks that if Burke had encountered Jesus Christ, he would have denounced Him as a dangerous innovator, that is, until he learnt that Our Saviour was descended from the Royal House of David. This is one of the few references I can find in Mary's writings to Jesus as a person. Her faith was always instinctively, if not explicitly, deist rather than Christian.

We have reached the core of this bruising conflict. But there is one other theme that runs through the *Rights of Men* that strikes me as original for its time. This is Mary's judgement on what politics is going to be like in the future.

She was not ashamed to proclaim a tremendous hopefulness: 'a glorious chance of attaining more virtue and happiness than has hitherto blessed our globe'. But it would come at the expense of our old illusions. In lamenting the fate of Marie Antoinette, Burke had lamented that 'the age of chivalry is gone. That of sophisters, economists and calculators, has succeeded; and the glory of Europe is extinguished for ever.' Yes, Mary responds coldly, and a good thing too. 'Whether the glory of Europe is set, I shall not now enquire; but probably the spirit of romance and chivalry is on the wane; and reason will gain by its extinction.' (p. 28) She returns to this theme at the end: 'the cultivation of reason dampens fancy . . . If we mean to build our knowledge or happiness on a rational basis, we must learn to distinguish the *possible*, and not fight against the stream. And if we are careful to guard ourselves from imaginary sorrows and vain fears, we must also resign many enchanting illusions.' (pp. 55–6)

This is an early warning or diagnosis of what Max Weber a century later was to call *die Entzauberung der Welt*, the disenchantment of the world. In her second great work, Mary was to declare that 'the science of politics is in its infancy'. When it grew to maturity, she expected that it would be a decidedly sober, if not dismal science.

FAREWELL TO ROUSSEAU

There is a foretaste, too, in *Rights of Men* that points forward to her other great work – showing how inextricably for her the rights of men were interwoven with the rights of women. In her closing pages, Mary takes a sideswipe at the ideas that Burke had aired in his early work on the Sublime and the Beautiful. How that essay degraded women: 'you have clearly proved that one half of the human species, at least, have not souls; and that Nature, by making women *little, smooth, delicate, fair* creatures never designed that they should exercise their reason to acquire the virtues that produce opposite, if not contradictory feelings', the virtues of fortitude, justice and wisdom. (p. 46) According to Burke, if women were to be loved, which was their chief purpose in life, they should 'learn to lisp, to totter in their walk, and nickname God's creatures'. (p. 45)

There was a huge amount more to be said on the subject. With Johnson's encouragement, she set to work on the *Vindication of the Rights of Woman*, which was to be her immortal masterwork. She did no special reading or historical research. This book, too, was written at a feverish pace, inside six weeks according to William

Godwin, but it may have been a bit more. Afterwards, she confessed that she was dissatisfied: 'Had I allowed myself more time, I could have written a better book, in every sense of the word.' Even her admirers have sometimes agreed. William Godwin wrote in his memoir of Mary that it was 'undoubtedly a very unequal performance, and eminently deficient in method and arrangement'. Yet it displayed 'the eminence of genius' and 'it seems not very improbable that it will be read as long as the English language endures'. Claire Tomalin contends that the book is 'more in the nature of an extravaganza' and that there is more logic packed into ten pages of Condorcet's essay *Sur l'admission des femmes au droit de cité*, written two years earlier. Jeremy Bentham, too, had turned his methodical mind to the political rights of women and prepared a series of notes, discussing the pros and cons of votes for women. But Mary's *Vindication* had much more to it than these male dabblings, apart from her force and passion, qualities that might be pooh-poohed by cautious crusty old men (Horace Walpole famously denounced her as 'a hyena in petticoats'). What Mary was demanding were not simply civic rights, such as the vote, property and inheritance rights, admission to closed male seats of power, though those were all part of it. What she was demanding was liberty, the acceptance of every woman as an independent spirit, who was just as free to make her own life as any man. That was a demand calculated to unnerve most men, then and now, and not a few women too.

If the minds of women were still inferior, there was a simple reason. 'One cause of this barren blooming I attribute to a false system of education, gathered from the books written on this subject by men who, considering females rather as women than human creatures, have been more anxious to make them alluring mistresses than affectionate wives and rational mothers.' (p. 71) In this book, Mary announced that she proposed to treat her own sex as rational creatures, 'instead of flattering their *fascinating* graces, and viewing them as if they were in a state of perpetual childhood, unable to stand alone'. (p. 73)

The argument was simple: 'In what does man's pre-eminence over the brute creation consist? The answer is as clear as that a half is less than the whole: in Reason.' (p. 76) And there could be no reasonable ground for excluding 'woman' from the definition of 'man'. After all, had not Talleyrand, to whom *Vindication* is bizarrely dedicated, observed that 'to see one half of the human race excluded by the other from all participation of government, was a political phaenomenon that, according to abstract principles, it was impossible to explain'. (p. 66) The time-serving, lecherous old ex-bishop had not done much about it, and nor had the French revolutionaries so far. Yet ultimately only prejudice could stand in the way of truth and logic. Alas, 'men, in general, seem to employ their reason to justify prejudices, which they have imbibed, they can scarcely trace how, rather than to root them out ... for a kind of intellectual cowardice prevails which makes many men shrink from the task'. (pp. 76–7)

No man had shrunk more obviously from the task than her one-time hero Jean-Jacques Rousseau. Like half the young women in Europe, she had adored the solitary sage. She was even prepared to forgive his maltreatment of Thérèse Levasseur. The poor man had tried 'to justify to himself the affection which weakness and virtue had made him cherish for that fool Theresa. He could not raise her to the common level of her sex; and therefore he labored [*sic*] to bring woman down to her's [*sic*].' (p. 260) But it was really *Emile* that was the disaster. Not only was the character of Sophie 'grossly unnatural', the system of education prescribed for her was absurd and immoral. She was to be made 'a coquetish slave in order to render her a more alluring object of desire' and to be taught nothing but obedience. 'What nonsense!' Mary explodes. (p. 91)

Rousseau says that woman ought to be weak and passive, because she has less bodily strength than man. From this he infers that 'she was formed to please and be subject to him; and that it is her duty to render herself agreeable to her master – this being the grand end of her existence'. (p. 150) As for their physical weakness, 'so far from being ashamed of their weakness, they glory in it; their tender muscles make no resistance; they affect to be incapable of lifting the smallest burthens, and would blush to be thought robust and strong'. (p. 151) Again Mary explodes, in a footnote this time: 'What nonsense!' (p. 151fn)

She gives no more credence to Rousseau's contention that women are intrinsically fonder of ornaments, mirrors and dressing up their dolls and themselves, and that they have no head for schooling: 'almost all of them learn with reluctance to read and write; but very readily apply themselves to the use of their needles'. (p. 153)

Other gurus of the day – Dr Fordyce, Dr Gregory – are dismissed with contempt: 'away with the lullaby strains of condescending endearment'. (p. 168) She particularly dislikes the dissimulation recommended by Dr Gregory in his *Legacy to his Daughters*: 'if you happen to have any learning, keep it a profound secret, especially from the men who generally look with a jealous and malignant eye on a woman of great parts and a cultivated understanding'. (p. 172) It was not, then, that such women did not exist, merely that they must keep their mouths shut – the last thing that Mary herself would dream of doing.

No less ridiculous were the men of science, like Dr John Berkenhout, who refused to let women learn botany because the language of stamens and pistils was too indelicate for the fair sex to get their heads round. What a gross idea of decency this implied. Wollstonecraft tells us proudly: 'I have conversed, as man with man, with medical men, on anatomical subjects; and compared the proportions of the human body with artists – yet such modesty did I meet with, that I was never reminded by word or look of my sex, of the absurd rules which make modesty a pharisaical cloak of weakness.' (p. 200 and fn) Like modern educators, she was convinced that proper sex education would sweep away the prurient sniggers. Adults should speak to children about 'the organs of generation as freely as we speak of the other parts of the body, and explain to them the noble use which they were designed for'. (Todd, p. 135)

She has contempt, too, for the weaker sisters from whom she would have expected better, such as Dr Johnson's friend Hester Thrale and Germaine de Staël, who all cravenly followed Rousseau's line. Only the republican Mrs Macaulay had earned her respect:

Catharine Macaulay was an example of intellectual acquirements supposed to be incompatible with the weakness of her sex. In her style of writing, indeed, no sex appears, for it is like the sense it

conveys, strong and clear. I will not call hers a masculine understanding, because I admit not of such an arrogant assumption
of reason; but I contend that it was a sound one, and that her
judgement, the matured fruit of profound thinking, was a proof
that a woman can acquire judgement, in the full extent of the
word. (*Vindication*, p. 180)

It was time 'to effect a revolution in female manners – time to
restore to them their lost dignity – and make them, as a part of
the human species, labour by reforming themselves to reform the
world'. (p. 113)

In this immense undertaking, there could be no gendered virtues,
not even modesty. 'For man and woman, truth, if I understand the
meaning of the word, must be the same.' (p. 119) It was for women
to grow up and 'leave the go-cart' (a sort of Zimmer frame on
castors, to teach children how to walk, not a miniature racing car,
as today).

Modern readers are taken aback by the ferocity of Wollstonecraft's
condemnation of the women of her day as simpering flirts – ignorant, deceitful, dissimulating and frequently immoral. They were
systematically degraded by the time they spent 'in making caps,
bonnets, and the whole mischief of trimmings, not to mention
shopping, bargain-hunting, etc. etc.' – when they could be exercising
their minds in gardening, experimental philosophy and literature.
(p. 147) But there is something bracing about her high-minded
scorn. Women, she insists, can be better than this. They can do
better than this, better as wives and mothers, and better out in the
world too.

'I may excite laughter, by dropping an hint, which I mean to
pursue, some future time, for I really think that women ought to
have representatives, instead of being arbitrarily governed without
having any direct share allowed them in the deliberations of government.' (p. 228) Alas, she never got around to pursuing the hint
in a second volume, but even in passing she links female suffrage
with the wider cause of equality. Women were, after all, 'as well
represented as a numerous class of hard-working mechanics, who
pay for the support of royalty when they can scarcely stop their

children's mouths with bread'. (Ibid.) That is to say, neither of these great sections of the population was represented in Parliament at all.

As for the sciences, why should women stop at botany (which was, despite Dr Berkenhout, already a popular pastime for enquiring women)? 'Women might certainly study the art of healing, and be physicians as well as nurses.' (p. 229) Politics, business, shop-keeping, farming – nothing was beyond the capacity of an educated woman. It should be said here that women, especially widows, had in the past run many such businesses. Mary was writing at a time when the circle of occupations proper to women was contracting, rather than expanding. It is a mistake to imagine that women's rights followed a uniform, if painfully slow, upward curve through the centuries.

'Education, education, education' was the Wollstonecraft mantra, just as it was to be Tony Blair's. Education must become 'a grand national concern'. Boarding schools, not just Eton, were nurseries of vice and deprived children of the affection and example of their parents. There must be proper day schools everywhere, and 'these should be national establishments, for whilst schoolmasters are dependent on the caprice of parents, little exertion can be expected from them, more than is necessary to please ignorant people'. (p. 247) Mary was never slow to tell people what was good for them. The Man in Whitehall knew best in such matters.

Such schools were to be co-educational all the way through. There were to be uniforms 'to prevent any of the distinctions of vanity'. At secondary level, those intended for mechanical trades or domestic employment ought to be removed to other schools, while 'the young people of superior abilities' would continue to be taught the sciences and the dead and living languages – a full-blown 11-plus division, in other words. Yet Mary also prefigures some elements of what was to be the progressive tradition – plenty of healthy romping on the school playing fields, a fair bit of teaching 'by conversations, in the socratic form', and school discipline to be run by the pupils. She would probably have been happy at Dartington or Summerhill, although exasperated if the academic standards were not kept up to scratch.

Wollstonecraft was certainly not unique in her concern for the schooling of women and the working classes. Many of those who were to be her opponents, such as Hannah More, minded about these things too. But where Mary was original was in her belief that education had to be the foundation of the great crusade to revolutionize the mindsets and the moral character of both sexes. If women were to live their lives fully, then men had to change too, and they would find their lives enriched as a result.

Again and again, she comes back to the overwhelming fact of inequality. 'There must be more equality established in society, or morality will never gain ground ... It is vain to expect virtue from women till they are, in some degree, independent of men.' (p. 221) There had to be a transformation of property relations, and a transformation of sexual relations too: 'all the causes of female weakness, as well as depravity ... branch out of one grand cause − want of chastity in men'. (p. 218)

Without a change in the property laws − the end of male dominance and of primogeniture − there could be no justice for the unlucky women in society, for the defenceless widows, for the unmarried sisters, and − here she embarks on her most shocking deviation from conventional mores − for the unmarried mother, the so-called fallen woman: 'highly as I respect marriage, as the foundation of almost every social virtue, I cannot avoid feeling the most lively compassion for those unfortunate females who are broken off from society, and by one error torn from all those affections and relationships that improve the heart and mind'. (p. 142) She went further, much too far for the vast majority of women who still believed that social ostracism was an indispensable deterrent to fornication: 'It does not frequently even deserve the name of error; for many innocent women become the dupes of a sincere, affectionate heart, and still more are, as it may emphatically be termed, *ruined* before they know the difference between virtue and vice.' (Ibid.) Such unfortunates ought not to be locked up in asylums and 'Magdalens', as homes for fallen women had just begun to be called. They should be offered a way back into society. They deserved justice, not charity.

In her book on the French Revolution, she went even further, offering a defence of adultery *in extremis*: 'who will coolly maintain, that it is just to deprive a woman, not to insist on her being treated as an outcast of society, of all the rights of a citizen, because her revolting heart turns from the man, whom, a husband only in name, and by the tyrannical power he has over her person and property, she can neither love nor respect, to find comfort in a more congenial or humane bosom?' (p. 333) Well, millions of respectable matrons did maintain exactly that, and not coolly either but with all the moral passion they could muster. If adultery was a legitimate item on the menu, then the family was dead. More congenial bosoms must stay out of bounds.

Today, much of what she wrote is the conventional wisdom, not just of those who would call themselves feminists. It was not the conventional wisdom then. And though the occasions for much of her outrage have diminished, there are a vision and a resonance in the *Vindication of the Rights of Woman* that have not faded, and an agenda that is, even now, far from finished. Woman was no longer to be 'the toy of man, his rattle'. (p. 100) 'Let woman share the rights and she will emulate the virtues of man, for she must grow more perfect when emancipated.' (p. 283) There at last on her final page is the word 'emancipated', for which generations of women were to fight and to chain themselves to distinguished railings that they might finally snap the chains that had confined them for so many centuries. I have not seen the word applied to women before, as opposed to slaves or prisoners, and nor has the *Oxford English Dictionary*.

'MRS IMLAY'

There was, though, an embarrassing gap in Mary's curriculum vitae to date. She had written a passionate outcry that went far deeper than the civil and political rights of women to touch the core of relations between the sexes. What she announced was a new kind of love based on warmth, intimacy and, above all, equality. Such a demand could only be based on personal experience. 'The world cannot be seen by an unmoved spectator, we must mix in the throng, and feel as men feel before we can judge of their feelings.' (pp. 187–8) But this appeal to experience was not based on her own. Apart from a few brief flirtations with hesitant curates and intense tea parties with young Dissenting intellectuals, she had had no close

relationship with any man. She had never been confident about her
looks: her beaky nose, her slightly boiled eyes, her tall gawky figure
had kept her from being pretty in the obvious way. From an early
age, she had joked about dying an old maid.

Here and there too, there is a certain spinsterly primness about
the *Vindication*. She lays stress on the need for women to be cleanly,
and she is keen on personal modesty, even when women are among
other women: 'Girls ought to be taught to wash and dress alone',
and she asks: 'How can *delicate* women obtrude on notice that part
of the animal oeconomy, which is so very disgusting?' (p. 205) She
has a bitter memory, too, of 'the jokes and hoyden tricks, which
knots of young women indulge themselves in, when in my youth
accident threw me, an awkward rustic, in their way'. (p. 206) There
is also an occasional suggestion that there is something intrinsically
disgusting about sex: 'True voluptuousness must proceed from the
mind ... what are the cold, or feverish caresses of appetite, but
sin embracing death ... without virtue, a sexual attachment must
expire, like a tallow candle in the socket, creating intolerable disgust.' (p. 281)

She took to dressing dowdily, with her hair down and her tall
figure wrapped in a shapeless long dress. When she first met the tiny
Swiss-German painter Henry Fuseli, he described her as 'a philosophical sloven, with lank hair, black stockings and a beaver hat'.
(Tomalin, p. 113) They were an odd couple. Apart from the height
difference, he was married to his former model Sophia Rawlins.
Mary fell in love with him the moment she saw him, and pursued
him with ardour, though with little serious response. Desperate to
live with Fuseli, she went round to his house and proposed to his
wife that she should move in and live with them as a threesome,
she providing the intellectual stimulation while Sophia attended to
the fleshly wants. Not surprisingly, Sophia threw her out in a fury.

Fuseli was talking too much, mostly about himself and his
work, to be upset by this bizarre episode. At any rate, he did agree
to go with her and Joseph Johnson on a jaunt to see the French
Revolution – still quite a popular outing in the summer of 1792.
They got as far as Dover, but there was news of trouble in Paris –
the upheavals that culminated in the September Massacres were just

beginning. Mary would happily have gone on, but the men were less bold, and the party returned to London.

When the *Vindication* came out, Mary was on her own again. She was thirty-three. The book's success did wonders for her self-confidence and her complexion. Her feckless brother Charles remarked on how handsome she had suddenly become. In her second bloom, eager as ever for adventure, she decided to go to Paris by herself, Massacres or no Massacres. 'I go alone neck or nothing is the word ... I am still a Spinster on the wing. At Paris, indeed, I might take a husband for the time being, and get divorced when my truant heart longed again to nestle with its old friends.' (Todd, p. 200)

She arrived in a dirty ill-lit city in December when all Paris was agog at the trial of Louis Capet, the *ci-devant* king of France. She saw Louis being driven through the silent streets lined with guards. She had taken a cheerfully callous view of the September Massacres, writing to her friend Roscoe: 'let me beg you not to mix with the shallow herd who throw an odium on immutable principles, because some of the mere instruments of the revolution were too sharp. – Children of any growth will do mischief when they meddle with edged tools.' (Tomalin, p. 154) But now she wept, and saw blood and horror everywhere.

This was no longer the blissful dawn of the Revolution, but its overcast afternoon. And it was in this violent, anxious city that Mary met Gilbert Imlay. He was an American speculator in real estate, flogging tracts of the backwoods to gullible Europeans. He claimed to have been a captain in the American army, and said his ultimate aim was to go home and farm, neglecting to mention that there was a heap of old debts and a lawsuit waiting for him if he did. He had written a travelogue about life in Kentucky and a novel, *The Emigrants*, which can claim to be just about the first American novel. He spouted progressive views, and he was tall, slim and handsome. He was also an experienced ladies' man in his late thirties. He was not, in short, *un homme sérieux*, and only someone as inexperienced as Mary could ever have pretended – or gone on pretending – that he was.

In Mary's ideal state of the future, such men would get the

brush-off. She had written in the *Vindication* that 'supposing, however, for a moment, that women were, in some future revolution of
time, to become, what I sincerely wish them to be, even love would
acquire some serious dignity, and be purified in its own fires; and
virtue giving true delicacy to their affections, they would turn in
disgust from a rake'. (p. 195) Unfortunately, that future revolution
of time had not yet occurred, and rakes were still doing nicely. For
as she also wrote: 'Men of wit and fancy are often rakes, and fancy
is the food of love.' (p. 196)

By April 1793, they were regularly seen around Paris together.
By May, they were lovers. It was in some lodgings on the Left Bank
that she first enjoyed those 'sensations that are almost too sacred
to be alluded to', for she wrote later that 'I slept at St Germain's,
in the very room (if you have not forgot) in which you pressed me
very tenderly to your heart'. (Tomalin, p. 187) After the affair was
over, he returned Mary's letters to her, so that we can still follow,
from her side at least, every twist and turn in the relationship. She
is touchingly grateful at first, always with a certain solemnity:
'Cherish me with that dignified tenderness, which I have only found
in you; and your own dear girl will try to keep under a quickness
of feeling, that has sometimes given you pain – Yes, I will be *good*,
that I may deserve to be happy.' (Letter II, published by Godwin in
Posthumous Works) Then anxious but still fond, as she becomes
aware that she is pregnant: 'Ever since you last saw me inclined
to faint, I have felt some gentle twitches, which make me begin to
think, that I am nourishing a creature who will soon be sensible of
my care.' (Letter V) She begins to sound alarmed and querulous as
Gilbert fails to answer her letters (although the interrupted state of
the mails is often to blame). Why must he always be away on business? Her hatred of money-grubbing comes to the fore: 'the demon
of traffic will ever fright away the loves and graces, that streak with
the rosy beams of infant fancy the *sombre* day of life'. (Letter XX)
She is obsessed by the fear that he is 'embruted by trade'. She is
slow to suspect the other possibility, that he may be dallying with
a new mistress. But soon she cannot avoid the thought that it may
be all over between them: 'The melancholy presentiment has for
some time hung on my spirits, that we were parted for ever, and

the letters I received this day, convince me that it was not without foundation ... I did not expect this blow from you' – though she has surely been dreading it for weeks. She ends: 'Perhaps this is the last letter you will ever receive from me.' (Letter XXXV) But she writes him thirty-three more letters before she finally concedes defeat and signs off: 'I part with you in peace' (Letter LXXVIII), which she doesn't really, because she is still threatening to haunt his dreams.

Yet while she was waiting for the baby and starting on this tormented correspondence, she still found time to embark on what she meant to be a multi-volume history of the French Revolution. She only completed the first volume, which ends well before the fall of the Girondins and the beginning of the Terror. So, in print anyway, she was not forced to confront the awful possibility that Edmund Burke, for all his defence of aristocratic privilege, might in some important respects be right: that it was not possible to tear up a whole nation by its historical roots without unleashing terrible consequences.

As late as the beginning of 1794, Mary remained optimistic about the long-term future. As she wandered along the empty corridors and up the silent staircases of Versailles, she wept for France 'over the vestiges of thy former oppressions'. But she still believed that 'Europe ought to be grateful for a change, that, by altering the political systems of the most improved quarter of the globe, must ultimately lead to universal freedom, virtue and happiness'. (p. 357) The coming of democracy would prevent wars too: 'in contemplating the extension of representative systems of polity, we have solid ground on which to rest the expectation that wars and their calamitous effects will become less frequent, in proportion as the people, who are obliged to support them with their sweat and blood, are consulted respecting their necessity and consequences'. (p. 356) She admitted that 'Europe will probably be, for some years to come, in a state of anarchy ...' but 'out of this chaotic mass a fairer government is rising than has ever shed the sweets of social life on the world'. (p. 319)

She loathed Robespierre and the Jacobins, but she had not foreseen anything like the full extent of the Terror. Nor did she acknowledge in her *History* the horrors that were taking place before her eyes. As she crossed the Place de la République, she had seen the blood from the guillotine sluicing across the pavement. Her sister feminist Olympe de Gouges and the irresistible Madame Roland had been among the women guillotined. It was Madame Roland who had bowed to the statue of Liberty before her execution and cried out: '*O Liberté, que de crimes on commet en ton nom!*' ('O Liberty, how many crimes are committed in thy name!') Among the 35,000 victims of the Terror, the execution of her friend Brissot and the twenty-one Girondin leaders in October 1793 was, she said later, 'one of the most intolerable sensations she had ever experienced'. (*Memoirs*, p. 244) Yet no shadow of these ghastly events to come found its way into the first (and only) volume of her *French Revolution*.

Nor did she foresee that the European war that was just beginning would last twenty years, spread throughout the globe and kill millions of people. There is no doubt that in this respect Edmund Burke was the better prophet.

What she did dread was a rather different possibility: that the Revolution might have replaced a cold-hearted aristocracy with a no less cold-hearted avaricious bourgeoisie. In a startling passage at the end, she launches a fierce critique of the new ruling class. It's worth quoting at length:

> The destructive influence of commerce, it is true, carried on by men who are eager by overgrown riches to partake of the respect paid to nobility, is felt in a variety of ways. The most pernicious, perhaps, is it's [*sic*] producing an aristocracy of wealth, which degrades mankind, by making them only exchange savageness for tame servility, instead of acquiring the urbanity of improved reason. Commerce also, overstocking the country with people, obliges the majority to become manufacturers rather than husbandmen; and then the division of labour, solely to enrich the proprietor, renders the mind entirely inactive. (*French Revolution*, p. 369)

She goes on to launch a direct assault on Adam Smith's most cherished principles:

The time which, a celebrated writer says, is sauntered away, in going from one part of an employment to another, is the very time that preserves the man from degenerating into a brute; for every one must have observed how much more intelligent are the blacksmiths, carpenters, and masons in the country, than the journeymen in great towns; and, respecting morals, there is no comparison ... thus are whole knots of men turned into machines, to enable a keen speculator to become wealthy; and every noble principle of nature is eradicated by making a man pass his life in stretching wire, pointing a pin, heading a nail, or spreading a sheet of paper on a plain surface. (Ibid., p. 370)

This supposedly uneducated female nobody has thus, in her very brief career, unleashed critiques of her three great near-contemporaries – Burke, Rousseau and Smith. She also prefigures Karl Marx's critique, eighty years later, of alienation under capitalism. There is not much doubt, I think, that if she had lived longer, she would have developed a full-blown assault on the inhumanity of industrial society. And all this completed, while pregnant, in a dangerous foreign city without the support of her absent, possibly faithless lover.

Gilbert Imlay had business in Le Havre, and unable to bear Paris any longer without him, she followed him there. Imlay thought that the sea air and his company might calm her down. At least she would no longer be writing those fretful accusing letters. It was in Le Havre that on 14 May 1794 – or 25 Floréal in the Revolutionary calendar – the baby was born to Citoyenne Imlay. In fact, they were not and never would be married, although Gilbert had registered her as Mrs Imlay at the American Embassy, so that she could come and go freely as a British woman could not, now that the two countries were at war.

Mary adored little Fanny, as the baby was called after the beloved Fanny Blood. At the age of thirty-five, she took to motherhood as passionately as she had taken to sex at the age of thirty-four. Fanny 'has got into my heart and imagination, and when I walk out without her, her little figure is ever dancing before me'. (Todd, p. 261) Mary could not resist hoping that Fanny might bring them closer together again: 'the little damsel . . . has been almost springing out of my arm – she certainly looks very like you – but I do not love her the less for that, whether I am angry or pleased with you'. (Ibid.)

But Imlay was off on business again, now back to Paris and then on to London. He was an erratic and brusque correspondent, whose letters gave small satisfaction even when they did arrive. She began to revert to her view that men were 'systematic tyrants and that it is the rarest thing in the world to meet with a man with sufficient delicacy of feeling to govern desire'. (Todd, p. 277)

In the end, if only to staunch the flow of miserable letters, Imlay invited her and Fanny to follow him to London. There in the house at 26 Charlotte Street that he had taken for them, she came to realize that he no longer loved her and was coldly offering her financial support only in order to be seen to be doing the right thing. She took an overdose of poison, laudanum probably (the suicide drug of choice at the time), but Imlay found her in time. Perhaps she meant to be found, perhaps not.

Amazingly, after this suicide attempt, she rallied to Imlay's cause. It was the strangest episode in the whole affair. As always, he had been operating close to the limit of legality. He had hatched a plan to evade the British blockade of France and import from neutral countries certain vital goods – grain, soap, iron – to be paid for in Bourbon silver, which would be exported, quite legally, to Sweden. To carry the silver and then the goods, he had bought a French cargo ship, *La Liberté*, renamed her the *Maria and Margarethe* (perhaps after Mary and her maid, Marguerite), and hired a Norwegian skipper, Peder Ellefsen, to sail her from Le Havre to Scandinavia under a Danish flag. Unfortunately, Ellefsen turned out to be a bigger rogue than Imlay and absconded with the ship and the silver. Mary agreed to go to Scandinavia (accompanied by baby Fanny and her French maid) to recover the stolen goods. She obviously hoped secretly that, if she succeeded, she might recover Imlay's love too. But it was an extraordinary venture for a mother with her child, especially a mother who hated the sort of speculative commerce that Imlay revelled in. Among other things, it was a criminal act for a British citizen, though not for an American, to collaborate in an operation to avoid the blockade. It was hare-brained, but it was magnificent.

We can still follow her voyage every step of the way across the rocky bays and fearsome mountains of the Scandinavian coasts, because she wrote a delightful travelogue, in between plenty more anxious letters to her 'husband'. In Imlay's cause, she badgered every mayor and judge, even secured an interview with Count Bernstorff, the effective ruler of Denmark and Norway. How much success did she achieve in her mission? We don't really know for sure. *Letters Written During a Short Residence in Sweden, Norway and Denmark* is one of her most delightful – and successful – books, but it does not go into the details of her commercial negotiations. But Per Nyström has shown that the *Maria and Margarethe* did turn up again, re-registered at Gothenburg in October 1795 to Elias Backman, Imlay's original partner in the business. Richard Holmes (p. 35) thinks that Mary may have brought off a settlement, and I like to think so too.

In fact, as her bizarre odyssey went on, Mary became even more disenchanted with trade, in particular with the effect it had on Gilbert: 'Ah! Shall I whisper to you – that you – yourself, are strangely altered, since you have entered deeply into commerce – more than you are aware of – never allowing yourself to reflect, and keeping your mind, or rather passions in a continual state of agitation.' (Todd, p. 348) For once, she had the sense not to send Gilbert this piece of character analysis.

When she and Fanny got back safely, she took the final humiliating step of questioning the cook whom Imlay had hired for them. The cook admitted that Imlay had a new mistress and had set up an alternative ménage. Typically, Mary rushed straight round to this other address, and found that the cook was right.

She wrote a suicide note to Gilbert, eloquent as ever:

> I write to you on my knees; imploring you to send my child and the maid with --- to Paris, to the care of Madame ----, 2 rue ----, section de ---. Should they be removed, ---- can give their direction.
>
> Let the maid have all my clothes, without distinction.
>
> Pray pay the cook her wages, and do not mention the confession which I forced from her – a little sooner or later is of no consequence. Nothing but my extreme stupidity could have

rendered me blind so long. Yet, whilst you assured me that you
had no attachment, I thought we might still have lived together.

I shall make no comments on your conduct; or any appeal
to the world. Let my wrongs sleep with me! Soon, very soon,
shall I be at peace. When you receive this, my burning head will
be cold.

I would encounter a thousand deaths, rather than a night
like the last. Your treatment has thrown my mind into a state of
chaos; yet I am serene. I go to find comfort, and my only fear is,
that my poor body will be insulted by an endeavor to recall my
hated existence. But I shall plunge into the Thames where there
is the least chance of my being snatched from the death I seek.
(Letter LXIX)

She went first to Battersea Bridge, but thought it too public, so
paid six shillings to be rowed upstream to Putney. It was night and
pouring with rain. Obsessively methodical as ever, Mary walked up
and down for half an hour to make her clothes sodden-heavy. Then
she paid the halfpenny toll to gain access to the wooden bridge and
jumped off the central arch. She floated downstream, unconscious,
her lungs full of water.

Amazingly, she was rescued by a fishing boat and carried to an
inn at Fulham. There she was restored by a medical man from the
Royal Humane Society, which had been set up a few years earlier for
this very purpose of reviving people who had fallen into the water,
whether on purpose or not. What a lot this tells us, both about the
rise of these new charitable institutions like the Foundling Hospital
and about the numbers of desperate young women who made it
worthwhile for the RHS medicos to be on call. And how cruel that
Mary should have come to seek the same fate as the unfortunates
she was fighting for.

Even then, after recovering, she did not give up. She certainly
resented being rescued into what she called 'living death'. But when
Imlay called to comfort her, she suggested that she and Fanny and
Gilbert and his mistress should all live together (shades of the three-
some she had proposed to Sophia Fuseli). Even more amazingly,
Imlay went along with the plan, far enough anyway for them to

start looking for a suitable house. But the crazy idea quickly fizzled out. Gilbert Imlay disappears from the story. Now Mary and Fanny really were on their own.

MRS GODWIN

Slowly Mary recovered her indomitable will. To everyone's surprise, after the handsome, charming Imlay, she took up with William Godwin, the celebrated author of *Political Justice*, a rather pernickety writer in his early forties, who wasn't handsome or charming at all, had never lived with a woman and was a sworn enemy of marriage. She took the initiative, though he later denied this, and in no time he was besotted: 'I never loved till now,' he wrote later. So, even more surprisingly, was she. 'Now by these presents let me assure you that you are not only in my heart, but my veins, this morning. I turn from you half abashed – yet you haunt me, and some look, word or touch thrills through my whole frame.' (Todd, p. 394) Looking at herself in the mirror the morning after, Mary recorded: 'If the felicity of last night has had the same effect on your health as on my countenance, you have no cause to lament your failure of resolution: for I have seldom seen so much fire running about my features as this morning when recollections – very dear, called forth the blush of pleasure, as I adjusted my hair.' (Todd, p. 402)

The 'failure of resolution' referred to here was the planned abstaining from sex at that time of the month to avoid Mary conceiving another child. Inadequate at the best of times, this popular method of birth control failed here too. They were married, to the consternation of all their friends, on 29 March 1797, at Old St Pancras Church, round the corner from their new home at 26 the Polygon, Somers Town. Like many another sensitive author, Godwin kept a separate apartment for himself a few doors away at 17 Evesham Buildings – 'we were both of us of opinion, that it was possible for two persons to be too uniformly in each other's society'. This bizarre couple had been dropped after their marriage by some of their fashionable friends such as the novelist Elizabeth Inchbald and the actress Sarah Siddons. But it was in genuine wedded bliss that they waited for the birth of Mary's second child. They expected it to be a boy and planned to call it William. But it was a girl, and so of course they called her Mary.

Mary Godwin was to be remembered for two things: marrying Percy Bysshe Shelley and writing *Frankenstein*. But she was not to remember her mother. For Mary Wollstonecraft died, aged thirty-eight, of septicaemia, eleven days after she was born. Godwin buried her in the churchyard at St Pancras where they had been married less than six months earlier.

He erected over her grave a plain square stone memorial that said simply:

MARY WOLLSTONECRAFT GODWIN
Author of a Vindication of the Rights of Woman
Born 27th April 1759
Died 10th September 1797

Two weeping willows were planted, one each side of the grave.

As she grew up in Godwin's house down the road, little Mary Godwin often visited the grave of the mother she never knew. When she was sixteen, she met Percy Bysshe Shelley and took to bringing him to the grave. And it was there at the graveside on 26 June 1814 that she declared she was dying with love for the poet and could not live without him. Shelley, himself only twenty-two, reminded her that he had a wife, Harriet, who was pregnant and in Bath at the time. Mary pleaded with wild gestures, why could not the three of them live together, she as his wife and Harriet as his sister? Shelley went along with the idea and sent a message to Harriet, who was furious and distraught. Nevertheless, Shelley and Mary became lovers the next day, and a month later set off for Dover and the Continent, but in a different threesome with Mary's step-sister, Claire Clairmont. She was also only sixteen, the daughter of Godwin's second wife and later to become Byron's mistress and the mother of their daughter Allegra, who died of typhus aged five. There are persistent rumours that Claire, too, had an affair with Shelley.

Mary would have known that her mother had in desperation proposed just such a *ménage à trois* to Gilbert Imlay, because Godwin described the disastrous episode in his memoir of his wife, though he does not fully disclose her similar proposal to Sophia Fuseli, who had been just as indignant as Harriet Shelley. So, remarkably, she like her mother had twice attempted a threesome. Nothing could be more offensive to the conventional sexual pairing of Western society, no greater blow struck for the supremacy of feeling over morality.

The gravestone is still in St Pancras churchyard, but Mary Wollstonecraft's body is not, nor is that of William Godwin, who was buried beside her thirty-seven years later. They were dug up in 1866 to make way for the new railway line coming in to Kings Cross, and removed by Sir Percy Florence Shelley, the only child of Mary Godwin and the poet, to lie with the Shelleys in the graveyard of the splendid neo-Gothic Church of St Peter's, Bournemouth. In death as in life, Mary was in the possession of men, her remains shifted in response to the new commercial pressures she detested.

A young architect called Thomas Hardy was tasked with supervising the removal of the bodies, and there after nightfall, by the light of flare lamps and given decent privacy by a high hoarding, he watched the dismal procession of the coffins that had been unearthed during the day, together with some loose skeletons carried on boards, including one that appeared to have two heads. The spectacle might be expected to have appealed to Hardy's macabre taste, but he could manage in response only a few jocular verses about the jumbling of bodies and tombstones. Luckily, Sir Percy had got wind of the proposed excavation and had removed the Godwin coffins to the balmier air of Bournemouth in good time.

A few yards from the Godwin monument, you can still see an amazing survival of this removal. Around the foot of a huge ash tree there are a hundred tomb-slabs jammed together and clasped by the writhing roots of the tree. It is known as 'Hardy's Tree', and it is far more evocative of the changes and chances of mortality than Godwin's bollard. How Mary Wollstonecraft would have loved its gothic oddity.

HER SECOND COMING

Godwin was so stricken by Mary's death that he could not bear to attend the funeral. But he was determined that she should not be forgotten. Within two weeks, he had begun work on his tribute to her. *Memoirs of the Author of 'A Vindication of the Rights of Woman'* came out only four months later, in January 1798. At the same time, he and the faithful Johnson brought out four small volumes of Mary's *Posthumous Works*, containing her letters to Imlay with all their passion, resentment and despair.

Though I find it hard to believe, it seems that neither Godwin nor Johnson foresaw the furore that followed. In his book, Godwin freely discussed Mary's love life, her pregnancies and her suicide attempts. Robert Southey denounced Godwin for 'a want of all feeling in stripping his dead wife naked'. Mary was condemned as 'a philosophical wanton', little better than a prostitute. In fact, the *Anti-Jacobin* indexed Godwin's book under 'Prostitution: see Mary Wollstonecraft'. The letters to Imlay drove home the terrible lesson as seen by conventional society: that the life of a free and equal woman as recommended by Wollstonecraft in her *Vindication* was in reality a cruel sham. Her own life had been a travesty of her ideals, and an awful warning to any woman who might be tempted to follow her.

Godwin made matters worse by exaggerating Mary's rejection of Christianity and by presenting her as a sentimental heroine, a sort of female Young Werther (Mary and Godwin had read Goethe's tear-jerker together when she was dying). Worst of all, he patronized her as a creature driven more by feeling than reason: 'The strength of her mind lay in intuition. She was often right, by this means only, in matters of mere speculation ... and yet, though perhaps, in the strict sense of the term, she reasoned little, it is surprising what a degree of soundness is to be found in her determination.' (Tomalin, p. 296) 'Reasoned little!!!' I can hear Mary snorting. If the term had been invented then, she would have denounced her dear husband as a male chauvinist pig.

So, women were not the equals of men. They could not have it all, or anything much in the way of civic and political rights. What they could have was the domestic sphere. There at least they were allowed to reign. As Clare Tomalin puts it: 'Mary died just in time to avoid the ludicrous sight of her sex being hoisted on to a new and supremely uncomfortable pedestal (those members of her sex, that is, whose menfolk could afford so to elevate them). Ladies, though intellectually inferior, were henceforth to be morally superior.' (Tomalin, p. 311) This became the prevailing orthodoxy, rammed home by a flock of prolific writers of advice to women. That advice found a huge audience. Hannah More's *Cheap Repository Tracts*, written as an antidote to the 'fatal poison' dispensed by Tom Paine, is said to have reached two million readers. Mary's *Rights of Woman* never sold more than a few thousand, though it remained in print for the next fifty years. (Todd, p. 185)

To all appearances, then, Mary had failed. Society had refused to budge in the direction she wanted; in fact, it had taken fright and retreated in the opposite direction. Yet there was, I think, a subtle undertow at work during this age of the 'separate spheres'. The Woman Question had at least been asked, and though conventional society recoiled from the answer Mary offered, some sort of answer had to be given. The sheer volume of published advice suggests a widespread uncertainty about the proper role for women in the modern world, and a need for fresh guidance.

The pedestal was doomed to crumble under its own weight. Complacent mid-Victorians might concede to the historian William Lecky's view that 'morally, the general superiority of women over men is, I think, unquestionable'. But if women were superior in this crucial department of life, why should they be treated as inferior in terms of civic and political rights? As John Stuart Mill remarked: 'There is no other situation in life in which it is the established order, that the better should obey the worse.' These superior beings, however fragrant and delicate they might be, could not be indefinitely barred from asking for more. So as the century wore on, women began to step down from the pedestal, put on knickerbockers and began to ride bicycles and play golf. The New Woman of the 1890s could not be held back, and nor could the next generation of suffragettes, though it was not until 1930 that women under thirty, the 'flappers', got the vote in Britain. In France, where the clarion call of equality had first been heard, and where several female champions like Olympe de Gouges had gone to the guillotine, women did not get the vote until 1945. Despite her incurable impatience, Mary had always said that it would take time.

The ongoing objection to Mary personally was to the wild and shocking character of her life. Her personal conduct had let the side down. Harriet Martineau thought that 'women of the Wollstonecraft order ... do infinite mischief, and for my part, I do not wish to have anything to do with them'. The cause of women's rights could be advanced only with the utmost discretion: 'women who would improve the condition of the sex must, I am certain, be not only affectionate and devoted, but rational and dispassionate'. But, gradually, Mary came to be appreciated for what she was. Her unrestrained freedom of speech and action was not just part of her, but perhaps the best part. George Eliot praised her 'strong and truthful nature' and 'her loving heart'. The embryonic women's movement believed that women had the right to be more than upright, uptight schoolmarms, and Mary had shown the way (though she certainly had her schoolmarmish side).

Yet, as she became an icon to succeeding waves of feminists, her version of feminism came under attack. Even her devoted editor, Professor Janet Todd, suggests in her introduction to *The Rights of Woman* that feminism has moved on. The progress of feminism between 1792 and 1992 had rendered much of her hope and analysis obsolete. 'If her feminism still presents difficulties, its basis presents even more: her rational, outdated, un-Freudian concept of human nature, so necessary for the kind of social progress she anticipated.' (*Vindication*, pp. xxix–xxx) Her rationalism now seems to us an absurd if not ignoble ideal.

Even if there is something in this critique, I don't think it's the heart of the matter. Wollstonecraft's 'revolution in female manners' is not offering a settled utopia. What she wants is freedom and equality based on justice. Women must have the right to make their own lives, just as any man does. Mary's interpretation of feminism does not guarantee happiness – she certainly achieved it only fleetingly herself. Nor is it based on a fixed view of sexuality or of the differences between the sexes. As we have seen, even in her brief flowering, her own views changed in the light of experience. All she offers is a ticket for the journey, not a bed of roses at the end of it. And in this, modern feminists are surely her heirs, and hers more than any other woman's.

Western women now have the right to vote and be voted for, to be a prime minister or a judge, or in some churches a bishop, or a jockey or the CEO of a FTSE-100 company, to take up kick-boxing or quantum physics, to choose their sexual orientation or even their gender, to marry or not to marry, to have a baby or not to have a baby, whenever and however they please, or not to take up any of these new options, for this is a permissive, not a coercive revolution. Sometimes these rights have been won or nearly won by arduous struggle, sometimes the rusty gates of the old citadels have swung open by themselves, as the defenders have scuttled off into the shadows. In these processes, for the first time in history, men are mostly bystanders, their only role to give the nod more or less reluctantly when the demand is made. It is a revolution unthinkable (or at any rate mostly unthought) little more than a century ago, and a revolution that cannot be rolled back, in a liberal democracy at least.

It has been a glorious revolution, with high spots of matchless exhilaration. Who can view without emotion the long lines of women waiting for hours outside the polling station to cast their votes for the first time in their lives? You do not have to be an Anglican, or even a Christian, to appreciate the spiritual intensity of the moment when a woman priest celebrates her first Holy Communion.

But feminism is not a panacea. The women's movement cannot liberate women (or men) from the wilful tug of the ego, nor provide a readymade guide to the duties that they continue to owe to their partners, parents and children. Life on the feminist front line has its disillusions as well as its joys. As for the other half of Wollstonecraft's mission, to civilise men, that can at best be described as a work in progress. The New Man does exist, but the old unreconstructed brute is still around, and in numbers. If there are today more marriages based on equality and mutual respect, there are certainly fewer marriages everywhere in the Western world, more divorces, more single parents, and more people leading solitary lives. Many feminists will argue that marriage is not the point. What matters is equality and independence. But Wollstonecraft herself certainly hoped that marriage would be a finer, nobler thing in the new society, not that it would wither away.

If Wollstonecraft did not come up with a definitive answer to how men and women should live together (or apart) on terms of equality, then nor has anyone else. What women can have, and insist on having, is the right to try it all, the right to score their own victories and make their own mistakes. That is what Mary Wollstonecraft insisted on too, which is why she remains the heroine of the whole story, even if we now call her a hero.

No feminist has appreciated the full-on Mary more than Virginia Woolf, in her marvellous essay in *The Common Reader*. Wollstonecraft's great works 'are so true that they seem now to contain nothing new in them – their originality has become our commonplace'. Her notorious wildness was not incidental but inevitable and intrinsic to her achievement. 'The life of such a woman was bound to be tempestuous. Every day she made theories by which life should be lived; and every day she came smack against the rock of other people's prejudices. Every day too – for she was no pedant, no cold-blooded theorist – something was born in her that thrust aside the theories and forced her to model them afresh.' Which is what each successive wave of feminists has sought or been forced to do. None of them, not Simone de Beauvoir or Germaine Greer or Gloria Steinem, has surpassed her in anger, in generosity, in curiosity, in wit and zest. Just as Charles Dickens called himself the Inimitable, she remains the Indomitable, the Princess who loathed princesses. As Woolf puts it so finely: 'She cut her way to the quick of life.'

IX

GIUSEPPE MAZZINI

and the religion of nationhood

'But why do you still seek the Fatherland and never find it? Why for you alone does the long martyrdom not bear the fruit of victory? What strange fatality overwhelms you, poor Israelites among the Nations, why does God deny to you the Patria conceded for centuries to peoples who have laboured less and started later than you? The divine life quivers in the bosom of your land more powerfully than anywhere else.'

It resounds even more in the Italian: '*Ma perchè cercate e non trovate la Patria? Perchè a voi soli il lungo martirio non frutta victoria? Quale strana fatalità s'aggrava su voi, poveri Israeliti delle Nazioni, perchè Dio vi neghi la Patria, concesso da secoli a popoli che oprarono e partirono meno di voi? La vita di Dio freme in seno alla vostra terra più che altrove potente.*' (*Ai Giovani d'Italia*, 1859, pub. 1872)

You imagine an audience of hundreds, perhaps thousands, of young Italians craning forward to catch the words flowing in a sweet, unending stream from the man in black on the platform. But that was not how it was. Most Italians, young or old, never caught a glimpse of the man who so irresistibly proclaimed their sense of nationhood and turned it into a sort of poetry. Nor had Giuseppe Mazzini seen much of Italy. From the time he went into exile from his native Genoa at the age of twenty-six, much of it spent in hiding, he seldom saw his homeland for more than a month or two, and even then could only walk the streets in disguise. He himself and everything he wrote were proscribed all over Europe, except in England, where he spent most of his remaining forty-one years. His letters and newspapers were smuggled across the Channel by Genoese sailors in barrels of pitch or pumice, or in bundles of sausages and drapery.

As a young man, he lost no time in joining the Carbonari, the secret society dedicated to turfing out all foreign oppressors and then unifying Italy under her own monarch, or perhaps even as a republic. The Carbonari had cells all over Italy and were instrumental in the failed revolts of 1820, 1821 and, most disastrous of all, 1831, after which they more or less faded out. Despite being called 'the charcoal-burners', the members were largely young aristocratic and middle-class idealists; the movement barely touched the peasantry. Even thirty and forty years later, in Garibaldi's heroic guerrilla bands there was scarcely a *contadino* to be seen.

Mazzini, known as Pippo to his parents and sisters, was a typical recruit. His father was professor of anatomy at Genoa, a stern man of liberal views whom Mazzini revered but found hard to get along with. Giuseppe was caught trying to recruit a government agent to the Carbonari, and was arrested. The Governor of Genoa told the professor that 'your son is too fond of walking by himself at night absorbed in thought. What on earth has he at his age to think about? We don't like young people thinking without our knowing the subject of their thoughts.' (King, p. 18) Giuseppe was locked up in the fortress of Savona, where he was quite happy watching the sea and the sky and taming a serin finch (a relative of the canary), which flew in through the gratings. For the rest of his life, he was to live in miserable lodgings, most often a bare bedsit (most of his possessions, including his overcoat, his watch and his mother's ring, were usually at the pawnbrokers), and he was more comfortably lodged when he was in jail. His only consolations were cheap tobacco and the cheeping of the canaries and linnets he tamed after he had fallen in love with that first serin finch.

In London, he spent his days in the British Museum, partly to keep warm. Whenever anyone gave him any money, he would instantly give it away again to the Cause or to the school in Hatton Garden (then as now the heart of Little Italy), which he had founded for poor Italian children who had been trafficked into semi-slavery as street musicians or trinket-sellers.

He never married and had only a couple of brief affairs. The deepest was with Giuditta Sidoli, a widow with four children who was also a political exile. Their affair seems to have produced a child, who died in infancy. This was only revealed long after his death by research into the archives of the police in Tuscany and Rome.

It is hard to exaggerate the ferocity with which the authorities pursued Mazzini all his life. During the 1831 uprising, he scarcely left his lodging in Marseilles, only venturing out when disguised as a woman or a Garde National. After the uprising had been crushed, he was condemned to death *in absentia*, the sentence being publicly read outside the Mazzini family home. He met his mother only once thereafter, during the 1848 Revolution. After that revolution too had been quelled, hundreds of victims suffered the *bastinado* (caning on the soles of the feet), which in some cases was fatal. Sometimes the victim's only offence had been to be caught with one of Mazzini's letters. Even after his death in 1872, after Italy had been unified under Victor Emmanuel II, the republic was still such a scandalous topic that town councils were forbidden to erect statues or name streets in his honour.

His letters were intercepted and read by the secret police all over Europe, including his love letters to Giuditta. Metternich in Vienna, Cavour and King Carlo Alberto and Victor Emmanuel in Turin – all revelled in his voluminous and eloquent correspondence. The British government, too, got hold of his private letters and passed their contents on to Vienna. The difference between Britain and the Continent was that, when Mazzini protested to Parliament, there was a huge furore in both Houses, during which the saintly Lord Aberdeen lied, claiming that no information from the letters had been passed on to a foreign power. Afterwards, Aberdeen confessed that 'this Mazzini affair has been the most unpleasant in which I have ever been engaged', and he deeply regretted his part in it.

Nor did the hounding of Mazzini ease off, as unification gathered momentum in the 1850s and 1860s. Cavour refused to cancel the new death sentence passed on Mazzini in 1858, agreeing with his king that Mazzini was an enemy of the state who should be 'executed without pity' if they caught him.

THE OLD REGIMES

For the defenders of the status quo, 'Italy' was not a dream but a threat. In a letter to his ambassador in Paris in 1847, Metternich famously warned that 'the word "Italy" is a geographical expression, a description which is useful shorthand, but has none of the political significance the efforts of the revolutionary ideologues try to put on it, and which is full of dangers for the very existence of the states which make up the peninsula'. (Metternich liked the phrase 'geographical expression' so much that he repeated it in a letter to Aberdeen in August that year.)

What a ghastly mixed bunch those states were, eight repressive dynasties all levered back into power by the Congress of Vienna: the Spanish Bourbons in Naples and Sicily; Napoleon's widow Marie Louise in Parma; Lombardy and Venice directly under the control of the Habsburgs; the pope restored to his domains sprawling across Central Italy; the grand duke of Tuscany; and the French-speaking king of Piedmont; plus Savoy and Sardinia, who had also been allowed to annexe Mazzini's Patria, the once independent republic of Genoa. The papal territories were probably the worst governed, the Piedmont collection the least bad. But all of them were run by cynical and corrupt aristocrats. These were the lands of Stendhal and Tosca and Scarpia and Casanova, riddled with foreign spies, homegrown informers and secret policemen, to a degree perhaps not surpassed until the East Germany of the Stasi.

The squalor that some travellers from Northern Europe found picturesque was the outward sign of a peninsula that was economically stagnant. Each state had its own currency and customs barriers, even its own system of weights and measures. In Marie Louise's tiny duchy, the traveller encountered seven customs stations in the thirty kilometres between Guastalla and Parma; one Englishman counted forty-three different scales of weights and measures in Lombardy–Venetia alone. Censorship was endemic everywhere, though less so in Tuscany.

As for there being an Italian nation waiting to be born, only a tiny minority of the twenty-odd million inhabitants spoke Italian rather than their local dialect, perhaps no more than 5 per cent. Even without the additional costs of the occupying Austrian army and the police states everywhere, disunity was holding Italy back in every sense.

Even those who hoped for some degree of reform and relief from the foreign oppressors could not conceive of a totally united Italy. The most that the so-called Moderates, men like Count Cesare Balbo, another prime minister of Piedmont, desired was eventual independence from Austria. Unification was 'an impossible absurdity'. (Mack Smith, p. 37) Even Cavour, later hailed as Italy's liberator, with a street in every city named after him, told Daniele Manin, the heroic defender of Venice, as late as 1856 that a completely united Italy was in the circumstances 'a nonsensical dream'. Those who dreamed that dream were ridiculed as '*italianissimi*'.

YOUNG MAZZINI AND YOUNG ITALY

So what did Mazzini have going for him, as he left his dear Genoa in February 1831, and crossed the Alps for the first time towards Lyons, where he joined the growing band of refugees? He might be penniless and, in England to start with, quite friendless apart from the Ruffini brothers who came with him (their brother had committed suicide in jail rather than betray his comrades, for which Mazzini never forgave himself). But first, last and always, he had himself. Throughout his life he struck everyone he met as remarkable, not least to look at:

> He was dressed in black Genoa velvet, with a large 'republican' hat; his long, curling black hair, which fell upon his shoulders, the extreme freshness of his clear olive complexion, the chiselled delicacy of his regular and beautiful features, aided by his very youthful look and sweetness and openness of expression, would have made his appearance almost too feminine, if it had not been for his noble forehead, the power of firmness and decision that was mingled with their gaiety and sweetness in the bright flashes of his dark eyes and in the varying expression of his mouth, together with his small and beautiful moustachios and beard. Altogether he was at that time the most beautiful being, male or female, that I had ever seen. (King, pp. 36–7)

His enemies mocked him for always dressing in black – in mourning
for his country. He was a *guastafeste*, a spoilsport, or *menagramo*,
a bringer of bad luck. But his conversation was as beguiling as his
face, by turns grave, gay and teasing. He was never downhearted
by his personal misfortunes, only by the stubborn refusal of Italy
to be born.

When he first arrived in England, 'this sunless and musicless island',
he was depressed by the lack of light: 'The whole city seems under a
kind of spell, and reminds me of the witches' scene in *Macbeth* ...
The passers-by look like ghosts – one feels almost a ghost oneself.'
(King, p. 74) The English were so drearily matter-of-fact, under the
dismal spell of Bentham and the Utilitarians. They had read no real
philosophy, no Vico, no Herder, no Hegel – 'here everyone is a sectar-
ian or a materialist'. But soon he came to love the English and their
liberal traditions, and they came to love him – Ruskin, John Stuart
Mill, Jane and Thomas Carlyle, George Eliot, who called him a true
hero. Swinburne described their friendship as 'the highest honour of
my life and one of its greatest and purest pleasures'. Jane Carlyle was
particularly fond of him and grateful for the tactful advice he gave
when Carlyle was being more than usually beastly to her, though she
was apprehensive about his relentless dedication to his cause: 'I never
saw a mortal man who so completely made himself into "minced
meat" for the universe.' (Mack Smith, p. 39)

He moved down from his various digs around the Tottenham
Court Road (24 Goodge Street, 183 North Gower Street) to a room
over a post office in Chelsea, so that he could visit the Carlyles once
a week and save on the bus fare. He even helped Thomas choose the
Italian books for the new London Library. Carlyle, who was no easy
man to please, thought him 'a man of true genius, an honourable,
brave and gifted man' but 'entangled in hopeless visions'.

Mazzini, alone and still under sentence of death, responded
with a touching warmth: 'Italy is my country, but England is my
real home, if I have any.' Like Marx, he came to love English seaside resorts such as Eastbourne and St Leonards, though he hated
Brighton. He even came to love the climate. He wrote once from
Italy: 'I think very often under these radiant skies of the London
fogs and always regretfully. Individually speaking, I was evidently

intended for an Englishman.' (King, p. 141) Writing to his English friends, he would sign himself Joseph, and the English translations of his works were credited to Joseph Mazzini.

But his English friends could not help him to invent Italy, except with occasional gifts of money, which instantly went to helping the ragged children of Little Italy, or to buying a job lot of old rifles for some doomed conspiracy, or to paying the costs of printing his newspapers and journals.

And what a lot of newspapers and journals he started: *La Giovine Italia*, *La Jeune Suisse*, *L'Apostolato Popolare*, *L'Italia del Popolo*, *Pensiero e Azione*, *La Roma del Popolo* – all of them founded, funded and largely written by Mazzini, often running up to 200 pages, appearing irregularly and after a year or two, not at all. Up to the last year of his life, he was scribbling deep into the night to fill his pages. Poorly printed, full of misprints because of being set by English or French compositors, they hit the mark none the less. All over the peninsula, Young Italy had its secret lodges spreading the word.

Mazzini repeatedly complained that his fellow countrymen were slow to see the light: 'Oh, how cold those Italians are, and how they hunt for excuses for their apathy. They will not see that they are slaves, without a name, accursed by God, and mocked among the nations.' (King, pp. 54–5) But the message did percolate, which was why Mazzini's name continued to terrify the authorities in Paris and Vienna as well as in Rome and Turin. He feared assassination and walked about in London with a sword-cane and kept the blinds drawn in his lodgings. The windows were also protected by netting, to keep the uncaged canaries from flying away. Here he sat in a fug of cheap tobacco (except when his admirers sent him a bunch of Havanas), plotting conspiracies from Piedmont to Sicily, and breaking off to sing to his guitar.

THE NATION FIRST AND LAST

What was that message? At its core, there was a very simple assertion, which was both a moral principle and a prophecy of the sweep of future events: 'The principle of nationality is sacred to me. I believe it to be the ruling principle of the future.' (Mack Smith,

p. 154) The Nation was the indispensable basis of the other elements of a good society, 'for without Nationality neither liberty nor equality is possible – and we believe in the Holy Fatherland, that is, the cradle of nationality, the altar and patrimony of the individuals that compose each people'. (*Duties*, p. 176)

What exactly did this mean? Mazzini spelled it out in uncompromising terms: 'I feel ready to welcome, without any fear, any change in the European map which will arise from the spontaneous general manifestation of a whole people's mind as to the group to which it feels naturally, not only by language, but by traditions, by geography, by tendencies, to belong.' (Mack Smith, p. 154)

Any change? That was quite a proposition if you looked at Europe, or any other continent, with its jumble of languages, allegiances, races and religions – and not least its disputed border territories. Such a deliberate upheaval would surely be devastating, unpredictable and bloody, as indeed it turned out to be.

Mazzini took up his belief in the central importance of nationhood very early in his adult life, and he cherished it to the end, but in the broadest and most generous terms. It was not simply that Italy deserved to be united and independent, preferably as a republic. It was that all other peoples deserved the same fulfilment. Alongside Young Italy, Mazzini set up, or tried to, Young Germany, Young Greece, Young Spain, Young Russia, Young Switzerland, Young Ukraine, Young Turkey, Young Austria, and even Young Argentina (though 5,000 subscribers in Buenos Aires and Montevideo preferred to join Young Italy). These were in his mind's eye to be the preliminaries to and props of Young Europe, which got going in 1834.

In *The Duties of Man*, published first in a string of articles from the 1840s on and collected in book form in 1860, he summarized his belief in a simple form designed for the general reader. It was hugely popular, went through over a hundred editions and was translated into twenty languages. It was of course banned in Piedmont.

The outlook was exhilarating: 'Natural divisions, the innate spontaneous tendencies of the peoples will replace the arbitrary division sanctioned by bad governments. The map of Europe will be remade. The Countries of the People will rise, defined by the voice of the free, upon the ruins of the Countries of Kings and privileged castes. Between these Countries there will be harmony and brotherhood.' (*Duties*, p. 52)

Yes, there might be a few little local difficulties here and there, but not in his homeland. 'To you who have been born in Italy, God has allotted, as if favouring you specially, the best-defined country in Europe. In other lands, marked by more uncertain or more interrupted limits, questions may arise which the pacific vote of all will one day solve, but which have cost, and will yet perhaps cost, tears and blood; in yours, no.' (*Duties*, p. 53)

Why was this? Because 'God has stretched round you sublime and indisputable boundaries; on one side the highest mountains of Europe, the Alps; on the other the sea, the immeasurable sea'. (Ibid.)

You could take a map of Europe and place a pair of compasses with one point on Parma and the other at the mouth of the river Var, and if you described a semi-circle with it in the direction of the Alps, and the point 'which will fall, when the semi-circle is completed, upon the mouth of the Isonzo, will have marked the frontier which God has given you'. (Ibid.)

No more disastrous experiment could be imagined. At the Var end, Mazzini's compass would sweep over most of the province of Nice and part of Savoy, both claimed by France. At the other end, the compass would take in even more contentious ground: what is now the Alto Adige and the Trentino, not to mention much of Slovenia, all then part of the Austro-Hungarian Empire and filled with a hotchpotch of nationalities. It was to gain these territories that Italy went to war in 1915, that terrible conflict in the pitiless icy mountains known as The White War. In no less than twelve battles fought along the river Isonzo (the last battle better known as Caporetto), Italy had 300,000 casualties (half their entire war losses) while the Austrians lost 200,000 men.

Sublime boundaries perhaps, but not indisputable ones.

In particular, Mazzini was criminally ignorant about the size of the large German-speaking population in what Austria called, not entirely without reason, the South Tyrol. Nor had he much clue about what he might be unleashing when he called for the liberation of the Balkans from Austro-Hungarian rule. Even those historians who continue to maintain that Europe merely drifted into the First World War cannot disguise the peculiar virulence of Serbian nationalism. In *The Sleepwalkers*, Christopher Clark dispels the illusion that the young men who assassinated the Archduke Franz Ferdinand in Sarajevo were maverick freelances. They were acting, at one remove, under the direction of the Serbian secret police. Mazzini did not, on the whole, approve of assassination, but he could scarcely have denied that Gavrilo Princip and his friends were heirs of the mission he had allotted to the youth of Europe.

Geography, though, was not to be the only, or even the most important, factor. 'Country is not a territory; territory is only its base; country is the idea that rises on that base, the thought of love that draws together all the sons of that territory.' (King, p. 301) 'Nationalities can be founded only for and upon and by the people.' (King, p. 300) The popular will was the only true test. Racial differences did not come into it. 'There is not a single country in Europe where an unmixed race can be detected.' Even the language was not decisive; Switzerland was a genuine nation, despite the diversity of languages and religions.

Which was all very well. But in these multi-ethnic, multi-tongued kingdoms, who was to decide who and what constituted the kingdom? That could be decided only by the people as a whole, or their elected representatives. Hence, 'the republic is the only legitimate and logical form of government'. (*Duties*, p. 78)

Mazzini also insisted with equal force that he was a patriot, not a 'nationalist', a word he used pejoratively from 1836 onwards to describe all those who wanted to encroach on the rights of other peoples. (Mack Smith, p. 12) Nothing must be allowed to harm 'the brotherhood of people which is our one overriding aim'. (Mack Smith, p. 13) National life and international life were two aspects of the same principle. Out of the new nation states would grow 'the United States of Europe, the republican alliance of the peoples', 'that great European federation, whose task it is to unite in one association all the political families of the old world, destroy the partitions that dynastic rivalries have made, and consolidate and respect nationalities.' (King, p. 309)

There would be an elected European assembly and a European

authority sitting at Rome. The nations of Europe would become eventually 'one vast market in which no one member could suffer or be fettered in developing its powers without inconvenience to the others'. The People's International League, which he founded in 1847, would not only enjoy unrestrained free trade but also unfettered immigration and emigration. (*Life and Writings*, VI, pp. 293–8) Although Mazzini loathed and despised everything Jeremy Bentham stood for, the President of the League was none other than Bentham's devoted editor, now Sir John Bowring.

Mazzini had, in short, foreseen pretty much every feature of the present-day European Union. What he had also understood, as many Eurosceptics have not, was that his European federation could, if handled rightly, mean not the dissolution but 'the rescue of the nation state' to quote the title of Alan Milward's contrarian masterpiece. Secure within agreed borders and living under a common code of commercial and international law, the nations of the federation could blossom, not in imposed uniformity but in their inherited quiddities.

So, we must give Mazzini credit for the uncanny accuracy of his long-term vision. But we cannot ignore his stupendous innocence about the force of the passions he was letting rip. To reach that chastened and pacific frame of mind that eventually engendered the European Union, the whole continent had to undergo two of the most ghastly wars in human history.

Was all this a tragic accident, a serial combination of unlucky botches? Or was the potential for tragedy on such a scale inherent in Mazzini's doctrine? We have no reason to doubt his sincerity when he says: 'I hate the monopolistic, usurping nation, that sees its own strength and greatness only in the weakness and poverty of others.' He denounced as stunted any nation that adopted a foreign policy 'of aggrandizement and selfishness'. (King, p. 303) We can certainly disregard the attempts of fascist supporters like the philosopher Giovanni Gentile to invent a 'fascist Mazzini'. The Duce himself sought to bolster his cred by claiming that he was one of the few men who had read all hundred volumes of Mazzini's works. Mazzini would surely have found Mussolini a wicked and vulgar charlatan.

Yet it remains true that by erecting the love of country into a religious mission, Mazzini did leave the way open for a monstrous perversion and extension of that mission. For this reason, we do need to look a little deeper into Mazzini's thought to grasp its more ominous implications.

THE NEW RELIGION

Like Marx and Bentham – like most Movers in fact – Mazzini did not pay much attention to his critics. Even in conversation he talked too much, in the most beguiling way, to take in much of what other people were saying. He even managed to silence Thomas Carlyle and Benjamin Jowett. Perhaps for that reason, he was a remarkably consistent thinker. He said much the same thing most of his life – there is not really an early or a later Mazzini. And most of what he said hung together. His rhetoric might be exuberant, even overblown. Karl Marx, his near neighbour in London (though we have no record of their ever meeting), denounced his 'false sublimity, puffy grandeur, verbosity and prophetic mysticism' (Mack Smith, pp. 200–1), which he thought made Mazzini an irrelevance in the new age of socialist materialism. But under the iridescent drapery we can detect the bones of a doctrine that deserves attention.

He begins by accepting the legacy of the French Revolution, what might be called the *acquis communautaire* of 1789. Whatever Bentham (and Mussolini and Hitler) might say, human rights do exist. They are precious and must never be discarded or overridden in any reformed society. Liberties matter. In *The Duties of Man*, Mazzini tells his audience of working men, 'there are things which constitute your individual being and are essential to human life. And over these not even the People has any right. No majority, no collective force can rob you of that which makes you *men*. No majority can decree a tyranny and extinguish or alienate its own liberty.' (pp. 78–9) These rights include personal liberty, freedom of movement, freedom of opinion and religious belief, freedom of the press, freedom of trade and freedom of association.

Mazzini also accepts the right to property as an eternal principle. He fiercely denounces communism, both on moral and economic grounds, because it denies liberty, closes the way to progress and petrifies society: 'If, instead of correcting evils and slowly modifying the constitution of property, you sought to abolish it, you would suppress a source of wealth, of emulation, and of activity, and you would be like the savage who to gather the fruit cuts down the tree.' (*Duties*, p. 104)

But rights are not enough. They are not even the more important half of the picture. If the rampant egoism that destroyed the French Revolution is to be curbed, duties must come first. Which is why he calls his treatise *The Duties of Man* and discusses duties before he comes to rights and liberties. And these duties have a sacred character. He tells the university students of Italy: '*La vita è missione; la vita è battaglia; la vita è la coscienza d'una santa idea, incarnata dall'amore e dalla costanza in fatti potenti.*' (*Scritti*, Vol IX, p.162)

These words – mission, struggle, conscience, incarnation, love, constancy – are the same words that a Christian preacher might use. But Mazzini tells us repeatedly that 'I am not a Christian, or rather I am a Christian plus something more'. (Mack Smith, p. 17) He admired Jesus as a great teacher, who brought the new ideas of brotherhood and forgiveness and humility into the world. But he did not think that Jesus was the son of God, except in the sense that we are all sons of God. 'We love Him as the best of our human brothers; we do not worship and fear Him as the inexorable Judge, or intolerant Ruler of the future.' (*Duties*, p. 304)

In *From the Council to God*, Mazzini's great polemic against the Catholic Church, it is not simply the corruption and cruelty of the papacy that he attacks but the Church's fatal misunderstanding of life: 'Life is movement, aspiration, progress. You deny progress; shrink in terror from all aspiration; crucify humanity upon Calvary; reject every attempt to detach the idea from the symbol and strive to petrify the living Word of God. You reduce all history (which is the successive manifestation of that Word) to a single moment.' (*Duties*, p. 298) Contrary to the teaching of the Gospels, the Church had always been on the wrong side, in hock to the rich and powerful, against the poor and oppressed. The Church had no grasp of *association*, one of Mazzini's favourite words. 'Your religion was the religion of individual man. It did not, it could not, at its origin, contemplate collective humanity.' (Ibid., p. 312) This fixation on the individual made the Church unable to focus on or even to accept social progress, or to understand the love of country that was integral to that progress.

Instead of being stuck on a single historical event, the crucifixion of Jesus, believers should join in a new form of worship and celebrate God's progressive revelation in the world. They should look back to the words of Jesus, especially in chapters 14–16 of St John's Gospel, which foreshadow God's future purposes: another Comforter will come, who will abide with you for ever; the branches that bear fruit will be pruned to bring more fruit; He will show you the things to come.

Now all this has much in common with the general current of Modernism in the Church and with the belated emergence of Christian social thought towards the end of the nineteenth century. What would a progressive state look like? Mazzini does not descend into much detail, but what he does sketch out is the sort of programme that Christian socialists then or social democrats in 1945 would endorse: a steeply graduated income tax, national systems of welfare and education, the nationalization of mines and railways, the promotion of co-operative enterprises.

Behind these worthy policies lies something much more momentous. As Ignazio Silone puts it: 'Mazzini's utopia was a world in which there would be nothing but free peoples. To them he transferred the religious legitimacy and authority which he withdrew from the papacy and from the dynasties that ruled in his time.' (Silone, p. 21) This transfer of moral power is unmistakeable, and Mazzini intends it to be permanent. From now on, our first loyalty is no longer to be to God as revealed in His Church but to God as revealed in the progress of Humanity with a capital H. In practical terms, this means that we are all conscripted into the service of the Nation, which is the vehicle of that progress. 'Dio e Popolo' – that was always Mazzini's slogan: 'God and the People', but it begins to look as though God *is* the People.

And if the Nation is to fulfil its destiny, it has the sacred right to call on us to make the supreme sacrifice. Irredentism – the redeeming of territory that rightly belongs to the nation – is part of its mission. The word '*irredentista*' was first coined by Italian nationalists after Mazzini's death. The man himself leaves us in no doubt what this means.

In his specific appeal *To the Italians*, which was the programme of his last journal, *Roma del Popolo*, founded a year before his death, he says: 'The Italian Mission is therefore: the Unity of the Nation, in its *material* aspect, by the reconquest of the Trentino, of Istria and of Nice.' (*Duties*, p. 245) In *The Duties of Man*, he tells his audience that 'you should have no joy or repose as long as a portion of the territory upon which your language is spoken is separated from the Nation'. (p. 55)

There is no opting out from this duty. 'Neutrality in a war of principles is mere passive existence, forgetfulness of all that makes a people sacred.' Any such shirking will not go unpunished. 'Sooner or later, a tremendous expiation will visit the cowardly desertion of the duty which God lays on peoples as on individuals.' (King, p. 305) And, indeed, post-war expiation, or *épuration* as the French called it after the Second World War, has taken a terrible toll, all thought of justice or mercy being tossed aside in the rush to take vengeance on collaborators.

It is notable that actual military conscription followed hot on this moral conscription. Mandatory military service for all men at the age of eighteen was instituted in Italy in 1865, and remained in force until 2005. It was Napoleon who had first imported into Italy the notion that every man ought to be compelled to serve his country militarily. But it was Mazzini above all who domesticated this imperative. Unification meant militarization. The wars of dynasties were typically affairs of pique and pride, often fought by mercenaries, many of them foreign mercenaries, and easily broken off when they were proving too costly. The wars of nations were sacred missions, which called on every citizen to fight to the end, however bitter. As the British government was to discover in 1915, all-out war, the *guerre à outrance*, is sustainable only by calling up the total manpower of the nation state.

At this point, we may be tempted to look back at the Genoa of Mazzini's youth. Elie Kedourie points out that 'he was living under a government which, as governments go, was not really intolerable: it did not levy ruinous taxation, it did not conscript soldiers, it did not maintain concentration camps, and it left its subjects pretty much to their own devices'. (Kedourie, p. 92) Even Mazzini's spell in the cooler was not such a harsh punishment. After all, Mazzini himself tells us: 'I had matter enough for three condemnations upon me: rifle-bullets; a letter in cipher ... the formula of the oath for the second rank of Carbonari; and, moreover, (for I was arrested in the act of leaving the house) a sword stick.' He managed to get rid of everything, which suggests, as he says, that the police 'had all the inclination, but not sufficient capacity for tyranny'. Was life in degenerate old Genoa so much worse than trudging through the icefields on the Isonzo battlefront, as described by Ernest Hemingway in *A Farewell to Arms*?

HIS HISTORIC MOMENT

Mazzini was sternly opposed to compromise. It was vital to stick to one's guns, literally, to seize every opportunity for action, even when the prospects of success were dismal. Keeping the momentum going was the thing. As botched uprising succeeded conspiracies that never even took off because the police had penetrated them from day one, Mazzini in his bedsit over the post office in Chelsea was battered by criticism from all over Italy. He was condemned in *The Times* by an Italian MP turned leader-writer as 'the Mephistopheles of Democracy'. Others denounced his skulking in London and sending out ill-armed men to be shot or tortured in hopeless raids.

Yet when revolution swept across Europe in 1848, nobody could say that Giuseppe Mazzini was found wanting. He was proud that the first uprisings broke out in Italy – in Milan, Genoa, Livorno and Venice. Insurgents in Palermo rose against the Bourbons, flying the Italian tricolor first flown fifty years earlier in Napoleon's Cisalpine Republic. King Ferdinand was scared into granting his subjects an 'irrevocable' constitution, followed with no less reluctance by the Grand Duke Leopold of Tuscany, and in March by Carlo Alberto in Piedmont. At the end of February, the French monarchy came to a dismal end. A fortnight later, an insurrection in Vienna forced old Metternich into exile and squeezed a constitution out of the emperor.

These revolts were spontaneous popular uprisings of the sort Mazzini dreamed of, and it was a great moment when he arrived in Milan on 7 April to a triumphal progress after seventeen years of exile. He immediately tried, without much luck, to reconcile the Moderates and the Republicans. He told Carlo Alberto in Piedmont that he would support him, as long as he agreed on complete unification, which was the last thing the nervy king wanted, fearing that such a campaign would end in a terrifying nationwide revolution led by Republicans. In another gesture of conciliation, Mazzini celebrated the feast of Corpus Christi alongside the Archbishop of Milan.

All too soon, these thrilling outbreaks were squashed, often with much brutality, and the pope and the kings ratted on the constitutions they had promised. The Austrians defeated Carlo Alberto at the miserable Battle of Custoza. But in Rome the already elected assembly opted for a republic and declared the temporal power of the papacy to be at an end. Pio Nono himself was still skulking in the French-held fortress of Gaeta.

Mazzini hurried to the city which he had always seen as the capital of a united Italy. It was his refrain that this would be Rome's third glorious age, the Rome of the People, after the Rome of the Popes and the Rome of the Caesars. He was forty-four years old, and, amazingly, this was his first visit to the Eternal City.

Some members of the assembly wanted to make him a dictator, but he proposed a triumvirate in the old Roman style. This was the beginning of his own Hundred Days, which G. M. Trevelyan called 'one of the great scenes of history'. Mazzini had never run so much as a post office before, but he governed with aplomb, moderation and common sense. He closed down the Papal Inquisition, stopped the executions for which the Papal States had been notorious, lifted censorship and distributed to the poor the proceeds of some Church property. He lived in one room in the Quirinale, dined at a local trattoria for two francs, and when Louis Napoleon besieged the city, lived on bread and raisins for the duration (not much change from his usual sparse diet). When the Republic took some French prisoners, Mazzini sent them bundles of cigars wrapped in handbills appealing for republican fraternity (a gesture first thought of by the

American Congress after taking some Hessian mercenaries during the revolutionary wars).

Napoleon III sent as his envoy Ferdinand de Lesseps, later the prime mover in the Suez Canal project. De Lesseps was much impressed by Mazzini, and had no idea that he had been sent merely to stall for time before General Oudinot's reinforcements arrived. For another month, the Romans struggled on against odds that eventually overwhelmed them. That was the end of the Roman Republic and of Mazzini's only taste of power. But it was a glorious end. The events of 1848 and 1849 had shown not only that Young Italy could set the whole peninsula ablaze, but also that the 'Mephistopheles of Democracy' was as wise a governor as he was brilliant a propagandist.

Grey and cadaverous now, grievously disappointed but undaunted, Mazzini slipped out of Italy and back to England, by way of Lausanne, where he made a start on translating the New Testament into Italian.

THE VICTORY OF THE MACHIAVELLIANS

Mazzini had another twenty years to live, and his one-man propaganda war never let up, but after 1849 he begins to fade from the pages of high politics. Ignazio Silone, writing ninety years later in the depths of the fascist era, had no hesitation in saying that 'As the most casual eye could see at once, Mazzini was irremediably and completely a beaten man'. (Silone, p. 39) Even his loyal biographer, Bolton King, regards his political manoeuvres in Italy after 1850 as mistaken and counterproductive: 'Had he gauged Italian sentiment more accurately, he would have spared himself the error, would have lost his deep distrust in Piedmont and its king, his bitter animosity to Cavour, his pitiable exaggeration of the strength of his own party.' (King, p. 155) The Republic had become impossible from the day that Victor Emmanuel swore allegiance to the constitution, and thereby proclaimed himself the champion of Italian aspirations. If Mazzini had been at the king's side, he could have done a lot of good. He wasn't going to beat them, so he should have joined them. In England, he was a spent force.

This may be a sound judgement in worldly terms, but it overlooks what a shoddy affair the final stages of unification were to be – not so much a glorious Risorgimento as an Establishment stitch-up. Young Italy was left on the sidelines, while Victor Emmanuel mopped up the duchies of central Italy. Cavour's deal with Louis Napoleon allowed Piedmont a free hand in return for giving up Savoy and Nice. Victor Emmanuel was a ceaseless and unscrupulous intriguer: he secretly offered a military alliance for war against either Prussia or France, then offered a different alliance to Prussia for war against Austria. In the end, he found himself fighting alongside Napoleon again, on the losing side in the Franco-Prussian War. In these head-spinning machinations, one is tempted to conclude that the real liberator of Italy was Bismarck, who smashed her two great oppressors, first Austria in 1866, then France in 1870.

Cavour did not live to see the ultimate success of his serpentine diplomacy. He died in 1861, aged only fifty. But he had a patriotic heart of sorts, concealed under his cynical exterior, and he would have delighted in the outcome.

For Mazzini, there was no such consolation. In his eyes, the new Italy had found its inspiration not in his beloved Dante but in Machiavelli. Where was the great, beautiful, moral Italy of his dreams? 'This medley of opportunists and cowards and little Machiavellis, that let themselves be dragged behind the suggestion of the foreigner – I thought to call up the soul of Italy, and I only see its corpse.' (King, p. 218) His people had let him down: 'It is my lot to consume my last days in the grief, supreme to one who really loves, of seeing the thing one loves most, inferior to its mission.' (King, p. 207) People expected him to rejoice, but 'nobody can understand how wretched I feel at seeing corruption, scepticism about the advantages of Unity, financial ruin, shame of subalternity, and moral anarchy increasing from year to year, and under a materialist immoral government, all the future of Italy disappearing'. (Mack Smith, p. 203)

As for popular democracy, that was a long time coming. At the time of unification, only 2 per cent of the population had the vote, increasing only to 7 per cent after the expansion of the franchise in 1882 – and half the members of parliament were appointed by the king. For the Republic, Italy had to wait until after the defeat of fascism – in fact, until 1948. The Mussolini years provided embarrassing evidence of how shallow the roots of Italian democracy were. Some writers, such as David Gilmour in *The Pursuit of Italy*, argue that even today Italian unity is insecurely rooted. From the Mafia to the Liga del Nord, regional loyalties continue to crop up in unwelcome ways.

This at least can scarcely be blamed on Mazzini. He had persistently argued that Italy could take her place as a flourishing nation only as a unified republic, with plenty of devolution to be sure, but as one nation, not a federation of distinct provinces.

His legacy, both for good and ill, lies not so much in the Italy we see before us today, nor even in the European institutions that then seemed so fanciful, but rather in the way he poeticized the idea of the nation into a religious faith. He was not himself a poet, though he was a prolific literary critic, but he loved poetry. He adored Byron above all other poets, not only for his verse, but for his heroic sacrifice for Greece. Religion was not dead, and nor was poetry, so long as both of them identified with the progress of the people. In future, the 'poor pale poetry of the individual' would give way to a 'grand social poetry, solemn, calm and faithful; recognizing God alone in heaven, and the people on earth'. ('Thoughts, addressed to the Poets of the Nineteenth Century', *Life and Writings*, I, p. 151) Poetry, like religion, had been conscripted into the service of social change; it 'had forsaken ancient Europe to animate the young and lovely Europe of the Peoples'. (Ibid., p. 150)

This is the legacy that was so gratefully taken up and cherished by later freedom-fighters who admired Mazzini, by Sun Yat-sen, by Gandhi and by Nehru, and many others across Europe and far beyond. They were happy to identify Mazzini as the man who had, more than any other, elevated their grubby and gruelling struggle to a sacred mission.

On his last trip to Italy – where he died, at Pisa, to be buried beside his mother in Genoa – Mazzini crossed the St Gotthard Pass on a sledge in deepest February. The sledge slipped on the ice and tumbled into a ravine. The lucky survivors took refuge in a hotel where the young Friedrich Nietzsche was staying. Nietzsche never forgot his conversations with Mazzini. He told his sister years later:

Of all fine lives, he envied most Mazzini's: that absolute concentration upon a single idea which becomes as it were a flame
consuming all that is personal in life. The poet turns his inner
urge to action into the characters he creates and so projects doing
and suffering outside himself. Mazzini expressed his in his own
life, which was the continual manifestation in word and deed,
of a most noble spirit. He was himself a tragic protagonist who
accepts grievous suffering in order to bring about fulfilment of
the ideal. (*Salvemini*, p. 192)

For Nietzsche, Giuseppe Mazzini was, in the nicest possible way,
a superman.

THE OTHER EXPLANATION

As we take leave of this enchanting, if sometimes exasperating character and his huge ambiguous legacy, we cannot ignore the fact that
there exists an entirely different explanation for the rise of nationalism. Historians who take the view that socio-economic factors are
usually, if not always, decisive in historical change think that this
applies to nationalism too. It is social and economic pressures that
shape the crises of 'modernization' through which emerging states
must pass. Flowery nation-talk is mere rhetorical decoration.

Ernest Gellner, for example, makes no bones about saying that
he is 'allergic to the history of ideas approach', because 'nationalism
as an elaborated intellectual *theory* is neither widely endorsed, not
of high quality, nor of any historic importance'. Gellner argues in
Nations and Nationalism that nationalist rhetoric is so saturated
with false consciousness that 'who said or wrote precisely what
doesn't matter much'. The only worthwhile question is why nationalism arose, not what's in it. From Mazzini to Enoch Powell, anyone
can spout reams of the stuff off the top of his head; it's all tosh.

In his *Nations and Nationalism Since 1780*, Eric Hobsbawm
went further: nationalism involves so much 'belief in what is
patently wrong' that 'no serious historian of nation and nationalism can be a committed political nationalist' – whereas the same
would, we presume, not apply to a committed political Marxist,

like Hobsbawm himself. Not merely is the content of its doctrines not worth studying; if you wish to be taken seriously, you must not believe a word of them. They have no explanatory, or any other sort of value. Religion is of little relevance either. It is simply not true, Gellner says, that 'once deities and kings are de-sacralised, then nations must inherit their aura'. People may become nationalistic and remain religious like the Poles, or be irreligious and not notably nationalistic like the Swedes.

For Gellner and for other historians, some but not all of a Marxist tendency, the 'secret of nationalism' remains what it always was: 'the new role of culture in industrialized society'. Premodern man is tumbled out of his hammock of kinship and forcibly enlisted in the nation. He has no other option but to learn the language and loyalties insisted on by this strange novelty among human institutions. His old, scattered, small-scale world, of familiar faces and customs and taboos – all that is crumbled away. He no longer knows his place, because there is no longer a place to know. It is not that he *chooses* to put all his eggs into this new basket. True, the orators and the folklorists will be busy persuading that the nation is the embodiment of his people's history and the true core of his identity. The reality is, though, that he has no alternative but to obey the materialist imperative. 'The socio-economic base is decisive,' Gellner pronounces, and, giving credit where it is not often given these days, 'that much is true in Marx.' The upsurge of nationalism is inexplicable without some grasp of the collapse everywhere of the old world. It would otherwise be an intolerable coincidence that peasants should be being made into Frenchmen, while Welshmen were being made into Britons, and, somewhat later, Shonas into Zimbabweans, and Xhosas into South Africans. Rhetoric and folk-lore could not begin to accomplish so much.

Kedourie, who is the particular target of Gellner, retorts in an afterword to a later edition of his *Nationalism* that the chronology in the real world does not fit Gellner's model. Nationalism in its modern form was, after all, first articulated in German-speaking lands when they were innocent of industrialization. Later, the nationalist passion swept through the Balkans, where there wasn't a factory to be seen. The pioneer nations of industrialization, such as

Britain and the United States, are precisely those where nationalist movements in this sense were virtually unknown.

Ideas do matter; they spread and have consequences. One simple idea that matters is the resentment of foreign occupiers, which is as old as recorded time. Among a hundred examples, we can think of the Jewish Revolt against the Romans in AD 66, or of the Dutch revolt against Spanish rule in the sixteenth century, or, two hundred years earlier, the one-man crusade of Cola di Rienzo, who led a rebellion against foreign domination, proclaimed the unity of Italy, and for a brief period ruled Rome with the same moderation and justice as Mazzini five centuries later. Like Mazzini the Triumvir, Rienzi, as he was more often known, borrowed his assumed title from Ancient Rome, that of Tribune. When he was toppled and taken for judgement to the pope, then in Avignon, his friend Petrarch lamented 'a crime worthy of the cross and vultures, that a Roman citizen should grieve to see his land, the rightful mistress of all others, enslaved to the basest of men'. (*Letters on Familiar Matters*, II, 13, p. 6, tr. Aldo S. Bernardo, 1982)

All this happened in the 1340s, surely a little early for the modernization process.

Like many other Italians of his day, Mazzini treasured the memory of Rienzi. And not just Italians. Bulwer-Lytton wrote a novel about him, which Wagner turned into one of his first operas. As a teenager, Adolf Hitler was bowled over by *Rienzi*, with its passionate message of national liberation, and later said that 'it was at that hour it all began'. He was given the original score of the opera and it was with him in the bunker in 1945. Who says that nationalism has no deep roots in history?

We note, too, that, in the case of his native Czech lands (he was brought up in Prague), Gellner is prepared to discuss the content of nationalist rhetoric and to ponder whether it corresponds more or less to the peculiarities of Czech culture. Was it too Protestant, too inward-looking, too focused on the Czech language? In his distaste for nation-talk, he does not go so far as to claim that all national cultures are indistinguishable. There are, it seems, nationalisms that are false and nationalisms that aren't. We may have all been through the same mincer, but we do not all end up the same, although the modern nation does display certain unvarying marks: a central, pervasive administration, a national language and education system. All nations are busy, if not always effective machines for standardizing their citizens.

But – and this seems to be critical for the socio-economic theory – this nation-building is a once-only process. Hobsbawm quotes with approval Bagehot's view of the nineteenth century as the age of 'nation-building'; for the developing nations, the process happened in the twentieth century, in some places is still happening. All the anxiety, all the passion, derives from the *transition*. Gellner concedes that patriotism is in some measure 'a perennial part of human life', but that very distinctive species of patriotism that we call nationalism 'becomes pervasive and dominant only under certain social conditions, which in fact prevail in the modern world, and nowhere else'.

Gellner modestly goes on to say that his argument does not explain why some nationalisms such as Hitler's and Mussolini's should have taken such a horrifically virulent turn. But surely it does. It is the agony of the transition, inflamed by a sense of injustice and exclusion, that induces the paranoia, the ferocity and the cruelty to the alien. The eggs are so fragile, the basket so ramshackle, and if it smashes, we are all bereft, in a world drained of warmth and meaning.

There does seem to be a comforting conclusion that follows from this argument. Now that most nations are securely built, their frontiers established even where they run heedlessly across tribal and linguistic boundaries, nationalistic inflammations may be expected to abate. And indeed, very gingerly, that is what Gellner does expect: 'The sharpness of nationalist conflict may be expected to diminish. It was the social chaos created by early industrialization, and by the unevenness of its diffusion which made it acute.'

Well, that's what we all hope. But is it really true? Gellner and Hobsbawm were writing in the relative calm of the 1980s and 1990s, at a time when economics was supposed to explain most things. Looking around us today – at Donald Trump, at Vladimir Putin, at Marine Le Pen, at Geert Wilders, at Nigel Farage and Brexit – one is struck rather by the opposite: that nationalist feeling is still flicker-quick to stir when stimulated. Few modern nationalists would echo Mazzini's complaints that his countrymen were too apathetic to respond to his appeal.

You could argue a rather different case: that national feeling may sometimes first erupt under the pressures of modernization and state-building, but once in the bloodstream it remains as persistent as the nastier forms of hepatitis. In those long-established Anglo-American states, where it took hold centuries earlier, it merely lies quiescent until provoked. The transition to modernity may be a once-and-for-all thing. But so, it seems, is the absorption of nationalism and its poetry. Whatever sophisticates may feel or hope, patriotism, to give it a kinder name, remains a heartfelt public passion, in the godless modern world still the most heartfelt. Which is why Mazzini lives.

X

KARL MARX

and the death of capitalism

LOOK FORWARD IN ANGER

The Russian traveller Pavel Annenkov first came across Karl Marx in Brussels in the mid-1840s when Marx was in his late twenties. Already the impression he made was indelible:

> With a thick mop of black hair on his hair, his hairy hands, dressed in a coat buttoned diagonally across his chest, he maintained the appearance of a man with the right and authority to command respect, whatever guise he took and whatever he did. All his motions were awkward but vigorous and self-confident, all his manners ran athwart conventional usages in social intercourse, but were proud and somehow guarded, and his shrill voice with its metallic ring marvellously suited the radical pronouncements over things and people which he uttered ... Before me stood the figure of the democratic dictator incarnate. (quoted Stedman Jones, p. 225)

Nearly thirty years later, another Russian émigré, Mikhail Bakunin, described a character whose *saeva indignatio* had somehow curdled: 'He is extremely ambitious and vain, quarrelsome, intolerant, and absolute, like Jehovah, the Lord God of his ancestors, and like him, vengeful to the point of madness. There is no lie or calumny that he would not invent or disseminate against anyone who had the misfortune to arouse his jealousy or his hatred, which amounts to the same thing.'

At about the same time, Jenny Marx, for whom the phrase 'long-suffering wife' might have been invented, lamented the misery of their lives and the hounding of her husband: '... police and democrats alike all bay the same refrain about his "despotic nature, his craving for authority and his ambition"! How much better it would have been, and how much happier he would be, if he had just gone on quietly and developed the theory of struggle for those in the fight.' (quoted Stedman Jones, p. 541)

But he had to be in the thick of the fight. In a family questionnaire, he said that his idea of happiness was 'to fight', while his idea of misery was 'submission' (he shared with Nietzsche and the late Christopher Hitchens a particular aversion to this key feature of the Christian faith). Nor was his pugnacity merely verbal. He was ready to smash several street lights during a pub crawl up the Tottenham Court Road, and if insulted he would revert to the duelling code of his Berlin youth: 'I shall be prepared to give you the satisfaction customary among gentlemen.' (quoted Stedman Jones, p. 526)

It was his unquenchable ferocity that sustained him through a life of grinding hardship, repeated disappointment, ever worsening health and, until his last few years, shabby obscurity. By the end of his life, his was a name to strike terror into bourgeois hearts across Europe, which gave him no little satisfaction. Yet at his funeral in Highgate Cemetery, there were only eleven mourners. At times, his thunderous certainty overwhelms his other, no less remarkable qualities: his intellectual curiosity, his acute literary sensibility, his capacity to soak up other people's ideas and metabolize them into his own, his willingness to change his mind without admitting it, his optimism that was both heroic and absurd. He was lionhearted if muddle-headed to the end. He never gave up. He was by no means the first observer to have voiced outrage at the appalling conditions endured by industrial workers. By the time he took his seat in the British Museum, the chorus of protest had become so deafening that Parliament could no longer ignore it. And he relied on the fieldwork of others, just as he borrowed his theoretical machinery from Hegel, Feuerbach, Saint-Simon, Ricardo and every other English economist of the day. But it was his ferocious public certainty that convinced the world that Marxism was a coherent, consistent and unstoppable doctrine.

That doctrine has kept an enduring fascination, not just because of its sulphurous moral indignation but because it combined two very different but equally seductive things: first, the claim in his masterwork *Das Kapital* (which I'll refer to as *Capital* from now on) to have uncovered, in a fashion both unprecedented and scientific, the 'great secret' of how, behind the reassuring formulae of the bourgeois economists, the capitalists exploited and expropriated their workers; and second, in *The Communist Manifesto* and Marx's other polemical and journalistic tirades, his prophecy of the inevitable downfall of capitalism and the triumph of the proletariat. The last would be first, and the old class antagonisms would be dissolved in a never-ending future of harmony and progress. Marxism was always firmly and intrinsically an atheistic creed. God had to be killed off before real philosophy could begin. But the echoes in Marx's scenario of the Fall and the Redemption are unmistakeable.

There had been nothing quite like it in the history of political ideas, in its forcefulness and the sweep of its assertions. It was all so much more exciting than the prosaic blueprints of the English reformers. Not the least exciting thing was the role reserved for intellectuals. The philosopher's duty now was to be *in* the world, not to interpret it but to change it – Marx was himself swept up in the great revolution of 1848 and served on the short-lived Committee of Public Safety in Cologne. Raymond Aron, the greatest of post-war French political writers, confessed that though he had never been a Marxist, he had been obsessed with the subject for thirty-five years. One of its charms, he thought, was that 'you can explain it in five minutes or study it for half a century'. Marxism was both deliciously simple and bafflingly difficult. And it was soused in anger.

As J. P. Plamenatz puts it:

The peculiarity of the Marxian social theory, and what makes it to the English, the French and the Americans an alien creed, lies not so much in the doctrines embodied in it, nor even in the manner of their embodiment, as in the emotions that find utterance through it. It is something altogether vaster, more elaborate, harsher and less accommodating than any French or

English brand of socialism; it is more demanding, arrogant and contemptuous; it thrusts aside with disdain whatever does not suit it, as if facts were not worth noticing unless they bore it out. It is a German theory, overwhelming in its profuseness, like a broad river in full spate carrying all before it. (p. xvii)

The impact that his best writings still make today is not to be denied. Even his sternest critics like Sir Karl Popper pay tribute to his burning desire to help the oppressed, his hatred of hypocrisy and the immense labours he devoted to forging what he believed to be scientific weapons to improve the lot of the vast majority of mankind. (*Open Society*, II, p. 82)

The mythology surrounding Marx and his doctrine was encrusted and fossilized by the Soviet regime, but the process began much earlier, even before Marx's death in 1883, and it accelerated over the next thirty years as the Social Democratic Party in Germany became the largest socialist party in the world and promoted Marx as the founder of their science of history. Engels claimed that by the time they met for the second time in the spring of 1845, 'Marx had already fully developed his materialist theory of history in its main features'. But Marx's latest biographer, Gareth Stedman Jones, argues that what came to be known as Marxism was largely created by Engels, beginning with his *Anti-Dühring* of 1878, his lacerating attack on the milder evolutionary socialism of Eugen Dühring, which simplified Marx's thought and converted it into a handy *Weltanschauung* for general use. Yet *Anti-Dühring* was read out to Karl Marx and approved by him (he actually wrote a part of it). So we cannot really argue that what Engels said and wrote after 1883 was not true Marxism. (Plamenatz, p. 6)

It was undoubtedly Engels who neatly tacked Marxism onto the end of Darwinism, to integrate it into the new scientific hegemony. At Marx's graveside, Engels declared roundly that 'Charles Darwin discovered the law of the development of organic nature upon our planet. Marx is the discoverer of the fundamental law according to which human history moves and develops itself, a law so simple and self-evident that its simple enunciation is almost sufficient to secure assent.' But in fact, Karl had been extremely ambivalent about

Darwin and did not really accept this continuity between natural history and human history. He resisted Darwin's implication that progress was 'purely accidental', and he had told Engels so. It is clear that Darwin's open-ended, evidence-based approach is the very reverse of Marx's economic determinism. In truth, not even Engels wanted to draw any close comparison between the class struggle of human beings and the biological struggle for life.

The story that Marx had wanted to dedicate *Capital* to Darwin was a long-standing canard based on a confusion between Marx himself and Edward Aveling, Eleanor Marx's dodgy partner and co-translator of *Capital*, who had written a student's guide to Darwin and wanted permission to dedicate it to the great man. (Wheen, pp. 363–9) As for Darwin, while he did write a polite letter thanking Marx for sending him a copy of *Capital*, Francis Wheen points out in his entertaining and informative 1999 Life of Marx that only the first 105 pages of the 822 pages of Darwin's copy are cut, and even the cut pages don't have any of the marginal scribbles that Darwin always wrote in any book that engaged him. He obviously just glanced at the first few chapters, then tossed off a thank-you letter.

This was not Engels' only 'improvement'. In editing volume three of *Capital*, where Marx had written that when the rate of profit fell, as it was bound to under capitalism, the system would be 'shaken' (*erschüttert*), Engels substituted 'collapsed' (*zusammengebracht*), suggesting a much more certain demise of the whole system. This was the origin of what became a hot topic from the 1890s to the 1930s as *Zusammenbruchstheorie*. Ironically, a key feature of Thomas Piketty's bestselling modern version of Marx, also called *Capital*, is that the rate of profit is destined to go on increasing, leading just like the original version to the relative immiseration of the working class. Neither prophecy seems entirely solid. The average rate of profit sometimes goes down, as it did towards the end of the nineteenth century, and sometimes goes up, as it did towards the end of the twentieth century. As with so much else in history, there is no discernible law that can be relied on.

In *Anti-Dühring*, Engels proclaims that under socialism, the state 'dies out' (*stirbt ab*), which seems different from Marx's '*Aufhebung des Staates*' (raising up or dissolving), even if neither term is really clear, despite the huge amount of ink spilled on expounding them. Yet we cannot entirely blame Engels. Marx often left his followers bewildered by his apparent zigzags and furtive shifts of position. The self-image of Marxism and of its founder is of the 'old mole' steadily burrowing underground, until it and he startle the bourgeoisie by breaking the surface. Yet at times, Karl appears rather more like a squirrel, leaping from branch to branch with a natural agility, wriggling through tight corners and with a bright eye for nuts and berries to be hoarded for future use.

HIS EARLY MASTERS

As a student in Bonn, Marx is instantly attracted by the materialism and atomism of the pre-Socratics, but he is wary of the determinism of Democritus and fastens on to Epicurus instead as the subject of his thesis, because he sees Epicurus as offering an escape into self-consciousness and human freedom. In a similar fashion, he works through Hegel and comes out the other side, transforming the master's cloudy historicism into a more down-to-earth account of how history develops, just as inexorably as Hegel claims, but propelled by social and economic forces that we are in a position to identify and analyse.

Georg Wilhelm Friedrich Hegel (1770–1831) dominated the intellectual life of his time in the German-speaking lands, especially in Berlin where Karl Marx studied for his doctorate. He contributed one idea of supreme importance to philosophy: that men do not start with a blank sheet of paper. There was no original moment at which human beings came together and signed a 'social contract'. We are the product of our historical inheritance. This idea was common to most of the Romantic thinkers of the late eighteenth century and was most memorably formulated, as we have seen, by Edmund Burke. But only Hegel erected this perception into an entire philosophical system. For Hegel, everything about us – our minds, our institutions, our economic system – comes from the unfolding of what he calls '*Geist*', or the World Spirit. For history is not a matter of one damn thing after another. There is a providence at work that is to lead us to true freedom. This intoxicating quasi-religious vision bewitched Marx and his contemporaries in Berlin and far beyond.

They were bewitched in particular by Hegel's 'dialectical method'. This sounds simple enough. The World Spirit moves in a three-beat rhythm: first, a *thesis* is proposed and gains acceptance in the minds of men. This comes to be criticized by opponents. That is the *antithesis*. There is a conflict between the two, and the outcome is a *synthesis* that reconciles and supersedes the two opposites at a higher level. Then the same process happens all over again. thus, History raises its game each time. It is a progress. Whatever happens to the Nation – and it is on the Nation that Hegel fixes his attention – has to happen, and it is good that it happens. 'The real is the rational.' Or to put it more brutally, might is right. The Hegelian is a worshipper of success. 'The History of the World is the World's Court of Justice.'

Especially right for Hegel is the actually existing Prussian state, which he adorned and adored and which made him its court philosopher. All other states were inferior, and whoever proposed to meddle with the glorious absolute monarchy of Friedrich Wilhelm III – for example, by proposing a new constitution – was contradicting the World Spirit. This laughable slavishness to the status quo was too much for Hegel's younger admirers. It was certainly too much for Karl Marx. Yet more than thirty years later, he still felt it necessary in the Author's Preface to *Das Kapital* to acknowledge his debt to and reverence for his old master, while protesting that 'my dialectical method is not only different from the Hegelian, but is its direct opposite'. Hegel's mystifications had turned true dialectic on its head: 'It must be turned right side up again, if you would discover the rational kernel within the mystical shell.' What he meant by this was that whereas Hegel proclaimed that thought determined the material world, Marx always believed that material circumstances basically determined and preceded our mindsets. The economic structure of any society generated its intellectual and political superstructure, and not the other way round. He wrote in *The Poverty of Philosophy*, composed in his late twenties, that 'it is the sovereigns who in all states have been subject to economic conditions, but they never dictated laws to them. Legislation, whether political or civil, never does more than proclaim, express in words, the will of economic relations'. (p. 83) Far from being the master of the nation's destiny, Friedrich Wilhelm was the puppet of its economic set-up.

That certainly does turn Hegel upside down, but in other crucial ways Marx kept strong traces of his Hegelian youth all his life. Like Hegel, he continued to believe that History was a global totality, that it had a single inevitable pattern and that it was working towards the full realization of human freedom. Like Hegel, he was ultimately both a determinist and an optimist. The development of human consciousness was the unfolding purpose of History, from the first cavemen and hunter-gatherers down to the frock-coated bourgeois of Berlin in the 1830s. The only difference – and it was a huge difference – was that, for Hegel, History had already reached its glorious terminus, while for Marx there was still a long way to go before the revolution ushered in the permanent dawn of socialism.

Quite how long they would have to wait for the dawn was a question that never ceased to vex Marx and Engels. Sometimes Karl thought that it was just around the corner. He wrote to Ferdinand Lassalle in 1858: 'History is evidently bracing itself to take again a new start, and the signs of decomposition everywhere are delightful for every mind not bent upon the conservation of things as they are.' (Avineri, p. 255) He had thought that the Crimean War might tip the scale in favour of revolution. Then he thought that the revolution would begin in Russia. In 1862, he thought it was about to break out in Germany, then a year later in Poland, five years later in Spain, then in 1877 in Russia again. All this was particularly embarrassing, because the outbreak of revolution was supposed to be an inevitable consequence of the stage of economic development reached by the country in question. His friend Wilhelm Wolff (to whose memory Marx dedicated the first volume of *Capital*, out of gratitude for a surprising legacy) took bets on which country the Moor, as the swarthy Marx was known to his circle, would next forecast a revolution breaking out in.

He retained from Hegel, too, the idea that History necessarily progressed by conflict. For Hegel, the Nation had to assert its soul by 'entering the Stage of History', that is, by asserting its dominance over other nations in battle. Winner took all, and rightly so. For Marx, the conflict was between classes, not between nations.

In fact, war between nations was an inconvenient intrusion in the Marxist scheme of things. Both Marx and Engels claimed that such wars, however ghastly, had little or no lasting effects on the serious business of History, the development of economic forces, which simply resumed where they had left off before the war.

Whether in war between nations (Hegel) or classes (Marx), the verdict of the Great Referee was not to be disputed. The winner deserved to win, and there was no appeal against the verdict. The slave economy of the ancient world gave way to the feudal system, which in turn gave way to bourgeois capitalism, which would in due course, and just as inevitably, give way to socialism. And every time the necessary superseding was brought about by conflict. 'The very moment civilization begins, production begins to be founded on the antagonism of orders, estates, classes, and finally on the antagonism of accumulated labour and actual labour. No antagonism, no progress. This is the law that civilization has followed up to our days.' (*The Poverty of Philosophy*, p. 61)

THE THEORY AND ITS DEFECTS

The difficulties in this thrilling chain of argument are not hard to spot. Since, for Marx, progress depends on advances in human knowledge, notably technical and scientific knowledge, how on earth can we reliably predict its future course? For we would have to possess such knowledge already, which by definition we do not. Marx did not know about the development of nuclear weapons that could blow up the world, for example. Nor can it be entirely true that the forces of production determine the sort of society we live in. Russian factories in the Soviet era worked in much the same way as British and American factories, although the systems of politics and property ownership were utterly different. Nor were the social systems of the past anything like as monolithic as Marx casually assumes. There were plenty of free peasants in the feudal era and thousands of freedmen as well as slaves doing the donkey work in the Roman Empire and the city states of Greece, not to mention plenty of merchants and bankers operating at every epoch we know of back to ancient Babylon – witness Marx's quoting of Aristotle's remark that usurers are rightly the most hated of men. (*Capital*, pp. 142–3) His association of specific technologies with particular social structures seems too glib. For example, in *The Poverty of Philosophy*, he claims in a famous phrase 'the handmill gives you society with the feudal lord; the steam-mill, society with the industrial capitalist.' (p. 109) Why? Capitalists all over the world made a good living out of handmills for centuries. It isn't even true that industrial capitalism was entirely sparked off by uppity bourgeois entrepreneurs. The exploitation of Britain's mineral resources was often pioneered and financed by ruthless feudal lords like the sixteenth-century Earl of Shrewsbury, who brought in expert workmen to apply new technologies to the coal and iron deposits of Sheffield. The voyages of merchant venturers and the colonial exploitation that followed were usually financed by noble patrons, including the royal family. Marx skates over the antiquity of the great global trade routes, such as the Silk Road to China, which can be traced back to the third century BC. If there is one constant theme in modern archaeology, it is the discovery in very early sites of artefacts from a multiplicity of different lands. The sweeping generalizations in *The Communist Manifesto* about the novelty of globalization need to be severely qualified. Equally, the flagrant accident of revolution breaking out in one country while its neighbour remained unmoved became so awkward for later Marxists that Lenin felt forced to enunciate a Law of Uneven Development, which of course is no law at all.

Nor is it true that progress is always driven by conflict. Sometimes it is, sometimes it isn't. Marx argues in *Capital* that technological innovation in eighteenth- and nineteenth-century England was provoked by the strikes of workers against the despotic factory system. But this is to ignore the restless search for improvements, long before, during and after the Industrial Revolution. Scientists then and now were motivated by the satisfaction of their discoveries as much as by the thought of the usefulness of their applications. Marx himself says that 'Watt's genius showed itself in the specification of the patent that he took out in April 1784. In that specification, his steam engine is described not as an invention for a specific purpose but as an agent universally applicable in Mechanical Industry. In it he points out applications, many of which, for instance the

steam-hammer, were not introduced till half a century later.'
(*Capital*, pp. 372–3) James Watt had no thought of frustrating the
militant Luddites; he was just prophesying what he hoped would be
a boon to future generations.

Marx records, too, the delight taken by the Greek poet 'Anti-
paros' (in fact Antipater of Thessalonica), a contemporary of
Cicero's, in the new invention of the waterwheel, which would liberate the local nymphs from their labours in the flour mill. (*Capital*,
p. 406) Vitruvius tells us that this invention combined the separate
Greek inventions of the toothed gear and the wheel turned by water.
Modern historians date the waterwheel, with its options of horizon-
tal or vertical axle, back to the second or third century BC. There
is no reason to suppose that its devising over several generations
was the result of industrial action by the millgirls of Byzantium or
Alexandria. It looks to us like a typical example of collaboration
by ingenious men in different communities over the years. This
is how progress is generally made, not only in technology but in
government, law, public welfare and the arts: not by conflict, but
by co-operation, by learning from mistakes, by refining promising
ideas, by what Sir Karl Popper calls 'piecemeal engineering'. Not
only is science an ongoing public collaboration between scientists
across the world, the practical uses of its discoveries often cannot be
foreseen. Far from being commissioned by profit-hungry capitalists,
the results of lab work are a free gift to subsequent generations.
By contrast, conflict, whether civil or military, far from assisting
progress, may deal progress a shattering blow for decades, if not
centuries. Look at the Dark Ages, in which humanity went backwards for hundreds of years. The Dark Ages, however, do not
feature much in the Marxist scheme of things.

Nor does Marx's simplification of the class system into two and
only two classes, the bourgeoisie and the proletariat, do justice to
the complexity of the class system in his day as in ours. In particular,
he fails to imagine a world in which the industrial proletariat constitutes not an overwhelming majority but a gradually diminishing
minority of the population. The rise of white-collar workers –
clerks, civil servants, teachers, administrators – was already
manifest in the 1860s and 1870s, and new suburbs were springing up

all around London to accommodate them, but he barely acknowl-
edges their existence. Marx did acknowledge that mechanization
would gradually lessen the number of workers required in factories,
but he more or less assumed that millions of those thrown out of
work by technology would simply remain destitute, part of 'the
industrial reserve army' of capitalism. He did not foresee, or even
try to foresee, the labour demands of an advanced industrial nation,
what we call a knowledge economy.

There is, besides, a painful gap in Marx's enormous oeuvre, and
it is just where you would expect to find him at his most eloquent
and intense. Nowhere does he give a full exposition of the nature
of class. In the eight hundred pages of the only part of *Capital*
published in his lifetime, there is scarcely a mention of the subject. There are, to be sure, sparkling insights thrown out in *The
Communist Manifesto* and brilliant journalistic accounts of the
class backgrounds of the actors in the Paris Commune. But as for a
thorough and systematic exposé of what class means, how it is to be
defined and exactly what role it is to play in the downfall of capitalism, we search in vain. Only in the incomplete Part III of *Capital*,
edited and published by Engels after Marx's death, does Marx get
down to what he must have regarded as a central task. Alas, just as
he begins, 'landed proprietors divide themselves into wine-growers,
farmers, owners of forests, mines and fisheries', we see the words
put in by the editor: 'At this point the manuscript ends.' In miserable
health, tortured by the intellectual difficulties he faced, many of
them self-inflicted, Marx found it almost impossible to get down to
serious work in his last years. After his death, Engels was distraught
to discover how little his old friend had actually finished of the long-
promised later parts.

All these peremptory simplifying habits of mind Marx had first
imbibed from Hegel when he was barely out of his teens. And
despite his insatiable passion for research, he never lost those habits,
because he only saw what he wanted to see. This is at once the
source of the hypnotic power of his ideas and the source of their
underlying weakness. We must also recognize that, while Marx
the journalist and pamphleteer was a master of moral indignation
and corrosive sarcasm, Marx the philosopher was a cloudy, clumsy

writer. Plamenatz describes brilliantly the difficulties that face even the most diligent reader:

> Marx the philosopher and Marx the economist speak an obscure, involved, mysterious language, a language that seems to mean more than it says and in fact says more than it means. It is the language of a man excited by his own ideas, deeply interested in what he wants to describe, but somehow unable to find the words that exactly express his meaning. Metaphors and similes abound; the same thought is now dressed up in one way and now in another. The writer seems always to be using several different sets of phrases and never to be satisfied that he has made his meaning clear until he has expressed it in all of them. And yet his use of each set is careless, as if he thought exact statement impossible in any, and hoped that what is misleading in one would always be corrected by using the others. (p. 115)

Marx inherits from Hegel and ultimately from Plato the assumption that the business of philosophy is to get to the essence of a thing. As Popper points out, this is not what scientists do: they simply name things by pointing to them, then set out to test how those particular things interact, to chart the regularities and irregularities in nature. Most of the time, science does not seek to penetrate into the essence of things; it merely seeks to form testable hypotheses about how they work.

By contrast, Marx spends the first hundred pages of *Capital* attempting to define the essence of 'value' and 'commodity' and leaves the reader not much wiser at the end of it. The 'labour theory of value', which Marx borrowed from the great David Ricardo, has perplexed economists for centuries. It seems only common sense to say, as we do, that much of the value attributable to any saleable commodity derives from the work put into it. The difficulty starts when Marx tries to assign a 'true value' to the contribution made by the hours worked by the factory operatives, as opposed to that made by the suppliers, designers, factory builders, entrepreneurs, managers, foremen, wholesalers, carriers and retailers, not to mention that of the teams who produced the various tools and machines and raw materials used in the manufacture and whose 'congealed labour', to use Marx's favourite phrase, also has to be reckoned with.

The model that Marx spends dozens of pages expounding in *Capital* is basically quite simple: we suppose that the worker works a twelve-hour day (pretty much the standard at the time). For the first ten hours, he is said to be working to support himself and his family, and that is what the capitalist pays him just enough to do. For the last two hours of his shift he is said to be working for free, and it is from this 'surplus labour' that the capitalist allegedly derives his profit, or 'surplus value'. Like most of Marx's devices, the 'last hour' idea was not original to him; the well-known economist Nassau Senior was another aficionado. But it is a ludicrously crude model. In the real world, the capitalist's profits (or lack of them) may come from a combination of any number of sources: from having got his factory premises and machinery cheap or dear, from the interest on his bank loans being low or high, from reducing his transport costs because of a new railway or canal opening, from a reduction or increase in the costs of his raw materials and semi-finished components, and, last but far from least, from the prices that wholesalers and retailers are prepared to pay for his goods and services. A change in customs tariffs or the exchange rate may blight or benefit his overseas sales. Nor is he entirely free to dictate the wage rates he pays his hands, for those rates will depend on the abundance or scarcity of suitable labour locally and from the strength of the relevant trade unions (already a force in mid-century, although not fully legalized until Disraeli's 1875 Act).

The relative importance of his labour costs may diminish over time, as new technology reduces the number of hands required. Marx fully recognizes this. Indeed, the distress of the redundant hand-loom weavers provokes some of his most scorching indignation. For this reason, he describes labour costs as 'variable capital', as opposed to the 'constant capital' of all the capitalist's other costs. But the point is that none of those other costs is constant either. All are subject to the vagaries of the market and to developments not only in technology but in commercial relations, between supplier and manufacturer, between business and the tax man, between nation states.

For all its obscurities and weaknesses, the idea of surplus labour remains central to Marx's thought all his life. This carries with it two consequences that make it harder to apply Marxism to modern life (never plain sailing in any case). First, Marx holds that the capitalist's profit derives entirely from those extra two hours (or whatever fraction of the working day we choose to assume that the labourer is no longer working to feed himself and his family). In a go-ahead business (and in the end all businesses have to modernize to survive), this 'variable capital' will gradually diminish in relation to the constant capital represented by ever more sophisticated and expensive machinery. Averaged out over the firm and then over the whole of industry, this rate of profit will gradually fall, and this fall spells the ultimate doom of capitalism. The belief that the rate of profit was inexorably destined to fall was shared by Marx's contemporaries, for the simple reason that the rate was in fact falling in those years. This argument can of course only hold as an enduring truth if you accept Marx's premise that the capitalist's profit is drawn solely from that particular moment in the productive process.

He first trumpeted his great discovery of this law in the *Grundrisse*, the 800-page 'sketch' of 1857–58: 'This is in every respect the most important law of modern political economy.' Yet he continued to worry about it to the end of his life. Marx had always been an inveterate non-finisher of his projects, but his failure to finish *Capital* to his satisfaction was spread over a good twenty years. And the 'law' of the falling rate of profit was the principal obstacle. In the Marx Papers in Amsterdam there are eleven manuscripts of Part III of *Capital*, almost all of them drafts and redrafts of the law of the falling rate of profit. Even Engels, who was putting the whole work together, had his doubts; improvements in transport and distribution meant that capital could be turned over twice as fast without any change in the labour force; new processes, for making chemical dyes among many others, could improve productivity without buying any new machinery. The economist Mark Blaug sighs: 'With hindsight, it is hard to believe that anyone could ever have doubted that capital-saving improvements are as normal a feature of technical change as labour-saving innovations.' (Seigel, p. 349)

The profit creamed off by the ruthless capitalist from 'surplus labour' was only one of a series of potential profits or losses that were clocked up in a chain of transactions, going back to the farmers who planted the flax seeds and the miners who dug the coal, not to mention the inventors of all the techniques deployed, the constructors of the roads, canals and railways that carry the goods – the list is endless. The underlying point is that the production of goods and services is a collaborative effort across time and space. The attempt to isolate any one element and discover its true, one might almost say Platonic, value is a will-o'-the-wisp. Indeed, every now and then Marx himself has to resort to what he calls 'exchange value' – what we call the market price – to explain how the system works in practice. In the last resort, how can one securely identify the economic value of something except by reference to what someone is prepared to pay for it? And this applies just as much to the value added by the labour of the factory worker as it does to the end-price paid by the customer in the shops. That is how our own Value Added Tax works (it was first known as the Cascade Tax, which gives a vivid idea of how it falls on a different taxpayer at each stage in the productive process), and it is difficult, if not impossible, to imagine any workable criterion other than the price that is actually paid. Nor can this be blamed on the invention of money, which for Marx is the root of most if not all evil. For even in a barter economy the terms of exchange will vary according to all sorts of factors – the state of the harvest, natural and unnatural scarcities caused by famine, warfare and disease.

The second consequence of concentrating all his attention on the moment in production process when the worker, typically for Marx a factory hand, turns the raw materials into the finished product is that he pays virtually no attention to commerce of any sort. For Marx, distributing, selling and advertising goods create no value at all (with the possible exception of transport). Working in a shop isn't real work because it produces no material goods. Aron points out that this idea remained a fundamental principle of Soviet statistics. (p. 699) Not coincidentally, the USSR was deplorably incompetent in meeting the demands of customers and in getting perishable goods into the shops before they rotted. The undervaluation of what we

call 'services' – today by far the largest component of Western economies – gives an air of abstracted unreality to Marx's model. His
dislike of the market was, if anything, even more pungent than his
dislike of private property. He hated competition in general for gen-
erating the individualism that had destroyed the sense of community
that was still to be found in premodern societies. His hostility was
faithfully copied by Lenin and the Bolsheviks, for whom commerce
was always the most disgusting of petit-bourgeois activities.

It is in his occasional writings, above all in *The Communist
Manifesto* and in the later pages of Part I of *Capital*, that Marx
shows his titanic, thunderous self-confidence. This was always
there. You have to admire the nerve of the teenage doctoral candidate who prefaces his dissertation with a declaration of his 'hatred
of all heavenly and earthly gods who do not acknowledge human
self-consciousness as the highest divinity'. He picked up this bracing
atheism from his closest friend at this time, Bruno Bauer, who, half
a century before Nietzsche, announced to the world that 'God is
dead for philosophy, and only the self as self-consciousness lives,
creates, acts and is everything'.

All this came from Feuerbach, as did the idea that man's
alienation from his true self derived from religion. Christianity,
in particular, fostered individualism and actively prevented the
emergence of a communal ethos, thus estranging man from his
true nature as a *Gattungswesen*, a 'Species-being'. Was this true of
all religion, or as Marx's other great friend, Arnold Ruge, argued,
particularly true of the Reformed churches, with their emphasis
on the individual conscience, which had dismantled the spiritual
community of the medieval church? The difficulty here is that all
monotheistic faiths are or were also intensely communal, not least
the Judaism into which Marx had been born.

In order to continue practising as a lawyer in Trier, an ancient
city in the Rhineland with a small Jewish community, his father
Hirschel had himself baptized as Heinrich, and later had his children baptized too. Like several fathers of famous curmudgeons
(Evelyn Waugh and Kingsley Amis come to mind), Heinrich was a
sweet-tempered and affectionate man, whose reproofs to his way-
ward son read rather charmingly. Karl was spectacularly ungrateful

and neglectful to his parents, except when he wanted cash, which was most of his life. But he did carry a daguerreotype of his father (it is buried with him at Highgate). His own fondness for children may have come from his happy upbringing.

For the faith of his fathers, a long line of respected rabbis, Karl had no fondness at all. If anything, Karl hated Judaism even more than Christianity. Money was the worldly God of the Jews, who were little better than 'hucksters'. Marx's admirers try to present his essay *On the Jewish Question* as a defence of the Jews and an attack on the civil disabilities from which they suffered. But the essay's brutish tone and his longing to see Judaism dissolved in a general dissolving of all religions leave a nasty taste, especially in the light of later history. The Jews remained his principal target, until he broadened his field of fire upon 'the bourgeoisie' as a whole. Then, in *The Communist Manifesto*, the bourgeoisie receive a startling upgrade. Having formerly portrayed them as narrow-minded philistines, Marx now salutes them as transformers of the world.

The sneers against Jews and blacks in his correspondence were often so repellent that later editors resorted to extensive censorship. August Bebel wrote to Karl Kautsky: '. . . by the way, I want to tell you – but please keep absolutely quiet about it – that some of the letters were not published, above all because they were too strong for us. The two old ones had at that time a way of letter-writing, to which I can in no way reconcile myself.'

Nor did Karl spare his old comrades. Almost everyone he worked with, except Engels who supported him financially for so long out of the profits of the Ermen & Engels mills, sooner or later came under his lash. Arnold Ruge, for example, with whom the Marxes had briefly lodged in the rue Vaneau, was described by Marx and Engels in one of their character sketches as 'ferret face': 'such a man is moreover richly endowed with all the vices, the mean and petty qualities, with the slyness and stupidity, the avarice and the clumsiness, the servility and the arrogance, the untrustworthiness and the bonhomie of the emancipated serf, the peasant: philistine and ideologist, atheist and slogan worker, absolute ignoramus and absolute philosopher all in one'. As Raymond Aron remarks in *Le Marxisme de Marx*: 'When Marx says something nice about somebody, he immediately has to say something nasty about someone else.'

Marx, though, was a good deal more loyal to his early ideas than to the men in whose company he had developed them: the supremacy of self-consciousness, the pernicious emptiness of all religions, the iniquitous individualism that those religions generated – these beliefs stayed with him all his life. So did the idea that 'political economy' was not an impartial science describing a permanent reality but was only a dressed-up justification of private property. The search for 'a humane Marxism' in the early manuscripts has attracted recent students who have been horrified by the excesses of communism in practice. This is by no means a wild goose chase. Yet it does not introduce us to a radically different Marx, rather it concentrates our attention on the Marx who is exploring what are to become the philosophical foundations of his harder political doctrine. He is, if you like, drilling through the rich topsoil on his way to the bedrock. But even these early writings are not free from problems.

LIFE UNDER SOCIALISM

In the case of the key notion of alienation (*Entfremdung* or *Entaüsserung* – he used both words for the same thing), it is not that Marx fails to tell us what he means by it:

> What constitutes the alienation of labour? First, that the work is *external* to the worker, that it is not part of his nature, and that consequently he does not fulfil himself in his life ... His work is not voluntary but imposed, *forced labour* ... We arrive at the result that man (the worker) feels himself to be freely active only in his animal function – eating, drinking and procreating, or at most also in his dwelling and in personal adornment – while in his human functions he is reduced to an animal. (Avineri, p. 106)

Marx's crucial premise in his early writings is that work constitutes man's essence: we are truly human only when we are engaged in self-chosen purposeful activity. To be a wage slave is to be estranged from one's true nature. It is notable that this talk of alienation vanishes almost entirely from Marx's writings after about 1845, as does all talk of human essence. Clearly he had come to the conclusion, quite rightly, that if man was an endlessly self-fashioning being, how could he have any such unchanging essence? He had, after all, ticked off Proudhon for that kind of talk: 'M. Proudhon does not understand that the whole of History is nothing but a continuous transformation of human nature.' After the Second World War (and a little before it too), Marx's early talk of alienation was picked up by an assorted crew of intellectuals – Jesuit priests, Left Bank intellectuals, even Jean-Paul Sartre himself. Themselves alienated by the bleak and brutish spectacle of communism in practice, they looked for a kinder, more humane version of the faith.

Marx was a progressive. He was contemptuous of sentimentalists who looked back to any sort of golden age. But he did think that we had lost something. There was something uniquely soulless about the modern world. At least in the Middle Ages there had still been direct human relations between the serf and the lord. But now cash was king. The money economy had destroyed any vestiges of an organic community. You can find exactly the same complaint in *Sybil*, that novel by another baptized Jew of much the same vintage, Benjamin Disraeli.

But it remained unclear – what exactly did an un-alienated person look like? How precisely were dull and menial tasks to be de-alienated under socialism? How indeed were they to be allocated? When asked who would polish the shoes after the revolution, Marx snapped back: 'You should.' (Wheen, p. 296) In Volume III of *Capital*, Marx states roundly that authoritarian factory discipline 'will become superfluous under a socialistic system in which the labourers work of their own accord'. (p. 83) But Engels, who had after all far more experience of factory life than Marx, clearly says that this kind of discipline is an inherent ingredient of large-scale industry and will not disappear when the social control of production is transformed (as indeed it never did disappear in Soviet Russia or anywhere else).

Marx, it has to be said, had a fairly woozy idea of what life would be like under socialism. Famously, in *The German Ideology* (1846), he hazards that 'in communist society, where nobody has one exclusive sphere of activity but each can become accomplished in any branch he wishes, society regulates the general production and thus makes it possible for me to do one thing today and another tomorrow, to hunt in the morning, to fish in the afternoon, rear cattle in the evening, criticize after dinner, just as I have a mind, without ever becoming hunter, fisherman, shepherd or critic'. (pp. 44–5) This bucolic utopia does not seem entirely serious. Do we really want to be treated by an amateur brain surgeon or flown by an occasional airline pilot? Is the abolition of the division of labour really something to be aimed for? Is it really so terrible that a person should have 'a particular, exclusive sphere of activity'? Isn't there something to be said for professional pride and training and dedication? This isn't just a youthful daydream of Marx's. Thirty years after *The German Ideology*, he writes in *The Critique of the Gotha Programme* in much the same terms about 'the higher phase of communist society, after the enslaving subordination of the individual to the division of labour, and therewith also the antithesis between mental and physical labour have vanished'. (Avineri, p. 233)

It is possible to interpret this demand for an end to the division of labour in a milder spirit. Perhaps Marx meant simply that everyone should have choices in their lives, that they should not be condemned to a lifetime in the mill or down the pit. But then this is pretty much what has happened today, especially after the disappearance of heavy industry and one-company towns, though that doesn't make life any easier for those who are left behind. Yet those who manage to make their way out of the post-industrial wasteland may gain access to those broader choices.

In any case, that dismissal of man's 'animal function' throws away three-quarters of what makes life worthwhile for most of us – love and family and home. Marx was not alone at the time in his assumption that the back-breaking grind of factory work degraded men to the condition of animals. Something of the sort is to be seen in Disraeli's description of Woodgate in *Sybil*. Marx had scarcely met any flesh-and-blood workers until he arrived in Paris in 1843. And then he was highly impressed: 'The brotherhood of man is no empty phrase but a reality, and the nobility of man shines forth upon us from their toilworn bodies.' Twenty years later, when he attended a trade union meeting chaired by John Bright, he records with a note of surprise, 'the working men themselves spoke *very well indeed* without a trace of bourgeois rhetoric'. More recent historians, such as E. P. Thompson and Jonathan Rose, have reminded us of the richness of nineteenth-century working-class culture. If this is alienation, one is tempted to say, it can't be all bad.

What the leaders of the radical workers complained of, from the Chartists onwards, was not alienation but exclusion from political power. The trouble was that the propertied classes refused to listen to what the workers actually said. Educated observers – Tocqueville, Macaulay, Carlyle – 'found it hard to think of workers or proletarians as other than wild, predatory and levelling'. But to his credit, though he was often slow to absorb political developments, Marx did listen to the radical artisans, the shoemakers, typesetters, weavers and watchmakers whom he came to like and respect (*pace* some of his detractors, he had no trace of snobbery). By the mid-1860s, we find Marx increasingly persuaded that the transition from the capitalist mode of production towards a socialist society had already begun and that, in England least, the transition might well be largely a peaceful one. In the 1867 preface to *Capital*, he refers to 'the process of revolution in England' as something that is happening. He experiences a growing admiration for British trade unions and is proud to have attracted their leaders into the International Working Men's Association. Trade unions, he says, are 'the schools of socialism'. He is fed up with Continental revolutionary activity. 'I prefer my agitation here through the "International Association" a thousand times.' 'If we succeed in re-electrifying the POLITICAL MOVEMENT of the ENGLISH WORKING CLASS, our ASSOCIATION will already have done more for the European working class, WITHOUT MAKING ANY FUSS, than was possible IN ANY OTHER WAY. And there is every prospect of success.' We cannot imagine the Marx of 1848 extolling the advantages of not making any fuss, let alone in capital letters.

How distant now seems the firebrand who wrote in the *Neue Rheinische Zeitung* of 7 November 1848: 'There is only one *means* by which the murderous death agonies of the old society can be *shortened*, simplified and concentrated and that is by *revolutionary terror*.' Even after the suppression of the revolutions of 1848, he looked forward gleefully to the violent cataclysm that was just around the corner. On New Year's Day 1849, he wrote in the paper: 'The table of contents for 1849 reads: Revolutionary rising of the French working class, World War!' For the next decade and more, he continued to argue in his addresses to the Communist League that 'the outbreak of a new revolution can no longer be very far away'. This revolution would demand 'the most determined centralization of power in the hands of the State authority' and 'a strong secret organization of the revolutionary party'. He looked back with nostalgia to the French Revolution and Robespierre's Committee of Public Safety – which had been recreated in 1848 in Vienna and in Cologne (where Marx was a member of it) and was to be revived once more in the Paris Commune. As far as the Continent was concerned, as late as 1874, he still looked forward to 'a *general European war*. We shall have to pass through it before there can be any thought of decisive overt activity on the part of the European working class.' The essential elements of what was to become Leninism, including 'the revolutionary dictatorship of the proletariat', continued to swirl in Marx's brain, though marked 'for the use of Continentals only'.

He had often referred derisively to 'the Holy Grail of universal suffrage'. He repeatedly mocks the 'parliamentary cretinism' of the deputies in the French National Assembly who were being duped by Louis Napoleon. But in England, it seemed, universal suffrage might do the trick and transform society. At the Hague Congress of the International in 1872, he made the distinction quite explicit: 'We know that the institutions, customs and traditions in the different countries must be taken into account; and we do not deny the existence of countries like America, England, and if I knew your institutions better I might add Holland, where the workers may achieve their aims by peaceful means.' But for most countries on the Continent, 'it is force which must be the lever of our revolution'.

Gareth Stedman Jones's biography of Marx is not the first to have pointed out Marx's 'English exceptionalism', but he is, I think, a pioneer in showing how thoroughly this new thought saturates Karl's later years and how far it undermines the claim of Marxism to enunciate a universal theory of historical development, rather than a more modest exploration of its varied possibilities. Yet even in the fiery heyday of 1848, we can discern a more plural and accommodating version of Marxism. *The Communist Manifesto* itself concedes that the measures required to raise the proletariat to the position of ruling class and win the battle of democracy 'will of course be different in different countries'. And several, if not all of the ten points suggested in the *Manifesto* as 'pretty generally applicable' could well be secured – and were indeed secured – in a parliamentary system with a widened franchise, for example, free education and a progressive income tax. Several others, such as public ownership, inheritance tax and central control of transport, came in, peacefully enough, with later Labour and Social Democratic governments in quite a few European countries.

Even in his direst prophecies of increasing pauperization under capitalism, Marx often covers himself in a get-out clause. In Chapter III of *Capital*, for example, he tells us that as the 'industrial reserve army' of the unemployed swells in relation to the numbers of active wage-earners, the official figures of pauperism are bound to increase too: 'That is the absolute general law of capitalist accumulation.' Then he adds: 'the action of this law, like any other, is naturally modified by particular circumstances'. And he does so, for the good reason that, after years of stagnation, the standard of living of the English working class did seem to be rising at that moment.

The structure of capitalism itself was changing during Marx's later life. The old arrangement of the capitalist and his family being sole owners of the factory, often living on the premises, was being replaced by the new pattern of company ownership residing with a bunch of shareholders, most of whom had nothing to do with the running of the company. The Joint Stock Company Act of 1844 and the Limited Liability Act of 1855 gave legal blessing to this divorce between ownership and management.

Marx catches up with these developments in Part III of *Capital*. Interestingly, he seems to suggest that this 'socialization' of capital may represent a transitional stage towards the actual producers recovering their rightful share: 'This ultimate development of capitalist production is a point of transition, which must necessarily lead to the reconversion of capital into the property of the producers.' Thus, Marx caught at least a glimpse both of what we call 'shareholder democracy' and 'the managerial society'. Which looks like another reason why Marx had such trouble in getting Part III into publishable shape. After all, if capitalism carried within itself the seeds of its own reformation, what need for any sort of revolution?

THE EXPERIENCE OF ENGLAND

We can, I think, associate some of this later mildness to the change in the Marx family's fortunes after they settled in London for good. Through the early years of his marriage to Jenny von Westphalen and the births (and all too often deaths) of their children, it is often difficult to recall whether they are in Berlin or Brussels or Paris or Cologne or Frankfurt, and whether or not Karl is still a Prussian citizen or reapplying to be one or actively being pursued by the authorities. He had been expelled from Paris, Brussels, Cologne and then Paris again, often at the instigation of the prime minister or the emperor himself. At one point, he applied for British citizenship and was turned down as a dangerous agitator, although he was permitted to go on living in Britain for the last thirty-four years of his life. In 1861, Karl writes to Ferdinand Lassalle (often the butt of his racist jibes) that he wants to stay in England: 'London, I CAN'T DENY IT, possesses an extraordinary fascination for me.' By 1853, his English is good enough for writing articles. By 1870, he writes *The Civil War in France* in a colloquial idiom that might have come from Thackeray or Surtees.

Jenny, too, felt no longing for her native Rhineland, and as for the surviving girls, Eleanor, Laura and little Jenny: 'The idea of their leaving the country of their precious Shakespeare appals them; they've become English to the marrow and cling like limpets to the soil of England.' In their early days in the city, they had lived on the edge. They had suffered a humiliating eviction from their lodgings in Chelsea, with their beds brought out on the pavement and loaded on a barrow by the bailiffs. For one coming from a grand baronial family in Trier (and the descendant of two Scottish dukedoms), Jenny had undergone a grinding change of fortune. She had already pawned her family silver in Frankfurt and sold her furniture in Cologne. In London, she again had to pop the silver. Unfortunately, some of the pieces bore the Argyll crest, and when Marx went to redeem it, he was arrested on suspicion of theft and flung into jail for a night.

Now life began to become a little easier. Several family legacies came in. Ermen & Engels was booming and Fred was as generous as ever. There were private schools and piano lessons for the girls. Karl even liked to claim that he was a canny investor on the Stock Exchange, once boasting of having made £400 in American funds and English stocks, though Stedman Jones suspects that the real source may have been another legacy. They moved out of Soho to the balmier air of Kentish Town. And Karl and Jenny were happy together. Even a Prussian spy writing in 1852 had to concede that 'as a husband and father, Marx, in spite of his wild and reckless character, is the gentlest and mildest of men'. Both Jenny and Karl suffered appalling ill health, not helped by the huge quantities of alcohol the doctors prescribed – bumpers of porter and claret and a spoonful of brandy every hour. But the family outings to Hampstead Heath, as described by Wilhelm Liebknecht, who looked after the children when Jenny went down with smallpox, sound idyllic:

Those walks to Hampstead Heath! Were I to live to a thousand I would never forget them ... The children used to speak about it the whole week and even the adults young and old used to look forward to it ... I generally led the way with the two girls, entertaining them with stories or acrobatics or picking wild flowers, which were more abundant then than now. Behind us came a few friends and then the main body: Marx and his wife and one of the Sunday visitors who was deserving of special consideration. In the rear came Lenchen and the hungriest of our party, who helped her carry the hamper ... Once food and drink had been partaken of, both sexes went in search of the most comfortable place to lie or sit. Those who did not prefer a nap got out the Sunday papers

bought on the way and spoke about politics. The children soon
found playmates and played hide-and-seek in among the gorse
bushes. (quoted Stedman Jones, p. 326)

Lenchen was the Marxes' faithful maid, Helene Demuth, who followed them through all their travails. While they were in London,
she gave birth to a son, Freddy. After Marx's death, she went to
keep house for Engels. Only on Engels' deathbed was it revealed – or
alleged – that Freddy was really Karl's son. The whole story derives
entirely from a letter written by Louise Freyberger, who took over
as Engels' housekeeper after Lenchen's death in 1890. The letter
was dated September 1898 but only surfaced in the 1960s. The only
independent confirmation comes from Freddy himself in later life
when he was ill. As with the story of Thomas Jefferson and Sally
Hemings, we have to discount the jubilation with which Marx's
many enemies fastened on the story. Remarkably, Lenchen is buried
along with Karl and Jenny in that huge tomb in Highgate. I am not
sure what that tells us about the truth. Not many great men are
buried with their servants. (Terrell Carver gives a robust dissection
of the evidence in Marx's favour; see 'Gresham's Law in the World
of Scholarship', marxmyths.org, 2005.) What is not disputed is that
it was Jenny who left instructions that when Lenchen died, she was
to be buried in the family tomb with herself and her husband. If she
knew that Freddy was Karl's son, would she have done that? But
then, perhaps she didn't know.

Karl was fond of English seaside resorts too. Ramsgate was his
favourite, as it was for Engels, who described to his mother 'the fake
Negro-minstrels, conjurors, fire-eaters, Punch-and-Judy shows and
nonsense of that sort'. Engels liked to take Jenny and his companion Lizzie Burns to the station bar at Ramsgate and treat them to
a small glass of port before leaving them to their own devices. At
these resorts they saw all classes mingling casually, and it is not too
fanciful, I think, to see these seaside excursions as part of a widening and mellowing of Marx's outlook on the world.

But of course it was English capitalism, the English factory system
and the English factory owners that were the prime target of Marx's
scorching fury and relentless contempt. The cotton mill owners of

Manchester, the forge masters of Sheffield, the lace millionaires who tortured the fingers of tiny children to make fancy frills and collars for the wives of the plutocrats – these were the villains who squeezed every last minute out of their employees' working day and who set women and small children to mind their implacable and dangerous machines deep into the night. England is the classic ground of the capitalist mode of production, Marx tells us in the introduction to *Capital*. This great book, only the first part in a projected four-part mammoth but already eight hundred pages long, is largely about England, not only because England was the most advanced industrial country in the world in the 1850s and 1860s (though soon to be overtaken by Germany and the United States), but also because Marx was living in England, and was destined to spend just over half his life there.

England was his focus for another reason too. She was also the most advanced country in the world in her willingness to examine herself. Her social statistics were an example to the rest of Europe, and it was these that Marx studied, day in and day out, from the moment the British Museum opened until closing time, despite the agonies of his incurable haemorrhoids (at home, he read standing up, which was not possible in the Museum). The condition of the poor in England might be wretched, but France and Germany had nothing to boast about:

> We should be appalled at the state of things at home [remember that *Capital* was first published in German], if, as in England, our governments and parliaments appointed periodically commissions of enquiry into economic conditions; if these commissions were armed with the same plenary powers to get at the truth; if it was possible to find for this purpose men as competent, as free from partisanship and respect of persons as are the English factory-inspectors, her medical reporters on public health, her commissioners of enquiry into the exploitation of women and children, into housing and food. (p. xviii)

These commissions and reports had practical outcomes, too. Already by the 1860s, the public pressure resulting from their

publication had forced Parliament to limit maximum hours of
work, especially for child workers (Marx himself did not think
it possible to prohibit child labour altogether; indeed, he thought
that early experience of work in moderation was character-
building), to set standards of hygiene and sanitation, and to
make some public provision for the education of the poor. Marx
thought that 'apart from higher motives, therefore, their own most
important interests dictate to the classes that are for the nonce the
ruling ones, the removal of all legally removable hindrances to the
free development of the working class'. (p. xviii) The later chapters
of *Capital* are full of the largely beneficial results of all these new
laws. Marx is fair-minded enough to make it clear that the very
worst of the factory era, in England at any rate, lies already in
the past. Ghastly as the lives of many workers still were, terrible
as were the diseases that still carried off workers in the mines,
potteries and steel mills, they had been even ghastlier twenty years
earlier when the young Fred Engels wrote *The Condition of the
Working Class in England*.

Marx's fair-mindedness makes the later chapters of *Capital* a
fascinating and often heartrending account of industrial England,
but it also begins to undermine the central girder of his theory.
Half against his will, what he shows us is that politics can work.
Parliament might be the executive committee of the ruling class,
as he claims, but it was an executive committee that responded
to reasonable pressures when it had to. Although so many of the
new industrial capitalists and directors of the East India Company
sat upon its benches and argued passionately that they would be
ruined if Parliament passed these new Bills to remedy abuses at
home and abroad, in the end Parliament passed those Bills, and
went on passing them even more emphatically after the franchise
had been widened in 1867 beyond the bourgeoisie to include some
working men. The legal recognition of trade unions under Disraeli's
Act of 1875 further enlarged the ability of working men to resist
abuses and claim a fairer share of the proceeds of technological
development. It looked less plausible now that the development of
capitalism would always make the workers absolutely or relatively
poorer. Yet Marx continued to maintain the line he had taken in his

KARL MARX 339

Address to the Working Classes (known as the *Inaugural Address*)
of October 1864:

> In all countries it has become a truth demonstrable to every
> unprejudiced mind, and only denied by those whose interest it
> is to hedge other people in a fool's paradise, that no improve-
> ment of machinery, no application of science to production, no
> contrivance of communication, no new colonies, no emigration,
> no opening of markets, no free trade, nor all these things put
> together, will do away with the miseries of the industrial masses;
> but that, on the present false basis, every fresh development of the
> productive powers of labour must tend to sharpen social contrasts
> and accentuate social antagonisms. (McLellan, 1973, p. 365)

Certainly, countries under the existing system would still suffer
slumps and booms. There would still be periods, often long
periods, of depressed wages and high unemployment. But on the
evidence of *Capital* itself, the long-awaited Bible of Marxism, it
was hard to detect any cumulative or inevitable historical process
that would prevent a decent parliament from remedying injustice
and tackling the periodic crises, so long as pressure was brought
to bear from outside, by trade unions, suffragettes and liberal
reformers. So long as the workers continued to have access to
the political system, and insisted on widening that access, it was
hard to identify the seeds of self-destruction that capitalism was
supposed to carry within itself.

Thirty years after Marx's death, the outbreak of the First
World War posed a double test to his theories. *The Communist
Manifesto* had claimed that 'the working men have no country'.
They belonged only to the universal class of the proletariat, and
by 1914 nearly a century of political agitation had made them conscious members of that class. They had no stake in the looming
capitalist-imperialist conflict, and it was their historic duty to stand
aside from it and use the occasion to bring about the long-awaited
revolution. Yet the German Social Democrats, the largest and most
politically conscious socialist party in the world, and one operating
in an advanced industrial economy, voted with little hesitation for

war credits to finance the conflict. They were responding, not to the bullying of the government, but to the patriotic wishes of their supporters. Patriotism trumped class, as it did on all sides in this terrible war.

And when the war was over and lost, even then the Social Democrats failed to bring off a proper revolution in Germany, whereas a handful of Bolsheviks in a conspicuously 'unripe' country brought off an earth-shattering upheaval, which was to terrify the rest of the world for the next seventy-five years. As Plamenatz points out:

> It was precisely because the German workers were numerous, well educated and politically organized, that they had no intention of making a revolution; they had gained too much without it, and they stood to gain much more ... It was precisely because the conditions that Marx thought necessary for a successful proletarian revolution did exist in Germany that there was no desire to make it; and it was also because they did not exist in Russia that Lenin was able to seize power in the name of Marx and the proletariat. (p. 187)

So what seems to decide events is not the ripeness or otherwise of a country's economy but the ripeness of its *politics*: a weak autocracy can be bowled over without much difficulty, while a developed parliamentary state is a much tougher nut to crack. So, if you take Marx's dichotomy between the material base and the political/intellectual superstructure – though this itself is a shaky distinction – then it seems to be the superstructure that often determines the destiny of the material base, and not the other way round.

Marx himself did sometimes stray from his rigid historical schema. In the last decade of his life, he became absorbed in Russia and other parts of the pre-capitalist world that had hitherto attracted his attention only fleetingly. Russian villages appeared to have long traditions of communal ownership reaching back into the mists of time. Now Marx began to think that similar traditions could be found all over the place. Only a 'judicial blindness' had prevented him from seeing that 'Right in my *own* neighbourhood, on the *Hunsrück*, the old Germanic system survived *until the last few years.*' (quoted Stedman Jones, p. 577) That pleasant hill country between the Moselle and the Rhine, where Edgar Reitz set his TV epic series *Heimat*, was, it seemed, Marx's *Heimat* in a deeper sense, a latter-day Eden still unspoilt by the serpent of private property.

Then Marx encountered the work of Nicolai Chernyshevsky and the enticing argument that, thanks to the influence of the advanced nations, backward countries like Russia could skip the intermediate stage and jump to a higher level of development, straight from the village commune to socialism. Karl not only agreed to the skipping hypothesis but changed the 'could' into a 'must'. Following on the emancipation of the serfs, a socialist revolution had to be made in Russia *before* capitalist development in the countryside destroyed the village commune. When the Russo-Turkish War broke out in 1877, Karl was certain that Russia would lose that war, which would act as a catalyst to revolution: 'This crisis is a new turning point. This time the revolution will begin in the East.' (quoted Stedman Jones, p. 582) For Russia at least, the bourgeoisie were shunted off into the wings of history. Now the peasants would make their own revolution. In fact, Russia won that war, and the revolution was delayed another forty years to 1917, when indeed the Chernyshevsky–Marx forecast did come true.

Later historians, notably Fustel de Coulanges, pretty well demolished the myth of the primeval commune. Far from being an example of collective ownership, the Russian *Mir* embodied collective serfdom, and in any case was of relatively recent origin and had been instituted by despotic czars. The German *Mark* was an equally unreliable exemplar, arising out of feudal institutions and permeated by private ownership of land. Anyway, even if the historical foundations had been sounder, the skipping theory would have dealt a death blow to the single strict historical pattern laid down by orthodox Marxism, and sternly policed by Engels. Never had it been truer that, as Karl himself said with a smidgen of pride: 'If anything is certain, it is that I myself am not a Marxist.' There now appeared to be at least three roads to socialism: the peaceful Anglo-American, the violent Continental, and the fast-track peasant-to-socialism route available to Russia and other backward nations. To be fair to Marx's powers of prophecy, if not to the robustness of his theory, all three were roads actually taken, in the wake of the world wars of the twentieth century.

It is hard to exaggerate how perplexed Marx seems to have been in his last years. Devastated by ill health and Jenny's death, he had lost so much of his old certainty. In 1870, he had taught himself Russian; by 1881, he had nearly two hundred Russian books on his shelves. He had written 30,000 pages of notes but was publishing nothing to speak of. When the Russian firebrand Vera Zasulich wrote in February 1881 to ask him to 'set forth your ideas on the possible fate of our rural commune and on the theory that it is historically necessary for every country in the world to pass through all the phases of capitalist production' (Shanin, p. 98), Marx dithered for a month, writing four drafts amounting to about 10,000 words, full of crossings-out and rewrites, before he finally sent her a letter barely a page long, pleading ill health and claiming that he had meant all that stuff about historical inevitability to apply only to Western Europe. 'The analysis in *Capital* therefore provides no reasons either for or against the vitality of the Russian commune.' All he could say, rather vaguely, was that he was convinced that 'the commune is the fulcrum for social regeneration'. (Shanin, pp. 99–123)

Yet in those drafts that he couldn't bring himself to send, he says forthrightly three or four times that Russia can 'build into the commune all the positive achievements of the capitalist system without having to pass under its harsh tribute'. In other words, Russia can skip, after all. But then, a couple of paragraphs later, he writes that 'the rural commune is at its last gasp'. And even when he is claiming that Russia can skip, it seems to be a backwards sort of skip. The new system, he tells us, quoting the American anthropologist Lewis Morgan, 'will be a revival in a superior form of an archaic social type. We should not then be too frightened of the word "archaic".' (Shanin, p. 104) What a far cry this is from the Marx of *The Communist Manifesto* and *Capital* who was so withering about the sentimentalists who harked back to the heyday of the medieval peasant.

Most unnerving of all for dedicated Marxists, the great man seemed anxious to withdraw from his prophetic role. The important thing, he told his Russian readers in 1877, is to study each historical development on its merits separately (as he had done with the evidence from England's advanced capitalist economy). 'Success will never come with the master-key of a general historico-philosophical theory.' (Shanin, p. 136) But that was the very key that his admirers thought he had forged for them.

FRED AND KARL

Intellectually, then, by the time of Marx's death it was all a terrible mess, and it is only thanks to the devious energies of Engels and the German Social Democrats who took over the guardianship of the shrine that it has taken us so long to realize what a mess it is. Note how smartly Engels moves, at the Founder's graveside, to associate Marxism with the overwhelming scientific prestige of Darwinism. Shortly before his own death, how sternly he warns the Russians against skipping: 'It is a historical impossibility that a lower stage of economic development should solve the enigmas and conflicts which did not arise, and could not arise, until a far higher stage.' In retrospect, it looks like a key move too to set up a joint Marx–Engels Archive and a joint *Marx-Engels-Gesamtausgabe*, which was destined to run into a hundred volumes and more. For all posterity, Engels would always be there to police his mentor's deplorable tendency to stray off-piste.

When they owed Engels so much, both literally and figuratively, it may seem ungrateful that Jenny should have described him as Karl's 'evil genius'. Apart from the ceaseless flow of cash, had he not championed Marx through the worst of times, intrigued to secure the two of them the leading role in the revolutionary vanguard, not least in wangling their commission to write *The Communist Manifesto*? And after Marx's death, did he not keep the Master's memory bright and cover up the shaming truth of how little of *Capital* Volumes II and III had actually been completed? If anyone, it was surely Engels who bequeathed a fully functioning ideology to the revolutionaries of the twentieth century.

Can we say, therefore, as Stedman Jones does, that what we call Marxism was largely created by Engels? Perhaps 'created' is not the right word; 'selected' or 'edited' might be better. There is, after all, very little in the accepted canon that was not, at some time or other, formulated by Marx himself. The gaps and difficulties in the doctrine are all there in his own work: the inadequacy of 'alienation' as an all-explaining concept of what's wrong; the deficiencies in Marx's definition of 'class', with which he was still wrestling in his last writings; the failure to prove that capitalism invariably leads to the absolute or relative immiseration of the proletariat; the difficulty of demonstrating the exact connection between the rise of religion and the emergence of private property; the failure, above all, to show exactly why capitalism carries the seeds of its own destruction, rather than long-term modification. As Isaiah Berlin points out in his Life, published in 1939 but still dazzling, Marx utterly failed to foresee either of those two great forces of the twentieth century: fascism and the welfare state. Obsessed as he was with the class struggle, he had little attention to spare for the persistence of national feeling or the growth of state power. Hence, he could not really understand the success of Bismarck or Louis Napoleon, preferring to dismiss them as mystifying mountebanks.

In all the thousands of pages that Marx wrote, just as there is remarkably little about the nature of class, so there is very little about the state. Those few words that he does give the subject tend to be dismissive, vague or hostile. The state, we are told, is the executive committee of the ruling class. The Paris Commune is praised for so speedily abolishing the police and the standing army, the key organs of the state – better still if they could finally suppress the power of the priests as well. Lenin enthusiastically seconded Marx's approval of the Commune's approach. For him, too, the old parliamentary bourgeois state had to be 'smashed'.

What of the state under socialism? Well, during the period of transition, the state will have to be nothing less than 'the dictatorship of the proletariat' – not a phrase that Marx uses often, in public anyway, but one whose meaning is clear enough. And after? Well, says Marx, retreating into untypical vagueness, you can't really describe what it will be like because History can only be established retrospectively. As Hegel tells us, the owl of Minerva only flaps her wings as twilight descends. But the state will in some way transcend itself, it will be *aufgehoben*, raised and reborn at a higher level.

But this resort to Hegelian cloudspeak won't really do. For what is clear is that socialist society will be planned. This 'planification' will replace the disorderly and anarchic carry-on of the free market. Communism is unthinkable without comprehensive planning. The state will therefore have to be active, vigilant and extensive – as indeed it has been in all known states that have called themselves Marxist. But exactly what this state planning will look like, neither Marx nor the more practical Engels give us a clue. Lenin, writing in *The State and Revolution,* on the eve of the Bolshevik Revolution, remained blithely optimistic:

> The great majority of the functions of the old state power have been so simplified and can be reduced to such simple operations of registration, filing and checking, that they can easily be per- formed by every literate person ... We ourselves the workers shall organize large-scale production on the basis of what capitalism has already created ... we shall reduce the role of state officials to a simple carrying out of our instructions as responsible, rev- ocable, and modestly paid 'managers' ... Such a beginning, on the basis of large-scale production, will of itself lead to the grad- ual 'withering away' of all bureaucracy, to the gradual creation of an order, an order without quotation marks, which will be different from wage-slavery, an order in which the functions of control and accounting – becoming more and more simple – will be performed by each in turn, will then become a habit and will finally die out as the *special* functions of a special section of the population. (III, 2, 4)

In practice, Lenin found himself devising one of the most power- ful, intrusive and bureaucratic states ever known. The 'managers' continued to exist and prosper, with or without quotation marks, and rose to become a separate class, the *nomenklatura*, enjoying the most delicious perks, even if not quite on the scale of the *ancien régime*. But Lenin had had to make it all up as he went along. As he was not slow to complain, he got no help from Marx.

Certainly Engels does not offer solutions to any of the problems in his lifelong friend's doctrine. He merely ignores them and
reissues what he takes to be the Authorized Version in a clearer,
more accessible form. Engels was a brilliant descriptive writer
and forceful polemicist, never better than in his early masterpiece,
The Condition of the Working Class in England, written when he
was only twenty-four. But he seldom supplies what remains of un-
ignorable value in all Marx's writings: his acute exploration of the
material roots of life and his explanation of how economic forces
generate and shape social relationships and events that do not seem
to have anything to do with economics. As Stedman Jones puts it,
Marx 'inaugurated a debate about the central economic and social
landmarks in modern history, which has gone on ever since'. Marx
has made us more painfully aware of the economic and social consequences of political decisions and of how hard those decisions
bear down on the poor and vulnerable. It is not so much that he
explains the system better – he borrows the best bits of his analysis
from Smith and Ricardo – more that he makes us emotionally alert
to the human impact.

Nor is his influence confined to economics and politics. Every corner
of the humanities is now coloured by the materialist approach – art
history, philosophy, literature and all the social sciences. Sometimes
this colouring is coarse and reductive, as happens with all orthodox-
ies; sometimes it distorts our vision to a painful degree; but often it
does lead to fresh understanding of how things came to be as they are.
It isn't an all-purpose calculus that can be relied on to return a reliable
answer to the things we really want to know about. Understanding
the material conditions of production may not give us much help in
understanding what is being produced. To know about the social and
economic history of fifteenth-century Netherlands may tell us a lot
about Rogier van der Weyden's patrons, but how much will it tell us
about his altarpieces? All the same, the Marxist approach remains a
permanent feature of our intellectual landscape. We may often resist
the claims of this approach, denouncing it as a new 'vulgar Marxism',
but, as with the atom bomb, we cannot un-know it.

THE TRAGIC LEGACY

The fate of 'Marxism' is, just as un-ignorably, a tragic one. Untold suffering has been inflicted in its name, all over the world, for three-quarters of a century. Such benefits as it did bring, mostly to poor and helpless peoples, could have been obtained by more modest and peaceable means. And the inherent defects of the ideology – its brutality, its intolerance, its vindictive cruelty – these, we now can see, cannot be dumped on Stalin, or even Lenin. They were there from the start, and they came straight from Karl Marx. Indeed, in some ways, as Plamenatz argues, Lenin was closer to Marx than any other great Marxist. (p. 7) Certainly Lenin himself believed that he was and explicitly took Marx's writings on the Commune (*The Civil War in France*) as the model for the violent overthrow of the bourgeois state that he demanded in *The State and Revolution*, composed in the summer of 1917 as a handbook for the October Revolution. It is clear that Marx applauded the motives behind every revolutionary terror from 1792 to 1871, even though he might dispute their tactical wisdom. Throughout the long peace of the nineteenth century from Waterloo to the Franco-Prussian War, he looked forward eagerly to a European war, or better still a world war, as a catalyst for the revolution. He persistently sneered at individual human rights as 'bourgeois' and 'egoistic'. Above all, the fundamental residue in his thought of his first master, Hegel, entrenched the insistence that history could have only one outcome. Sooner or later, however long delayed or diverted, the last class antagonism would be dissolved in the dictatorship of the proletariat. Thereafter, any resistance to the true socialism that would inevitably follow could legitimately be suppressed as 'counter-revolutionary'.

Many of his sparring partners understood this and foretold how it would all end. Bakunin said, in 1868 at the second Congress of the League for Peace and Freedom: 'I hate communism because it is the negation of liberty ... I am not a communist because communism concentrates and causes all the powers of society to be absorbed by the state.' As early as 1844, Arnold Ruge, later to be abused as a ferret-faced philistine, wrote to Feuerbach of his then friend Karl's communism and of Fourier's socialism that 'these two tendencies end up with a police state and slavery. To liberate the proletariat from the weight of physical and intellectual misery, one dreams of an organization that would generalize this very misery, that would cause all human beings to bear its weight.' Thus, even before the writing of *The Communist Manifesto*, the long-term tendencies were identifiable.

The most extraordinary thing is that, right at the beginning of his career, in the *Economic Manuscripts* of 1843–44, Marx himself seems to have foreseen how badly the nationalization of everything might turn out. If the revolution comes too early, before the development of productive forces are adequate, he tells us, 'all the old shit' (*die ganze alte Scheisse*) will come flooding up again. In a tangled passage, he warns us against the consequences of such a premature 'crude communism':

> Communism is the positive expression of the abolition of private property, and in the first place of universal private property ... the domination of private property looms so large that it aims to destroy everything which is incapable of being possessed by everyone as private property. It wishes to eliminate talent etc. by force ... This communism, which negates the personality of man in every sphere, is only the logical expression of private property, which is this negation. Universal envy settling itself as a power is only a camouflaged form of cupidity which re-establishes itself in a different way. The thoughts of every individual private property are at least directed against any wealthier private property, in the form of envy and the desire to reduce everything to a common level ... Crude communism is only the culmination of such envy and levelling-down. (Avineri, pp. 223–4)

This 'crude communism' is to be only the first stage before being superseded by the higher communism in which all disharmony and division is eliminated. Quite why this first stage, with all its backbiting and jealousy, should disappear so easily is never made clear. If all previous human history has been driven by conflict and envy, why should individual men and women suddenly shed those unpleasant qualities, almost overnight in historical terms, when they have shown no improvement under 'crude communism'? What cannot be denied is that 'crude communism' bears a hideous resemblance to life in Soviet Russia, as described by Alexander Zinoviev, Alexander Solzhenitsyn and many other disillusioned critics of the regime. All the spying, the petty jealousies, the paranoia – not just on the part of the regime but between ordinary citizens – seem therefore not to have represented a ghastly perversion of Marx's theories but a logical consequence of them after a premature revolution in a huge 'unripe' country. It is small consolation to think that Karl Marx himself once caught a glimpse of this.

There was, as we have seen, a time in his life, in the 1860s, when he too began to understand the possibilities of a peaceful transition to democracy. But to work those possibilities up into a new synthesis, he would have had to junk the fiery rhetoric of his twenties and thirties. He would have had to admit that he had been, in large part, wrong. And among all the gifts bestowed on this extraordinary man, climbing down was not included.

XI

MOHANDAS GANDHI

and the non-violent path

A PECULIAR HINDU

What a strange saviour. One cannot help asking the question Sunil Khilnani asks: 'How, by what twist of historical fate, did this frail, ungainly man with teapot ears, whose figure wrapped in handspun cloth evoked a faded archetypal memory of saintliness, wander into the modern world; and how, for a time, did he electrify it?' ('Introduction', *Autobiography*, p. 1) How did Mohandas Gandhi's message of peace and the spinning wheel ever gain a hearing in a century of total war and relentless technological advance? To be blunt, he was an ugly little man, no more than 5ft 5 inches tall, with a big nose and a profile that dwindled into an absent chin. His voice was weak, and in public he could not launch into a sentence without a repeated sibilance; defending a client in court, he would go, 'essess-ess, your worship, ess-essess, this poor woman was attending an invalid sister. . .' (Ram Guha, *Gandhi Before India*, p. 91) As a law student in London, he was so shy that at committee meetings of the Vegetarian Society he had to write down what he wanted to say and ask someone else to read it out. (Fischer, p. 41) Even in later life, when addressing huge audiences he was often inaudible. His admirers complained that he persisted in speaking in a low, monotonous voice, 'never waves his arms, seldom moves a finger'. (Guha, *Gandhi Before India*, p. 542) In two spells at the Bombay Bar, he failed to secure any briefs, which was why he tried his luck in South Africa.

But he wasn't as frail as he looked or sounded. His followers were constantly surprised by the huge distances he could walk or bicycle, and the speed he went at. He recovered from punishing fasts after a glass of orange juice. In the same way, he startled friends and enemies by his decisiveness, his refusal to budge, but at the same time by his patience, his willingness to wait for the right moment, his readiness to change his mind.

Mohandas came from the Gujarat, in the west of India. His grandfather, father and uncle were all first ministers in small states there. They were Modh Banias, a subdivision of the merchant/banker caste, inferior to the priest and warrior castes, but superior to the menial Shudras, let alone to the outcaste Untouchables. If he wanted to follow in the family footsteps, he needed a professional qualification. The law was best, and, oddly enough, the quickest way to qualify was to go to London, where the indulgent Inns of Court admitted foreign students after eating a few dinners in their halls and passing some undemanding exams.

On his way, he had to pass though Bombay, where the local Modh Banias got wind of his plan and took a dim view of it. Their religion forbade voyages abroad across the *kala pani*, the black water. If he went, he would be obliged to eat meat and drink alcohol with Europeans, possibly even smoke cigars with them. Gandhi, still in his teens, but already married with a baby son, was quite unmoved by their threats, even when the head Bania swore at him and declared him an outcaste. Not only did Gandhi go off to England quite undeterred, on his return he never bothered to seek readmission to that section that had banned him, although, according to the rules, none of his relatives could ever have him in their houses again. (*Autobiography*, pp. 48–53, 94–5)

Though he never ceased to perform his devotions with punctiliousness and genuine reverence, Gandhi turned out to be the least conforming Hindu who ever lived. He thought that child marriages, including his own, were an abomination. He thought that women deserved every human right available, and he greatly admired the suffragettes he saw at work in England. As for caste, in moods of exasperation, he would exclaim that 'Caste is a drag upon Hindu progress, and untouchability is an excrescence'. (17 September 1927, *Gandhi Reader*, p. 211) The original caste divisions, the

Varnas, were defensible only as social-solidarity groupings (not unlike medieval guilds in the West). There could be no question of one being superior to another. 'All *Varnas* are equal, for the community depends no less on one than on another.' (Ibid., p. 218) 'I believe implicitly that all men are born equal . . . I consider that it is unmanly for any person to claim superiority over a fellow-being.' (16 September 1927, *Gandhi Reader*, p. 207) The modern caste system was 'a hideous travesty of the original . . . We have distorted it today and made ourselves the laughing stock of the world.' (Ibid.) There was no such thing as untouchability in the sacred scriptures, the *Shastras*. It was a blot on Hinduism.

In fact, he went further. Caste practices had nothing to do with religion, even if they were sanctioned in the scriptures. 'Nothing in the *Shastras* which is manifestly contrary to universal truths and morals can stand.' ('Caste has to go', *Coll. Works*, 62, p. 121)

Who was to be the judge of those universal truths and morals? The individual seeker after truth, otherwise known as M. K. Gandhi. As Partha Chatterjee puts it: 'To Gandhi then truth did not lie in history, nor did science have any privileged access to it. Truth was moral, unified, unchanging and transcendental. It was not an object of rational inquiry or philosophical speculation. It could only be found in the experience of one's life, by the unflinching practice of moral living.' ('Gandhi and the critique of civil society', *Subaltern Studies*, III, p. 172)

In other words, you found out truth as you went through life – or as Gandhi's critics liked to put it, he makes it up as he goes along. Gandhi does not dispute this: 'Truth is what everyone for the moment feels it to be.' (20 April 1933, *Coll. Works*, 54, p. 456) He heartily agreed with Emerson (one of his favourite writers) about foolish consistency being the hobgoblin of little minds. When he was reproached with changing his mind, he replied: 'At the time of writing, I never think of what I have said before. My aim is not to be consistent with my previous statements on a given question, but to be consistent with the truth as it may present itself to me at a given moment. The result is that I have grown from truth to truth.' (Fischer, p. 380) Gandhi's critics particularly disliked the subtitle of his autobiography: *The story of my experiments with truth*. That sounded to them dangerously like tampering with something sacred.

When Gandhi proclaims the Truth, usually with a capital T, he is not offering a set of principles that are to be universally applicable; he is offering an example of how to live, whether by fasting, or spinning cotton, or leading a non-violent march of protest, or by abstaining from sex with his long-suffering wife, Kasturba. Or as the philosopher Akeel Bilgrami puts it: 'Truth for Gandhi is not a cognitive notion. It is an experiential notion. It is not propositions purporting to describe the world of which truth is predicated, it is only our own moral experience which is capable of being true.' (p. 4164) Bilgrami characterizes this as an enterprise of stunning ambition and originality, though he is doubtful about its plausibility. But Gandhi is only reverting to an older sense of 'truth' as meaning 'true to the right path' rather than 'true to the facts'; fidelity rather than veracity. That is how medieval philosophers used the word; the modern sense of scientific accuracy only crept in in the fourteenth century or thereabouts (see Richard Firth Green, *A Crisis of Truth*, 1999). Gandhi's usage is not unlike Jesus's in St John's Gospel: 'I am the way, the truth, and the life.' (14:6)

At first Gandhi disliked Christianity, and found the Old Testament hard going. But the Sermon on the Mount, he said, 'went straight to my heart'. (Fischer, p. 51) He adopted the Beatitudes as his standard mantras of humility and forgiveness. He came to love English hymns too, and would often have them sung at prayer meetings in the various ashrams he founded or at the end of a fast. Particular favourites were 'When I Survey the Wondrous Cross', 'Lead, Kindly Light' and 'Abide with Me'. Interspersed with the hymns there would be readings from the Qur'an and the Upanishads. In Ramachandra Guha's view: 'No Hindu before or since has had such a close, intense relationship with the Abrahamic religions.' (*Gandhi Before India*, p. 531) There were limits to this engagement, however. He resisted the efforts of sympathetic Christian ministers to convert him. He could not accept the idea of Jesus as the only son of God, for were we not all sons of God? For Gandhi in any case, there could be no question of a personal God in the Christian sense. His dearest spiritual counsellor was the jeweller-poet Raychandbhai, a Jain, who taught him that God was not a physical being, 'had no abode outside the self', and was emphatically not the creator of the universe, which had arisen from natural processes. (ibid., p. 86) Even Raychandbhai did not enjoy the position of Gandhi's guru. Gandhi firmly maintained that 'the throne has remained vacant'. (Fischer, p. 53) He was his own man, and nobody else's.

For all his disdain for Western culture, he picked up many of his running themes from modern Western writers: from Ruskin's *Unto This Last*, to Tolstoy's *The Kingdom of God Is Within You*, to Thoreau's essay on civil disobedience (though he had conceived the idea before he read Thoreau). Gandhi was also a great lover of Bunyan. Both the language and the idea of the Pilgrim's Progress through Vanity and Despond seemed to describe his own path through life.

What are these themes? That salvation lies in your own hands, not the hands of priests and bishops; that manual labour is as good as intellectual labour and in fact better for both the soul and the body; that the simple life of the village is healthier than the moral and physical corruption of the big cities. Gandhi himself had always been a city-dweller and had scarcely spent a night in an Indian village before his later campaigns. Like many of the simple-lifers he borrowed from, he came from the urban bourgeoisie. We have met these ideas before, in Rousseau and Jefferson, for example. But only Gandhi weaves them together in an alluring homespun blanket. He does more: he lives the idea. Literally, he walks the walk, if ever anyone did.

ACTION MAN

What strikes one first about Gandhi, though, is not any kind of woozy sentimentality, but rather an extraordinary *briskness*. His speed of action and reaction, his obsession with practical ways and means are startling. He was never in truth a great book-reader, as he said himself, and set little store by book learning. At the school he founded on the commune outside Johannesburg, which he christened Tolstoy Farm, he never felt the want of textbooks; he doubted whether he and his pupils had ever read a book from cover to cover. (*Autobiography*, p. 308) What he was above all was a man of action. That was why he loved the *Bhagavad Gita*, because it was all about action.

He was obsessive about punctuality, obsessive too about rendering exact accounts of every rupee he was given. And he was a networker par excellence, rising instantly to the top of any organization he got into. He was always in a hurry. When he passed his bar exams, he enrolled in the High Court the next day and sailed for home the day after. (*Autobiography*, p. 88)

He reacted with an explosive prickliness to any slight or insult. In South Africa, when he went into court magnificently arrayed in frock coat and turban, and the judge told him to take off the turban, he refused and wrote straight to the newspapers to complain about his treatment. (*Autobiography*, pp. 110–11) The case he had been invited to South Africa to work on, primarily as a translator, was a vicious dispute between two Gujarati cousins, involving complex questions of accounting, a science of which Gandhi was wholly ignorant. Within a week, he had mastered the intricacies of book-keeping and recommended a settlement that the bemused cousins went along with. On his way to Maritzburg, then the capital of Natal, he was turfed out of his first-class seat and immediately sent a long telegram of protest to the general manager of the railway, who grovelled. (Ibid., pp. 113–14) Then he was made to freeze on the outside of the stagecoach on to Johannesburg because he was a 'coolie'. Another tussle, and in the end Gandhi got an inside seat – at the expense of a 'Hottentot' who was made to sit on the footboard. (Ibid., pp. 115–16)

Like the other Indians in South Africa, the young Gandhi's life was a succession of petty humiliations. But unlike most of his compatriots, he fought back. At the time of his arrival, the whites were increasingly edgy, not only because of the growing number of Indians in Natal – more than 35,000 as against 47,000 Europeans – but because of their commercial zip. In Durban, there were already more than four hundred Indian shops. (Guha, *Gandhi Before India*, pp. 66, 92) The first elections in the state brought to power a government 'calling for a steadfast opposition to an indiscriminate Asiatic invasion'.

This opposition was not confined to the backwoods. Joseph

Chamberlain, now the Colonial Secretary in London, said 'he quite sympathized with the determination of the white inhabitants of these Colonies, which are in comparatively close proximity to millions and hundreds of millions of Asiatics, that there shall not be an influx of people alien in civilization, alien in religion, alien in customs'. (Ibid., p. 126) Lionel Curtis, Fellow of All Souls, then the Assistant Colonial Secretary of the Transvaal and a devoted protégé of Lord Milner's, was later to be idolized as the inventor of the Commonwealth idea. But it was he who devised the Asiatic Ordinance or Black Act, designed to shut the door against the invasion, arguing that self-government by and for the Indians was 'no more in their nature than it is in the nature of a billiard cue to stand on end without support'. (Ibid., p. 205) Winston Churchill, too, was making his debut on the colonial political scene, as Chamberlain's under-secretary. He told the House of Commons, shortly before meeting Gandhi for the first time in 1906, that 'it is very desirable to keep the white and Coloured quarters apart, as the practice of allowing European, Asiatic, and native families to live side by side in a mixed community is fraught with many evils'. (Ibid, p. 222) In short, the British elite was racist to the core and determined to keep South Africa a white man's country (the Africans did not come into the equation).

As soon as he arrived in South Africa, Gandhi had been straight into the action. He whipped off an open letter to all legislators declaring that it was the hard work of the Indians that had made Natal 'the Garden Colony of South Africa', meanwhile quoting Schopenhauer and Bishop Heber in defence of Indian culture. (Ibid., p. 75) He got up a monster petition against the Bill to remove Indian voting rights, signed by 8,000 Indians, and despatched it to Lord Ripon, Chamberlain's predecessor as Colonial Secretary, who admitted that the Bill looked bad: 'The great thing is to avoid exclusion in terms of race.' (Ibid., p. 77) Couldn't they soften the Bill by introducing a property or length-of-residence qualification instead?

Already we can see Gandhi's unrivalled ability to embarrass the British, by appealing to the liberal principles they were supposed to uphold. He gradually piled up this weight of guilt on the masters of the universe. Twenty years later, the Bishop of Madras had to confess: 'I see in Mr Gandhi, the patient sufferer for the cause of righteousness and mercy, a truer representative of the Crucified Saviour, than the men who have thrown him into prison.' (Ibid., p. 491) The viceroy himself, then Lord Hardinge, said that 'the passive resisters in South Africa had the deep and burning sympathy of India and also of those who like myself, without being Indian, sympathise with the people of India.' (Ibid.) Gandhi had thus come, over his two decades in South Africa, to exert a three-way moral leverage in London, South Africa and the Raj.

THE HARSH PATRIARCH

After his first three years abroad, Gandhi returned to India to see the wife and children he had left behind – he had two sons now – and to stir the indignation of the Indian public against the maltreatment of their fellow citizens overseas. In Natal, he was already a star and was soon to become so in India too. But to Kasturba he was a relative stranger. He had kept his vow to abstain from wine, women and meat while abroad, but it would be hard to claim that his family had been much in his thoughts. In London to start with, he had blithely passed himself off as a bachelor. (*Autobiography*, p. 73) Kasturba was illiterate, and he was exasperated by the failures of his efforts to teach her. He confessed that he expected doglike devotion from her: 'A Hindu wife regards implicit obedience to her husband as the highest religion.' (Ibid., p. 177) Kasturba, however, was more recalcitrant than he had bargained for. When the grateful community showered him with diamonds and gold chains, he wanted to give them back, but she wanted to keep them for her future daughters-in-law. When they took in Christian houseguests, she refused to clean their chamber pots, and he dragged her out of the house in a rage. (Ibid., p. 255) She made huge sacrifices for him over the sixty years of their marriage, and joined the first group of women who went to jail for the cause, coming out dreadfully emaciated and close to death. When she was dying, he refused to allow her to be given penicillin – a repeat of the family's refusal to save his father's life by allowing the surgeon to perform a relatively simple operation on his fistula.

But it was his treatment of his sons, especially the eldest, Harilal, that is really chilling. He frowned on both Harilal's marriages, disowned him at the age of eighteen, gave him little credit for being willing to go to jail for the cause even more than he had, and publicly humiliated him in the pages of *Indian Opinion*, accusing him of wanting to get rich quick by dubious means and warning off potential collaborators from being deceived by the Gandhi name. Harilal took to the bottle and became a Muslim. He turned up drunk at his mother's deathbed, and had to be turned away. He died derelict in a TB hospital in Bombay in June 1948, a few months after his father was assassinated. The second son, Manilal, survived treatment that was scarcely less unfeeling and in later life marvelled how much nicer his father was to his young helpers than he had ever been to them. Gandhi acknowledged that he had sacrificed their literary education (he had not allowed Harilal to train for the bar in London as he had), but he had no regrets. 'I am quite clear that I have not been negligent in doing whatever was needful for building up their character.' (Ibid., p. 285)

He had few regrets about his neglect of Kasturba either. When he was in Volksrust jail for refusing to pay a fine, he was told that she had suffered a haemorrhage and might not live. His friend suggested that he pay the fine and join her. Gandhi said this was impossible: 'When I embarked upon the struggle, I counted the cost. If Mrs Gandhi must leave me without even the consolation a devoted husband could afford, so be it.' (Guha, *Gandhi Before India*, p. 307) One senses a certain unholy relish in his sacrifice. 'Yes, a man who wishes to work with detachment must not marry. My point is that you cannot attach yourself to a particular woman and yet live for humanity.' (Ibid., p. 515)

THE AFRICAN ABSENCE

There was, however, one rather large section of humanity that was conspicuous by its absence from Gandhi's concerns. In his time, Africans outnumbered Europeans in South Africa by ten to one; they outnumbered the beleaguered Indians by even more. Yet in the five hundred pages of Gandhi's account of his work in South Africa, the blacks play virtually no active part; we find only a few pages describing their habits in kindly but patronizing terms, and the only black who has even a walk-on part in Gandhi's autobiography is the 'Hottentot' shoved out of the stagecoach. Far from campaigning for a better deal for the Africans, at a public meeting in Bombay (26 September 1896) on his return to India, Gandhi complained of the representative institutions' 'desire to degrade us to the level of the raw Kaffir whose occupation is hunting, and whose sole ambition is to collect a certain number of cattle to buy a wife with, and then pass his life in indolence and nakedness'. (Ibid., p. 104)

This was one of the speeches Gandhi was too shy to deliver himself and had a Parsi friend read out for him. Far from there being any observable black–brown solidarity, the Himalayan explorer Francis Younghusband found at a dinner in Gandhi's well-furnished English villa that the Indian merchants not only resented being called coolies, 'but while they complain of being classed separately from Europeans, they are much offended at Kaffirs being classed with them'. (Ibid., p. 130) When Gandhi started *Indian Opinion* in 1903, there was no mention of the blacks among its aims.

When the Zulus rose in revolt in April 1906, Gandhi instantly offered to raise an ambulance corps for the government. He explained his motives to the readers of *Indian Opinion*: 'It is not for me to say whether the revolt of the Kaffirs is justified or not. We are in Natal by virtue of British power. Our very existence depends upon it. It is therefore our duty to render whatever help we can.' (Ibid., p. 194) But the Zulu revolt was about precisely the same type of grievance that Gandhi had already led such an effective Indian protest against: an annual poll tax of £1 per head. The figure for the Indian poll tax had been £3 per head. The aim had been to induce the Zulus to take up paid employment in the mines and elsewhere to remedy the labour shortage. Unlike the Indians, the Zulus had unwisely resorted to violence. At the end, thirty-one government troops lay dead, against nearly 4,000 Africans. It had been the usual one-sided fight between machine guns and spears. 'This was no war but a man-hunt,' Gandhi himself reported. (*Autobiography*, p. 289) The ambulance corps did great work, because the whites had no desire to tend the wounded Zulus, still less attend to the sores of the blacks who been sentenced to flogging. 'This work, therefore, eased my conscience,' Gandhi concluded. (Ibid.)

But it did not prick him to engage more actively with the Africans. He did speak warmly of John Dube, the black leader who had acquired 300 acres close to his own settlement and who became the first president of the Native Natal Congress, which later developed into the African National Congress. Yet although they were such close neighbours, Dube and Gandhi seldom met (admittedly Gandhi was away in the Transvaal much of the time). Nor can I trace any evidence of Africans among Gandhi's intimate circle, either at Phoenix or Tolstoy Farm. When Gandhi finally left South Africa in July 1914, he left in triumph. The government had just caved in to all the demands of the Indians: the abolition of the £3 tax; Indian marriages now to be recognized under the law; free passage for any Indian who wanted to go back home. Gandhi was feasted and cheered all over South Africa – by Europeans, Indians, merchants, mineworkers, shopkeepers, by Hindus of all castes, by Muslims, Christians and Parsis. But not by Africans.

THE AMBULANCE MAN

The Zulu rebellion was not the first occasion on which Gandhi served in an ambulance corps. At the outbreak of the Boer War on 17 October 1899, he held a meeting in Durban to discuss helping the British. To assist their rulers in their hour of need, he argued, would prove that the Indians were not just money-grubbers and not just a deadweight upon the Europeans. This was a golden opportunity to demonstrate their loyalty. Within three months, five hundred Indians had volunteered for an ambulance corps. Gandhi managed one section. He loved the action. They marched more than twenty miles a day carrying the wounded back to the dressing station, most notably from Spion Kop. The former prime minister of Natal, Sir John Robinson, who had been elected to stem the Indian inflow, now congratulated Mr Gandhi 'upon his timely, unselfish and most useful action in voluntarily organizing a corps of bearers for ambulance work'. (Guha, *Gandhi Before India*, p. 137) Gandhi later told an audience in Calcutta that 'as a Hindu, I don't believe in war, but if anything can even partially reconcile me to it, it was the rich experience we gained at the front'. (Ibid., p. 148)

The objections raised to Gandhi's inconsistency were not appeased by his blithe admission that he didn't believe in being consistent. When it came to 1914, there were plenty of Congress supporters who thought that Indians ought not to fight for their oppressors. Gandhi was in England at the time and persisted with the argument that at least 'Indians residing in England should do their bit during the war'. (*Autobiography*, p. 316) He firmly rejected the line taken by the IRA that 'England's danger is Ireland's opportunity'. On the contrary, 'It was becoming and far-sighted not to press our demand while the war lasted.' (Ibid., p. 317) So he began to train yet another ambulance corps.

Back in India, he attended the war conference called by the Viceroy, Lord Willingdon. He pledged to start an Indian recruitment campaign and afterwards wrote a long letter to Willingdon, setting out his terms: 'I recognize that in the hour of its danger, we must give, as we have decided to give, ungrudging and unequivocal support to the Empire of which we aspire in the near future to be partners in the same sense as the Dominions overseas.' (Ibid, p. 403) It was to be an explicit bargain. He wanted the Congress to withdraw for the duration all its resolutions in favour of Home Rule. 'If we serve to save the Empire, we have in that very act secured Home Rule.' (Ibid., pp. 403–4)

The reforms proposed after the war by Edwin Montagu, the secretary of state, and Lord Chelmsford, the new viceroy, scarcely fulfilled Britain's side of the tacit bargain, though they did represent modest steps towards self-government. But in any case, Gandhi had revealed once more that non-violence was not for him a universal creed that admitted of no exceptions; it was a tactic, a noble and effective one perhaps, but still a tactic. The practical outcome, though, of Gandhi's indefatigable recruitment campaign was that half a million Indians fought for the Allies.

SATYAGRAHA: ITS MEANING AND PRACTICE

'I have nothing new to teach the world. Non-violence is as old as the hills.' (1936, quoted M. V. Karnath, *Gandhi: A Spiritual Journey*, 2007, p. 195) Right from the start, Gandhi insists that his teaching is deeply embedded in the Indian tradition. Back in September 1906, when a packed meeting in Johannesburg resolved on mass resistance against Lionel Curtis's Asiatic Ordinance, Gandhi told the readers of *Indian Opinion* that the resolution 'is, and at the same time is not, unique. We consider it unique, because nowhere else in the world have Indians so far resolved, as they have done now, to go to gaol rather than submit to a law. On the other hand, we do not consider it unique because a number of similar instances are found [in our history]. When we are dissatisfied with anything, we resort to *hartal* [a sort of general strike].' (Guha, *Gandhi Before India*, p. 209) Gandhi points out, quite rightly, that this was the traditional method used in the native states to obtain redress of a grievance. The history of the Raj was littered with such episodes (see, for example, the work of Ranajit Guha, especially *Elementary Aspects of Peasant Insurgency in Colonial India*, 1983).

Gandhi also claimed that the Indian peasants had always been peaceful in their resistance, and that they were schooled in this by their scriptures. The message that he took from the *Gita* was strictly pacific, though as with most sacred scriptures there was plenty of room for other interpretations. He thought, though, that the term 'passive resistance' was too narrow, that it did not rule out hatred and thus might break out in violence. He and his circle devised instead the word '*satyagraha*' or 'truth-force' (*Autobiography*, p. 292) as a more powerful and far-reaching alternative. It was under this banner that he led his campaigns in South Africa and later in India. He called the ashram that he founded in his home district of Ahmedabad 'the Satyagraha Ashram'. The principle of *satyagraha* runs through the most extended statement of his beliefs, *Hind Swaraj*, or 'Indian Self-Rule', published in Gujarati in *Indian Opinion* in December 1909 and proscribed by the government of Bombay in March 1910, which only spurred Gandhi on to have the book translated into English.

The book is in the form of a dialogue between the Reader who puts up a series of objections and the Editor who answers them. The overall message is that 'the force of love and pity is infinitely greater than the force of arms'. (Mukherjee, *Gandhi Reader*, p. 45) Real Home Rule was not simply a matter of kicking the English out. It was a matter of self-rule and self-control. Like Edith Cavell in the West, Gandhi declares that 'patriotism is not enough, I must have no hatred or bitterness towards anyone'. And the only way to achieve true self-rule was *satyagraha*. 'My creed is non-violence under all circumstances. My method is conversion, not coercion,' he persisted twenty years later. (12 January 1928, *Gandhi Reader*, p. 74) As we have seen, 'under all circumstances' was not strictly true, but it was true as far as the immediate struggle for national independence went. In that endeavour, the Indian people had to show grace and goodwill under pressure, and never to slip into hatred of their opponents.

By these means, India would set an example to the world:

Through the deliverance of India, I seek to deliver the so-called weaker races of the earth from the crushing heels of Western exploitation in which England is the greatest partner. If India converts, as it can convert, Englishmen, it can become the predominant partner in a world commonwealth of which England can have the privilege of becoming a partner if she chooses. India has the right, if she only knew, of becoming the predominant partner by reason of her numbers, her geographical position and culture inherited for ages. This is big talk, I know. (Ibid.)

This was an ambition that Nehru was to perpetuate in his championing of the Non-Aligned Movement, which took wing in the 1950s and today includes nearly two-thirds of the members of the UN. When Gandhi first outlined the vision, it must have seemed very big talk indeed.

Satyagraha was not simply a question of civil disobedience, of refusing to obey an obnoxious law and being ready to pay the legal penalty with good humour. The *satyagrahi* had to show that they had exhausted every alternative method of protest first and that they bore their jailors no ill will.

In Gandhi's hands, *satyagraha* was always meticulously planned. He insisted on rigorous punctuality, strict adherence to the plan, and accounting of every rupee spent. He had no hang-ups about accepting donations from maharajas and nawabs and tycoons like the Tatas, father and son, and G. D. Birla, the big industrialist in whose house he was murdered. He was so beyond corruption that these associations never really tainted him.

Hind Swaraj is full of rants against modern technology and its corrupting effects as opposed to the pure and simple life of the Indian village. But in practice he travelled everywhere by train and fired off cables to everyone who mattered. He was the unashamed beneficiary of the modernizing programme of Lord Dalhousie in the previous century.

He was no disdainer of the dark arts of PR either. At a protest meeting in Jo'burg's West End Bioscope Hall, a photo of the *satyagraha* ladies in jail was flashed up on the screen (Guha, *Gandhi Before India*, p. 475), probably one of the first propaganda ads ever screened. Gandhi's devoted secretary Sonja Schlesin, one of his many Jewish colleagues, took photographs of the bruises of the victims of white violence and sent prints to the newspapers and to the government. (Ibid., p. 483)

See how minute his instructions are, for example, to Albert West, the British editor of *Indian Opinion*:

> With reference to the £3 tax, the first step is not to advise the men to refuse to pay the tax but for the [Natal Indian] Congress to send a petition to the Prime Minister, signed by all the Indians in Natal – say, 15,000 signatures. There should be a mass meeting held. The Congress should then ask the Indians in the other Provinces to support. We must then await the reply from the Prime Minister. Then there should be a petition to Parliament next year, and if Parliament rejects the petition, there should be an appeal to the Imperial Government by the Congress aided by the other Associations in South Africa. Finally the refusal to pay the tax! (Ibid., p. 425)

His instructions could go into the smallest detail down to the logistics, the prisoners' diet and religious needs. West was to meet the marchers at the Transvaal border but just watch as a spectator, and buy onward tickets for them if they were not arrested. 'Mrs Gandhi will be purely fruitarian. Jeki [their daughter-in-law] and others will not touch bread.' (Ibid., p. 466)

These careful preparations were designed to enable the *sat-yagraha* to proceed calmly and come to a successful and graceful end, which it so often did. But Gandhi had a deeper purpose; to engage as many people as possible in the process, and to draw the finest responses from them. The *satyagrahi* were to act as if proper systems of justice and democratic consultation were already in place, so that the authorities were under a moral obligation to respond in the same spirit, because all concerned subscribed to a shared set of legal, moral and religious values. The Indians in South Africa were not to think of themselves as alien or inferior, nor were the Untouchables in India.

Non-violence as practised by Gandhi exerted a kind of enforced *intimacy* between the rulers and the ruled. General Jan Smuts, the Boer War hero, then Colonial Secretary of the Transvaal, greets Gandhi 'as if we were old chums', even though Smuts shares the Europeans' goal of making the Transvaal 'a white man's country'. When Gandhi is in jail, Smuts sends him a couple of religious books, and Gandhi asks the boys at Phoenix to make the General a pair of stout leather sandals, which he wears at his farm every summer. (Ibid., p. 322)

Yet at the same time, Smuts feels intensely uncomfortable in their dealings. Introducing a Bill that gave the Indians about half of what they were asking for, Smuts confessed: 'There is no more awkward position for a Government than a movement of passive resistance . . . In more primitive times one would have met it by simply issuing a declaration of war. But in these times it is impossible to do that, and therefore the situation becomes a very difficult one for us to handle.' (19 August 1908, Ibid., p. 300) Meeting Gandhi in Cape Town three years later, Smuts told him that 'it has hurt me more than you to imprison these people. It has been the unpleasantest episode of my life to imprison men who suffer for their conscience.' (27 March 1911, Ibid., p. 407)

Satyagraha is a politics of *embarrassment*. The authorities and their supporters are to be shamed into behaving as their moral and religious codes instruct them to behave. This may take a very long time, as Gandhi warned. He repeatedly explains that he is a believer in 'slow politics', that changes of heart come only gradually and after persistent pressure, and that it is always a mistake to press for too much, too soon. It was not until 1986 that the Dutch Reformed Church finally changed its support for apartheid and opened its doors to people of all races.

The effect on the *satyagrahi* themselves is more immediate. They are mobilized, emboldened, brought to life as political beings. Even if this or that particular protest fails to achieve its goal, there are always more to come, and there is no going back. *Satyagraha* is not a series of one-offs. It ratchets up the awakening of the soul.

THE VEGETARIAN OPTION

Western readers of Gandhi, particularly his early readers, tended to admire (or sometimes to deplore) his struggle for national independence and human rights, and to discard as irrelevant or cranky, and to poke fun at, his 'other' side: the loincloth, the theosophy, the vegetarianism, the obsession with sexual continence, the spinning wheel and the homespun cloth. Look again at Churchill's notorious outburst in 1931: 'It is alarming and also nauseating to see Mr Gandhi, a seditious Middle Temple lawyer, now posing as a fakir of a type well known in the East, striding half-naked up the steps of the viceregal palace, while he is still organising and conducting a defiant campaign of civil disobedience, to parley on equal terms with the representative of the King-Emperor.'

Churchill's objection is clearly as much sartorial as political. Gandhi reveals himself to be a fraud by affecting a manner of dress that he would never have dreamed of wearing in the Middle Temple. True, when Gandhi was studying in the Middle Temple, he was impeccably turned out from the Army & Navy Stores with a top hat, gold watch chain and a proper bow tie, which he struggled to tie correctly. But he wasn't in the Middle Temple any more, he was back home in the most populous nation on earth (as it was then and has now in 2017 become again), where people wore dhotis and shawls just like he did and half of them never touched meat or eggs and believed that it was wrong to take the life of a fly. *Ahimsa* – non-striking – was a cardinal principle of all the great old religions of India. The idea of non-violence being a cranky fad would itself have seemed cranky, if not to Mr Churchill, who, Gandhi claimed as early as 1922, 'understands only the gospel of force'. (Mukherjee, *Gandhi Reader*, p. 105)

Gandhi delighted in calling himself a quack and a crank. He loved experimenting with all sorts of diets and medical treatments. After reading a popular guide to midwifery, he had no hesitation in delivering Kasturba's last child unaided. Some of his interventions may strike us as crazy or cruel, such as denying Kasturba beef tea when she was desperately ill and penicillin when she was dying. Other therapies he recommended are now regarded as admirable: fresh air and exercise, a light diet of fruit and nuts. He ground his own flour, baked his own bread, spun his own yarn, loved DIY. Some of his teachings seemed retro to his contemporaries, and not always easy to revive. Even in the rural India of his day, it was already a struggle to find spinning wheels and hand looms that worked and teachers who could instruct his ashram in how to work them. But such crafts appeal to us in the West now too, in theory at least.

Vegetarianism, as a moral theory as well as a dietary preference, has an increasing reach these days. We may not go along with Gandhi's hostility to vivisection, but the stench of the slaughter-houses offends our nostrils more than it used to, and we are uneasy about the environmental costs of rearing livestock to feed an ever-growing global population.

It was one of Gandhi's objections to Christianity that, unlike the Buddha, 'one fails to notice this love for all living beings in the life of Jesus'. (*Autobiography*, p. 157) If Gandhi had managed to get to grips with the Old Testament too, I don't imagine that he would have cared for the carte blanche that God gives to Adam and Eve in Genesis 1:28: 'And God said unto them, Be fruitful and multiply, and replenish the earth and subdue it: and have domin-ion over the fish of the sea, and over the fowl of the air, and over every living thing that moveth upon the earth.' It was Gandhi's view that Man had done enough multiplying already. Though he was hostile to artificial methods of contraception, his emphasis on sexual continence was intended to control the population as well as to purify the soul.

His veneration of the Indian village romanticized the often-wretched reality. He was well aware of this. At the end of his life, he admitted to Nehru that 'my ideal village still exists only in my imagination'. (5 October 1945, *Gandhi Reader*, p. 289) But he still stood by the model of society that he had outlined in *Hind Swaraj* over thirty years earlier: 'if India, and through India, the world, is to achieve real freedom, then sooner or later we shall have to go and live in the villages'. (Ibid.)

This sounds now, and sounded then, pretty implausible. But there is more to Gandhi's argument than nostalgia. His underlying claim is that Man can survive, and deserve to survive, on this planet only if he treads more lightly upon it. That lighter footprint is the guiding principle of today's environmental movement – we call it sustainability – just as it was the founding principle of India's old religions. Nobody ever did more to link the two than M. K. Gandhi.

The fallible Mahatma

By the end of the Great War, people were talking of Mohandas Gandhi as the 'Mahatma', the 'Great-Soul', roughly equivalent to 'Saint'. This canonization was given an imprimatur by Rabindranath Tagore, but it had already entered common speech. The Mahatma's *pratap* (power and glory) began to acquire extraordinary resonance. Peasants mobbed trains, even in the middle of the night, to catch a glimpse of him. To get a *darshan* of a saint or a holy image was worth a great deal, as it was to medieval Christians.

Miracles began to be attributed to his influence. The Mahatma could split boiling pans, lift thatched roofs, transform wheat fields into fields of sesame, make sweets shower down from heaven and, contrariwise, shower shit upon the ungodly and those who dared criticize him. The project of Indian independence began to be known as 'Gandhi's Swaraj', as opposed to the official programme of the Congress. (Amin, *passim*)

The first *satyagraha* on Indian soil was in support of the sharecroppers of Champaran in northern Bihar, near the border with Nepal. An illiterate sharecropper named Raj Kumar Shukla dogged Gandhi, pleading with him to go there and take up their cause.

Eventually Gandhi consented to take a train from Calcutta to Patna where he met a prosperous local lawyer, Rajendra Prasad, later to become president of the Congress Party and later of all India. In Champaran, the landlords had been compelling the peasants to plant three-twentieths of their land with indigo and surrender the indigo as rent. Germany then developed a synthetic indigo and the landlords wanted cash instead, which the peasants didn't have. When Gandhi arrived, he was immediately told to leave, and when he refused was summoned to court. He telegraphed Prasad, wired the viceroy. Prasad and other local prominenti volunteered to go to jail with Gandhi – a typical case of his ability to enlist the gentry to his cause. The Lieutenant-Governor dropped the case and ordered an inquiry, which assembled a mountain of damning evidence against the planters. In the settlement, the planters assumed that Gandhi would demand the uttermost rupee, but when they offered to pay back only 25 per cent of their ill-gotten gains, he accepted – a typical case of his determination that every *satyagraha* should end gracefully and with minimum ill will. Within a few years, indigo planting had ceased, and most of the planters had abandoned their estates to the peasants. Not a stick was raised in anger, not a head broken.

But when *satyagraha* was launched on a larger scale, not even Gandhi's masterful orchestration could guarantee a trouble-free outcome. The agitation against the Anarchical and Revolutionary Crimes Act 1919, better known as the Rowlatt Acts, turned out badly. The Acts were typical pieces of post-war panic legislation, named after the judge on whose report they were based. They gave the authorities wide-ranging powers to lock up terror suspects without trial. Constitutional opposition was soon exhausted. So Gandhi organized a nationwide *hartal*, or one-day stoppage, for 6 April 1919.

At first it seemed to work beautifully. In his autobiography, Gandhi exulted that 'the whole of India from one end to the other, towns as well as villages, observed a complete *hartal* on that day. It was a most wonderful spectacle ... Delhi had never witnessed a *hartal* like that before. Hindus and Musulmans seemed united like one man.' (p. 414)

But then the police opened fire on the *hartal* procession. Delhi went into lockdown. Gandhi moved on to rally support in the Punjab, where feelings were running strong. He was stopped at the border on the orders of the Governor, Sir Michael O'Dwyer, and so he was not able to go on to Amritsar. Now reports of violence were beginning to come in from all over the country. Gandhi went back down to his home city of Ahmedabad, where the leading citizens pleaded with him to suspend the *satyagraha*. Gandhi said he needed no telling, 'for I had already made up my mind to suspend *satyagraha* so long as people had not learnt the lesson of peace'. (Ibid., p. 421) Nevertheless, O'Dwyer was not the only person who blamed Gandhi for the violence and counter-violence sweeping across the Punjab and culminating in the Massacre of Amritsar, which left 379 people dead, or more than 1,000 according to the Congress.

Rather than simply blaming the appalling actions of Brigadier Reginald Dyer, Gandhi spoke of a 'Himalayan miscalculation' on his own part. What he called 'mobocracy' would always lead to disaster. 'Before restarting civil disobedience on a mass scale, it would be necessary to create a band of well-tried, pure-hearted volunteers who thoroughly understood the strict conditions of Satyagraha.' (Ibid., p. 423)

Despite its disastrous climax, the agitation against the Rowlatt Acts did ultimately prevail. Dyer's conduct was unanimously condemned by the official inquiry, and after a decent interval the Rowlatt Acts were repealed. O'Dwyer was assassinated in 1940 by an Indian activist.

For all Gandhi's hopes, there was no reliable way of making sure that non-co-operation on a large scale did not spiral out of control into violence. Nor was there any guarantee that the authorities would respond by rational negotiation rather than lurching into panicky repression. Non-violence had its successes and its failures. Only in retrospect can we see it as a source of sustained, if intermittent pressure on the British to quit India.

Nor can the failure of the British to speed up the timetable towards self-rule and Dominion status be blamed on inter-war viceroys. Chelmsford, Reading, Irwin, Willingdon and Linlithgow might have been an unimaginative bunch, varying in their sympathies towards Indian aspirations, but they were responsible to London, where the reactionary caucus led by Churchill and Birkenhead lurked and growled over their cigars. Birkenhead, the former F. E. Smith, was secretary of state for India from 1924 to 1928, and what time he spared from the golf course he devoted to frustrating the mild ambitions of the Montagu–Chelmsford programme for constitutional advance. 'What man in this House', he asked his fellow peers after he had left office, 'can say that he can see in a generation, in two generations, in a hundred years, any prospect that the people of India will be in a position to assume control of the Army, the Navy, the Civil Service, and to have a Governor-General who will be responsible to the Indian government and not to any authority in this country?' (Fischer, p. 274) Churchill directed his firepower upon Gandhi personally. In 1935, he declared: 'Gandhism and all that it stands for must ultimately be grappled with and finally crushed.' (Fischer, p. 390)

Throughout the long and dismal period of British prevarication and Indian disappointment leading up to the Government of India Act of 1935 (itself hardly a consummation devoutly to be wished by either side), Gandhi never stopped. He tirelessly negotiated with everyone, the British in London and Delhi, the Indian National Congress of which he was now and then the master, and the Untouchables with their brilliant but difficult leader, B. R. Ambedkar, and the Muslim League with its slightly less brilliant and even more difficult leader, Mohammed Ali Jinnah. Of his seventeen fasts (two of them in South Africa), some of the longest, stretching up to twenty-one days, took place in this period. At the end of them, he would appear speechless and almost lifeless, but after a sip of orange juice his wiry frame recovered with amazing rapidity. Four of the fasts were in support of his crusade for the Untouchables, the *Harijan*, but they failed to resolve his long-running dispute with Ambedkar whether the Untouchables should vote separately or should join a single electoral roll, as Gandhi wanted. Three of the fasts were in support of Hindu–Muslim unity, or rather against the growing divide. The others were mostly penitential, to atone for the violent conduct of others – anarchists, strikers, assassins or would-be assassins. The prosperous lawyers and merchants who bolstered and bankrolled him were sometimes happy to go to jail with or for him, but the fasting was not to their taste. Just as well no doubt. They were not in training for it, as Gandhi was.

Of all his initiatives in this period, the one that strikes me as nearly beautiful (if that adjective can ever be applied to anything in politics) was the Salt March. At the end of 1929, the Congress, orchestrated by Gandhi, had for the first time passed a motion in favour of unabridged independence and secession from the British Empire. How was this new chapter in India's history to be firmed up and imprinted in the minds of the people?

Tagore, visiting Gandhi at the ashram on 18 January 1930, asked Gandhi what he had in mind for the coming year, rather like a critic asking an impresario what he had up his sleeve for the new season. Gandhi replied: 'I am furiously thinking night and day, and I do not see light coming out of the surrounding darkness.' But there was violence in the air, and he felt he had to find a way of channelling the resentment into non-violent action.

What he did, on 3 March 1930, was to write a letter to the Viceroy, Lord Irwin, later as Foreign Secretary Lord Halifax, warning him that civil disobedience would begin in nine days against the iniquitous Salt Tax. The government had assumed a monopoly over the production and sale of salt and exploited it by a swingeing tax that bore hardest upon the sweating peasants.

The Mahatma set out from the ashram with seventy-eight followers and walked the two hundred miles to the sea at Dandi. When they reached the beach, they prayed. Gandhi waded into the sea, then came back to the beach and picked up a handful of salt left by the waves. In doing so, he had broken the law that made it a punishable offence to possess salt not obtained from the British government stores. What more brilliant demo could there be of the absurdity of imperial rule than its appropriation of the most naturally occurring substance on the planet?

Following Gandhi, villagers all along India's endless sea coast went out with their pans to make salt. There were mass arrests. Congress volunteers openly sold salt on the city streets. The police raided the Congress HQ where they were making salt on the roof.

The pinch that Gandhi himself had gathered became a collectable item and was sold to the highest bidder for 1,600 rupees. Nehru was arrested under the Salt Act and was jailed for six months. Unrest spread all over India. The Viceroy was estimated to have 60,000 protesters in his jails. The police beat up the protesters with rifle butts and *lathis* and in one or two places opened fire, but except in Chittagong, there was no violence by the protesters. Civil disobedience had worked in the most uproarious way. Moral authority had slipped from the hands of the Raj. And all from a handful of salt.

THE TERRIBLE DIVIDE

Gandhi had always insisted on the unity of India and her people. In *Hind Swaraj*, he claimed that 'we were one nation before they [the English] came to India ... It was because we were one nation that they were able to establish one kingdom ... Subsequently they divided us ... we Indians are one as no two Englishmen are.' (Mukherjee, *Gandhi Reader*, pp. 24–5) In historical fact, the entire peninsula had never been under a single ruler until the British came. There were parts of southern India that even the great Ashoka never conquered. How much, in the cultural sense, did Indians think of themselves as one people? That was harder to assess. If they did, when did such a sense take hold? How far did Hindus and Muslims share that sense?

The Mahatma continued to claim that 'Hindu-Muslim unity is the breath of our life'. (26 December 1924, *Gandhi Reader*, p. 266) And it was essential for true *Swaraj*: 'I see no way of achieving anything in this afflicted country without a lasting heart unity between Hindus and Musulmans of India'. (29 May 1924, *Gandhi Reader*, p. 265) But did that heart unity really exist? Gandhi worked so desperately hard to achieve it, precisely because he doubted its reality. Back in South Africa, where the relatively small communities of Indians might have been expected to cling together, 'I had realized early enough that there was no genuine friendship between the Hindus and the Musulmans.' (*Autobiography*, p. 398) Before 1910, his mentor in India, G. P. Gokhale, was already worrying about 'the fierce antagonism between Hindus and Mahomedans'.

Some Hindu organizations were 'frankly anti-Mahomedan, as the Muslim League is frankly anti-Hindu, and both are anti-national'. (Letters to William Wedderburn, 24 May 1907 and 24 September 1909, quoted Guha, *Gandhi Before India*, p. 370)

Lord Curzon had certainly fomented this friction in 1905 by dividing Bengal into the mixed West and the Muslim-majority East, later to become East Pakistan, and later still Bangla Desh. The British were unashamed about following the ancient imperial principle of 'divide and rule', although some viceroys like Lord Dufferin claimed that they weren't. But this was why the Morley-Minto reforms of 1909 divided the nation into separate electorates for the legislative councils, with the Muslims guaranteed reserved seats in excess of their 25 per cent of the population. Morley, the secretary of state in London, and Minto, the Viceroy, could claim that they were only responding to the demands of the Muslim community led by the Aga Khan. Morley, the biographer of Gladstone, was liberal to his bones, but his ambitions for India were decidedly limited. He reassured Curzon that 'if it could be said that this chapter of reforms led, directly or indirectly to the establishment of a parliamentary system in India, I for one would have nothing at all to do with it'.

The last thing the British wished to encourage was a sense of shared nationality among those they ruled. They wanted to damp down any feeling of *demos*. In fact, we can look all the way back to Cleisthenes to see that a common electoral roll is the essential building block of a real democracy.

Hindus and Muslims had certainly come together at times under the pressure of events. During the Great Mutiny of 1857, they had fought side by side, taking up each other's battle cries. Gandhi's untiring efforts to reach out to Muslims at all levels were not without effect. In the early days of the Congress, Muslims had been prominent in numbers. But there was undoubtedly a Hindu swagger about the Congress leadership that gradually caused Muslims to drift away, not only to take refuge in the Muslim League but to give the League a fresh impetus towards separation.

Jinnah was not an attractive personality, certainly when compared to Gandhi or Nehru. He was a forbidding and resentful character, apparently unaware of the paradox that he, a non-religious man who ate pork and drank alcohol, should be agitating to set up a separate religious state, while the devout Gandhi was insistent on a united secular state.

Like Gandhi, Jinnah was a Gujarati from Kathiawar. Like so many Muslims, his family had been recent converts to Islam. Jinnah is a Hindu name. Despite this – or perhaps because of it – they came to hate each other. In their long talks together in September 1944, stretching over a fortnight, Gandhi formed the view that Jinnah was an 'evil genius, though not a fraud'. (Fischer, p. 469) Jinnah thought Gandhi was a fraud, or perhaps a devious humbug. Gandhi simply could not accept Jinnah's view that 'by all the canons of international law, we [the Muslims of India] are a nation with our own distinctive culture and civilization, language and literature, art and architecture, names and nomenclature, sense of value and proportion, legal laws and moral codes, customs and calendar, history and traditions, aptitudes and ambitions'. (Fischer, p. 431)

Deep down, you feel that Gandhi really thought that the Muslims were a bunch of apostates: 'I find no parallel in history for a body of converts and their descendants claiming to be a nation apart from the parent stock.' (Ibid.) Would there be a third nation in India if several million people adopted Christianity (as indeed they did in South India)? In Gandhi's attitude, however much he tried to suppress it, we can detect more than a touch of the patronizing attitude that had driven so many Muslims out of the Congress.

So the terrible slide towards Partition began, unstoppable either by the British who had helped to start it, or by the Congress that had by now more or less fulfilled Jinnah's claim to be a purely Hindu party, and certainly not by Gandhi's forlorn fasts. Quite why it had become so unstoppable may become clearer from the last chapter of this book.

Gandhi never concealed his feelings. And he certainly did not conceal his sense of total failure. 'I have not convinced India. There is violence all around us. I am a spent bullet.' (Fischer, p. 454) He blamed the caste Hindus for their lack of charity towards the Untouchables, and he blamed their patronizing attitude towards the

Muslims too: 'The Moslems are religious fanatics, but fanaticism cannot be answered with fanaticism. Bad manners irritate. Brilliant Moslems in Congress became disgusted. They did not find the brotherhood of man among the Hindus ... Hindu separatism has played a part in creating the rift between Congress and the League.' (Fischer, p. 469)

Partition was 'a spiritual tragedy'. His thirty-two years of work had come to 'an inglorious end'. (Fischer, p. 507) He could not find it in his heart to take any part in the celebrations of Independence Day. On that 15 August he was in Calcutta, trying to quell the violent mobs that had broken out. He went on to do the same round Delhi, the Mahatma deploying his *pratap* one last time. In January the following year, he began his last fast, 'a fast unto death'. In fact, he ended the fast when the rioting stopped and a peace agreement was signed in Gandhi's presence at the house of his patron G. D. Birla. It was the bullet from a disenchanted Hindu journalist twelve days later that did for him.

Of our twelve Prime Movers, only Jesus and Gandhi died violent deaths. It may be no coincidence that they are the only two to have preached non-violence and forgiveness. In India, though, the assassin's bullets have remained an all too common currency, striking down British proconsuls and Indian prime ministers with equal remorselessness.

STILL WITH US

Gandhi's despair was not simply that Partition should have come, with its million deaths and its appalling displacement of populations. He also lived long enough to dislike the sort of India that he saw emerging: militaristic, jealous of its boundaries, urban-minded and degenerating into endemic corruption. If he had lived on to see how successive Indian governments were to behave in Kashmir, how his protégé Nehru was to provoke a foolish and disastrous war with China, his tears would have been bitterer still. As they would if he had known that India would continue to maintain one of the largest standing armies on the planet and would become the world's largest importer of arms. As for India's vaunted parliamentary system, were so many legislators ever under indictment as in the Lok Sabha?

Gandhi admired Mazzini greatly as the unifier of Italy, who was yet 'so broad-minded that he could be regarded as the citizen of every country'. (Guha, *Gandhi Before India*, p. 180) Personally, Mazzini was 'adorable', and yet the Italy of Mazzini 'remains in a state of slavery' and the working classes were as unhappy as ever, in a perpetual state of misery and revolt. (Mukherjee, *Gandhi Reader*, p. 39) In his last days, Gandhi was coming to think that the same could be said of India, which had not even been united.

In India today, the Mahatma remains an idol celebrated on postage stamps and banknotes, but his life and teaching are largely ignored and certainly not imitated by the thrusting entrepreneurs of Gurgaon and Bangalore. As for the peasants, India still has more poor people than any other country, though that is mostly because she has more people – Gandhi's methods of birth control didn't work either.

What I find interesting, though, is how Gandhi still catches his critics on the raw. Those critics come, oddly enough, almost equally from right and left, from the heirs of Winston Churchill and the heirs of Karl Marx. In a curious way, their critiques seem to blur into one another.

Gandhi's illusion, they both tell us, was to imagine that non-violence, however ingeniously practised, could transform the world. The Marxist historian Perry Anderson says in a long polemic extended over three issues of the *London Review of Books* that 'Satyagraha had not been a success. Each time Gandhi had tried it, the British had seen it off. In the end independence did not come from passive resistance, let alone sexual abstinence.' (*LRB*, 5 July 2012) Indians had more reason to be grateful to the brilliant Subhas Chandra Bose and his Indian National Army, which fought alongside the Japanese in the jungle and which was disgracefully edited out of the Indian national story by the Nehru regime. In the First World War, the Indians would have done better to imitate the example of the Irish and use England's danger as their opportunity. 'The price of liberation was not small in Ireland – division of the country and civil war. But it was tiny compared with the bill that would eventually be paid in India.' (Ibid.)

Andrew Roberts, the Tory biographer of Churchill and Lord Salisbury, argues that 'for all his lifelong campaign for Swaraj, India could have achieved it many years earlier if Gandhi had not continually abandoned his civil-disobedience campaigns just as they were beginning to be successful. With 300 million Indians ruled by over 0.1 per cent of that number of Britons, the subcontinent could have ended the Raj with barely a shrug if it had been politically united.' (*Wall Street Journal*, 26 March 2011) What this implies, of course, is that Gandhi should have carried on the civil disobedience after Amritsar, thus provoking British violence on a far more terrible scale. Roberts is on record as approving Dyer's actions, claiming that far more than 379 would have been killed if he had not fired on the crowd. So the Indians would have had to wade through blood to get their freedom.

Like Anderson, Roberts dismisses Gandhi as a mystagogue and a sexual weirdo, claiming among other things that he had a passionate homosexual affair with his admirer Hermann Kallenbach. These allegations seem rather shakily based, but leaving them aside and also any suggestion that Gandhi was some sort of mystic (he always denied any direct knowledge of God, and, as we have seen, his definition of Truth was a severely moral and practical one), what we are left with is a simple proposition: that in politics important matters, such as national independence, are decided strictly by economic and military forces. By contrast, any conversion of hearts and minds dwindles into insignificance. India gained her independence because Japan, aided by the INA, had shattered British military power in South Asia and because Britain was economically exhausted after the war.

Force was and is the decisive factor. Churchill was right. Marx was right. Gandhi's fasts and marches, his praying and hymn-singing were airy-fairy irrelevances. This knock-'em-down style of argument has itself plenty of punch. It elbows aside dissent from the delicate-minded.

Yet in the last part of his polemic, Anderson himself steps back to note, with exemplary fairness, certain other persisting features of India since independence.

First, India has remained a democracy, a remarkably stable one, considering its huge and diverse population. Anderson traces this back, without hesitation, to the beginnings of the Indian state: 'The stability of Indian democracy came in the first instance from the conditions of the country's independence. There was no over-throw of the Raj but a transfer of power by it to Congress as its successor.' ('After Nehru', *LRB*, 2 August 2012) In other words, the peacefulness of that transfer had long-term consequences, and those consequences were benign.

Next, one of the outstanding features of that democracy is the intense engagement of the poor. In other democracies, the worst-off tend to be turned off. 'In India alone, the poor form not just the overwhelming majority of the electorate, they vote in larger num-bers than the better-off.' (Ibid.) Despite the appalling corruption, poverty and inequality, the poor remain loyal participants in the system. At every Indian roadside you see crowds gathering round the candidates for election.

Third, the persistence of caste is a source of strength rather than weakness, a stabilizing factor. India is in fact 'a caste-iron democ-racy'. Reforms of the system have followed Gandhi's general lines, but the system is sanitized, not destroyed.

Finally, though India's constitution is strongly centralized, as Nehru insisted, and though the central government has not hesitated to overrule or even replace provincial governments that have displeased it, Anderson notes that 'in outcome, the union became something like a creatively flexible federation'. The prov-inces are governed with a zestful individuality, often by colourful and charismatic characters who are quite happy to take on Delhi. Their party congresses have an oomph that has been drained from party conferences in some European countries, notably Britain.

If you take these four factors together, it is rather harder to keep Gandhi out of the picture. These are the things he stood for – peaceful transformation, the mobilization of the poor, respect for the villages and their traditions, devolution of power. If you look at the *quality* of Indian democracy, Gandhi does seem to live more than a little.

By contrast, the long-term influence of force-fuelled takeover seems more questionable. In Ireland, to take Anderson's own

example, the Easter Rising and its brutal suppression, the Civil
War and the Black and Tans have cast terrible long shadows, not
simply in the renewal of the Troubles for the last thirty years of the
twentieth century but in the unburied memories that have haunted
and divided families and communities in Ireland and poisoned
Anglo-Irish relations, not to mention precipitating the flight of Irish
Protestants from the South. At the official level, it was a century
before the two governments dared to repeat George V's visit to
Dublin, so strong was the fear of assassination (a justified fear in
view of the murder of Mountbatten and his family). Is the bloody
birth of Israel any better as a template? For decades, the country was
run by veterans of one terror gang or another. Fifty years after the
Six Day War, the prospect of Israel living in peace with her neighbours and her Arab population remains as far off as ever.

I can do no better on this whole question than quote what Gandhi
said in 1922:

> Mr Churchill, who understands only the gospel of force, is quite
> right in saying that the Irish problem is different in character
> from the Indian. He means in effect that the Irish, having fought
> their way to their swaraj thorough violence, will be well able to
> maintain it by violence, if need be. India, on the other hand, if she
> wins swaraj in reality by non-violence, must be able to maintain
> it chiefly by non-violent means. This Mr Churchill can scarcely
> believe to be possible . . . (9 March 1922, *Gandhi Reader*, p. 105)

Let us match up Churchill and Gandhi one last time. It was
Churchill who pressed hardest for armed intervention to reverse
the Russian Revolution. It was Churchill who insisted that Wing-
Commander (not yet 'Bomber') Harris should bomb the hell out
of the rebel tribes in Mesopotamia. It was Churchill who sent the
troops to quell the South Wales miners before the Great War and
wanted to crush the General Strike after it. How long the memories of those on the receiving end of all this, and how minimal the
benefits at the time.

Whereas in the case of Gandhi, one is tempted to agree with
Ramachandra Guha that the persistent urge to write him off is

driven by annoyance at his continued popularity, or, worse still, by the thought that his influence might actually be growing.

In the United States, for years after the Civil War, the rights of blacks actually went backwards. Their chances of voting in Virginia, for example, diminished under successive revisions of the state constitution, which might have pleased Thomas Jefferson, if not George Mason. It was only when the civil rights movement developed its own version of *satyagraha* that legislators were emboldened to pass laws and police chiefs felt compelled to uphold those laws, opening polling booths, churches, buses, diners and schools to all races.

The twentieth century taught us that *satyagraha* works against almost any opponents: racist governors in the Deep South, Communist Party bosses in Eastern Europe, generals in Burma, stubborn Boers in South Africa. It takes leaders of extraordinary courage and stamina, such as Martin Luther King, Nelson Mandela and Aung San Suu Kyi – all declared admirers of the Mahatma, although Gandhi would have had something to say about the treatment of the Rohingya – to stick with it until they do overcome. But the basic techniques are always the same: peaceful protest, civil disobedience (civil in two senses: non-military and non-rude), no demonization of opponents, appeal to the spirit and the letter of the law, readiness to suffer hardship and imprisonment without bitterness. Gandhi's techniques.

In a worldwide study in 2011, the human rights organization Freedom House calculated that of sixty-seven countries that had made the transition to democracy, civic resistance had been the key strategy in at least fifty. In nine out of ten of these resistance movements, there was a strong bottom-up component. And two-thirds of the successful countries had resistance movements that were wedded to non-violent methods. Resistance movements which used violence were much less successful. Of course, non-violence hasn't always achieved permanent results – in the Arab Spring, for example – any more than it always worked for Gandhi. But at the very least the failed initiatives have laid down a marker for future reprise.

The great events of the last years of the twentieth century – the fall of the Berlin Wall, the collapse of communism and of apartheid – came as a total surprise to almost all of us, including those who had all their lives been hoping for them to happen. It seemed implausible that such granite regimes should so quietly implode. The guns, the tanks, the barbed wire looked so solid, so impregnable. Nobody could imagine that it would all end with a whimper, not a bang.

We had forgotten Gandhi.

XII

MUHAMMAD IQBAL

and the dream of Islam

THE MUSLIM TOTAL ECLIPSE

The slaughter in the trenches was terrible, but the aftershock of the Great War was terrible too. By the day of the Armistice in November 1918, three great empires had crashed, leaving behind rage and resentment that were to take the rest of the century to burn out. For us in the West, the implosion of the Russian, the Austro-Hungarian and the German Empires within a year of each other was such a relentless, all-consuming spectacle that we had little attention left to spare for the fourth collapse. Yet today, a hundred years later, it is the fallout from the end of the Ottoman Empire that haunts us.

For millions of Muslims everywhere, this was the greatest heart-ache. Their allegiance to the Sultan in Constantinople as their Caliph might be largely nominal, sentimental even, but it occupied a part of their hearts and would not go away lightly. From the Muslim perspective, Sultan Mehmed's abdication in 1922 was only the final piece in a pattern of malign events, in which the Great Powers seemed engaged in a conspiracy, whether tacit or deliberate, to destroy Muslim power and independence all over the world.

In 1911, France had assumed control over Morocco. In October that same year, Italy bombarded Tripoli and took over most of present-day Libya. By the following year, Bulgaria, Greece, Montenegro and Serbia had not only achieved their independence from the Ottoman Empire but felt strong enough to form themselves into a Balkan League and seize Turkey's remaining European territories.

These successive hammer blows were witnessed by the Western powers with unconcealed glee. Ever since Gladstone's campaign against Turkish atrocities in Bulgaria, liberal opinion in the West, fed on a diet of ill-digested classical memories, had been pro-Greece, pro-Christian and anti-Turk, and in a larger sense, anti-Muslim too, or so Muslims could be forgiven for feeling. On the outbreak of the Great War, of the four empires that were destined to collapse, only that of the Ottomans was openly expected or hoped for. Asquith, the British prime minister, told the House of Commons on 9 November 1914: 'I do not hesitate to predict that the Ottoman government will perish by the sword. It is they and not we who have rung the death knell for Ottoman dominion, not only in Europe but in Asia. With the disappearance of Turkey, there will disappear, as I hope and believe, the blight which for generations past has withered some of the fairest regions.' Turkey was not only 'the sick man of Europe'– a thought first voiced by Czar Nicholas I back in 1853 – she had become rotten, corrupt and oppressive, a patient who now deserved to be put out of her misery and her wretched subjects rescued from theirs.

Muslims beyond the borders of the Ottoman Empire had reason to be gloomy too. Lord Crewe, the secretary of state for India, claimed that 'Mahomedan opinion in India remains fairly steady simply because it is in a state of confusion about the future, and has by no means squarely faced the prospect, tolerably obvious and not unwelcome to us, of the final exit of the last great Muslim power.' (Quoted Niemeijer, p. 120) But Crewe was not himself facing the full reality. Ever since 1857, Muslims in India had seen only a grim future. They had lost the proud glitter and the lucrative employments of the Moghul courts. They felt distrusted by the Raj, although thousands of Hindus too had fought against the British in the Great Mutiny. Under the new colonial regime, Hindus were embarrassingly more agile in taking advantage of the new commercial opportunities. Even the movement for Indian independence seemed to the Muslims as much a threat as a promise. Hindus outnumbered Muslims by three to one, and the supposedly non-denominational Indian National Congress looked increasingly like a Hindu nationalist movement. The founding of the Muslim League in 1906 seemed like a feeble counterweight. Its first move was for the League's President, the Aga Khan, to demand separate electorates for the Muslims in the new elections for the provincial councils, for fear they would otherwise be swamped. The British were only too happy to oblige, thankful that the traditional imperial 'divide and rule' tactic was, on this occasion, being suggested by the ruled rather than the rulers.

Meanwhile, to the north and west, the Raj had beaten the Afghans to a standstill in the Third Afghan War. Britain was extending her influence over Iran in pursuit of the recently discovered oil deposits. And to the north, the Muslim provinces of Russia, which had been ravaged by the Cossacks for centuries, were soon to find that conscription into the new USSR was no kinder to their faith or their prosperity. In the Middle East, the Treaty of Sèvres in 1920 executed an Anglo-French carve-up, by imposing multiple mandates under the League of Nations, over Palestine and Iraq for Britain, and over Syria and Lebanon for France. These protectorates soon became indistinguishable from colonies, and rebels in any of them were liable to be bombed by the protecting power – the first systematic bombing of civilian populations. It was small consolation for Indian Muslims that General Allenby's troops who occupied Palestine and much of Syria and Mesopotamia (soon to become Iraq) were overwhelmingly Muslims of the Indian Army.

One can only gasp that thirty-odd years later, the French and the British (now plus the Israelis) should have chosen Sèvres again to sign up to another carve-up, this time of Egypt and the Suez Canal. But then tact was never a forte of the Great Powers. We ridiculed George W. Bush for awaking painful memories by describing his War on Terror as 'a crusade'. Rather worse, I think, were General Allenby's reported words on entering Jerusalem: 'The wars of the Crusades are now complete.'

Most painful of all for the Muslims was the Balfour Declaration of 1917 that a homeland must be found for the Jews, and not in Uganda or Madagascar or one of the other far-away places that had been suggested, but in Palestine, sacred territory to Muslims as well as to Christians and Jews. Arthur Balfour was, it should be added, moved not just by humane instincts but by cloudier emotions in which an anti-Muslim streak was clearly visible. He too looked forward to the 'setting free of the populations subject to the tyranny of the Turks; and the turning out of Europe of the Ottoman Empire as decidedly foreign to Western civilization'. (Niemeijer, p. 80)

THE POET OF TODAY, YESTERDAY AND TOMORROW

In this murky outlook that greeted them at every corner of the compass, Muslims looked for consolation. And they found it, in abundance, in the shape of a young poet from the Punjab. To this day, Muhammad Iqbal is regarded as the greatest poet to write in Urdu after Ghalib, and one of the greatest to write in Persian since Hafiz. He is revered as the man who invented the idea of Pakistan, and who gave hope to Muslims everywhere. In Pakistan, 9 November is Iqbal Day, his birthday. Throughout his poetry, Iqbal rehearses the historic grievances of Islam; he recalls the great days of the caliphates; and he promises that greater days will come again for the faithful, if only they get up off their knees. He was not exaggerating when he claimed:

> I have no need of the ear of To-day,
> I am the voice of the poet of To-morrow. (*Secrets*, p. 3)

It is hard to exaggerate the impact of his verse, even in translation (although he was lucky in his translators). It is at the same time sweetly lyrical, caustic, sulphurous and soaring. He uses the traditional poetic vocabulary of roses and nightingales, moonbeams and dewdrops, familiar to English readers from Omar Khayyam, but there is none of the *Rubaiyat*'s amiable fatalism. This is poetry tooled up for action, contemptuous of the languors of 'art for art's sake'.

Muhammad Iqbal was born in 1877, in Sialkot, in the northern Punjab, near the border with Kashmir. Here the wounds of the recent past were as raw as anywhere in India. His family, like many others then living in Sialkot, were originally Kashmiri and had fled the vicious misrule of the Dogra dynasty. Again, like many others, they had converted generations earlier from Hinduism (as many as 75–90 per cent of Indian Muslims were estimated to have come from convert families). Sialkot was a prominent military station and had been chosen as one of the three testing stations for the new cartridges that caused so much anguish to Hindus and Muslims alike. For this reason, it was one of the first stations to erupt in open mutiny. The ferocious Brigadier John Nicholson virtually wiped out the rebellious cavalry at a ford on the river Ravi, called Trimu Ghat, shooting stragglers on the water like sitting ducks. The Ravi often flows through Iqbal's lyrics, but never, I think, streaked with blood as it was on that day.

Iqbal's first verses were unashamedly patriotic. In 1904, 'Our Homeland', or 'Song of India', as it was later known, became an an instant hit, with its opening line – 'Our country, India, is the best in the whole world' – possibly inspired by *'Deutschland über Alles'*, although Iqbal did not actually visit Germany until four years later, in the course of his studies at Trinity College, Cambridge. Like Gandhi, he was an example of how a talented lad from a modest background could, with a bit of luck and a local whip-round, get to university or law school in England. His father, Nur Muhammad, was an unambitious man who made caps for veils and occasionally had Sufi-style visions. In Cambridge, Iqbal mingled with McTaggart and Russell; he delved into the mysteries of space time with Eddington; in Germany he was bewitched by Bergson and Nietzsche. No poet of the twentieth century, not even Eliot, can have been better read in Western philosophy. And no poet of the twentieth century can have been more determined to discard most of what he read. He boasted that 'I broke the spell of modern learning, I took away the bait and broke the trap'. (*Tulip*, p. 155) He urged others not to be seduced either:

> I will take nothing from Europe, except – a warning!
> You enchained to the imitation of Europe, be free,
> Clutch the skirt of the Koran, and be free! (*Javid Nama*,
>   I, 1270)

Today, Iqbal's 'Song of India' is the official quick march of the Indian Army, set to music by Ravi Shankar. (Sevea, p. 209) His next venture in the patriotic line was unlikely to be adopted by any Indian regiment. The Islamic community's song begins: 'We are Muslims, the whole world is our country'. (Mir, p. 11) Iqbal's fateful journey from nationalism to pan-Islamic supranationalism is contained in those two contrasting opening lines.

His verse soon came to encompass the setbacks and sufferings of Muslims in every community. In 'Before the Prophet's Throne', he mourned the bombing of Libya and 'the martyred blood of Tripoli'. (*Poems*, p. 68) When Iqbal read the poem to a congregation of a thousand in the Imperial Mosque, Lahore, many, including the poet, were in tears at the thought of the suffering of their faraway fellow Muslims. After the French bombed Damascus in 1925, Iqbal poured scorn upon the building of a mosque in Paris, for who had built this 'palace of idols' but 'the same robbers whose hands have turned Damascus into a desert'? ('Paris Mosque', *Poems*, p. 73)

He mocked the contrast between the moral pretensions of the Europeans and the brutality of their colonial actions. Europeans shed hypocritical tears for all peoples groaning under oppression. But Syria and Palestine, supposedly freed from the 'savage grasp' of the Turks, were now 'pining, poor things, in the clutches of "civilization"' – that is, of their French and British occupiers under the mandates of the League of Nations. ('Civilization's Clutches', *Poems*, p. 76)

In his epic poem, *Javid Nama*, Iqbal creates his own version of Dante's *Divine Comedy* (its own form probably drawn from an earlier Arab model). Iqbal's alter ego, Zinda Rud ('living stream'), is guided by the medieval poet Rumi through the planets, meeting heroes and traitors, travelling through hells and utopias. He meets among others Pharaoh and Lord Kitchener, both drowned for their sins. In the presence of the Persian mystic Shah-i-Hamadan, he laments the fate of his own Kashmiri people under alien Hindu rule:

> My soul burns like rue for the people of the Vale ...
> The lament in my flute is on their behalf.
> Since they have lost their share of selfhood
> They have become strangers in their own land ...
>   (*Javid Nama*, II, 2901)

India, his family's country of adoption, was no more to be envied under British rule. India seemed fated to permanent occupation by a foreign power, 'always the brightest jewel in someone's crown'. ('Reproach', *Poems*, p. 96)

Nor were the modernizers of the Muslim world entirely acceptable to Iqbal. The ambitious army officers who had fought their way to the top in Turkey and Iran were not to his taste, though he respected their military victories:

> The morning breeze is still in search of a garden,
> Ill lodged in Ataturk or Reza Shah,
> The soul of the East is still in search of a body. ('The East',
>   *Poems*, No. 87)

That sort of secular renewal – commercial collaboration with the West, using Western script, banning the fez (Iqbal's preferred headgear) – did not bring the soul renewal that he had in mind. Ataturk (formerly Mustafa Kemal) is singled out in *Javid Nama*. He sang of a great renewal, but

> No, the Turks have no new melody in their lute,
> What they call new is only the old tune of Europe.
>   (*Javid Nama*, II, 1117)

What Iqbal wanted all his life was the old tune of Islam. His most powerful lyrics of all are exercises in nostalgia, yearnings for the great days of medieval Islam. When he stands in the Great Mosque of Cordoba, now a Christian cathedral (as indeed it had been before the Moors conquered Cordoba), he looks back to the glories of Moorish Spain:

> Even today in its breeze fragrance of Yemen still floats,
> Even today in its songs echoes live on of Hejaz.
> Under the stars your realm lies like a heaven; alas!
> Ages are fled since your courts heard their last prayer-call
>   sound ... ('The Mosque of Cordoba', *Poems*, p. 41)

Perhaps the most stirring of these souvenir poems is 'Sicily', where he links all the lost glories to a project of renewal. The nightingale voices of the poets have shed bitter tears for the fate of Baghdad and Delhi and Granada. Now it is his turn to bring their glories back to life:

> So to sorrow with you fate has chosen Iqbal ...
> Tell your grief then to me, who am grief ...
> Stir my veins – let the picture glow bright with fresh colour,
>   the ancient days' record declare!
> I go with your gift to the Indies and I who
> weep here will make others weep there. ('Sicily', *Poems*,
>   pp. 13–14)

And not simply make them weep, but stir them to action. For what had been could be again, renewed and refreshed. The Western bourgeoisie might seem to have the upper hand, but all was not lost:

> But now come! For ways are changing in the assembly of
>   the earth
> And in Orient and Occident your own age comes to birth.
> From the womb of this old universe, a new red sun is born.
> For extinguished stars, oh heaven, how much longer will you
>   mourn? ('Khizar, the Guide', *Poems*, p. 22)

Even standing in the Great Mosque, the poet is itching to follow the marching bell of the new caravan:

> Destiny's curtain till now muffles the world to be;
> Yet, already, its dawn stands before me unveiled. ('The
>   Mosque of Cordoba', Ibid.)

I have quoted from Iqbal's verse at length, to give some idea of its force and jingle. What needs also to be got across is its unaccommodating insistence on the undiluted faith of the Qur'an.

> Allow the song of this solitary nightingale to pierce through
>   the hearts of the listeners!
> Let the call of this marching bell awake the hearts from
>   deep slumber,
> And be freshened up with a new covenant but thirsting for
>   the same old wine. ('The Complaint', Shafique, p. 73)

The sound of this bell would be heard all over the Muslim world, among the Turkic peoples of central Asia for example. Iqbal was for a time an enthusiast for Enver Bey, the leader of the short-lived pan-Turanian movement, which aimed to unite all the Muslim peoples beyond the Caucasus. In 'The Tartar's Dream', he evokes the ghost of Timur (Tamburlaine):

> Suddenly quivered the dust of Samarkand,
> And from an ancient tomb a light shone, pure
> As the first gleam of daybreak, and a voice
> Was heard: 'I am the spirit of Timur!
> Chains may hold fast the men of Tartary,
> But God's firm purposes no bonds endure:
> ... Call in the soul of man a new fire to birth!
> Cry a new revolution over the earth!' (*Poems*, p. 57)

No wonder Iqbal is still revered across Central Asia. His most recent biography, by Khurram Ali Shafique, comes emblazoned with the official support and the flags of Afghanistan, Azerbaijan, Iran, Kazakhstan, the Kyrgyz Republic, Pakistan, Tajikistan, Turkey, Turkmenistan and Uzbekistan.

The fact that Timur was one of history's great mass murderers does not deter Iqbal at all. He idolizes great Muslim rulers, however cruel, and even if they ruled over non-Muslim populations. By contrast, he damns their betrayers, such as Jafar, who betrayed the Nawab of Bengal to Robert Clive at Plassey, and Sadiq, who betrayed Tipu Sultan to the young Arthur Wellesley at Seringapatam. What Iqbal worships is Muslim power and what he mourns is its loss.

In his first collection to be translated into English, *Asrar-i-Khudi*, or *Secrets of the Self*, he attacks all quietism, especially the sentimental softness of the Sufis; for life was power made manifest, and its mainspring was the desire for victory. Mercy out of season was 'a coldness of Life's blood, a break in the rhythm of Life's music'. (*Secrets*, pp. 91–2)

Again and again, Iqbal emphasizes the need for Muslims to be hard. In his poem 'The Diamond and the Coal', the diamond tells the coal to 'be hard as a stone, be a diamond', for 'In solidity consists the glory of Life; Weakness is worthlessness and immaturity'. (*Secrets*, pp. 105–7)

In leafing back through the Muslim past, Iqbal rejects any hint of liberalism or tolerance, for example, that of the Emperor Akbar, who famously encouraged inter-faith debate in his palace at Fatehpur Sikri, or that of Akbar's great-grandson Dara, who tried to work out a reconciliation between Hinduism and Islam. Instead, Iqbal recommends Dara's brother, the Emperor Aurangzeb (Alamgir), a brute who murdered most of his own family in his devastating wars of conquest:

> When that the impious seed of heresy,
> By Akbar nourished, sprang and sprouted fresh
> In Dara's soul, the candle of the heart
> Was dimmed in every breast, no more secure
> Against corruption, our Community
> Continued; then God chose from India
> That humble-minded warrior, Alamgir,
> Religion to revive, faith to renew,
> The lightning of his sword set all ablaze
> The harvest of impiety. (*Mysteries*, p. 17)

Iqbal insists on the uniformity of Muslim culture. Individual Muslims had a duty thoroughly to assimilate the culture of Islam. 'The object of this assimilation is to create a uniform mental outlook, a peculiar way of looking at the world, a definite standpoint from which to judge the value of things which sharply defines our community, and transforms it into a corporate individual, giving it a definite purpose and ideal of its own.' (*Speeches, Writings and Statements of Iqbal*, ed. L. A. Sherwani, 1977, p. 126) Or, as he put it in 'The Pillars of Islam': 'Peoples must have one thought, and in their minds pursue a single purpose'. (*Mysteries*, p. 12) One cannot help thinking here of the general will that is to prevail in Rousseau's ideal society, or indeed Marx's. Certainly Iqbal, like Rousseau, does not shrink from insisting that people should be 'forced to be free'. For Iqbal, indeed, Rousseau was 'the father of modern political thought'. (Sevea, p. 144)

Just believing was not enough, however: 'Mere belief in the Islamic principle, though exceedingly important, is not sufficient. In order to participate in the life of the communal self, the individual mind must undergo a complete transformation, and this transformation is secured, externally by the institutions of Islam, and internally by the uniform culture which the intellectual energy of our forefathers has produced.' (Shafique, p. 44)

And which forefathers exactly would those be? In his famous *Six Lectures on the Reconstruction of Religious Thought in Islam*, delivered in various Indian cities in 1930, Iqbal makes the answer absolutely clear. He spotlights

a movement of immense potentialities which arose in the 18th century, from the sands of Nejd, described by Macdonald as 'the cleanest spot in the decadent world of Islam'. It is really the first throb of life in modern Islam. To the inspiration of this movement are traceable, directly or indirectly, nearly all the great modern movements of Muslim Asia and Africa, e.g., the Sennusi movement, the Pan-Islamic movement, and the Babi movement, which is only a Persian reflex of Arabian Protestantism. The great puritan reformer, Mohammad Ibn-i-Abdul Wahab, who was born in 1700, studied in Medina, travelled in Persia, and finally succeeded in spreading the fire of his restless soul throughout the whole world of Islam. (pp. 213–14)

The Wahhabi! The hard men of the Arabian desert. Again and again, Iqbal instructs us to follow the Arabs, in thought and lifestyle. We are to beware the subtle fantasies of Persia which have transgressed the boundaries of the Prophet's teaching. Instead, 'conform thyself with Arab ways, to be a Muslim true'. (*Mysteries*, p. 45)

Iqbal was consistently on the side of austerity and the Wahhabi, and so on the side of Ibn Saud in the battle for control of Arabia, for the Saudis had been linked with Ibn Abd al-Wahhabi himself and with his sect from the beginning. The poet had deplored the collusion of Husain, the last Sharif of Mecca, with the British in the Arab war against the Turks in 1916, complaining that 'the lord of Mecca barters the honour of Mecca's faith'. (*Poems*, p. 18)

In reality, Britain was only anxious to back the winning horse in the Arabian stakes, and was willing to promise any party to protect the Holy Places in return for support against the Turks. They were quite happy to switch to Ibn Saud when the Wahhabi lord came out of the Nejd Desert and seized the Holy Places and most of Arabia. His minder, Captain William Shakespear, the political agent in Kuwait, was no less enamoured of this desert hawk than T. E. Lawrence had been of Husain.

Iqbal was anti-British at all times, and it was a surprise to everyone when he accepted a knighthood for his services to poetry in 1922. He did not call himself a Wahhabi, nor an adherent of the other austere sect in the region, the Salafi. Nor was he an unqualified supporter of the Deobandi, the hard-line equivalent in Northern India. What mattered, though, was that he lent his vast prestige as a poet to a purified and puritanical version of Islam. Some thought of him as having liberal tendencies. But the thrust of his poetry – and it is his poetry that makes him the prophet of the Islamic renaissance – was always in praise of hardness and austerity.

Ironically, the Allama, the honorific title awarded to religious scholars by which he is still widely known, was personally a rather indolent character, married three times, quite portly, fond of lying on his couch with his hookah and gossiping, averse to exercise and charming rather than austere in his manner.

Did his endorsement of the Wahhabi mean, for example, that in Iqbal's ideal Muslim society, the position of women would be much like it is in present-day Saudi Arabia? Well, yes, it did.

He spells this out very clearly in his remarkable lines on mother-hood in 'The Pillars of Islam':

Take any peasant woman, ignorant,
Squat-figured, fat, uncomely, unrefined,
Unlettered, dim of vision, simple, dumb;
The pangs of motherhood have torn her heart,
Dark, tragic rings have underscored her eyes;
If from her bosom the Community
Receive one Muslim zealous for the Faith,
God's faithful servant, all the pains she bore
Have fortified our being, and our dawn
Glows radiant in the lustre of her dusk. (*Mysteries*, p. 64)

This heroic epitome of simple faith is immediately contrasted with
the modern woman:

Now take the slender figure, bosomless,
Close-corseted, a riot in her glance,
Her thoughts resplendent with the Western light;
In outward guise a woman, inwardly
No woman she; she hath destroyed the bonds
That hold our pure Community secure;
Her sacred charms are all unloosed and spilled;
Bold-eyed her freedom is, provocative,
And wholly ignorant of modesty. (Ibid.)

Such a woman is unfitted to be a mother, and no star will shine upon
the evening of her days. In fact:

Better it were this rose had never grown
Within our garden, better were her brand
Washed from the skirt of the Community. (Ibid.)

Iqbal confirms this position in prose: the so-called 'emancipation
of the Western woman' was an experiment likely to fail, but not
before it had done incalculable harm: 'the muslim woman should
continue to occupy the position in society which Islam has allotted
her ... All subjects which have a tendency to de-womanise and to
de-muslimise her must be carefully excluded from her education.'

(Mir, pp. 134–5) We are reminded here of the restricted curriculum that Rousseau proposes for Sophie in *Emile*.

The Allama is proud of the great days of Islamic culture and of Islam's achievements in science and technology. He claims that Islam is open to the future, largely because it looks forward to no new messiah. The finality of the Prophet is at its core. There is no disabling dualism in the faith, no division between matter and spirit. The Qur'an, Iqbal insists, is a very *physical* book. Islam is therefore just as suitable to the modern world as it was to the middle ages. Several Western observers go along with this. Ernest Gellner, for example, agrees that the theology and organization of Islam are 'closer to the ideals and requirements of modernity than those of any other world religion. A strict Unitarianism, a (theoretical) absence of any clergy, hence, in principle, equidistance of all believers from the deity, a strict scripturalism and stress on orderly law-observance, a sober religiosity, avoiding ecstasy and the audio-visual aids of religion – all these features seem highly congruent with an urban bourgeois life style and with commercialism.' (*Plough, Sword and Book*, 1988, p. 216)

But at the same time, there is an undeniable, indeed self-vaunted, exclusiveness and a harshness and rigidity about the Wahhabi version of the faith, which Iqbal recommends so passionately. This comes unmistakably to the fore when Iqbal addresses the great question of his day, and ours: what sort of state should Muslims aspire to live in?

THE LOST CALIPH

The recent pretensions of so-called ISIS to restore the medieval Caliphate are widely ridiculed. An institution buried under the rubble of centuries surely hasn't a hope of resurrection. It tends to be forgotten, except by historians, that the Caliphate (or Khilafat) was a live issue in much more recent times. After the Turkish defeat in the Great War, a movement to save the Caliphate began in India, under the energetic leadership of the Ali brothers, Muhammad Ali and Shaukat Ali. In the interests of Hindu–Muslim unity, Gandhi, who knew and liked the brothers, engineered the support of the

Indian National Congress for the cause, although of course it was of
no interest at all to Hindus. A delegation was despatched to London
led by Muhammad Ali. Lloyd George and Curzon could not have
been less interested, and preferred to complain about Turkish
atrocities in Greece and Armenia. The Central Khilafat Committee
(CKC) resolved on a policy of non-co-operation with the Raj. The
results were feeble. Few Indians wanted to give up their jobs or hand
back their medals. There was another delegation to London with
equally wretched results. The whole campaign fizzled out in 1924
when Ataturk gained control and the Turkish National Assembly
abolished the Caliphate.

Iqbal had shown early sympathy for the movement and served
as the secretary of the Punjab branch of the CKC for a time, but
like many others he came to think of this sort of pan-Islamism as
'moonshine', an iridescent bubble that sooner or later was bound
to pop. Other prominent Muslims were harsher. Jinnah called it
'a false religious frenzy' which could bring no benefit to India in
general or to Muslims in particular. Iqbal himself resigned, fed up
with the naivety of the CKC leaders.

Yet the brief flowering of this rather absurd campaign did leave a
few things behind: a yearning for Muslim solidarity beyond national
borders for one thing, and a sharper consciousness of the discomfort
of living in a nation where Muslims were in a minority and where
the majority wanted to highlight its own culture. If Muslims no
longer had any loyalty to a non-existent Caliph in a distant country,
what precisely was the loyalty they owed to the state they actually
lived in?

THE INVENTION OF PAKISTAN

What was to be done? In 1930, in his *Six Lectures*, Iqbal set out the
realities as he saw them: 'The idea of Universal Imamate has failed
in practice. It was a workable idea when the Empire of Islam was
intact. Since the break-up of this Empire independent political units
have arisen. The idea has ceased to be operative and cannot work
as a living factor in the organization of modern Islam.' (p. 221) In
fact, these ruptures appeared between Muslim states 'for the sake

of a mere symbol of power which departed long ago'. The logical conclusion was that 'For the present every Moslem nation must sink into her own deeper self, temporarily focus her vision on herself alone, until all are strong enough to form a living family of republics.' (Ibid., p. 223)

So far, so good. But what was a Moslem nation exactly? In his famous address as president to the All-India Muslim League that same year, Iqbal argued that Islam is not like Christianity. It isn't a religion of private conscience and private practice. It comes with its own intrinsic code of law and creates a certain kind of social order. The religious ideal cannot be separated from the social order. 'Therefore, the construction of a polity on national lines, if it means a displacement of the Islamic principle of solidarity, is simply unthinkable to a Muslim.' (Anjum, p. 203)

V. S. Naipaul, in *Beyond Belief*, describes this as 'an extraordinary speech for a thinking man to have made in the twentieth century. What Iqbal is saying in an involved way is that Muslims can live only with other Muslims ... What is really in the background of this demand for Pakistan and a Muslim polity, what isn't mentioned, is Iqbal's rejection of Hindu India.' (p. 269)

Later in this same speech, Iqbal takes the issue head on:

> The Muslim demand for the creation of a Muslim India within India is, therefore, perfectly justified ... I would like to see the Punjab, North-West Frontier Province, Sind and Baluchistan amalgamated into a single State. Self-government within the British Empire, or without the British Empire, the formation of a consolidated North-West Indian Muslim State appears to be the final destiny of the Muslims ... I therefore demand the formation of a consolidated Muslim State in the best interests of India and Islam. (Anjum, pp. 205–7)

This is the moment from which the invention of Pakistan is often dated and accordingly credited to Iqbal. He died of kidney failure in 1938 and so never lived to see the birth of his country. He does not in fact refer to Pakistan by name (the first traceable usage of that word appears to come four years later). Nor does he refer to what was to become East Pakistan at all. Nor was he the first person to call for partition. That credit or discredit goes, oddly enough, to a fiery Hindu Nationalist, Lala Lajpat Rai, who in 1924 proposed 'a clear partition of India into a Muslim India and a non-Muslim India'. Lala Lajpat Rai also broke fresh and bloody ground by suggesting that Punjab and Bengal should both be partitioned and that the populations of Hindus and Muslims should be transferred on a massive scale. (Shafique, pp. 115–17) Iqbal later dipped his own toe into those murky waters. In a letter to Jinnah in 1937, he did say that 'it is obvious that the only way to a peaceful India is a redistribution of the country, on the lines of racial, religious and linguistic affinities'. (Anjum, p. 227) The idea that such a 'redistribution' could be peaceful could occur only to a poet. But then it may be possible that poets have less moral imagination than other people.

Had the Allama not paused to consider his own family's personal experience of the pain, loss and upheaval involved in migrating from Kashmir to the Punjab, or how this would be multiplied a millionfold by the simultaneous jostling of two huge communities, or how intercommunal violence on a horrific scale would be inevitable? The suspicion must be that the Allama had not paused to think at all. Enough for him to have thrown his enormous prestige behind a terrifying idea, which from then on became thinkable for the first time.

As Iqbal Singh points out in *The Ardent Pilgrim*, one of the few even faintly critical biographies of Iqbal that anyone has dared to publish: 'There is more here, in fact, than contradiction and inconsistency. There is self-deception, unconscious, subtle but unmistakable self-deception. This applies both to Iqbal himself, in so far as he associated himself with the Pakistan demand and those who turn to Iqbal's philosophy for ideological justification of Pakistan. The underlying argument in both is crudely demagogic, though it might be phrased in the most glittering language of idealism.' (p. 161) 'In reality he succeeded only in stimulating the growth of a very virulent species of nationalism among his community.' (Ibid., p. 234)

All the Allama's public prestige had been poured into his backing for the idea that Muslims could and should live in an exclusively

Muslim state, where Islam was not only the state religion but also its governing ideology, with *sharia* overseen and enforced by a council of religious scholars. Iqbal tried to brush aside the accusation that he was calling for theocracy, claiming that 'in this sense all state, not based on mere domination and aiming at the realization of ideals, is theocratic.' (*Six Lectures*, p. 217)

But this is mere quibbling. As Naipaul points out, 'there was something else that Iqbal had never considered: that in the new state the nature of history would alter, and with that altering of the historical sense, the intellectual life of the country would inevitably be diminished. The mullahs would always hold the ring. All the history of the ancient land would cease to matter. In the school history books, or the school "civics" books, the history of Pakistan would become only an aspect of the history of Islam.' (p. 329)

THE GRATITUDE OF THE AYATOLLAHS

Just how much a real live theocracy owes to Iqbal is shown by his huge popularity, amounting to hero worship, in Iran. The ayatollahs today proudly acknowledge their debt to the poet from Lahore. The current supreme leader, Ayatollah Ali Khamenei, opened the first conference on Iqbal in Teheran in 1986 by declaring that in its 'conviction that the Qur'an and Islam are to be made the basis of all revolutions and movements', Iran was 'exactly following the path that was shown to us by Iqbal'. (Sevea, p. 210) The chief ideologue of the revolution, Ali Shariati, describes Iqbal as the figure who brought a message of 'rejuvenation', 'awakening' and 'power' to the Muslim world. The poet's work was in itself a 'jihad' for their salvation. Iqbal had not fallen into the fallacies of Marxism or modernism; he had provided the model for a purified but this-worldly Islam that could hold its own against the West.

Iqbal would not have disdained any of this praise. He had, after all, written a poem entitled 'Jehad', in which he lamented that 'in our world now the sword has no more virtue' and 'our hearts have lost all memory of delight in death'. ('Jehad', *Poems*, p. 62)

THE BLOOD-RED PLANET

There is no hindsight involved in recognizing Iqbal as a forerunner of the frightful rhetoric and practice of Islamic terrorists today. Right from the beginning, even his translators quailed. Reynold Nicholson in 1920 warns his readers that Iqbal, then quite unknown in the West, was 'a religious enthusiast, inspired by the vision of a new Mecca, a world-wide theocratic utopian state in which all Moslems, no longer divided by the barriers of race and country, shall be one.' (*Secrets*, X) The book had taken the younger generation of Moslems by storm, and they regarded Iqbal as their messiah. Nicholson wondered whether those admirers would be satisfied by a distant vision of the City of God. Iqbal denounced nationalism, but his admirers were already protesting that he did not mean what he said.

Thirty years later, after the catastrophe of partition, a no less distinguished translator of Iqbal, Arthur Arberry, warned in his introduction of the 'revival lately of the spirit of irreconcilable hostility which found its most dramatic and bloody expression in the crusades'. (*Mysteries*, xiii) He points out Iqbal's oversimplification, stridency and dogmatism: 'When a politician poses and is accepted as a prophet, it is irresponsible of him to continue to indulge in the puerilities of the soap-box, unless he is ambitious, like Hitler, to stage a fantastic *Götterdämmerung*.' (Ibid., xiv) It was because of Iqbal and his fellow militants that 'we live in dangerous times, and may well be heading for the greatest collision since Richard fought Saladin'. (Ibid., xvi) And this from an admirer of Iqbal's poetry who had devoted years to the most exquisite Englishing of it.

The implications of Iqbal's rhetoric were grasped at once by his first English reviewers. E. M. Forster, writing in the *Athenaeum* in December 1920, spotted that Iqbal had been energized by Nietzsche: 'He tries to find, in that rather shaky ideal of the Superman, a guide through the intricacy of conduct. His couplets urge us to be hard and live dangerously, tigers, not sheep; we are to beware of those sheep who, fearing our claws, come forward with the doctrine of vegetarianism . . . we are to shun culture. And though love is indeed good, it has nothing to do with Mercy.'

Goldie Lowes Dickinson, writing in *The Nation* that same month, is harsher. He too fingers Nietzsche as the source of Iqbal's hard-man act: 'The doctrine of hardness, of individuality, of the need of conflict and of the benefit of an enemy run all through the poem.' Lowes Dickinson is quite right about this. Iqbal's dialogue between the coal and the diamond is lifted straight from *Also Sprach Zarathustra*. Lowes Dickinson goes on: 'Only Moslems are worthy of the Kingdom. The rest of the world is either to be absorbed or excluded. And the emphasis on personality, the contempt for mysticism and quietism, the call to conflict and hardness, is the appeal of a patriot to an oppressed people to rise and assert themselves. Quite clearly Mr Iqbal desires and looks forward to a Holy War, and that a war of arms.'

Writing in *The Nation*'s Christmas issue, Lowes Dickinson concludes by suggesting that, after the horror of the Great War, wistful Westerners might be once more looking for a star in the East. 'What do they find? Not the star of Bethlehem, but this blood-red planet.' (24 December 1920)

After these reviews reached him, Iqbal protested that he had not got it all out of Nietzsche. In fact, he had written on the Sufi doctrine of the Perfect Man long before he had ever heard of Nietzsche. But the indictment sticks. These bloodshot poems have nothing of the Sufi about them, and a great deal of Nietzsche's vatic, overwrought, pseudo-Biblical rhetoric. The mild herbivores of old Bloomsbury had got Iqbal's number right from the start. The tragedy is that so few of his fellow Muslims realized where he was leading them. The most charitable assumption is that Iqbal probably didn't either. Blindness goes with being a bard, after all. Poesy's wings are indeed viewless, just not in the sense that Keats intended.

In praise of trade-off

The hopes were so high, the ambition so exhilarating, and the logic so irresistible. If science could unlock the secrets of nature, why could it not also find the key to human social relations? If painstaking research could predict the movements of the planets, unearth the upheavals of rocks millions of years ago, explain the evolution of the birds and the bees, not to mention of Man himself, surely to construct a science of politics would be a doddle. We have seen how Jeremy Bentham could scarcely wait to introduce the restless, inquisitive spirit of the natural sciences into the new moral sciences of law, politics and economics.

The Prime Movers were not content with old Aristotle's snail's-pace accumulation of evidence, nor with Montesquieu's cautious description of how societies actually worked. Rousseau for one decried Montesquieu for failing to make that crucial leap from 'is' to 'ought'. Which is another way of saying what Marx was to say, that 'philosophers have only interpreted the world; the task, however, is to change it'. Movers wanted to persuade people into the right path, to teach them how to organize their societies, and to reinforce their advice with the authority of science.

Most of them had a strong sense of being pioneers, of being the first to glimpse the Promised Land. 'The science of politics is in its infancy,' Mary Wollstonecraft declared, with the implication that her generation was fated to bring it to maturity. Rousseau's Emile tells us that 'the science of political right is yet to be born, and it is to be presumed that it never will be born'. But Rousseau himself never lacked the confidence that his Legislator would be a supreme engineer of souls.

The most conspicuous claim to scientific authority was that advanced by Marx, and more stridently after his death by Engels. Ever since, Marxist politicians and propagandists have spoken of 'scientific socialism', as though the existence of such a thing were an accomplished fact. Yet as Karl Popper pointed out in *The Open Society* (and by implication in *The Logic of Scientific Discovery*), Marxism bears few marks of true science: it seems to offer few falsifiable theses, tends to be slippery and slapdash in its terminology, and prefers denunciation to critical debate. Nothing could be less like Darwin's painstaking measurement of finches and minute examination of the nocturnal habits of worms.

Yet posterity has, to a large extent, taken Marxism at its own valuation. The same is true of capitalism and Utilitarianism. The great spokesmen of these creeds are accepted as unimpeachable precursors of the Modern. Their works are re-edited and republished in enormous collected editions, often with little close reading or genuine critique.

One of the most striking things about them is what a narrow time-belt so many of them were born into. Half of my chosen Movers were born within fifty years of each other, between 1710 and 1760. The remarkable period of their flowering in the second half of the eighteenth century has sometimes been tagged as 'the Birth of the Modern'. By this historians and political analysts mean the dawning of a consciousness that we can recognize more or less as our own. It is a particularly self-conscious sort of consciousness, which is aware of its sharp difference from 'traditional' society and rather proud of that difference.

Yet if we have learnt anything from the Prime Movers, it is surely to question the notion that there is a single modernity. Nothing is more glaring than how conflicting and diverse are these Modernities struggling to be born. In the commotions of their own times, they were already viciously at odds: Burke against Rousseau, Wollstonecraft against Burke, Bentham against Burke and vice versa. These quarrels have not diminished in intensity with the years.

The division of labour, for example. For Adam Smith, it is the beginning of civilization and progress. For Rousseau, it is the greatest calamity to have afflicted mankind. Today, neo-liberalism, as its enemies call it, is founded on the endless specialization, the unfettered play of the free market. The haters of industrial capitalism look forward as keenly as Marx and Rousseau ever did to abolishing the division of labour and restoring Man to his natural wholeness.

For the dominant tradition in the West, to be modern is to live in a society that is drained of religious meaning and in which public life is wholly secular. For millions of Muslims, by contrast, religion is at the heart of the civic order, just as Iqbal said it should be. If Marx would have been happy to see the extirpation of religion from politics in the West, he has had no such luck in persuading posterity that nationhood is a pernicious illusion. From the moment that the German Socialists voted for war credits in 1914, nation has always trumped class. Yet intellectuals remain reluctant to confront the reality that nationality is a prime component of modernity.

Even gender today no longer looks such a settled question. The vanguard of sexual modernists has moved on from an ideal of equality between the sexes to a new ideal of gender fluidity, in which gender becomes something freely alterable and self-chosen, not an indwelling given.

Modernity in general begins to look less like a comfortable terminus in which we can catch our breath and congratulate ourselves on having arrived safely, and more like a camp pitched on a windswept slope under enemy fire.

We have, in short, a double problem, one that gets worse the more Prime Movers you look at, and the deeper you go into their thought. Not only are even the greatest of these doctrines defective in themselves; their core principles are stubbornly and irremediably in conflict with one another. I am constantly amazed that it should have taken us so long to acknowledge this fact. Again and again, political commentators have tried to argue away these conflicts, to insist that at some higher level they can be brought into a gratifying synthesis. Take the notorious conflict between freedom and equality. Repeatedly, philosophers of socialism, most notably R. H. Tawney, have insisted that 'real freedom' is actually part of 'real equality'. Far from being in conflict, Tawney tells us, one is inconceivable without the other. This seems to stretch the meaning of freedom beyond the realms of the plausible. As Isaiah Berlin argued in a legendary footnote:

> Nothing is gained by a confusion of terms. To avoid glaring inequality or widespread misery I am ready to sacrifice some or all of my freedom: I may do so willingly and freely: but it is freedom that I am giving up for the sake of justice or equality or the love of my fellow men. I should be guilt-stricken, and rightly so, if I were not, in some circumstances, ready to make this sacrifice. But a sacrifice is not an increase in what is being sacrificed, namely freedom, however great the moral need or the compensation for it. Everything is what it is: liberty is liberty, not equality or fairness or justice or human happiness or a quiet conscience. (*Two Concepts of Liberty*, 1958, p. 103fn; *The Proper Study of Mankind*, 1997, p. 197)

Isaiah Berlin's underlying argument is that many desirable values, each of them precious to us in itself, are simply 'incommensurable', or incompatible, with one another. We find this hard to accept. For we have as a species an incurable longing to find a single valid answer to the problems of living together – a Theory of Everything, or TOE, as the scientists call it. But in political life at least, no such TOE exists. We are stuck with contradiction and diversity. And we are more likely to find workable solutions if we recognize this reality and work with it, rather than against it.

Berlin's critics – and there have been quite a few, both on the left and on the right – argue that his attitude leads him, whether he likes it or not, into an uncomfortable relativism, from which he is powerless to escape. If any political value, or set of values, is as good as any other, then how can Berlin justify the liberalism he himself so passionately believes in, or the Zionism that he also passionately believes in (and that looks sure to collide with the liberalism)? But this is a caricature of Berlin's view. He isn't saying that any of these principles is as good as any other, depending on the circumstances. What he is saying is that each of them has genuine enduring worth, but we should not conclude from this that they can always be reconciled with one another, because very often they can't.

In any case, the position of the absolute believer is an uncomfortable one too. How can his preferred principle claim to be universally valid if it has not met the challenge of rival principles, if he has not argued through, in good faith, the differences between them, and accepted any modification or compromise that may turn out to be necessary? How can the absolutist know he is in the right if he has not joined the free conversation of ideas? Yet this is just what most if not all Prime Movers will not do. They refuse to engage with their critics, acknowledging their existence only to denounce them in the most vituperative style. Instead, they declaim at the top of their voices that theirs is the only wisdom that dissolves all conflicts and solves all man's problems.

This is a claim that Berlin sharply disputes:

It seems to me that the belief that some single formula can in principle be found whereby all the diverse ends of man can be harmoniously realized is demonstrably false. If, as I believe, the ends of life are many, and not all of them are in principle compatible with each other, then the possibility of conflict – and of tragedy – can never wholly be eliminated from human life, either personal or social. The necessity of choosing between absolute claims is then an inescapable characteristic of the human condition.' (*The Proper Study of Mankind*, p. 237)

That is what freedom is for, not because it makes us happier or morally better but because it enables us to choose, which is part of being human.

In modern times, it is Berlin who has put this argument most memorably. But though the argument is a rarity, it is not a complete novelty. Rather, it is an insight that is fitfully glimpsed, and only by those who have paused to reflect carefully on the nature of politics. At times, Edmund Burke can himself be as tendentious as any other Mover; he will caricature his opponents, select the evidence to suit his case, ignore unhelpful data. Yet in one of the quieter passages of his *Reflections on the Revolution in France*, he catches the unavoidable complexity of politics brilliantly. The task of a statesman is, he says, to 'see that the parts of the system do not clash' and that 'the evils latent in the most promising contrivances are provided for as they arise'. There have to be trade-offs, to use our modern term for it. The aim should be that 'one advantage is as little as possible sacrificed to another. We compensate, we reconcile, we balance. We are enabled to unite into a consistent whole the various anomalies and contending principles that are found in the minds and affairs of men.' Successful nations were not remarkable for the elegant simplicity of their political systems. What they could boast of was 'not an excellence in simplicity, but one far superior, an excellence in composition'. (*Works*, V, p. 306)

We can in fact go back to the dawn of political thought and find something very similar in Aristotle's *Politics*. As we have seen in the chapter on Pericles and the invention of democracy, Aristotle set his students to research all the different constitutions of the Greek city states scattered across the Aegean at the time. There were said to be no less than 158 of these studies, but only one of them has survived in full, the study of the Athenian constitution. It is to this survival that we owe much of our knowledge of how politics actually worked in Athens. The whole research programme was a remarkable exercise in the study of comparative political institutions, probably the first ever.

Aristotle did not undertake that programme in order to award a laurel wreath to the best type of constitution. He wanted to draw out the features from the wealth of material collected that *together* made for good government. It was to be an effort that might best be described as 'syncretic' or 'synthetic', joining together diverse elements in a new compound.

For the ancient Greeks who coined these words, they described useful and even admirable things; *synkretizo*, for example, means 'combine in the face of a common enemy'. But modern speech has given them a sourer connotation of 'artificial' or 'false'. The *OED* describes the applications of 'syncretic' to philosophy or religion as 'almost always derogatory'. By contrast, Aristotle himself tells us that 'they are nearer the truth who combine many forms; for the state is better which is made up of more numerous elements'. (*Politics*, II, 6.18) 'Some people say that the best constitution is a combination of all existing forms, and they praise the Spartan version, because it is made up of oligarchy, monarchy and democracy.' (II, 6.17) For us in modern Britain, the government can be seen as the monarchic element, the Parliament as the democratic element, and the judges and other public authorities provide the oligarchic element. Aristotle would have had no patience with the *Daily Mail*'s description of the Appeal Court judges as 'enemies of the people' for condemning as illegal the government's action in presuming to trigger Article 50 in the Brexit process without consulting Parliament. For him, this would have been a perfect example of a mixed tripartite system in action. He uses the word *memeigmenen*, an inflection of the verb *mignumi*, from which we derive 'mix'; he also uses *synkeisthai*, 'lie together' or 'fit together' like the bones of a skeleton.

We shouldn't think that Aristotle is starry-eyed about the Spartans or their system. They were inclined to corruption and to make war on their neighbours (though the Athenians were just as bad). In any case, their democratic manners might derive more from their social habits of dining together and living in intimacy than from their system of government. Aristotle always tries to pay close attention to the facts on the ground as opposed to the theory. And it is his repeated criticism of his old master, Plato, that the blueprints of *The Republic* and *The Laws* do not correspond to the realities of human experience. You feel that if Plato had not been his tutor, he would have been a good deal harsher on him.

Modern readers find Plato more fun, as well as more elevating, and often describe Aristotle as 'dry, crabbed in style'. (*Retrieving the Ancients: An Introduction to Greek Philosophy*, Part IV, David Roochnik, 2004) Which is part of the reason why I have not included Aristotle among the Prime Movers, although I revere him as much as any political philosopher, as have thousands of readers before me: Dante famously calls him '*I maestro di color che sanno*', 'the master of those who know'. But Aristotle does not set out to move us; he enquires, he analyses, he refines and very often he undermines received wisdom. He has not even the flamboyance of the show-off sceptic. He does not pretend not to know what he does know, which you feel Socrates will do to make a point. He simply doggedly puts down his conclusions based on the best evidence he can gather together; when his evidence is scanty or mistaken, he is quite often wrong. But he never twists the evidence to drive his argument forward. Although he is not an experimental scientist in the modern sense, he is a scientist in the truest sense: that he is ready to be proved wrong by the evidence.

It is worth reading Aristotle to see what a Mover is not. For Aristotle's dry, unhurried style, so full of qualifications and exceptions, is a pattern of intellectual enquiry. And it draws our attention to the nagging problem about even the greatest of the Prime Movers I have chosen: they are intent on arguing a case, incurably reluctant to admit weaknesses in or exceptions to that case, still less willing to consider that there might be malign consequences to the theory or course of action they are recommending, or to consider that alternative theories might undermine their arguments.

What they refuse to accept is that every vision has its snag. Each of these great ideas is rich in potential for making us happier, but if pushed to the extreme with blinkered passion, each also possesses terrible destructive power: witness the human wastelands of communism, the corpse mountains piled up by the ferocity of nationalism, the sewage and shanty towns generated by unregulated free markets.

Politics may sometimes be about brotherhood, or equality or free enterprise or national identity, but it is always about the reconciliation of principles that do not fit together. The zealot will denounce every compromise or trade-off as a sell-out. Yet trading off is no betrayal; it is itself a principle and an overarching one. I'd go further. The trade-off is not just a grubby necessity; it is the noblest part of the politician's vocation.

ACKNOWLEDGEMENTS

I have been immensely lucky in my mentors. At Oxford, Robert Shackleton, Alban Krailsheimer and David Luke kindled my interest in eighteenth- and nineteenth-century political thought. In London, Mel Lasky encouraged me to write for *Encounter* about all sorts of ideas from usury to brotherhood. I enjoyed a continuing extramural education by becoming friends with that nest of singing birds at the LSE: Maurice Cranston, Elie Kedourie, Shirley and Bill Letwin, Ken Minogue and Michael Oakeshott. In the Commons press gallery, the incomparable company of Frank Johnson and Alan Watkins was another sort of education. To this roll of the great departed, I must now sadly add that of my beloved agent David Miller, to whom this book is dedicated and whose affection and conversation knew no bounds.

For this book, I owe a special debt to Mary Beard for guiding me through the ancient world, to Pankaj Mishra for drawing my attention to the importance of Iqbal, to Rudrangshu Mukherjee for his advice on Gandhi and late Marx, and to Charlie Smith for sharing his researches on Cleisthenes and the Alcmaeonids.

Part of the chapter on Burke first appeared in the *London Review of Books*. Part of the chapter on Marx first appeared in the *Times Literary Supplement*. Both have since undergone quite a bit of revision. Like old buildings, old thinkers are perpetually *in restauro*.

SELECT BIBLIOGRAPHY

In most cases, I have listed the Collected Works, but for ease of reference I have also included editions of some of the better known individual works.

I PERICLES and the invention of democracy

Aristotle, *Politics*, tr. Benjamin Jowett, 1905; tr. Ernest Barker, 1946
——, *The Athenian Constitution*, tr. P. J. Rhodes, 1984
Azoulay, Vincent, *Pericles of Athens*, tr. Janet Lloyd, 2014
Barker, Ernest, *The Political Thought of Plato and Aristotle*, 1959
Beard, Mary, *SPQR: A History of Ancient Rome*, 2015
Beloch, Karl Julius, *Griechische Geschichte*, Vol. 2, 1914
Bradeen, Donald W., 'The Popularity of the Athenian Empire', *Historia*, Vol. 9, 1960, pp. 257–69
Burckhardt, Jacob, *The Greeks and Greek Civilization*, tr. Sheila Stern, 1998
Cary, M. et al. eds., *Oxford Classical Dictionary*, 1949
de Ste Croix, G. E. M., *Athenian Democracy and Other Essays*, 2004
——, 'The Character of the Athenian Empire', *Historia*, Vol. 3, 1954
Ehrenberg, Victor, *From Solon to Socrates*, 1968
——, *Sophocles and Pericles*, 1954
Fornara, Charles W., and Samons, Loren J. II, *Athens from Cleisthenes to Pericles*, 1991
Forrest, W. G., *The Emergence of Greek Democracy*, 1966
Grote, George, *History of Greece*, 12 volumes, 1846–56
Hamilton, Alexander, Madison, James and Jay, John, *The Federalist Papers*, ed. Clinton Rossiter, 1961
Herodotus, *The Histories*, tr. Tom Holland, 2013

Kagan, Donald, *Pericles of Athens and the Birth of Democracy*, 1990
——, *The Peloponnesian War*, 2003
Larsen, Jacob O., 'Cleisthenes and the Development of the Theory of Democracy at Athens', in *Essays in Political Theory presented to George Sabine*, ed. Kawitz and Murphy, 1947, pp. 1–17
O'Neil, James L., *The Origins and Development of Ancient Greek Democracy*, 1995
Ostwald, Martin, 'The Reform of the Athenian State by Cleisthenes', in *Cambridge Ancient History*, second edition, ed. John Boardman, 1988, pp. 303–46
Plutarch, *Lives*, tr. A. H. Clough, 2015
Quinn, T. J., 'Thucydides and the Unpopularity of the Athenian Empire', *Historia*, Vol. 8, 1964, pp. 257–66
Raaflaub, Kurt A., Ober, Josiah and Wallace, Robert W., eds., *Origins of Democracy in Ancient Greece*, 2007
Roberts, J. T., *Athens on Trial: the Anti-democratic Tradition in Western Thought*, 1994
Samons, Loren J. II, ed., *Cambridge Companion to the Age of Pericles*, 2007
——, *Pericles and the Conquest of History*, 2016
——, *What's Wrong with Democracy?*, 2004
Sinclair, T. A., *A History of Greek Thought*, 1951
Thucydides, *The History of the Peloponnesian War*, tr. Rex Warner, 1954

II JESUS and the brotherhood of man

Beard, Mary, et al., *Religions of Rome*, 2 volumes, 1998
Beigel, R., *Rechnungswesen and Buchführung der Römer*, 1994
Chadwick, Henry, *The Church in Ancient Society*, 2001
——, *The Early Church*, 1967
Confalonieri, Luca Badini, *Democracy in the Christian Church*, 2012
Daniélou, Jean and Marrou, Henri, *The Christian Centuries Vol. I*, tr. Vincent Cronin, 1964
D'Entrèves, A. P., *Natural Law*, 1951
Finley, M. I., *The Ancient Economy*, 1985
Fletcher, Richard, *The Conversion of Europe*, 1997
Heichelheim, Fritz E., *An Ancient Economic History*, 3 volumes, 1965
Hollingworth, Miles, *Saint Augustine of Hippo*, 2013

Johnson, Paul, *A History of the Jews*, 1987

Kloft, Hans, *Die Wirtschaft der Griechisch-Römischen Welt*, 1982

Lietzmann, Hans, *A History of the Early Church*, Vols. 1 and 2, tr.
    B. L. Woolf, 1961

Millett, Paul, *Lending and Borrowing in Ancient Athens*, 2002

Milton, John, *The Doctrine and Discipline of Divorce*, Everyman
    Edition, 1927

Mount, Ferdinand, *The Subversive Family*, 1982

Nelson, B. N., *The Idea of Usury*, 1949

Pliny, *Letters*, tr. Betty Radice, 2003

Rothbard, Murray N., *Economic Thought before Adam Smith*, 1995

Temin, Peter, 'Financial Intermediation in the Early Roman Empire',
    Journal of Economic History, Vol. 64, No. 3, 2004, p. 15

Ten Brink, Candida, *Die Begründung der Marktwirtschaft in der
    Römischen Republik*, 1994

Tertullian, *Apologeticus*, tr. A. Soulard, 1917

Zgur, Andrej, *The Economy of the Roman Empire in the first two
    centuries AD*, 2007

III JEAN-JACQUES ROUSSEAU and the self supreme

Cassirer, Ernst, *The Question of Jean-Jacques Rousseau*, tr. and ed.
    Peter Gay, 1954

Cranston, Maurice, *Jean-Jacques: The Early Life and Work of
    Jean-Jacques Rousseau 1712–1754*, 1983

——, *The Noble Savage: Jean-Jacques Rousseau in Exile and Adversity
    1754–1762*, 1991

——, *The Solitary Self: Jean-Jacques Rousseau 1762–1778*, 1997

Rousseau, Jean-Jacques, *A Discourse on Inequality*, tr. and ed. Maurice
    Cranston, 1984

——, *Basic Political Writings*, ed. Donald A. Cress, 2011

——, *Emile, or On Education*, tr. and ed. Allan Bloom, 1979

——, *Julie, ou La Nouvelle Héloïse*, ed. Flammarion, 1999

——, *Les Rêveries du promeneur solitaire*, ed. Marcel Raymond,
    1948

——, *The Social Contract*, tr. H. J. Tozer, 1998

Vaughan, Charles Edwyn, *Studies in the History of Political Philosophy
    before and after Rousseau*, ed. A. G. Little, 1925

——, ed., *Du Contrat Social*, 1918

——, ed., *The Political Writings of Jean-Jacques Rousseau*, 1915

IV ADAM SMITH and the invisible hand

Phillipson, Nicholas, *Adam Smith: An Enlightened Life*, 2010

Rae, John, *Life of Adam Smith*, 1895

Raphael, D. D., *Adam Smith*, 1985

Ross, Ian Simpson, *The Life of Adam Smith*, 1995

Smith, Adam, *Essays on Philosophical Subjects, with An Account of the Life and Writings of the Author, by Dugald Stewart*, ed. Joseph Black and James Hutton, 1795

——, *Lectures on Rhetoric and Belles-lettres*, ed. John M. Lothian, 1963

——, *The Glasgow Edition of the Works and Correspondence*, 1976–87

——, *The Theory of Moral Sentiments*, 1759

——, *The Wealth of Nations*, 1776; Everyman Edition, intro. William Letwin, 1975

Winch, Donald, 'Adam Smith', *Oxford Dictionary of National Biography*

V EDMUND BURKE and the stickiness of society

Bevan, Ruth A., *Marx and Burke*, 1977

Bourke, Richard, *Empire and Revolution: The Political Life of Edmund Burke*, 2015

Bromwich, David, *Moral Imagination*, 2014

——, *The Intellectual Life of Edmund Burke*, 2014

Burke, Edmund, *Works*, 12 volumes, 1808–13

——, *Writings and Speeches*, ed. Paul Langford, 9 volumes, 1981–1991

Furber, Holden, ed. *The Correspondence of Edmund Burke*, 1958–78, 10 volumes

Dwan, David and Insole, Christopher J., eds., *The Cambridge Companion to Edmund Burke*, 2012

Ehrman, John, *The Younger Pitt*, 3 volumes, 1969, 1983, 1996

Burke, Edmund, and Burke, William, *An Account of the European Settlements in America*, 2 volumes, 1757

Hampshire, Stuart, *Modern Writers and Other Essays*, 1969

Kirk, Russell, *The Conservative Mind: From Burke to Santayana*, 1953

Montesquieu, *De l'Esprit des Lois*, ed. Gonzague Truc, 2 volumes, 1956

Norman, Jesse, *Edmund Burke: Philosopher, Politician, Prophet*, 2013

O'Brien, Conor Cruise, *The Great Melody: A Thematic Biography of Edmund Burke*, 1992

VI THOMAS JEFFERSON and the endless revolution

Adams, William Howard, *The Paris Years of Thomas Jefferson*, 1997

Boyd, Julian et al. eds., *The Papers of Thomas Jefferson*, 41 volumes to date, 1950–

Hitchens, Christopher, *Thomas Jefferson: Author of America*, 2007

Jefferson, Thomas, *The Writings of Thomas Jefferson*, ed. Paul Leicester Ford, 12 volumes, 1904–05

Kranish, Michael, *The Flight from Monticello*, 2010

Linklater, Andro, *Owning the Earth*, 2014

Maclay, William, *Journal of William Maclay, 1789–1791*, ed. E. S. Maclay, 1927

Malone, Dumas, *Jefferson and His Times*, 6 volumes, 1948–81

O'Brien, Conor Cruise, *The Long Affair: Thomas Jefferson and the American Revolution, 1785–1800*, 1996

Onuf, Peter S., ed., *Jeffersonian Legacies*, 1993

Padover, Saul K., ed., *Thomas Jefferson on Democracy*, 1939

Rossiter, Clinton, *1787: The Grand Convention*, 1987

——, ed., *The Federalist Papers: Alexander Hamilton, James Madison, John Jay*, 1961

Shackelford, George Green, *Jefferson's Adoptive Son: The Life of William Short, 1759–1848*, 1993

Vidal, Gore, *Inventing a Nation: Washington, Adams, Jefferson*, 2003

Wills, Garry, 'Uncle Thomas's Cabin', *New York Review of Books*, 18 April 1974

VII JEREMY BENTHAM and the management of happiness

Atkinson, Charles Milner, *Jeremy Bentham: His Life and Work*, 1905

Bentham, Jeremy, *A Fragment on Government*, ed. Ross Harrison, 1988

——, *An Introduction to the Principles of Morals and Legislation*, ed. J. H. Burns and H. L. A. Hart, 1970

——, *Bentham's Auto-Icon and related writings*, ed. J. E. Crimmins, 2002

——, *Collected Works*, ed. J. R. Dinwiddy and J. H. Burns, 1968, 33 volumes to date, projected total of 70

——, *Deontology; or the Science of Morality*, 1834

——, *Economic Writings*, ed., W. Stark, 3 volumes, 1952–54

——, *Panopticon; or, the Inspection-House*, Dodo Press, 2008

——, *Works*, ed. John Bowring, 11 volumes, 1838–43

Crimmins, James E., 'Bentham on Religion: Atheism and the Secular Society', *Journal of the History of Ideas*, Vol. 47, No. 1, Jan–Mar 1986, pp. 95–110

Dinwiddy, John, *Bentham*, 1989

Everett, Charles Warren, *Jeremy Bentham*, 1966

——, *The Education of Jeremy Bentham*, 1931

Hazlitt, William, *The Spirit of the Age*, Everyman Edition, 1910

Himmelfarb, Gertrude, 'On Reading Bentham Seriously', *Studies in Burke and His Time*, Vol. 14, Winter 1972–73, pp. 185–6

Letwin, Shirley Robin, *The Pursuit of Certainty*, 1965

Lucas, Philip and Sheeran, Anne, 'Asperger's Syndrome and the Eccentricity and Genius of Jeremy Bentham', *Journal of Bentham Studies*, Vol. 8, 2006

Mack, Mary P., *Jeremy Bentham: An Odyssey of Ideas, 1748–1792*, 1962

Marmoy, C. F. A., 'The "Auto-Icon" of Jeremy Bentham at University College, London', *Medical History*, Vol. 2, 1958

Mill, John Stuart, *Utilitarianism, On Liberty, Representative Government*, Everyman Edition, 1972

Montefiore, Simon, 'Prince Potemkin and the Benthams', *History Today*, Vol. 53, 8 August 2003

Oakeshott, Michael, *Rationalism in Politics*, 1962

Rosen, Frederick, *Jeremy Bentham and Representative Democracy*, 1983

——, 'Jeremy Bentham', *Oxford Dictionary of National Biography*

Ryan, Alan, ed., *Utilitarianism and Other Essays: John Stuart Mill and Jeremy Bentham*, 1987

Schofield, Philip, *Utility and Democracy: The Political Thought of Jeremy Bentham*, 2006

Semple, Janet, *Bentham's Prison*, 1993

Steintrager, James, *Bentham*, 1977

Werrett, Simon, 'Potemkin and the Panopticon', *Journal of Bentham Studies*, Vol. 2, 1999

VIII MARY WOLLSTONECRAFT and the rights of woman – and men too

Cameron, K. N, ed., *Shelley and His Circle*, 4 volumes, 1961–70

Condorcet, Marquis de, *Oeuvres Complètes*, Paris, 1847

George, Sam, 'Cultivating the Botanical Woman: Rousseau, Wakefield and the Instruction of Women in Botany', *Zeitschrift für Pädagogische Historiographie*, Vol. 12, No. 1, 2006

Godwin, William, *Memoirs of the Author of 'A Vindication of the Rights of Woman'*, 1798

——, ed., *Posthumous Works of the Author of 'A Vindication of the Rights of Woman'*, 4 volumes, 1798

Nyström, Per, *Mary Wollstonecraft's Scandinavian Journey*, Royal Society of Arts and Sciences of Gothenburg, *Humaniora*, No. 17, 1980

Paine, Thomas, *Common Sense*, 1776

——, *The Rights of Man*, 2 volumes, 1791, 1792

Taylor, Barbara, 'Mary Wollstonecraft', *Oxford Dictionary of National Biography*, 2004

Todd, Janet, *Mary Wollstonecraft: A Revolutionary Life*, 2000

Tomalin, Claire, *The Life and Death of Mary Wollstonecraft*, 1974

Wollstonecraft, Mary, *A Vindication of the Rights of Men, A Vindication of the Rights of Woman, An Historical and Moral View of the Origin and Progress of the French Revolution*, ed. Janet Todd, 1993

——, *Collected Letters*, ed. R. M. Wardle, 1979

——, *Works*, ed. Marilyn Butler and Janet Todd, 7 volumes, 1989

Wollstonecraft, Mary and Godwin, William, *A Short Residence in Sweden*, and *Memoirs of the Author of 'The Rights of Woman'*, ed. Richard Holmes, 1987

Woolf, Virginia, 'Mary Wollstonecraft', *The Common Reader*, Second Series, 1932

IX GIUSEPPE MAZZINI and the religion of nationhood

Gellner, Ernest, *Encounters with Nationalism*, 1994

——, *Nations and Nationalism*, 1983

Gilmour, David, *The Pursuit of Italy*, 2011

Hobsbawm, E. J., *Nations and Nationalism since 1780*, 1990

Kedourie, Elie, *Nationalism*, 1960; expanded edition, 1993

King, Bolton, *Mazzini*, 1902

Mack Smith, Denis, *Mazzini*, 1994

Mazzini, Giuseppe, *Ai Giovani d'Italia*, 1887

——, *Scritti editi ed inediti*, 18 volumes, 1861–91

——, *The Life and Writings of Joseph Mazzini*, ed. Emilie Ashurst, 6 volumes, 1891

—— (as Joseph Mazzini), *The Duties of Man and other essays*, tr. Ella Noyes et al., Everyman Edition, 1907

Minogue, K. R., *Nationalism*, 1967

Salvemini, Gaetano, *Mazzini*, tr. I. M. Rawson, 1956

Silone, Ignazio, ed., *The Living Thoughts of Mazzini*, 1939

Thompson, Mark, *The White War: Life and Death on the Italian Front 1915–1919*, 2008

Trevelyan, G. M., *Garibaldi's Defence of the Roman Republic*, 1907

Weber, Eugen, *Peasants into Frenchmen: The Modernization of Rural France, 1870–1914*, 1977

X KARL MARX and the death of capitalism

Anderson, Perry, *Lineages of the Absolute State*, 1974

——, *Passages from Antiquity to Feudalism*, 1974

Aron, Raymond, *Le Marxisme de Marx*, 2002

Avineri, Shlomo, *The Social and Political Thought of Karl Marx*, 1968

Berlin, Isaiah, *Karl Marx*, 1939

Borkenau, Franz, *World Communism*, 1962

Carver, Terrell, ed., *The Cambridge Companion to Marx*, 1991

——, 'Gresham's Law in the World of Scholarship', marxmyths.org, 2005

Engels, Frederick, *The Condition of the Working Class in England*, 1845; first English translation, 1887

——, *The Origin of the Family, Private Property and the State*, tr. Alec West, 1942

Lenin, V. I., *Works*, 2 volumes, 1947

Lukács, George, *History and Class Consciousness*, tr. Hermann Luchterhand, 1971

McLellan, David, *Karl Marx*, 1973; revised edition, 2006

Marx, Karl, *Capital*, Vol. 1, tr. Samuel Moore and Edward Aveling, 1887

——, *Critique of Hegel's Philosophy of Right*, tr. and ed. J. O'Malley 1970

——, *Grundrisse*, tr. and ed. David McLellan, 1971

——, *On the Civil War in France*, ed. Christopher Hitchens, 1971

——, *The Poverty of Philosophy*, 1847

Marx, Karl and Engels, Friedrich, *The Communist Manifesto*, tr. Samuel Moore, 2015

——, *Karl Marx-Friedrich Engels, Collected Works*, tr. Richard Dixon et al., 50 volumes, 1975–2004

Plamenatz, John P., *German Marxism and Russian Communism*, 1954

Popper, Karl, *The Open Society and its Enemies*, 2 volumes, 1945

——, *The Poverty of Historicism*, 1957

Seigel, Jerrold, *Marx's Fate*, 1993

Shanin, Teodor, *Late Marx and the Russian Road*, 1985

Singer, Peter, *Marx: A Very Short Introduction*, 1980
Stedman Jones, Gareth, *Karl Marx: Greatness and Illusion*, 2016
Wheen, Francis, *Karl Marx: A Life*, 1999

XI MOHANDAS GANDHI and the non-violent path

Amin, Shahid, 'Gandhi as Mahatma', *Subaltern Studies*, Vol. 3, 1984, pp. 1–61
Anderson, Perry, 'Gandhi Centre Stage', 'Why Partition?', 'After Nehru', *London Review of Books*, 5 July, 19 July, 2 August 2012
Bilgrami, Akeel, 'Gandhi, the Philosopher', *Economic and Political Weekly*, Vol. 38, No. 39, Sept–Oct 2003, pp. 4159–65
Brown, Judith M., *Gandhi's Rise to Power*, 1972
——, *Modern India*, 1985
Brown, Judith M. and Parel, Anthony J., eds., *The Cambridge Companion to Gandhi*, 1997
Chatterjee, Partha, 'Gandhi and the critique of civil society', *Subaltern Studies*, III, p. 172
Fischer, Louis, *The Essential Gandhi*, 1962
——, *The Life of Mahatma Gandhi*, 1950
Gandhi, Mohandas K., *An Autobiography: The Story of My Experiments with Truth*, 2001
——, *From Yeravda Mandir*, tr. V. G. Desai, 1932
——, *Satyagraha in South Africa*, tr. V. G. Desai, 1928
——, *The Collected Works of Mahatma Gandhi*, Ministry of Information and Broadcasting, Government of India, 100 volumes; online at Gandhiserve
Gandhi, Rajmohan, *Mohandas: A True Story of a Man, his People and an Empire*, 2007
Guha, Ramachandra, *Gandhi Before India*, 2013
——, *India after Gandhi*, 2007
Guha, Ranajit, 'Discipline and Mobilise', *Subaltern Studies*, Vol. 7, 1992, pp. 69-120
Mehta, Ved, *Mahatma Gandhi and His Apostles*, 1977
Mukherjee, Rudrangshu, *Nehru and Bose: Parallel Lives*, 2014
——, *The Penguin Gandhi Reader*, 1994
——, 'Gandhi's Swaraj', *Economic and Political Weekly*, Vol. 44, No. 50, 12–18 December 2009, pp. 34–9
Parel, Anthony J., ed., *Hind Swaraj, and Other Writings by M. K. Gandhi*, 2009

XII MUHAMMAD IQBAL and the dream of Islam

Allen, Charles, *God's Terrorists: The Wahhabi Cult and the Hidden Roots of Modern Jihad*, 2006

Anjum, Zafar, *Iqbal: The Life of a Poet, Philosopher and Politician*, 2014

Hassan, Parveen Feroze, *The Political Philosophy of Iqbal*, 1970

Iqbal, Muhammad, *Javid-Nama*, tr. and ed. Arthur J. Arberry, 1966

——, *Poems from Iqbal*, tr. V. G. Kiernan, 1955

——, *The Mysteries of Selflessness*, tr. and ed. Arthur J. Arberry, 1953

——, *The Reconstruction of Religious Thought in Islam*, Lahore 1930, Oxford 1934

——, *The Secrets of the Self*, tr. and ed. Reynold A. Nicholson, 1920

——, *Tulip in the Desert*, tr. and ed. Mustansir Mir, 2000

Minault, Gail, *The Khilafat Movement: Religious Symbolism and Political Mobilization in India*, 1982

Mir, Mustansir, *Iqbal*, 2005

Mishra, Pankaj, *From the Ruins of Empire*, 2012

Naipaul, V. S., *Beyond Belief: Islamic Excursions among the Converted Peoples*, 1998

Niemeijer, A. C., *The Khilafat Movement in India 1919–1924*, 1972

Qureshi, M. Naeem, *Pan-Islam in British-Indian Politics: A Study of the Khilafat Movement 1918–1924*, 1999

Ruthven, Malise, *Islam in the World*, 2006

Schimmel, Annemarie, *Gabriel's Wing*, 1963

Sevea, Iqbal Singh, *The Political Philosophy of Muhammad Iqbal*, 2012

Shafique, Khurram Ali, *Iqbal: His Life and Our Times*, 2014

Sherwani, L. A., ed., *Speeches, Writings and Statements of Iqbal*, 1977

Singh, N. Iqbal, *The Ardent Pilgrim*, 1951

Winstone, H. V. F., *Captain Shakespear*, 1976

INDEX